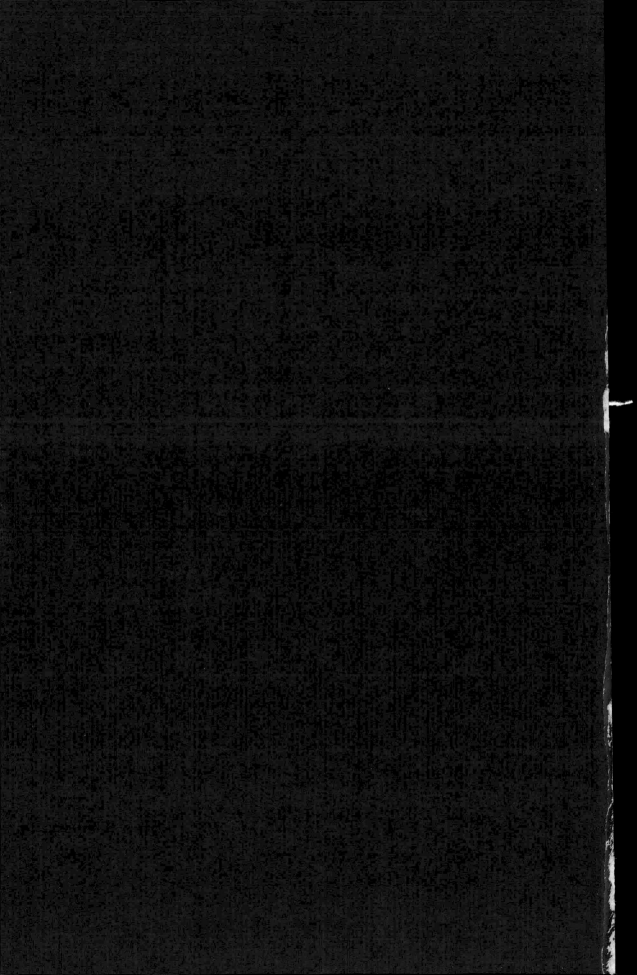

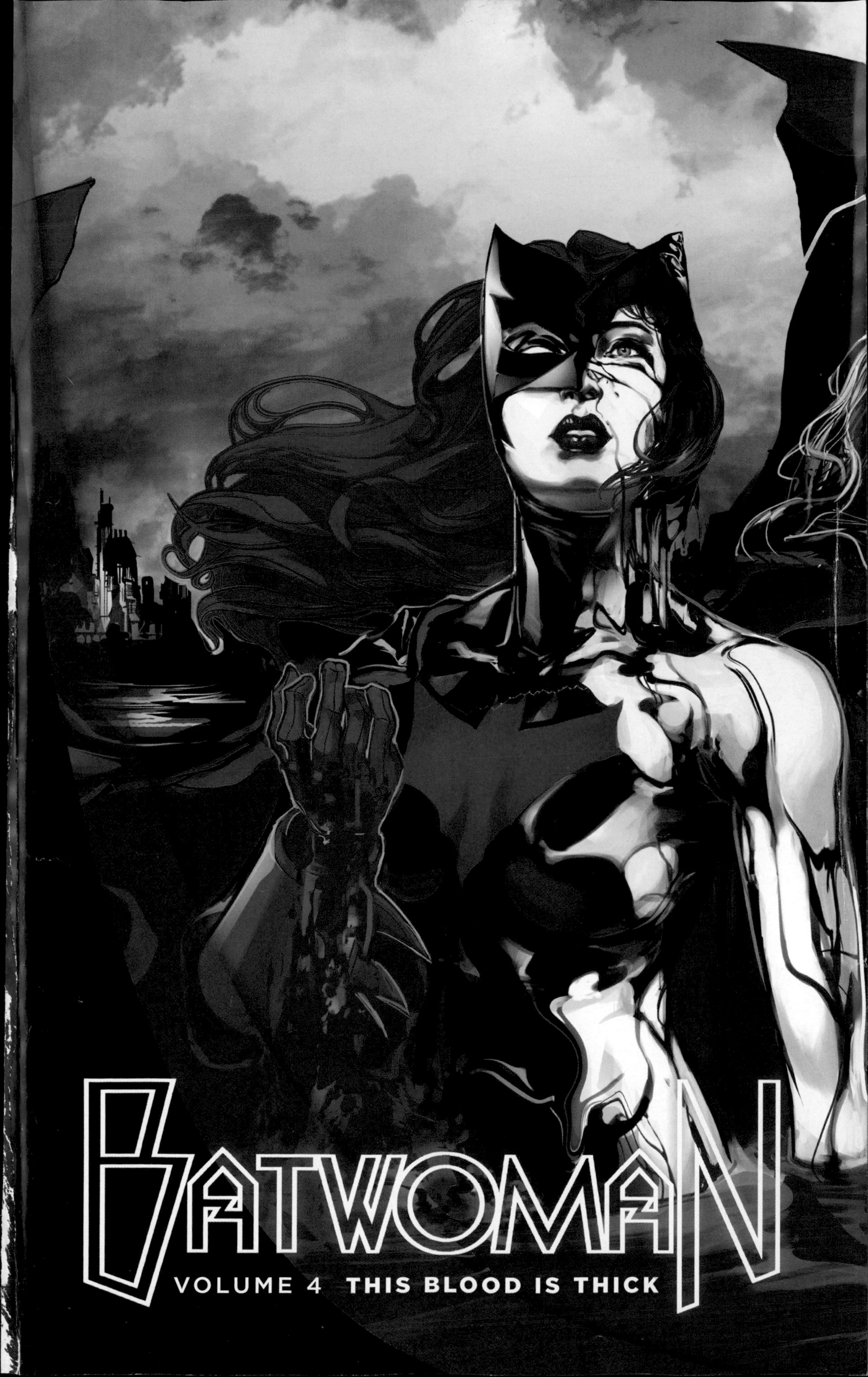
BATWOMAN
VOLUME 4 THIS BLOOD IS THICK

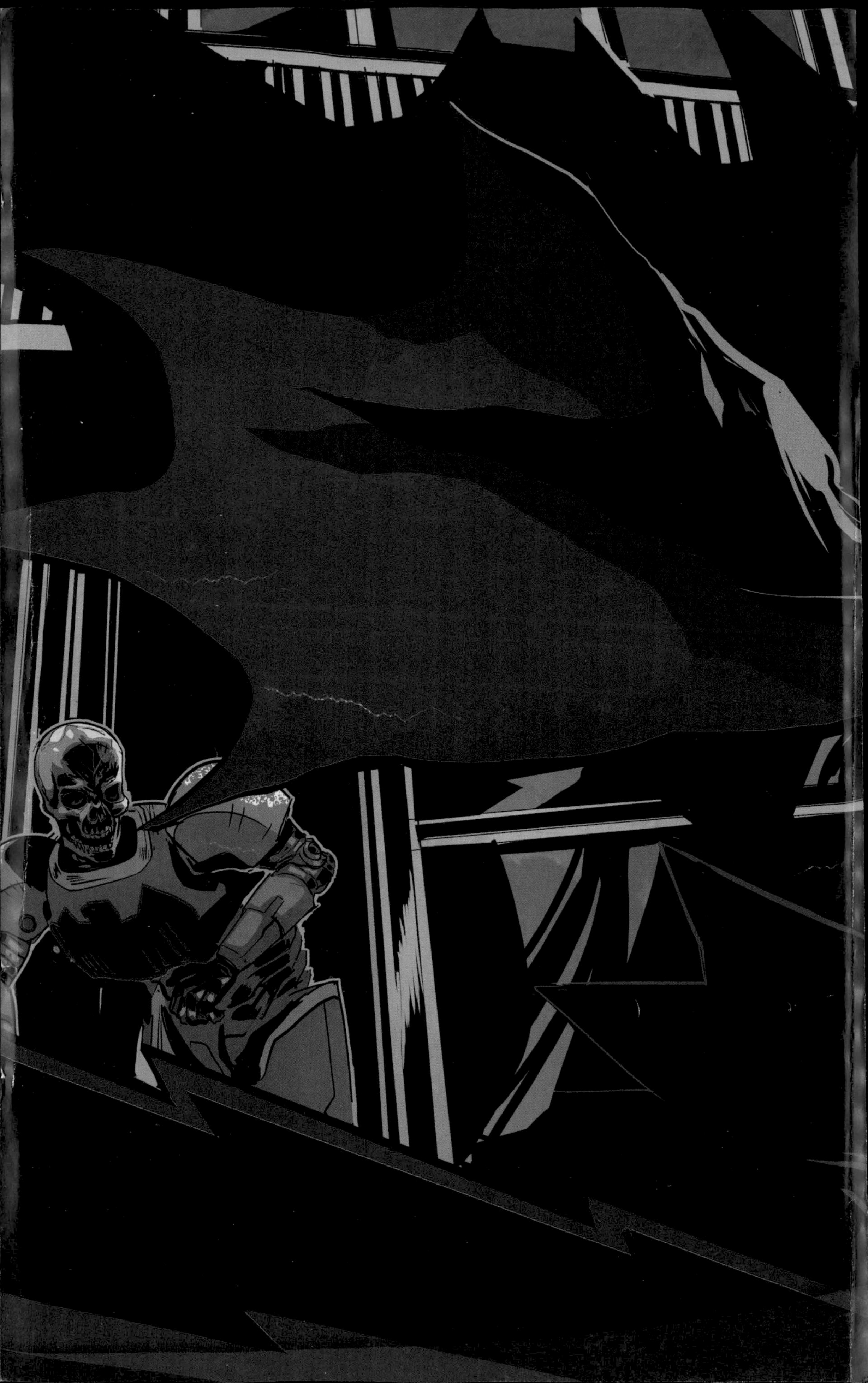

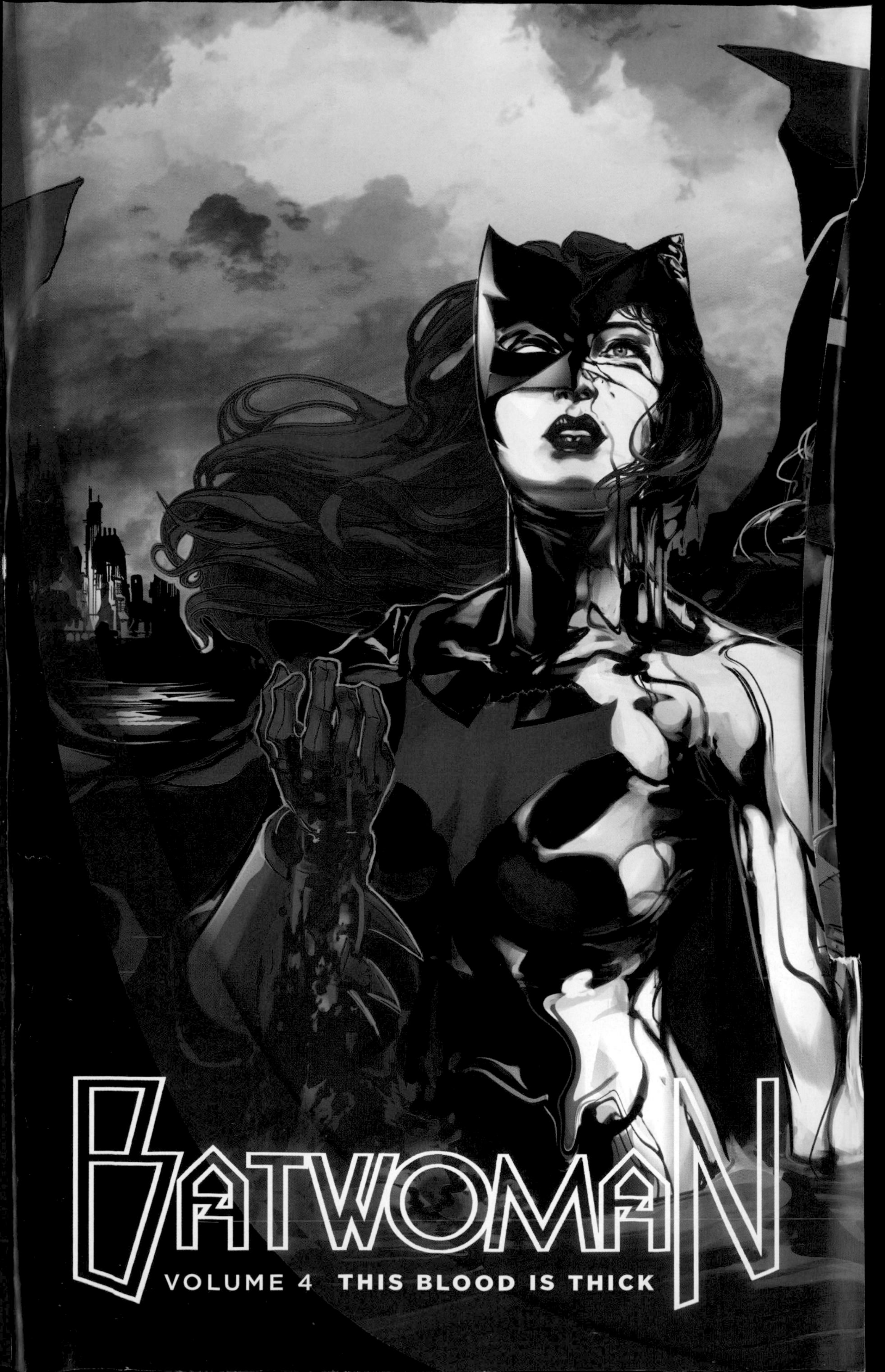
BATWOMAN
VOLUME 4 THIS BLOOD IS THICK

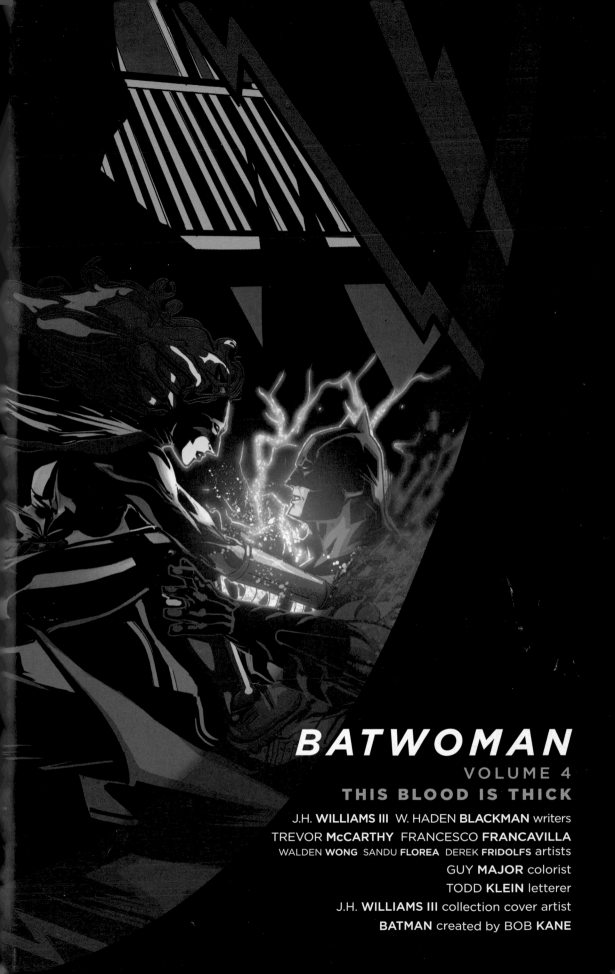

BATWOMAN
VOLUME 4
THIS BLOOD IS THICK

J.H. **WILLIAMS III** W. HADEN **BLACKMAN** writers

TREVOR **McCARTHY** FRANCESCO **FRANCAVILLA**

WALDEN **WONG** SANDU **FLOREA** DEREK **FRIDOLFS** artists

GUY **MAJOR** colorist

TODD **KLEIN** letterer

J.H. **WILLIAMS III** collection cover artist

BATMAN created by BOB **KANE**

MIKE MARTS Editor – Original Series DARREN SHAN Assistant Editor – Original Series
ROWENA YOW Editor ROBBIN BROSTERMAN Design Director – Books
ROBBIE BIEDERMAN Publication Design

BOB HARRAS Senior VP – Editor-in-Chief, DC Comics

DIANE NELSON President DAN DIDIO and JIM LEE Co-Publishers
GEOFF JOHNS Chief Creative Officer
JOHN ROOD Executive VP – Sales, Marketing and Business Development
AMY GENKINS Senior VP – Business and Legal Affairs NAIRI GARDINER Senior VP – Finance
JEFF BOISON VP – Publishing Planning MARK CHIARELLO VP – Art Direction and Design
JOHN CUNNINGHAM VP – Marketing TERRI CUNNINGHAM VP – Editorial Administration
ALISON GILL Senior VP – Manufacturing and Operations HANK KANALZ Senior VP – Vertigo and Integrated Publishing
JAY KOGAN VP – Business and Legal Affairs, Publishing JACK MAHAN VP – Business Affairs, Talent
NICK NAPOLITANO VP – Manufacturing Administration SUE POHJA VP – Book Sales
COURTNEY SIMMONS Senior VP – Publicity BOB WAYNE Senior VP – Sales

BATWOMAN VOLUME 4: THE BLOOD IS THICK

DC Comics, 1700 Broadway, New York, NY 10019
A Warner Bros. Entertainment Company.
Printed by RR Donnelley, Salem, VA, USA. 2/21/14. First Printing.

HC ISBN: 978-1-4012-4621-1
SC ISBN: 978-1-4012-4999-1

SUSTAINABLE Certified Chain of Custody
FORESTRY At Least 20% Certified Forest Content
INITIATIVE www.sfiprogram.org
SFI-01042
APPLIES TO TEXT STOCK ONLY

Library of Congress Cataloging-in-Publication Data

Williams, J. H., III.
Batwoman. Volume 4, This blood is thick / JH Williams, W. Haden Blackman ; illustrated by Trevor McCarthy.
pages cm
Collects Batwoman #18-24"
ISBN 978-1-4012-4621-1 (hardback)
1. Graphic novels. I. Blackman, W. Haden. II. McCarthy, Trevor. III. Title. IV. Title: This blood is thick.
PN6728.B365W58 2014
741.5'973—dc23
2013049639

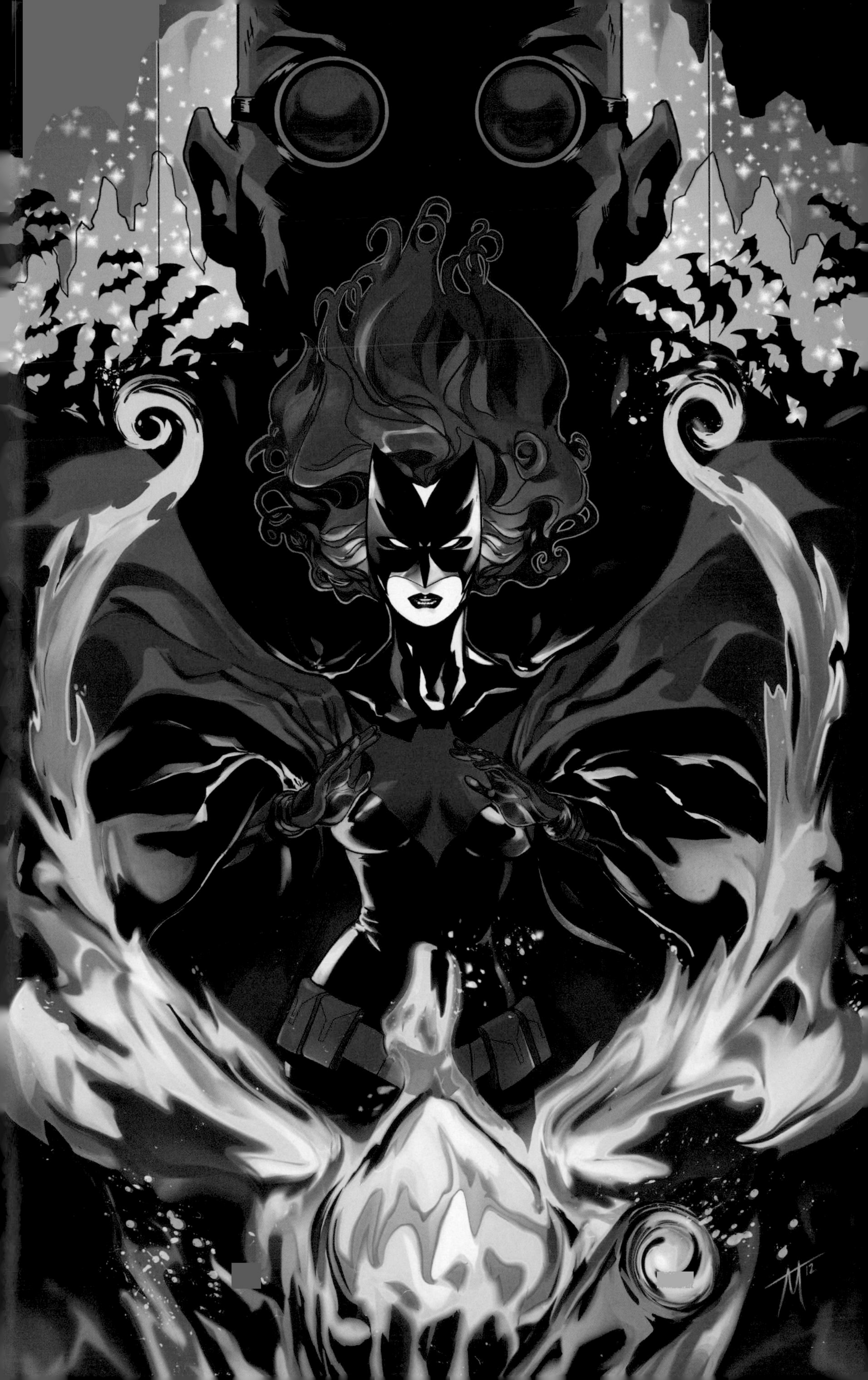

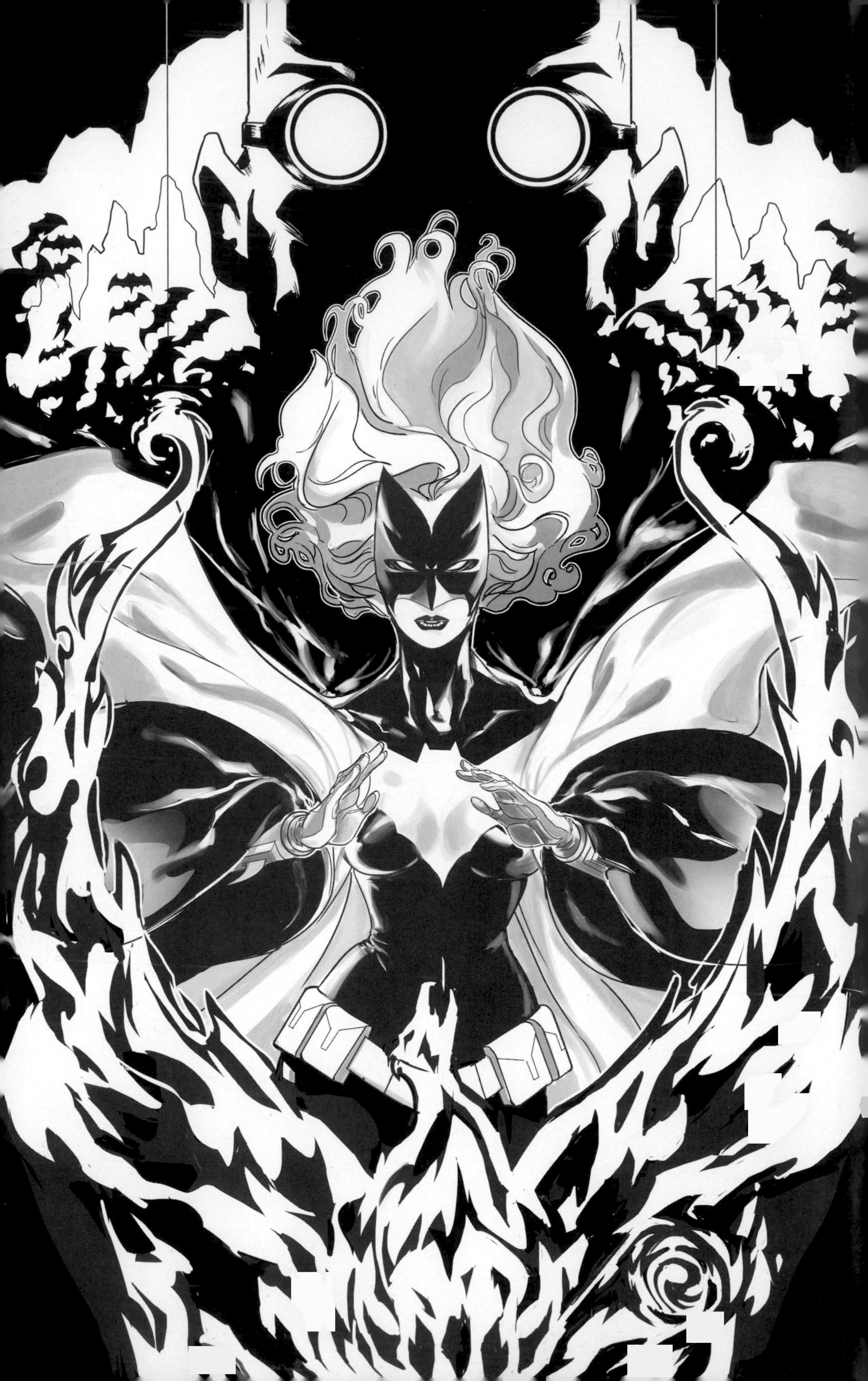

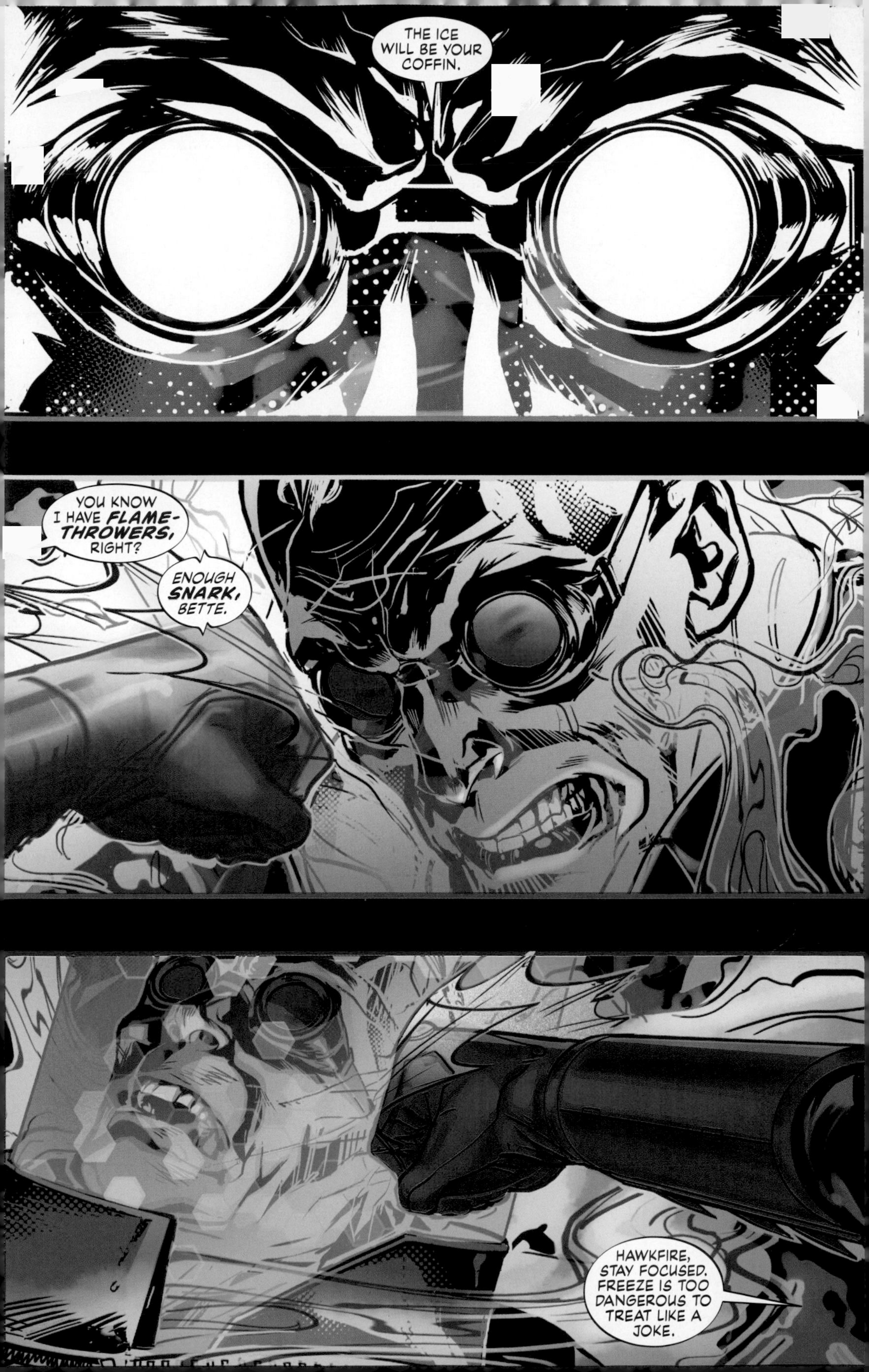
THE ICE WILL BE YOUR COFFIN.
YOU KNOW I HAVE FLAME-THROWERS, RIGHT?
ENOUGH SNARK, BETTE.
HAWKFIRE, STAY FOCUSED. FREEZE IS TOO DANGEROUS TO TREAT LIKE A JOKE.

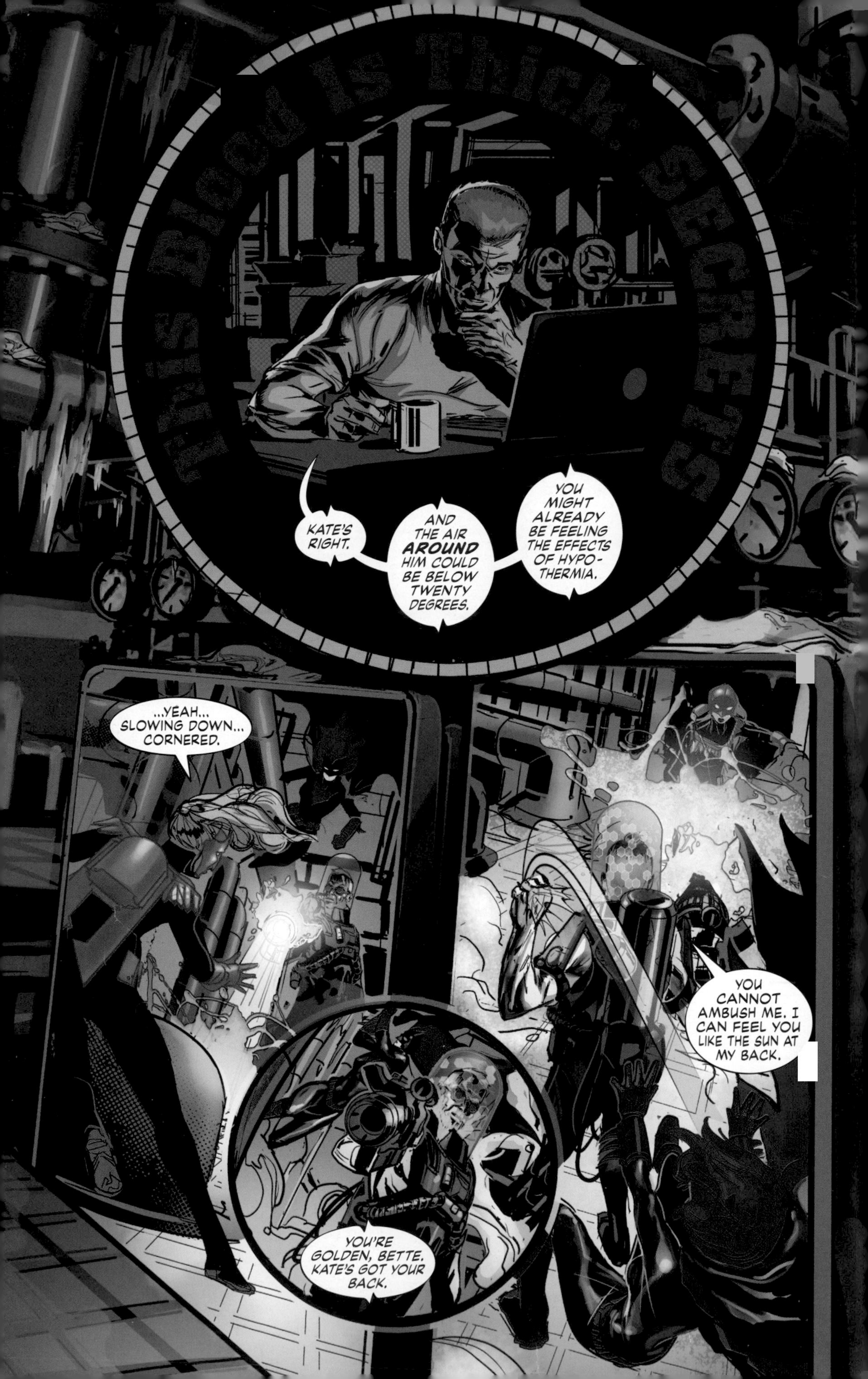
THIS BLOOD IS THICK. SECRETS
KATE'S RIGHT.
AND THE AIR AROUND HIM COULD BE BELOW TWENTY DEGREES.
YOU MIGHT ALREADY BE FEELING THE EFFECTS OF HYPO-THERMIA.
...YEAH... SLOWING DOWN... CORNERED.
YOU CANNOT AMBUSH ME. I CAN FEEL YOU LIKE THE SUN AT MY BACK.
YOU'RE GOLDEN, BETTE. KATE'S GOT YOUR BACK.

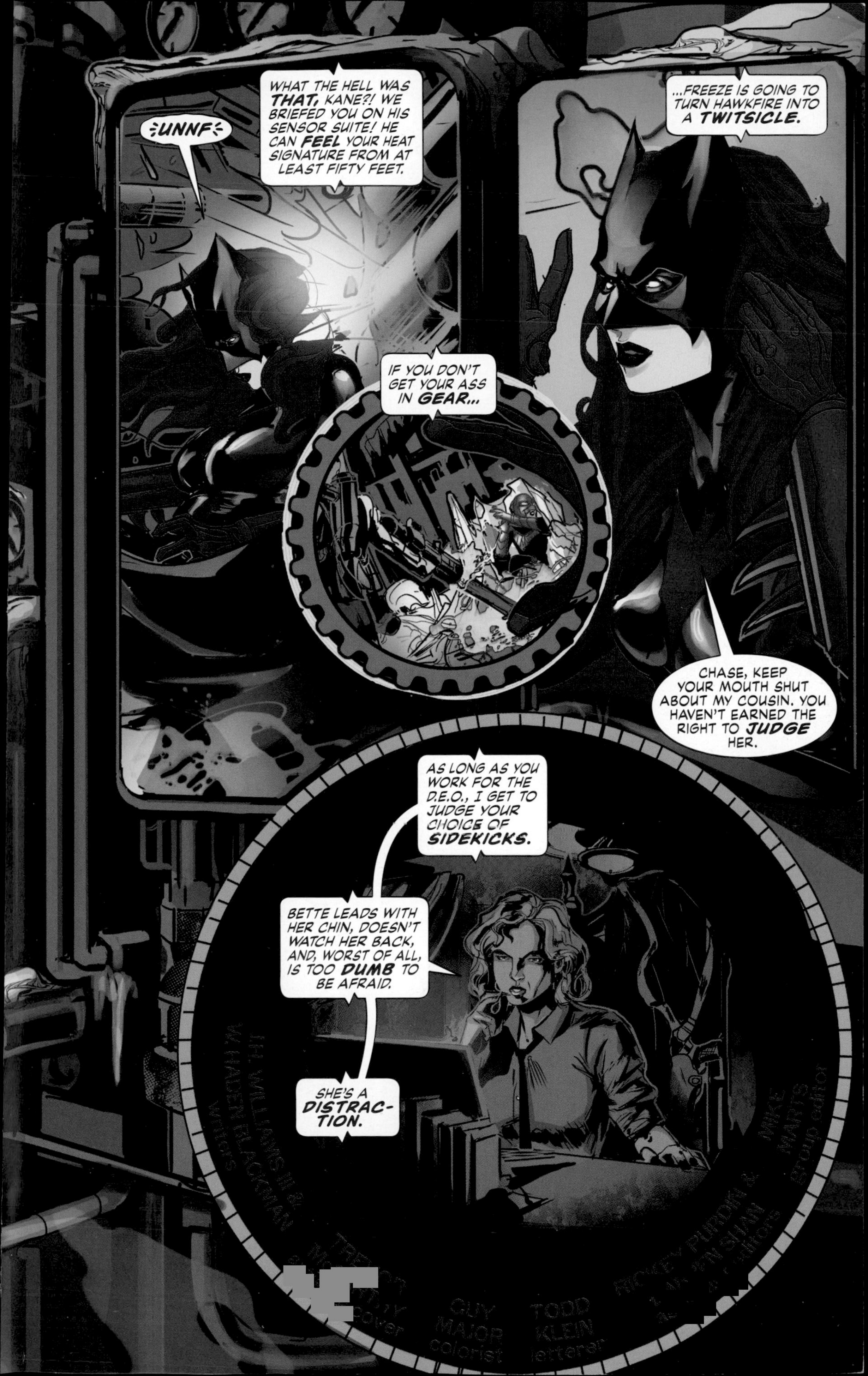

UNNF
WHAT THE HELL WAS THAT, KANE?! WE BRIEFED YOU ON HIS SENSOR SUITE! HE CAN FEEL YOUR HEAT SIGNATURE FROM AT LEAST FIFTY FEET.
IF YOU DON'T GET YOUR ASS IN GEAR...
...FREEZE IS GOING TO TURN HAWKFIRE INTO A TWITSICLE.
CHASE, KEEP YOUR MOUTH SHUT ABOUT MY COUSIN. YOU HAVEN'T EARNED THE RIGHT TO JUDGE HER.
AS LONG AS YOU WORK FOR THE D.E.O., I GET TO JUDGE YOUR CHOICE OF SIDEKICKS.
BETTE LEADS WITH HER CHIN, DOESN'T WATCH HER BACK, AND, WORST OF ALL, IS TOO DUMB TO BE AFRAID.
SHE'S A DISTRACTION.
J.H. WILLIAMS III & W. HADEN BLACKMAN writers
GUY MAJOR colorist
TODD KLEIN letterer
MIKE MARTS group editor

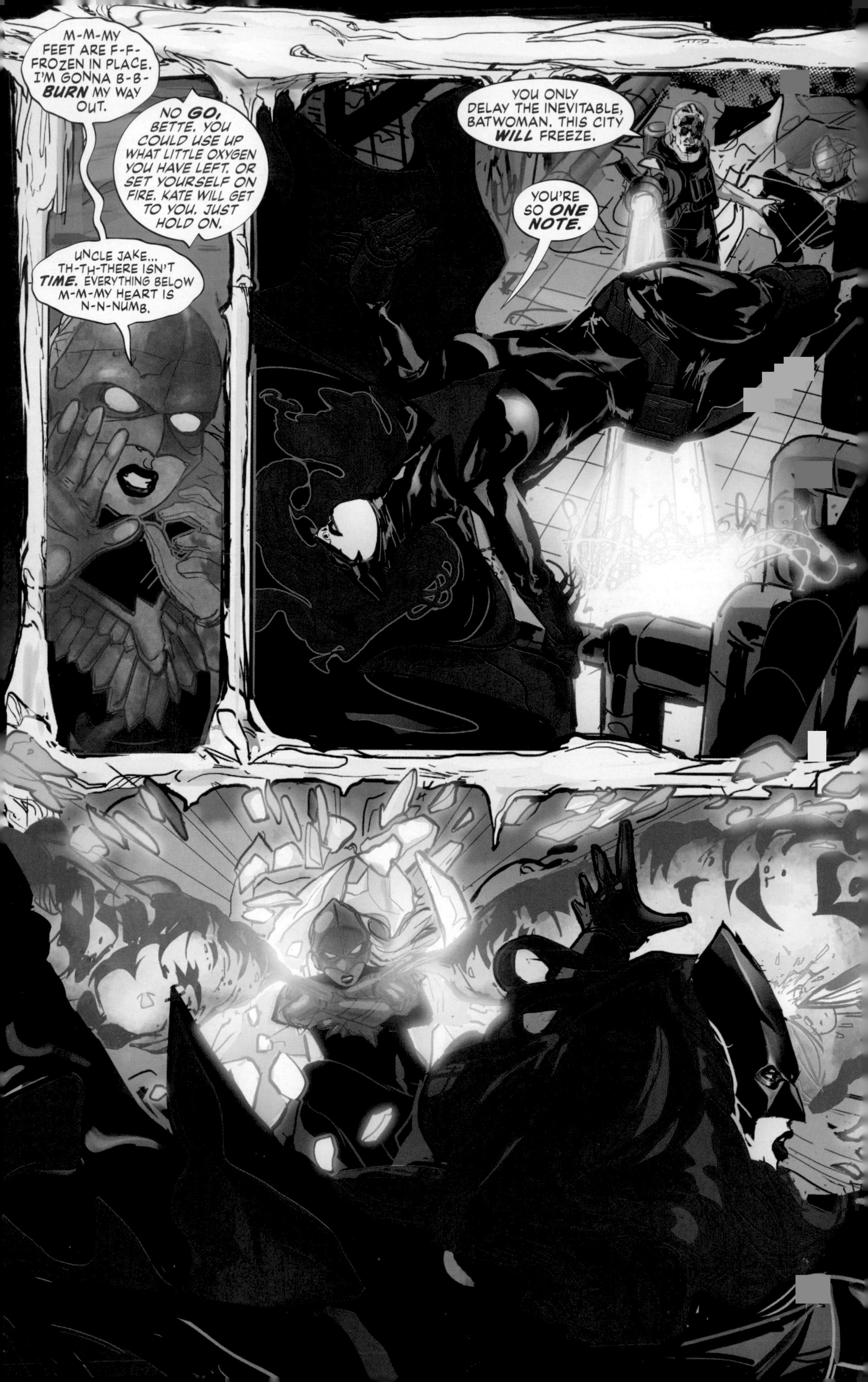
M-M-MY FEET ARE F-F-FROZEN IN PLACE. I'M GONNA B-B-**BURN** MY WAY OUT.
NO **GO,** BETTE. YOU COULD USE UP WHAT LITTLE OXYGEN YOU HAVE LEFT. OR SET YOURSELF ON FIRE. KATE WILL GET TO YOU. JUST HOLD ON.
UNCLE JAKE... TH-TH-THERE ISN'T **TIME.** EVERYTHING BELOW M-M-MY HEART IS N-N-NUMB.
YOU ONLY DELAY THE INEVITABLE, BATWOMAN. THIS CITY **WILL** FREEZE.
YOU'RE SO **ONE NOTE.**

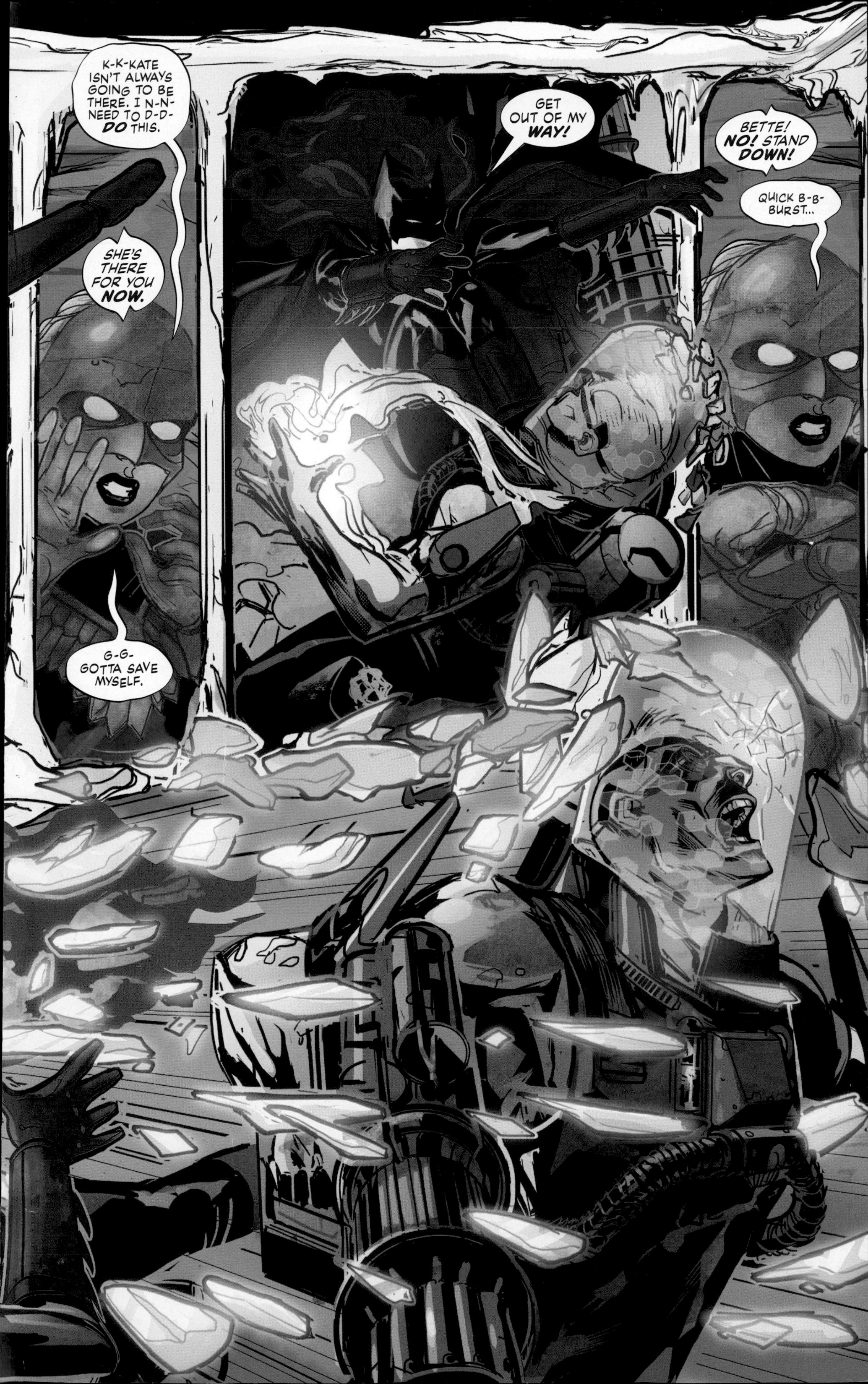
K-K-KATE ISN'T ALWAYS GOING TO BE THERE. I N-N-NEED TO D-D-**DO** THIS.
SHE'S THERE FOR YOU **NOW.**
G-G-GOTTA SAVE MYSELF.
GET OUT OF MY **WAY!**
BETTE! **NO!** STAND **DOWN!**
QUICK B-B-BURST...

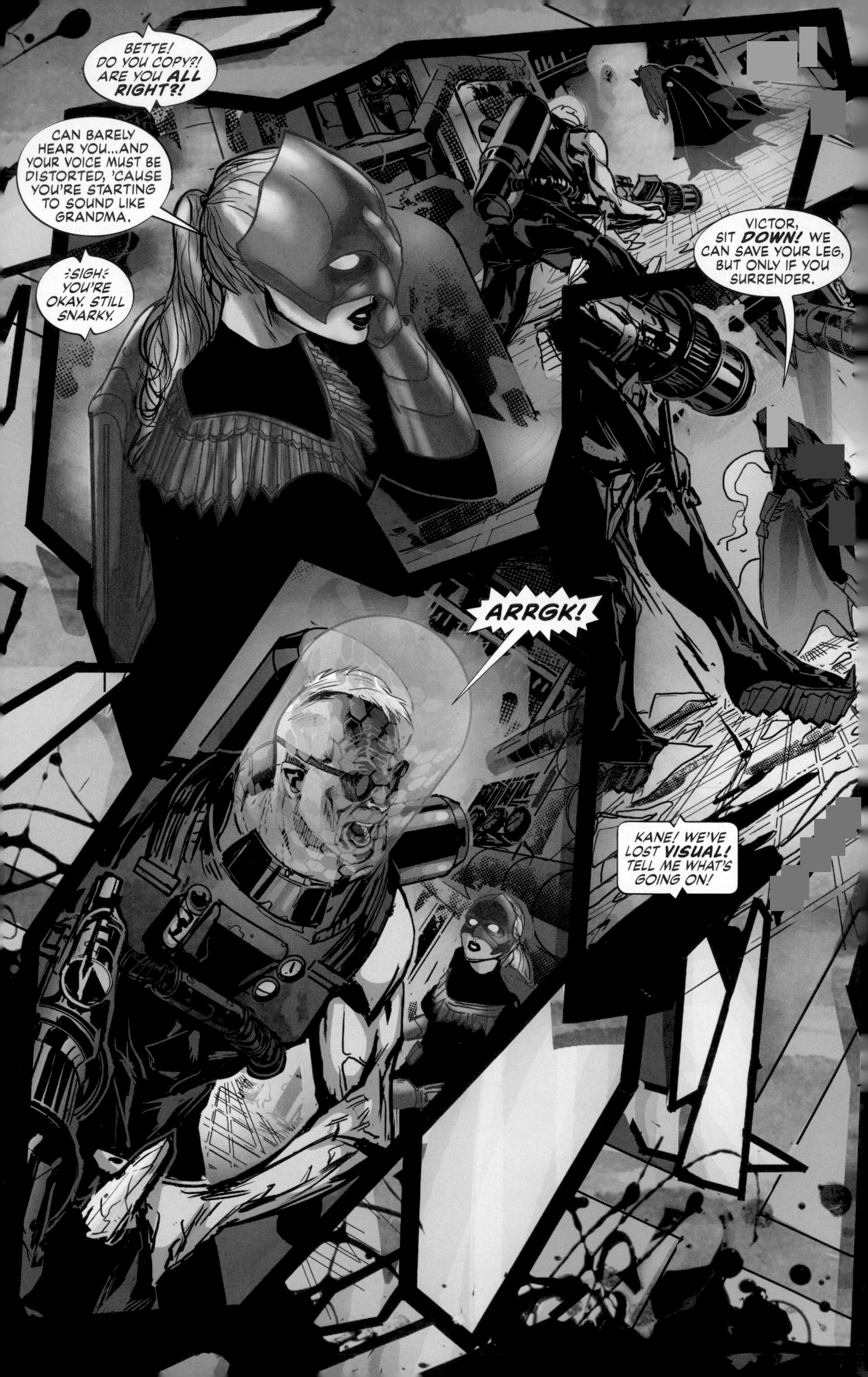
BETTE! DO YOU COPY?! ARE YOU ALL RIGHT?!
CAN BARELY HEAR YOU...AND YOUR VOICE MUST BE DISTORTED, 'CAUSE YOU'RE STARTING TO SOUND LIKE GRANDMA.
-SIGH- YOU'RE OKAY. STILL SNARKY.
VICTOR, SIT DOWN! WE CAN SAVE YOUR LEG, BUT ONLY IF YOU SURRENDER.
ARRGK!
KANE! WE'VE LOST VISUAL! TELL ME WHAT'S GOING ON!

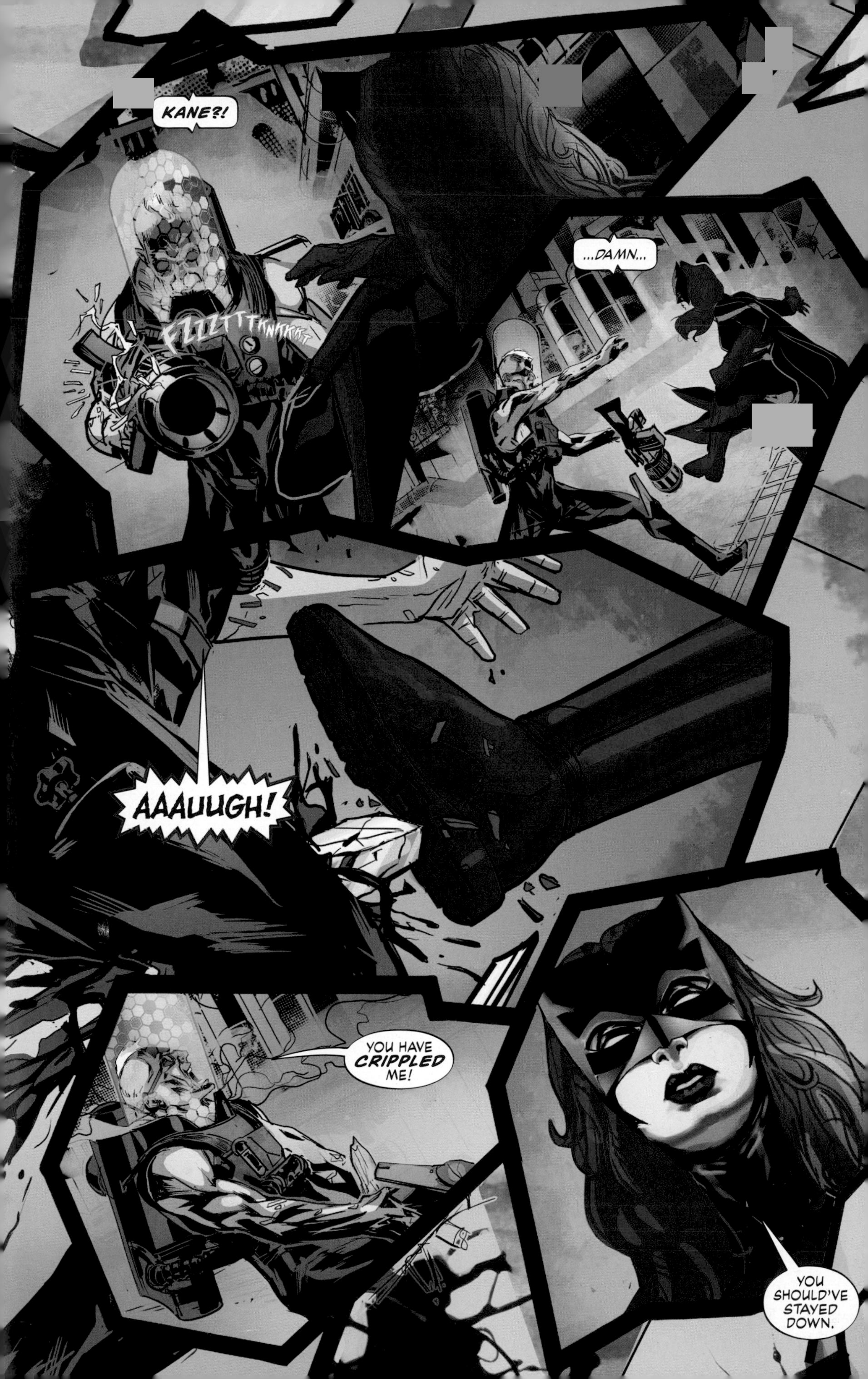
KANE?!
...DAMN...
AAAUUGH!
YOU HAVE CRIPPLED ME!
YOU SHOULD'VE STAYED DOWN.

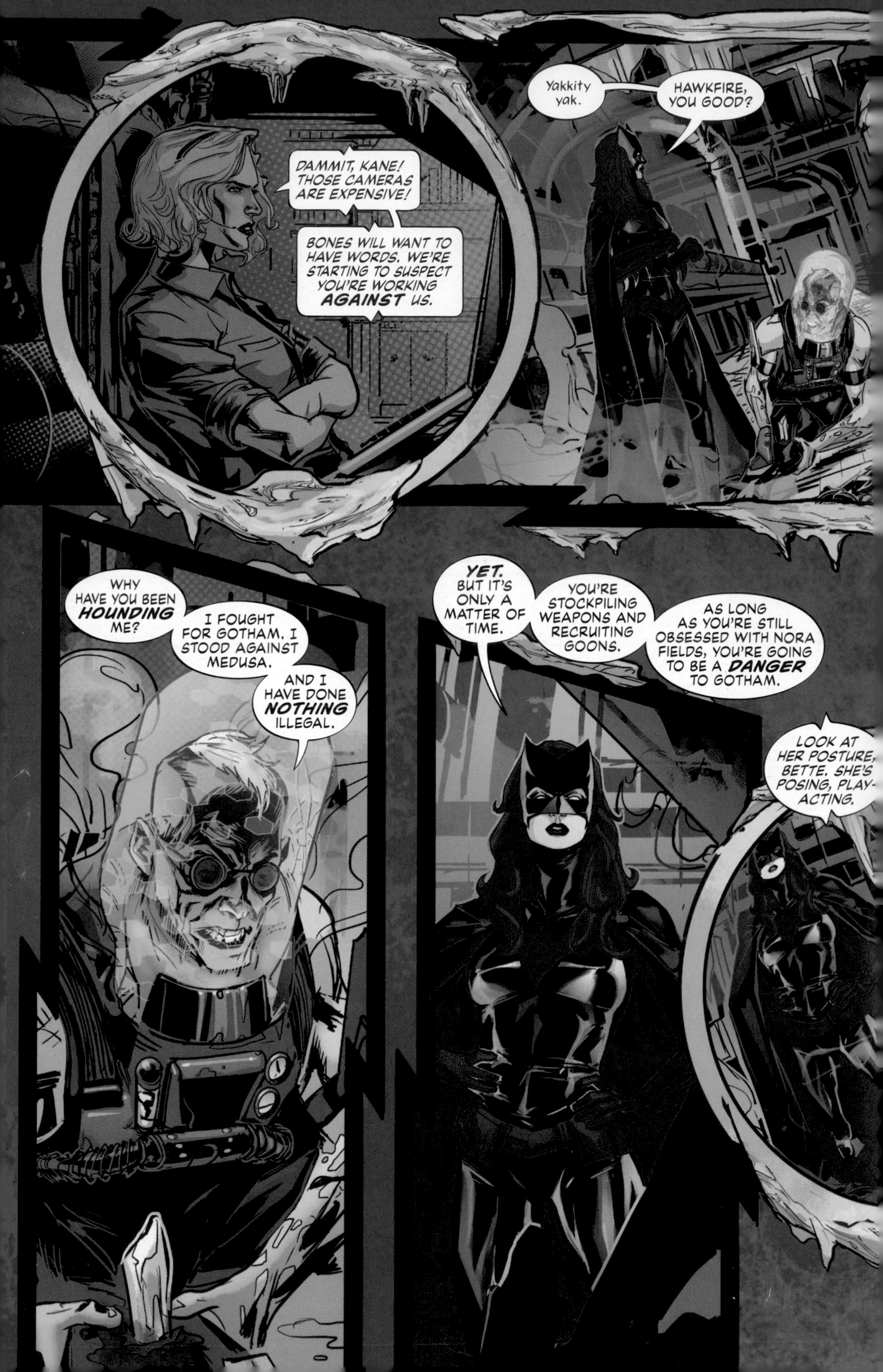
DAMMIT, KANE! THOSE CAMERAS ARE EXPENSIVE!
BONES WILL WANT TO HAVE WORDS. WE'RE STARTING TO SUSPECT YOU'RE WORKING **AGAINST** US.
Yakkity yak.
HAWKFIRE, YOU GOOD?
WHY HAVE YOU BEEN **HOUNDING** ME?
I FOUGHT FOR GOTHAM. I STOOD AGAINST MEDUSA.
AND I HAVE DONE **NOTHING** ILLEGAL.
YET. BUT IT'S ONLY A MATTER OF TIME.
YOU'RE STOCKPILING WEAPONS AND RECRUITING GOONS.
AS LONG AS YOU'RE STILL OBSESSED WITH NORA FIELDS, YOU'RE GOING TO BE A **DANGER** TO GOTHAM.
LOOK AT HER POSTURE, BETTE. SHE'S POSING, PLAY-ACTING.

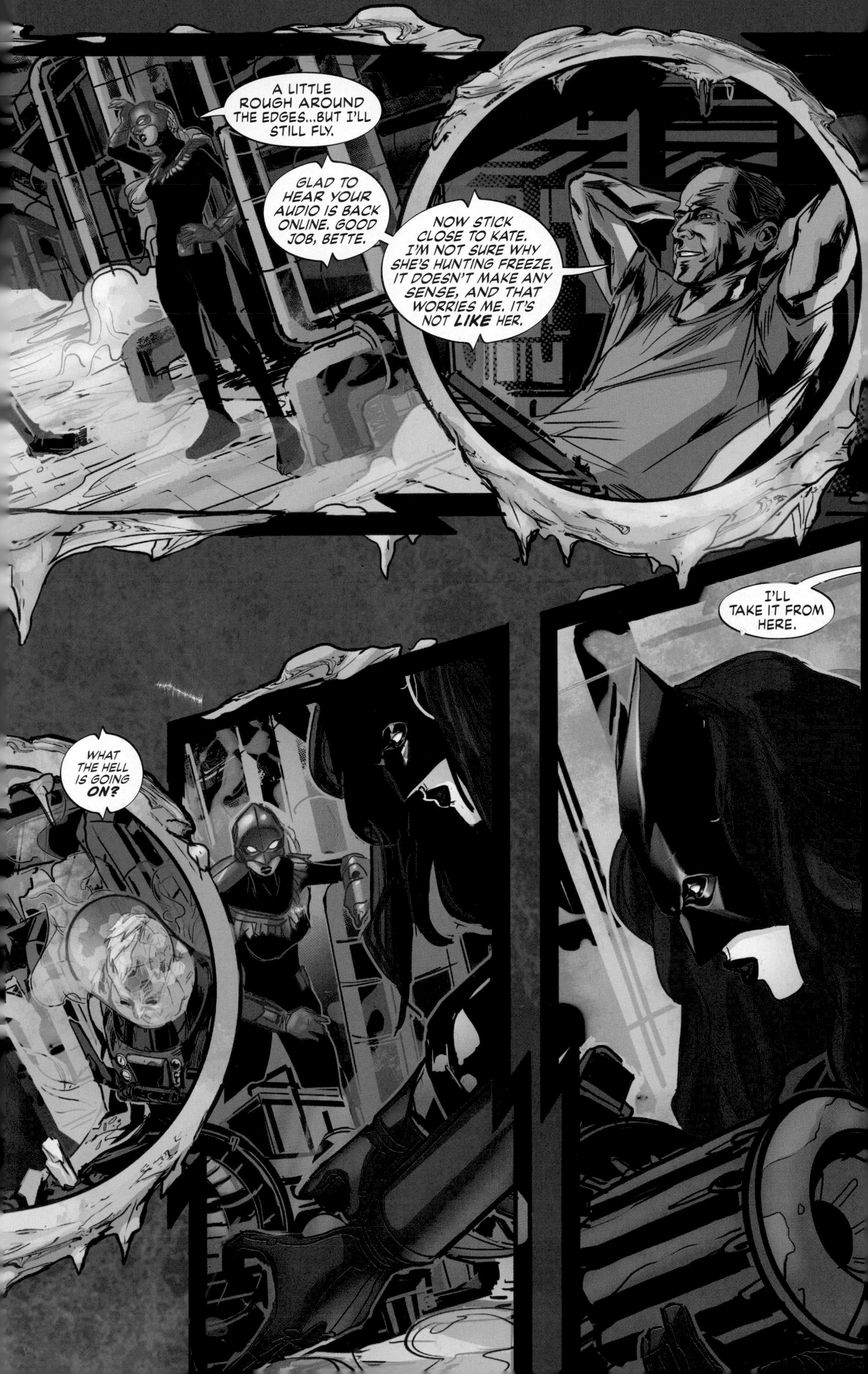
A LITTLE ROUGH AROUND THE EDGES...BUT I'LL STILL FLY.
GLAD TO HEAR YOUR AUDIO IS BACK ONLINE. GOOD JOB, BETTE.
NOW STICK CLOSE TO KATE. I'M NOT SURE WHY SHE'S HUNTING FREEZE. IT DOESN'T MAKE ANY SENSE, AND THAT WORRIES ME. IT'S NOT LIKE HER.
I'LL TAKE IT FROM HERE.
WHAT THE HELL IS GOING ON?

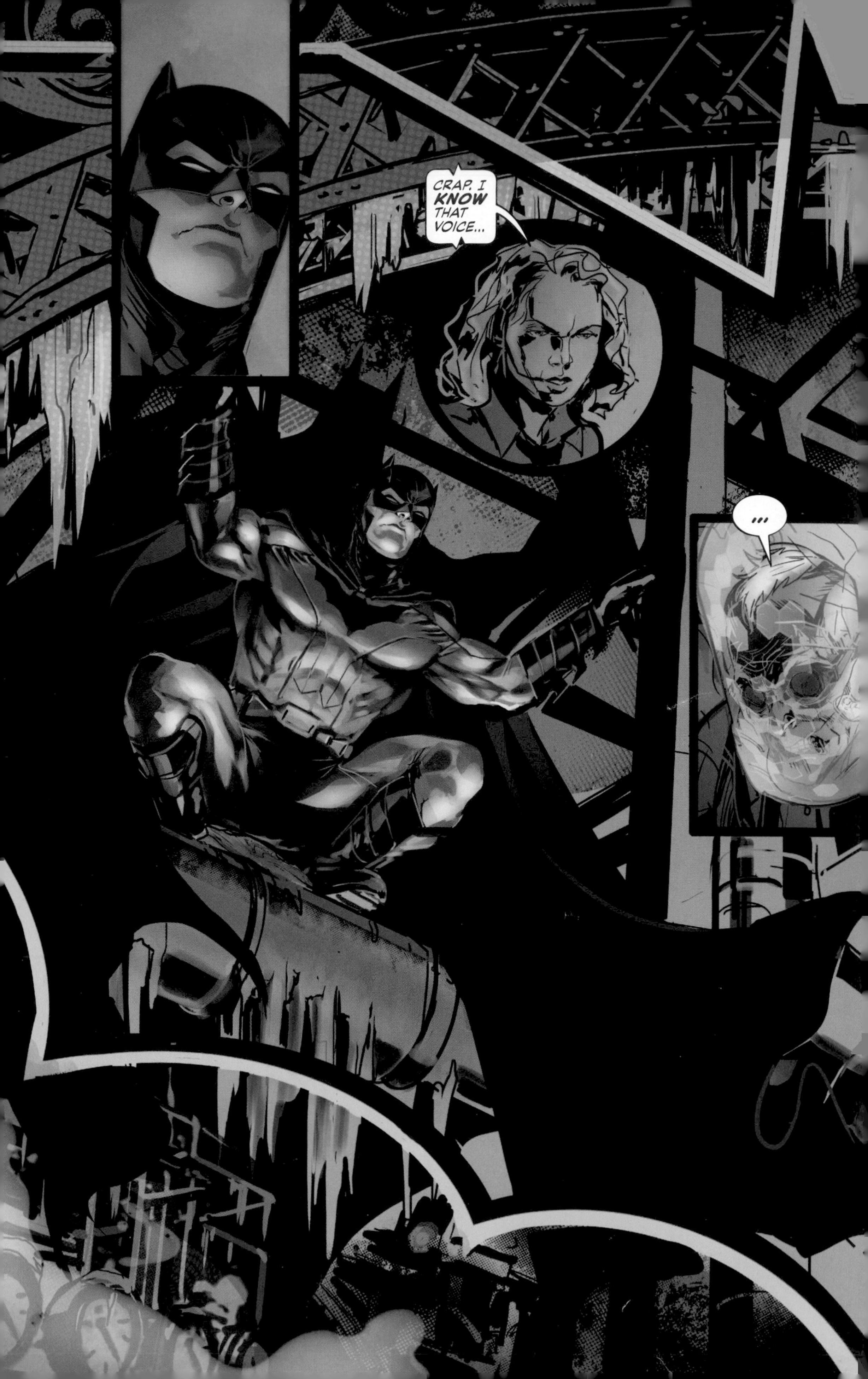
CRAP. I KNOW THAT VOICE...
...

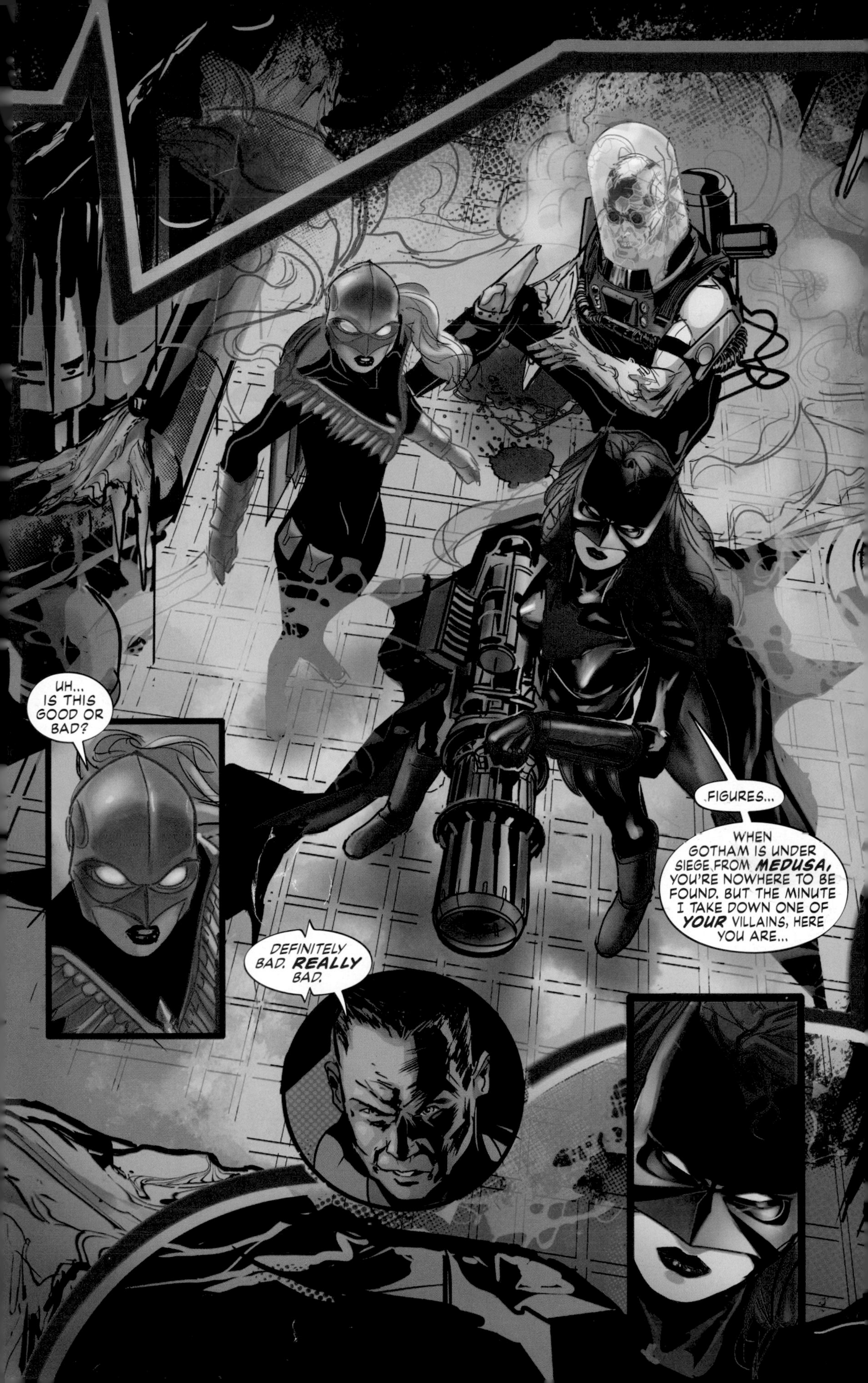
UH... IS THIS GOOD OR BAD?
DEFINITELY BAD. REALLY BAD.
FIGURES...
WHEN GOTHAM IS UNDER SIEGE FROM MEDUSA, YOU'RE NOWHERE TO BE FOUND. BUT THE MINUTE I TAKE DOWN ONE OF YOUR VILLAINS, HERE YOU ARE...

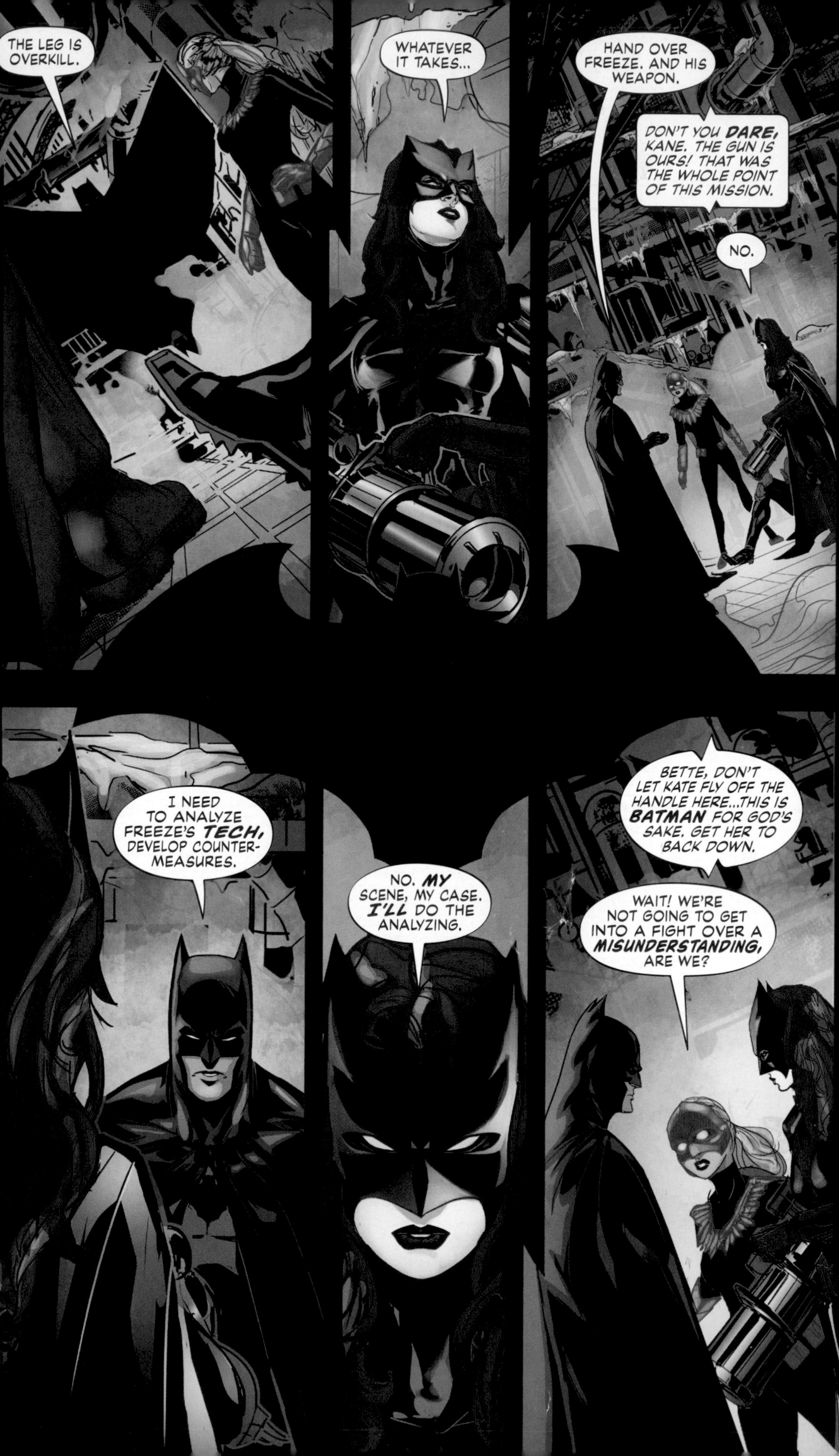
THE LEG IS OVERKILL.
WHATEVER IT TAKES...
HAND OVER FREEZE. AND HIS WEAPON.
DON'T YOU DARE, KANE. THE GUN IS OURS! THAT WAS THE WHOLE POINT OF THIS MISSION.
NO.
I NEED TO ANALYZE FREEZE'S TECH, DEVELOP COUNTER-MEASURES.
NO. MY SCENE, MY CASE. I'LL DO THE ANALYZING.
BETTE, DON'T LET KATE FLY OFF THE HANDLE HERE...THIS IS BATMAN FOR GOD'S SAKE. GET HER TO BACK DOWN.
WAIT! WE'RE NOT GOING TO GET INTO A FIGHT OVER A MISUNDERSTANDING, ARE WE?

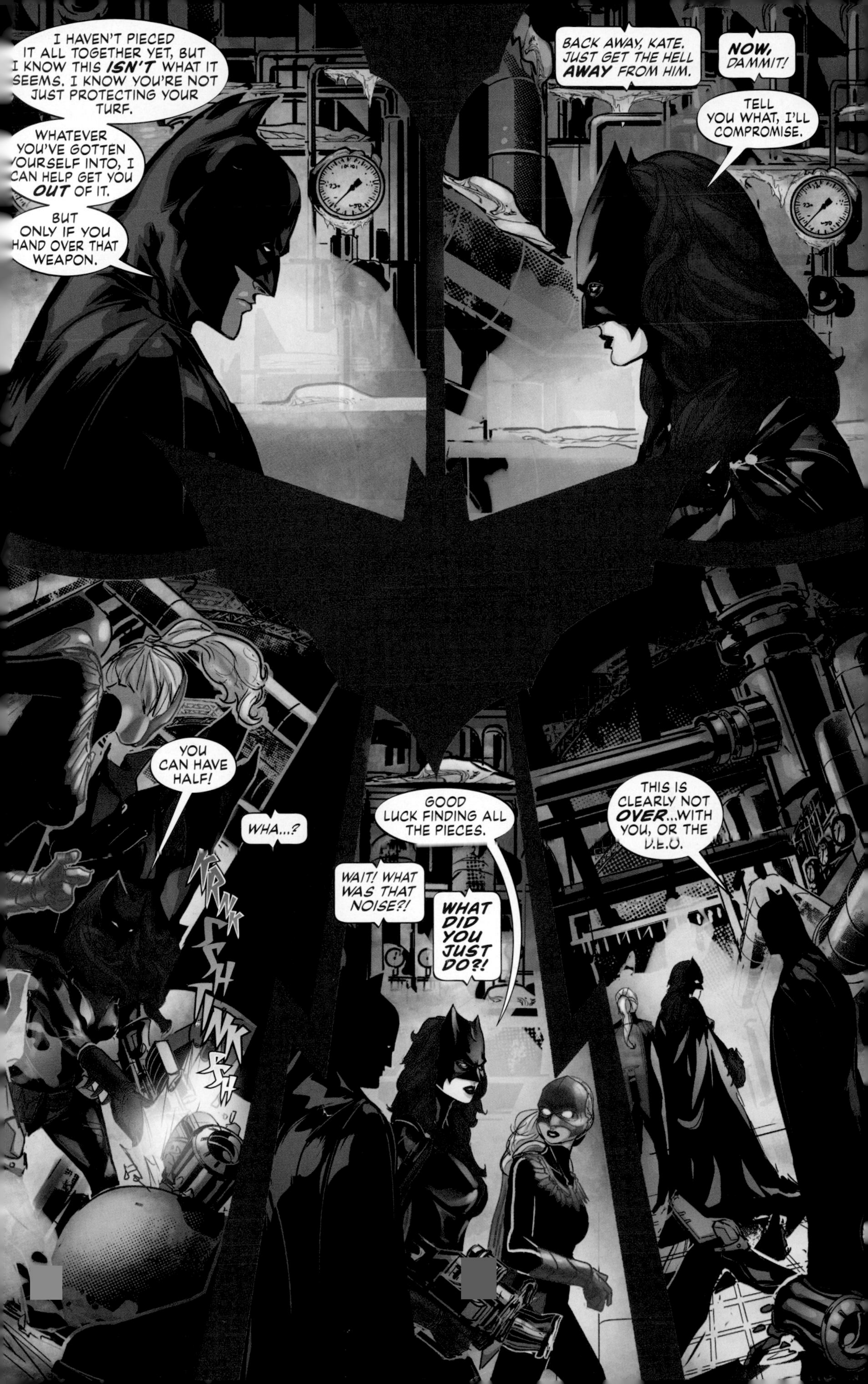
I HAVEN'T PIECED IT ALL TOGETHER YET, BUT I KNOW THIS *ISN'T* WHAT IT SEEMS. I KNOW YOU'RE NOT JUST PROTECTING YOUR TURF.
WHATEVER YOU'VE GOTTEN YOURSELF INTO, I CAN HELP GET YOU *OUT* OF IT.
BUT ONLY IF YOU HAND OVER THAT WEAPON.
BACK AWAY, KATE. JUST GET THE HELL *AWAY* FROM HIM.
NOW, DAMMIT!
TELL YOU WHAT, I'LL COMPROMISE.
YOU CAN HAVE HALF!
WHA...?
KRNK
SSH
TINK
SSH
GOOD LUCK FINDING ALL THE PIECES.
WAIT! WHAT WAS THAT NOISE?!
WHAT DID YOU JUST DO?!
THIS IS CLEARLY NOT *OVER*...WITH YOU, OR THE D.E.O.

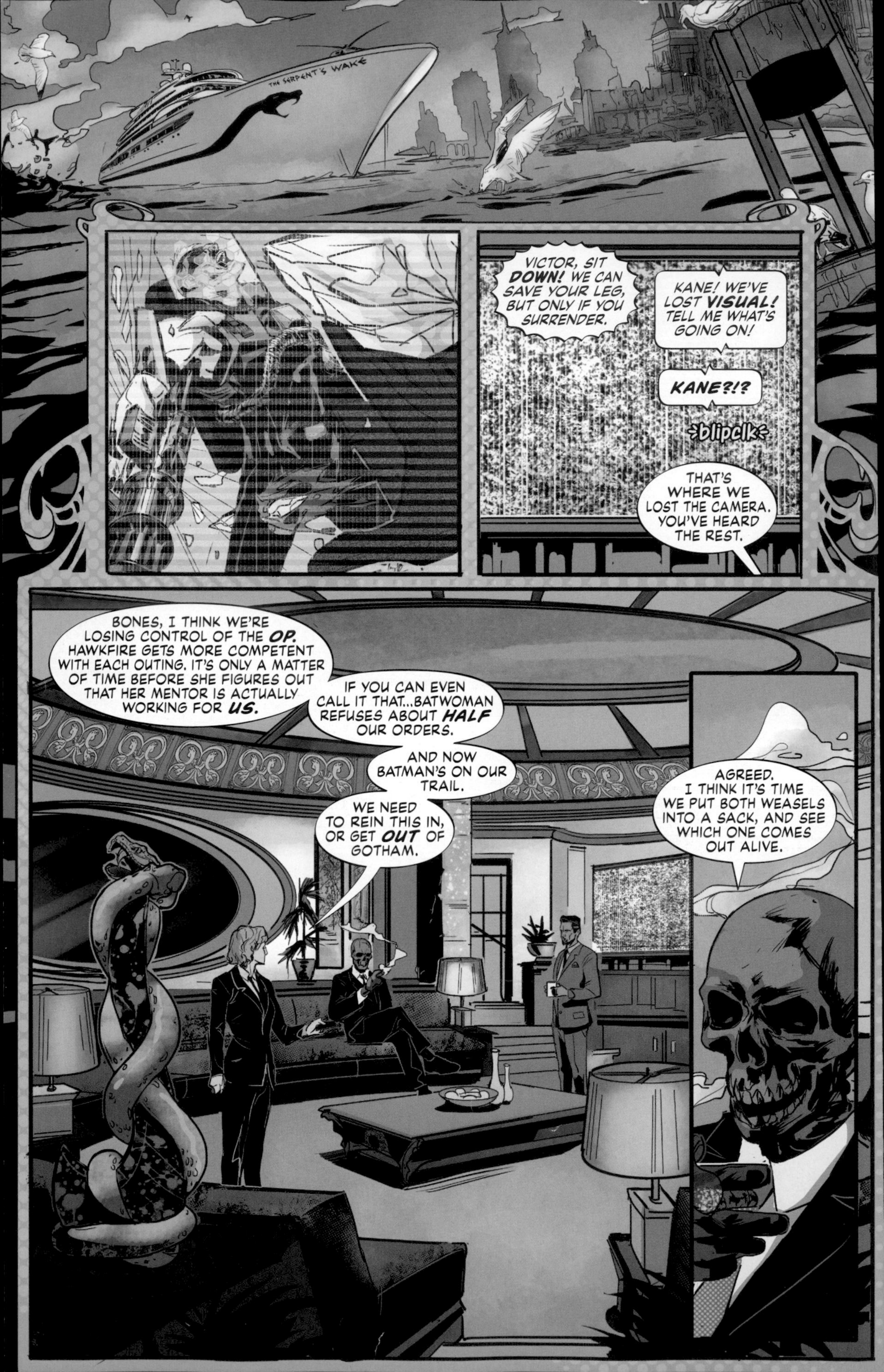
THE SERPENT'S WAKE
VICTOR, SIT DOWN! WE CAN SAVE YOUR LEG, BUT ONLY IF YOU SURRENDER.
KANE! WE'VE LOST VISUAL! TELL ME WHAT'S GOING ON!
KANE?!?
blipclk
THAT'S WHERE WE LOST THE CAMERA. YOU'VE HEARD THE REST.
BONES, I THINK WE'RE LOSING CONTROL OF THE OP. HAWKFIRE GETS MORE COMPETENT WITH EACH OUTING. IT'S ONLY A MATTER OF TIME BEFORE SHE FIGURES OUT THAT HER MENTOR IS ACTUALLY WORKING FOR US.
IF YOU CAN EVEN CALL IT THAT...BATWOMAN REFUSES ABOUT HALF OUR ORDERS.
AND NOW BATMAN'S ON OUR TRAIL.
WE NEED TO REIN THIS IN, OR GET OUT OF GOTHAM.
AGREED. I THINK IT'S TIME WE PUT BOTH WEASELS INTO A SACK, AND SEE WHICH ONE COMES OUT ALIVE.

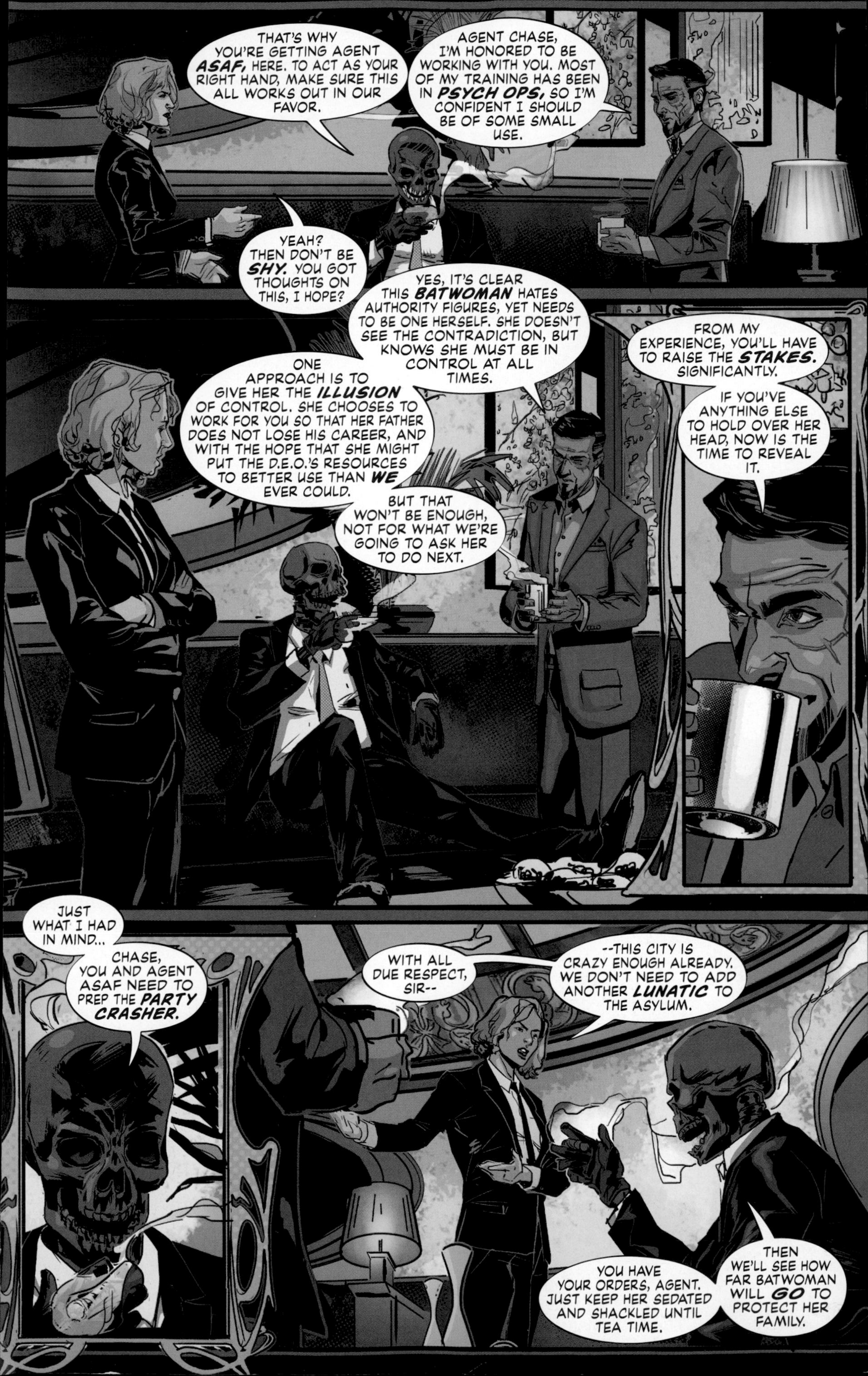
THAT'S WHY YOU'RE GETTING AGENT ASAF, HERE. TO ACT AS YOUR RIGHT HAND, MAKE SURE THIS ALL WORKS OUT IN OUR FAVOR.
AGENT CHASE, I'M HONORED TO BE WORKING WITH YOU. MOST OF MY TRAINING HAS BEEN IN PSYCH OPS, SO I'M CONFIDENT I SHOULD BE OF SOME SMALL USE.
YEAH? THEN DON'T BE SHY. YOU GOT THOUGHTS ON THIS, I HOPE?
YES, IT'S CLEAR THIS BATWOMAN HATES AUTHORITY FIGURES, YET NEEDS TO BE ONE HERSELF. SHE DOESN'T SEE THE CONTRADICTION, BUT KNOWS SHE MUST BE IN CONTROL AT ALL TIMES.
ONE APPROACH IS TO GIVE HER THE ILLUSION OF CONTROL. SHE CHOOSES TO WORK FOR YOU SO THAT HER FATHER DOES NOT LOSE HIS CAREER, AND WITH THE HOPE THAT SHE MIGHT PUT THE D.E.O.'S RESOURCES TO BETTER USE THAN WE EVER COULD.
BUT THAT WON'T BE ENOUGH, NOT FOR WHAT WE'RE GOING TO ASK HER TO DO NEXT.
FROM MY EXPERIENCE, YOU'LL HAVE TO RAISE THE STAKES. SIGNIFICANTLY.
IF YOU'VE ANYTHING ELSE TO HOLD OVER HER HEAD, NOW IS THE TIME TO REVEAL IT.
JUST WHAT I HAD IN MIND...
CHASE, YOU AND AGENT ASAF NEED TO PREP THE PARTY CRASHER.
WITH ALL DUE RESPECT, SIR--
--THIS CITY IS CRAZY ENOUGH ALREADY. WE DON'T NEED TO ADD ANOTHER LUNATIC TO THE ASYLUM.
YOU HAVE YOUR ORDERS, AGENT. JUST KEEP HER SEDATED AND SHACKLED UNTIL TEA TIME.
THEN WE'LL SEE HOW FAR BATWOMAN WILL GO TO PROTECT HER FAMILY.

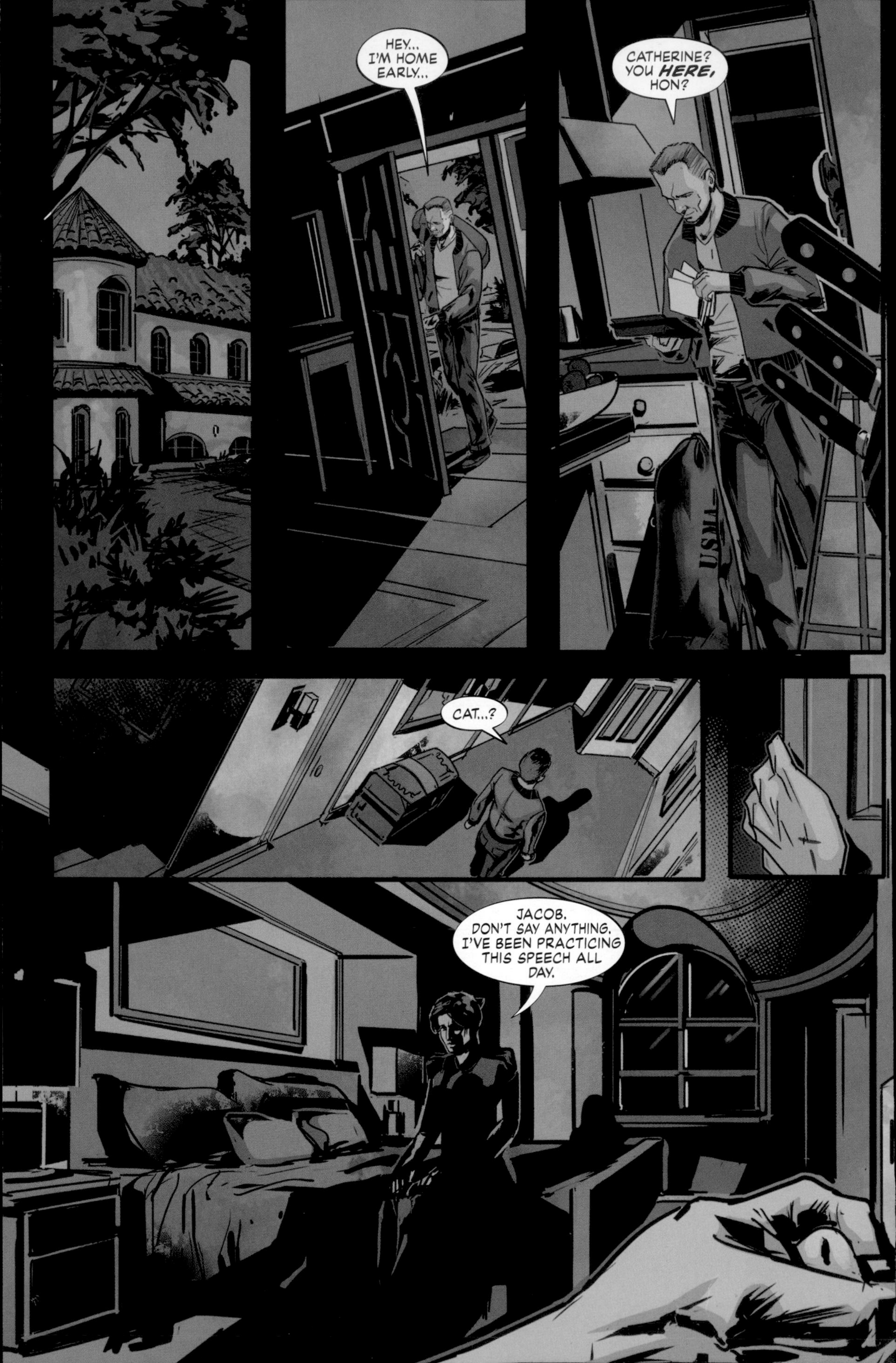
HEY... I'M HOME EARLY...
CATHERINE? YOU **HERE,** HON?
CAT...?
JACOB. DON'T SAY ANYTHING. I'VE BEEN PRACTICING THIS SPEECH ALL DAY.

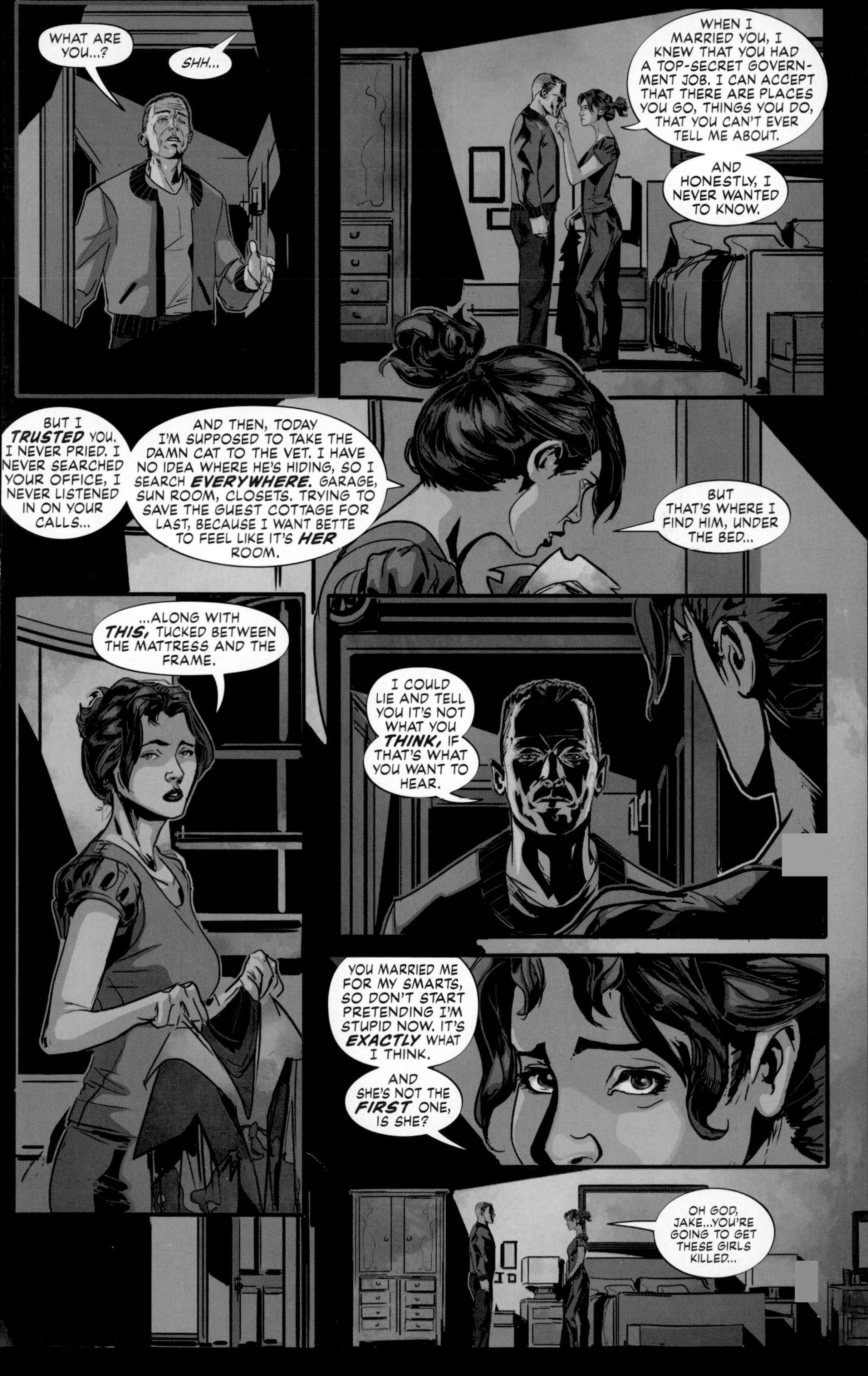
WHAT ARE YOU...?
SHH...
WHEN I MARRIED YOU, I KNEW THAT YOU HAD A TOP-SECRET GOVERNMENT JOB. I CAN ACCEPT THAT THERE ARE PLACES YOU GO, THINGS YOU DO, THAT YOU CAN'T EVER TELL ME ABOUT.
AND HONESTLY, I NEVER WANTED TO KNOW.
BUT I TRUSTED YOU. I NEVER PRIED. I NEVER SEARCHED YOUR OFFICE, I NEVER LISTENED IN ON YOUR CALLS...
AND THEN, TODAY I'M SUPPOSED TO TAKE THE DAMN CAT TO THE VET. I HAVE NO IDEA WHERE HE'S HIDING, SO I SEARCH EVERYWHERE. GARAGE, SUN ROOM, CLOSETS. TRYING TO SAVE THE GUEST COTTAGE FOR LAST, BECAUSE I WANT BETTE TO FEEL LIKE IT'S HER ROOM.
BUT THAT'S WHERE I FIND HIM, UNDER THE BED...
...ALONG WITH THIS, TUCKED BETWEEN THE MATTRESS AND THE FRAME.
I COULD LIE AND TELL YOU IT'S NOT WHAT YOU THINK, IF THAT'S WHAT YOU WANT TO HEAR.
YOU MARRIED ME FOR MY SMARTS, SO DON'T START PRETENDING I'M STUPID NOW. IT'S EXACTLY WHAT I THINK.
AND SHE'S NOT THE FIRST ONE, IS SHE?
OH GOD, JAKE...YOU'RE GOING TO GET THESE GIRLS KILLED...

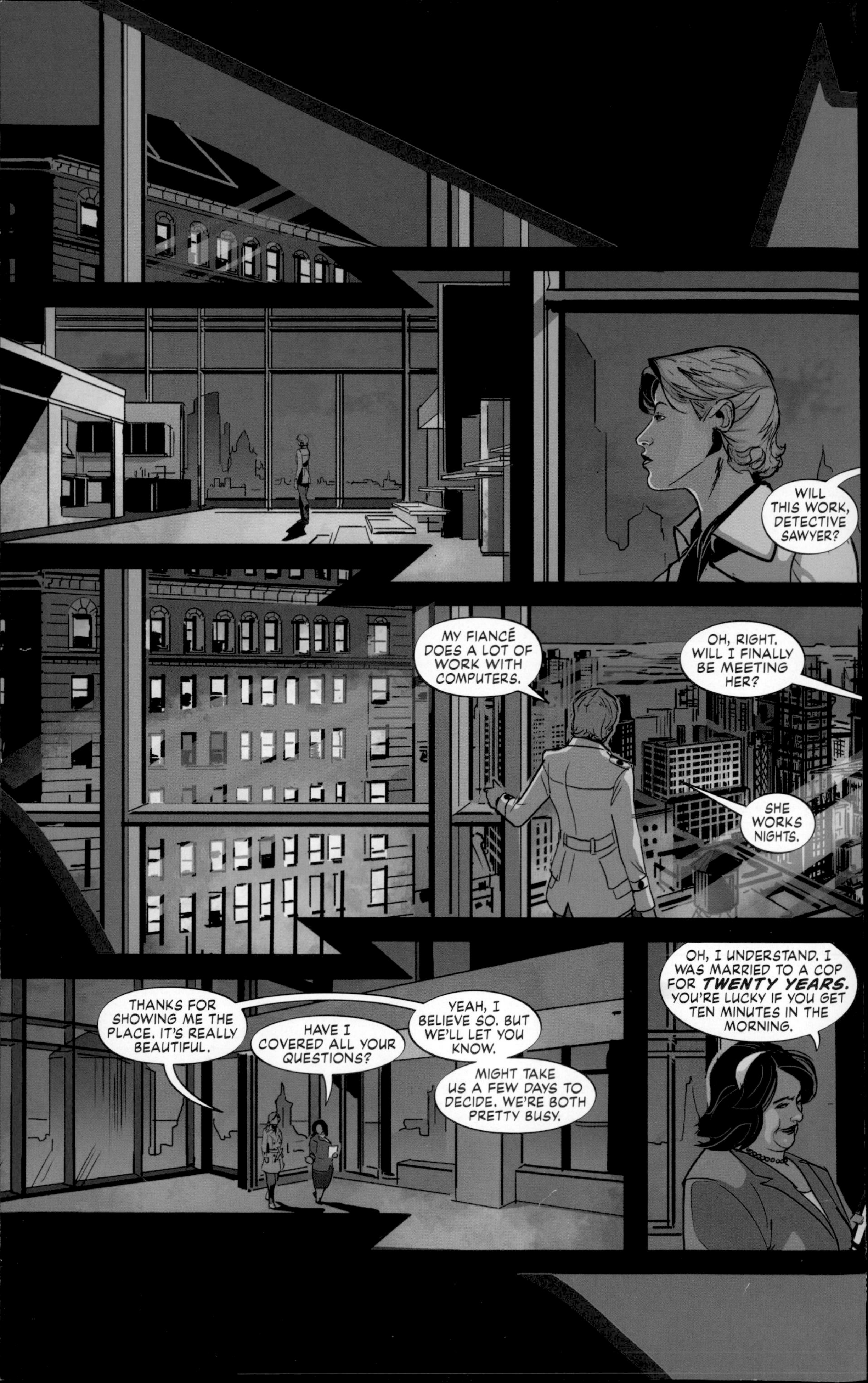
WILL THIS WORK, DETECTIVE SAWYER?
MY FIANCÉ DOES A LOT OF WORK WITH COMPUTERS.
OH, RIGHT. WILL I FINALLY BE MEETING HER?
SHE WORKS NIGHTS.
OH, I UNDERSTAND. I WAS MARRIED TO A COP FOR TWENTY YEARS. YOU'RE LUCKY IF YOU GET TEN MINUTES IN THE MORNING.
THANKS FOR SHOWING ME THE PLACE. IT'S REALLY BEAUTIFUL.
HAVE I COVERED ALL YOUR QUESTIONS?
YEAH, I BELIEVE SO. BUT WE'LL LET YOU KNOW.
MIGHT TAKE US A FEW DAYS TO DECIDE. WE'RE BOTH PRETTY BUSY.

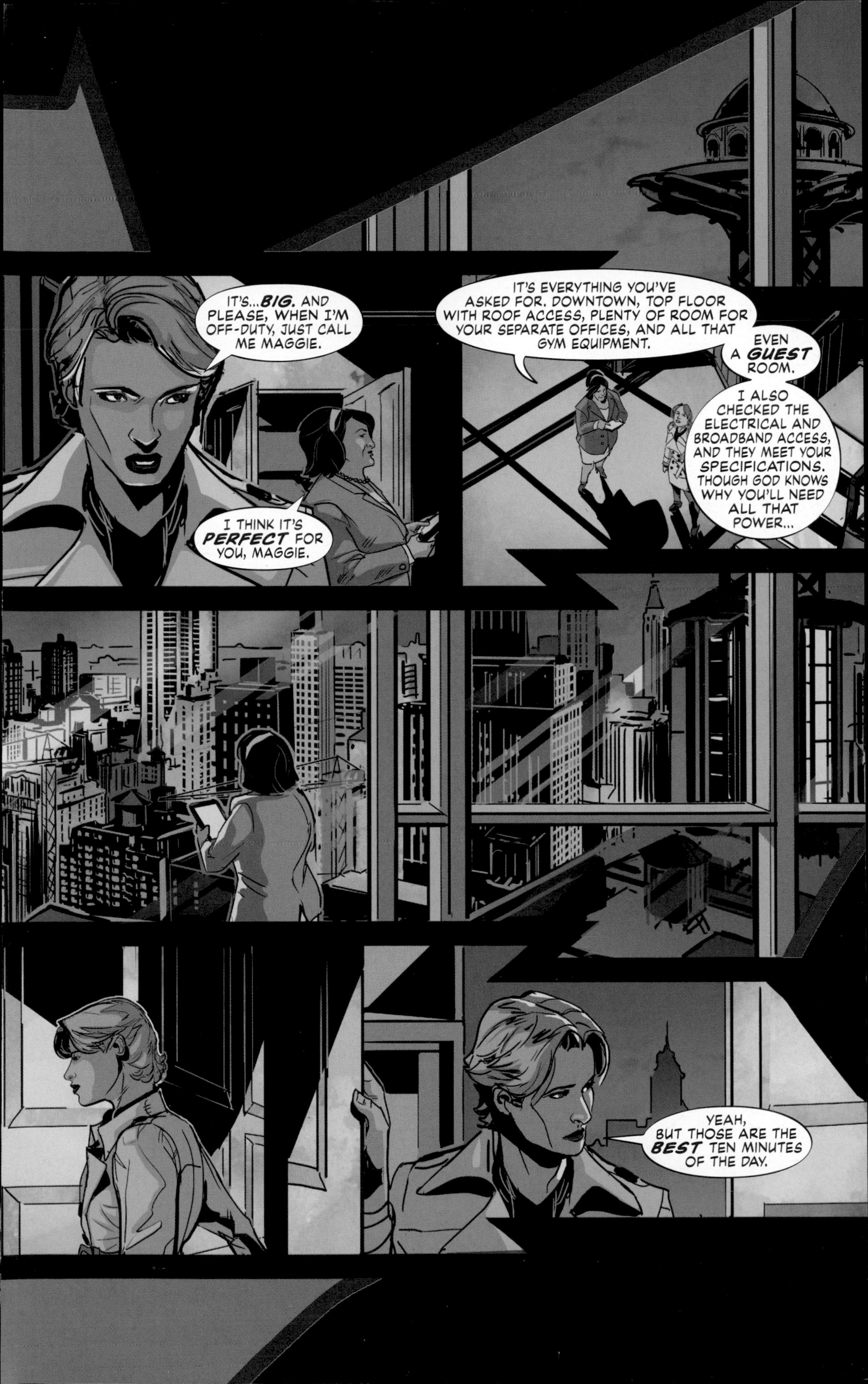
IT'S...BIG. AND PLEASE, WHEN I'M OFF-DUTY, JUST CALL ME MAGGIE.
I THINK IT'S PERFECT FOR YOU, MAGGIE.
IT'S EVERYTHING YOU'VE ASKED FOR. DOWNTOWN, TOP FLOOR WITH ROOF ACCESS, PLENTY OF ROOM FOR YOUR SEPARATE OFFICES, AND ALL THAT GYM EQUIPMENT.
EVEN A GUEST ROOM.
I ALSO CHECKED THE ELECTRICAL AND BROADBAND ACCESS, AND THEY MEET YOUR SPECIFICATIONS. THOUGH GOD KNOWS WHY YOU'LL NEED ALL THAT POWER...
YEAH, BUT THOSE ARE THE BEST TEN MINUTES OF THE DAY.

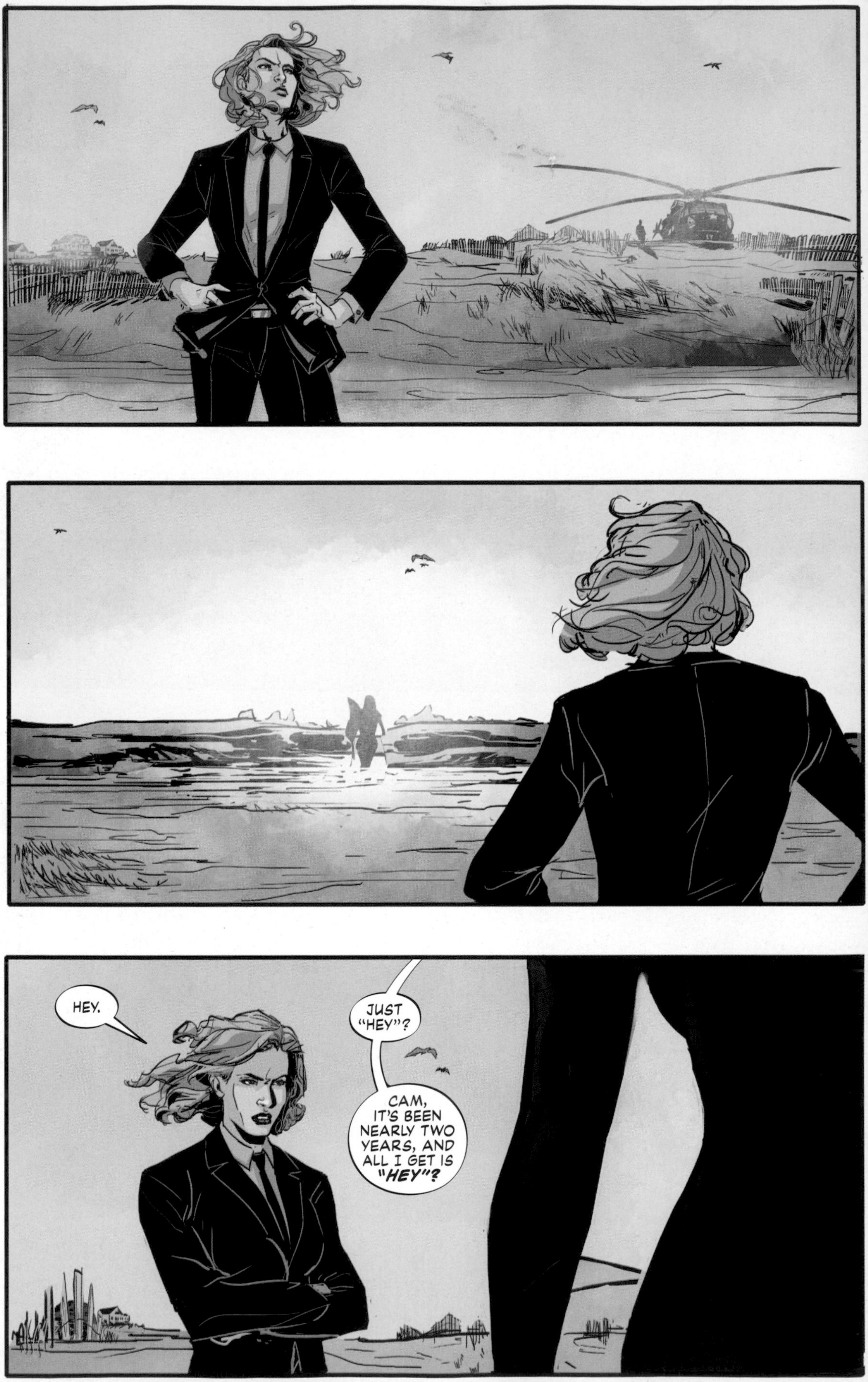
HEY.
JUST "HEY"?
CAM, IT'S BEEN NEARLY TWO YEARS, AND ALL I GET IS "HEY"?

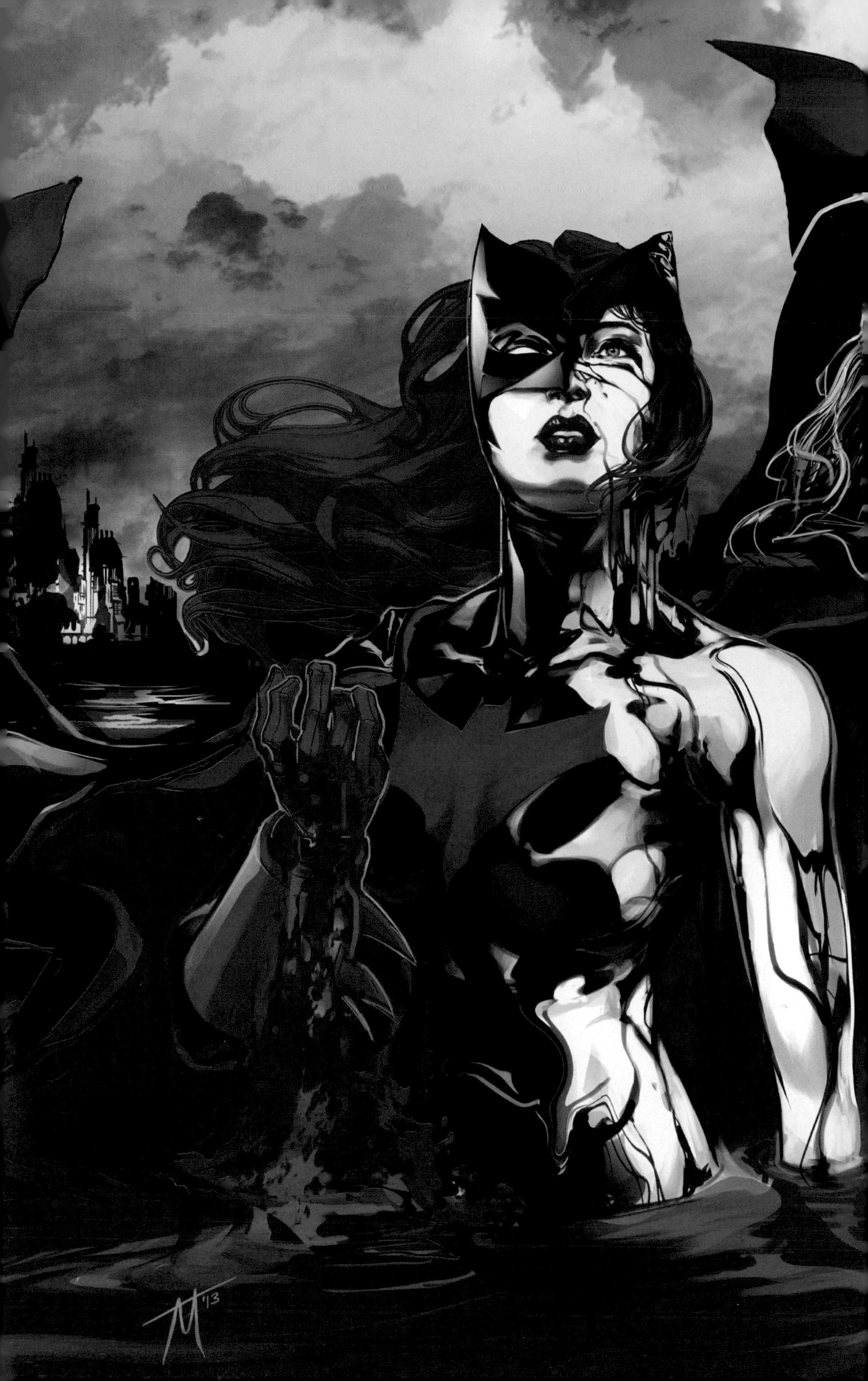

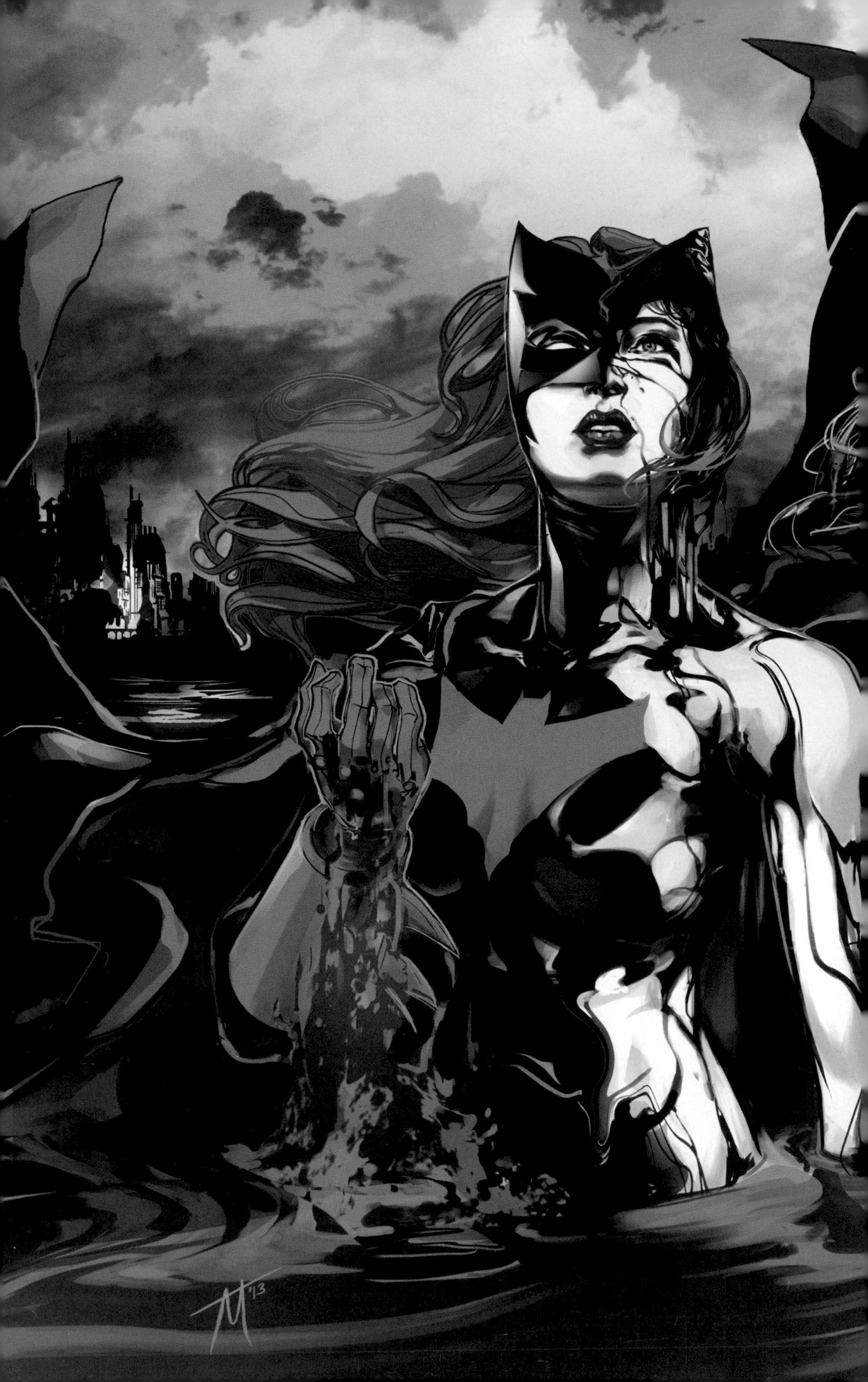

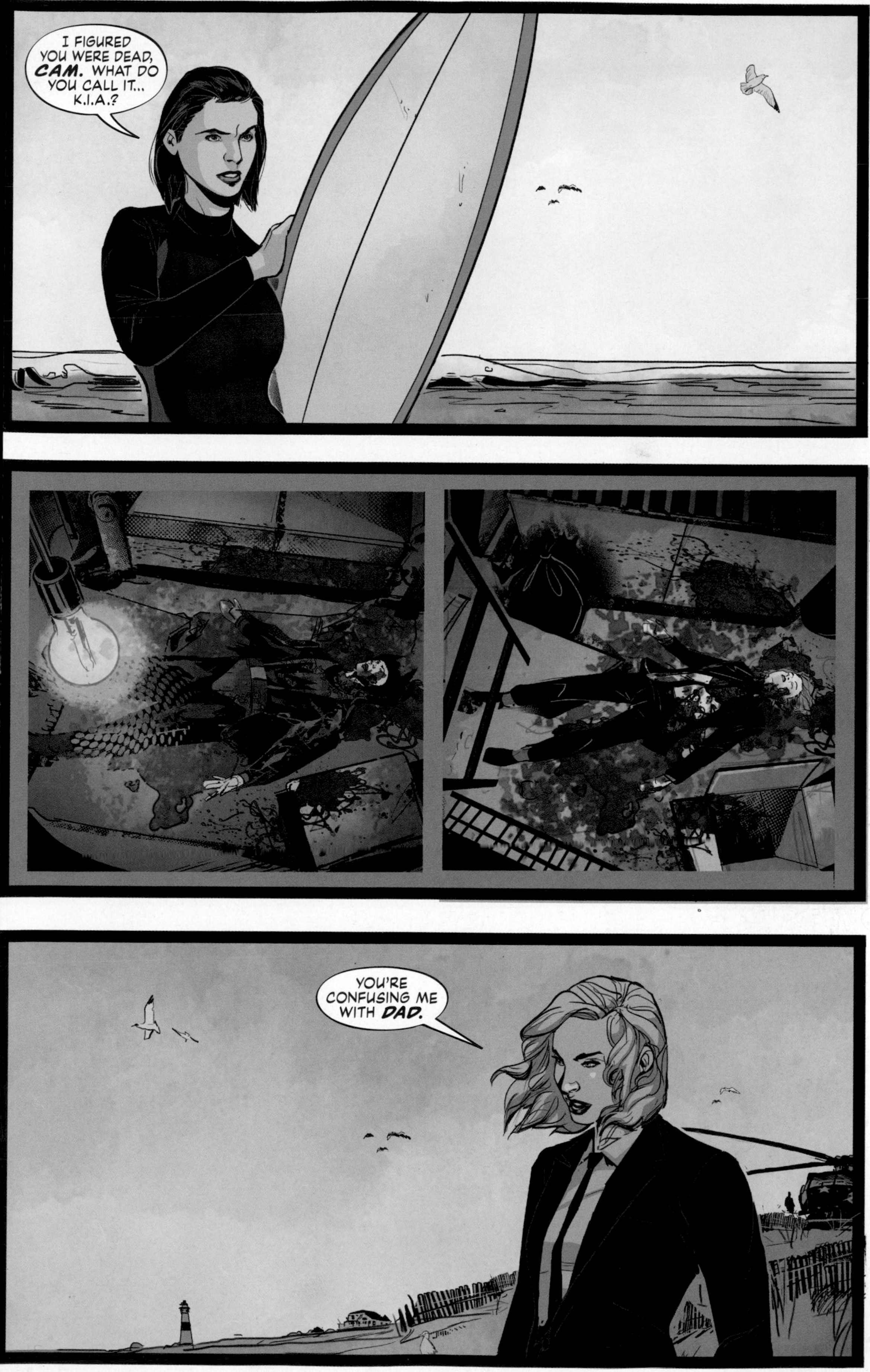
I FIGURED YOU WERE DEAD, **CAM.** WHAT DO YOU CALL IT... K.I.A.?
YOU'RE CONFUSING ME WITH **DAD.**

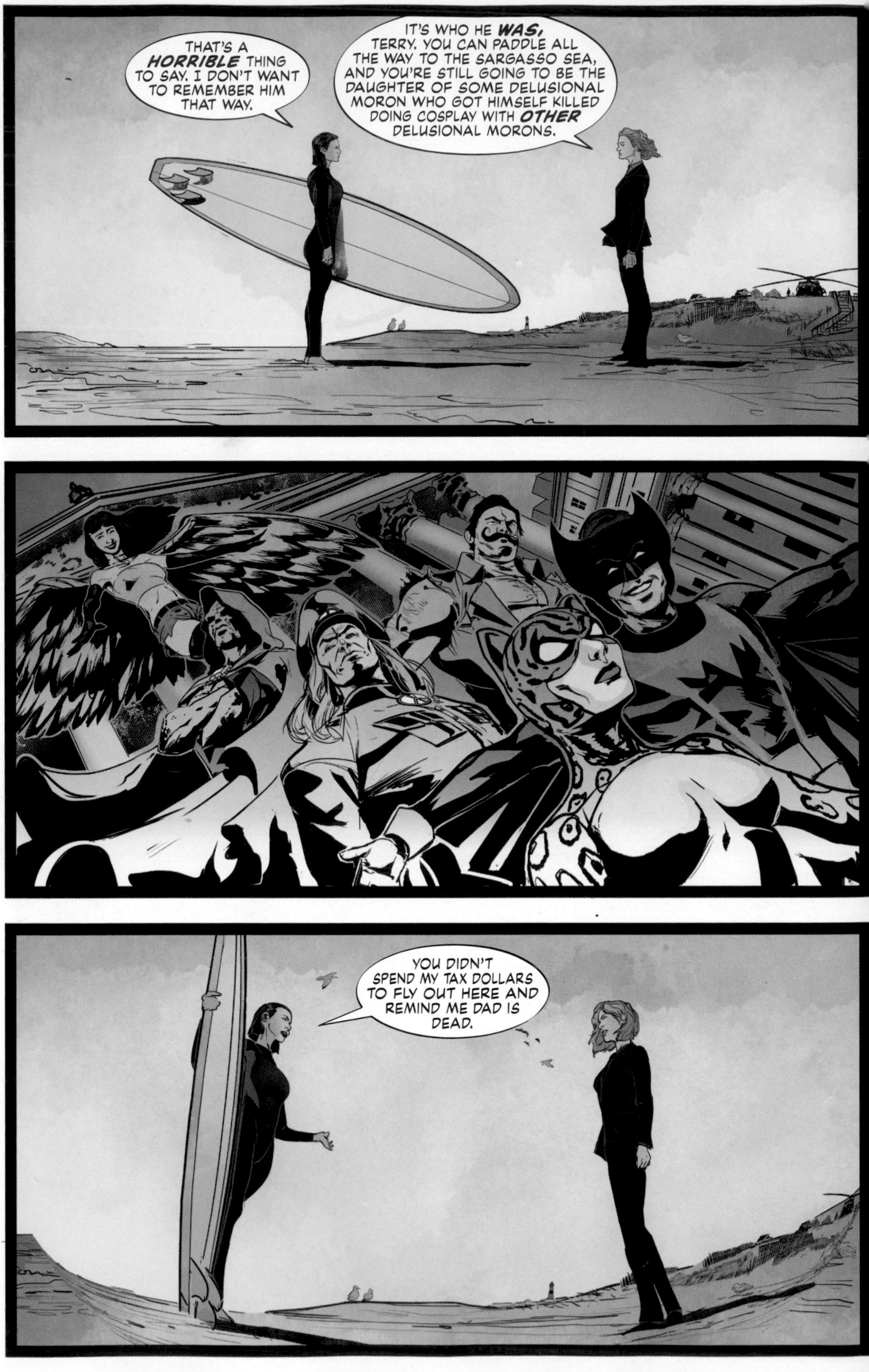
THAT'S A HORRIBLE THING TO SAY. I DON'T WANT TO REMEMBER HIM THAT WAY.
IT'S WHO HE WAS, TERRY. YOU CAN PADDLE ALL THE WAY TO THE SARGASSO SEA, AND YOU'RE STILL GOING TO BE THE DAUGHTER OF SOME DELUSIONAL MORON WHO GOT HIMSELF KILLED DOING COSPLAY WITH OTHER DELUSIONAL MORONS.
YOU DIDN'T SPEND MY TAX DOLLARS TO FLY OUT HERE AND REMIND ME DAD IS DEAD.

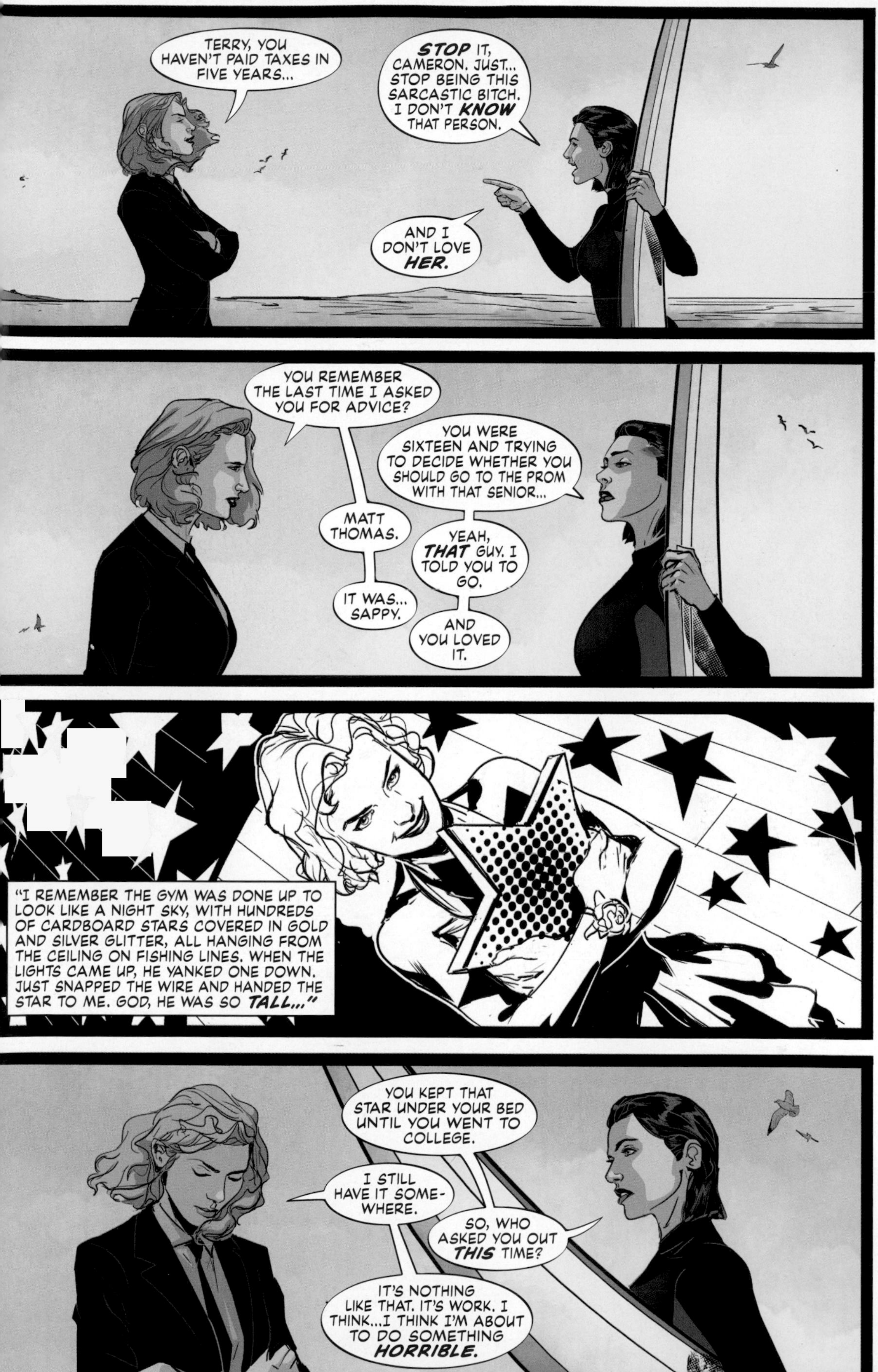

TERRY, YOU HAVEN'T PAID TAXES IN FIVE YEARS...
STOP IT, CAMERON. JUST... STOP BEING THIS SARCASTIC BITCH. I DON'T KNOW THAT PERSON.
AND I DON'T LOVE HER.
YOU REMEMBER THE LAST TIME I ASKED YOU FOR ADVICE?
YOU WERE SIXTEEN AND TRYING TO DECIDE WHETHER YOU SHOULD GO TO THE PROM WITH THAT SENIOR...
MATT THOMAS.
YEAH, THAT GUY. I TOLD YOU TO GO.
IT WAS... SAPPY.
AND YOU LOVED IT.
"I REMEMBER THE GYM WAS DONE UP TO LOOK LIKE A NIGHT SKY, WITH HUNDREDS OF CARDBOARD STARS COVERED IN GOLD AND SILVER GLITTER, ALL HANGING FROM THE CEILING ON FISHING LINES. WHEN THE LIGHTS CAME UP, HE YANKED ONE DOWN. JUST SNAPPED THE WIRE AND HANDED THE STAR TO ME. GOD, HE WAS SO TALL..."
YOU KEPT THAT STAR UNDER YOUR BED UNTIL YOU WENT TO COLLEGE.
I STILL HAVE IT SOME-WHERE.
SO, WHO ASKED YOU OUT THIS TIME?
IT'S NOTHING LIKE THAT. IT'S WORK. I THINK...I THINK I'M ABOUT TO DO SOMETHING HORRIBLE.

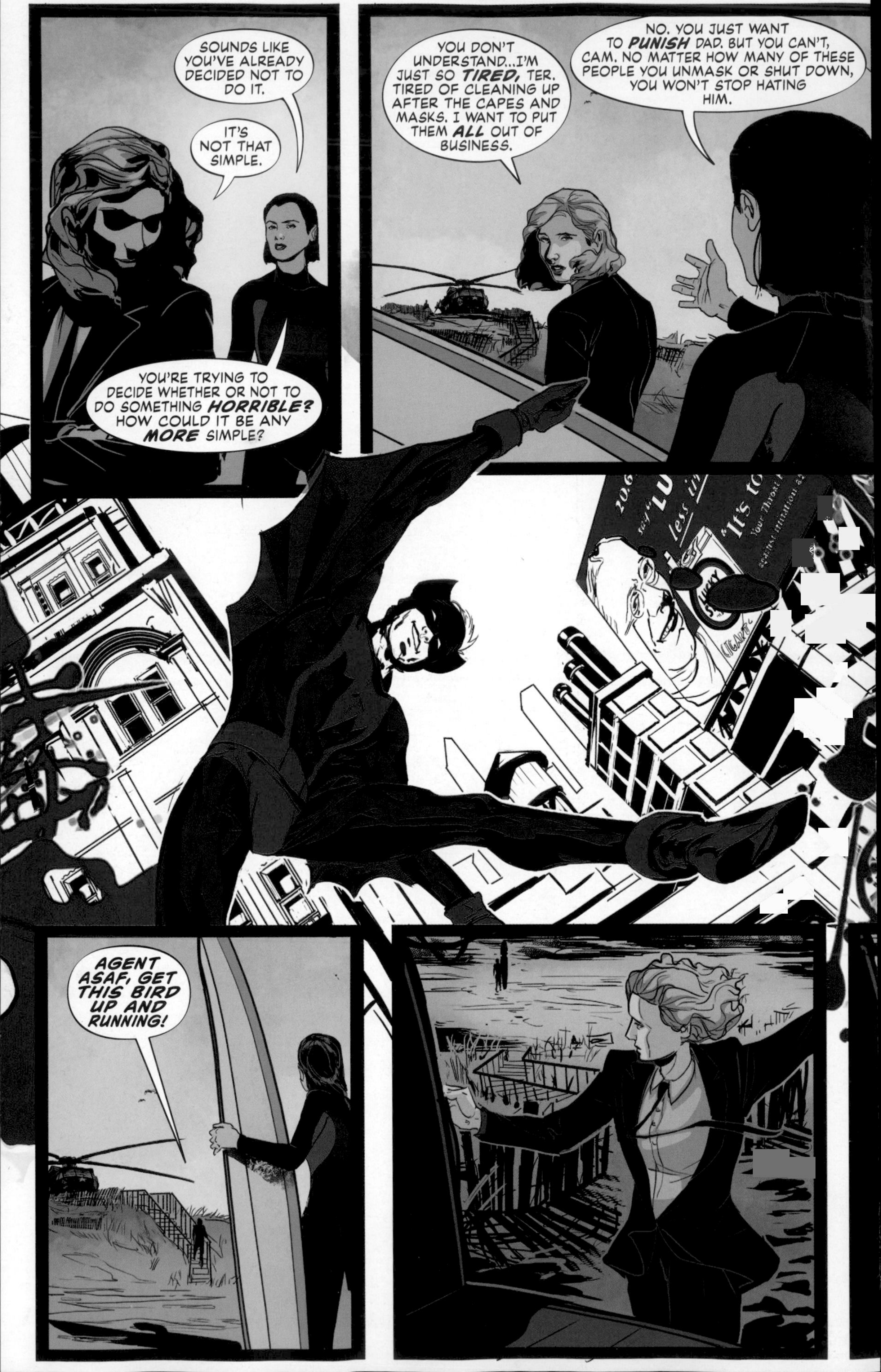
SOUNDS LIKE YOU'VE ALREADY DECIDED NOT TO DO IT.
IT'S NOT THAT SIMPLE.
YOU'RE TRYING TO DECIDE WHETHER OR NOT TO DO SOMETHING HORRIBLE? HOW COULD IT BE ANY MORE SIMPLE?
YOU DON'T UNDERSTAND...I'M JUST SO TIRED, TER. TIRED OF CLEANING UP AFTER THE CAPES AND MASKS. I WANT TO PUT THEM ALL OUT OF BUSINESS.
NO. YOU JUST WANT TO PUNISH DAD. BUT YOU CAN'T, CAM. NO MATTER HOW MANY OF THESE PEOPLE YOU UNMASK OR SHUT DOWN, YOU WON'T STOP HATING HIM.
AGENT ASAF, GET THIS BIRD UP AND RUNNING!

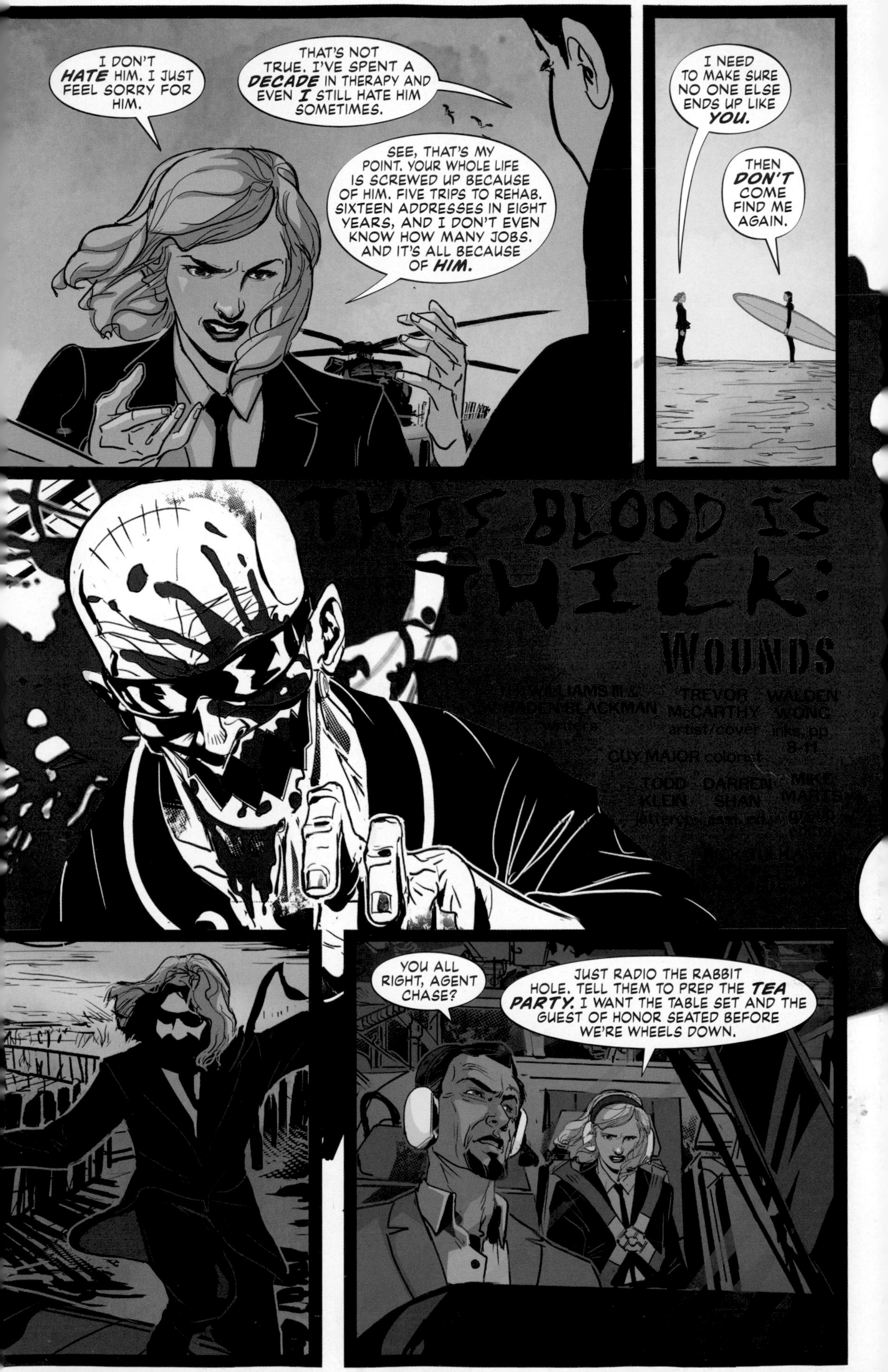
I DON'T HATE HIM. I JUST FEEL SORRY FOR HIM.
THAT'S NOT TRUE. I'VE SPENT A DECADE IN THERAPY AND EVEN I STILL HATE HIM SOMETIMES.
SEE, THAT'S MY POINT. YOUR WHOLE LIFE IS SCREWED UP BECAUSE OF HIM. FIVE TRIPS TO REHAB. SIXTEEN ADDRESSES IN EIGHT YEARS, AND I DON'T EVEN KNOW HOW MANY JOBS. AND IT'S ALL BECAUSE OF HIM.
I NEED TO MAKE SURE NO ONE ELSE ENDS UP LIKE YOU.
THEN DON'T COME FIND ME AGAIN.
THIS BLOOD IS THICK:
WOUNDS
TREVOR McCARTHY artist/cover
WALDEN WONG inks, pp 8-11
GUY MAJOR colorist
TODD KLEIN
DARREN SHAN
MIKE
YOU ALL RIGHT, AGENT CHASE?
JUST RADIO THE RABBIT HOLE. TELL THEM TO PREP THE TEA PARTY. I WANT THE TABLE SET AND THE GUEST OF HONOR SEATED BEFORE WE'RE WHEELS DOWN.

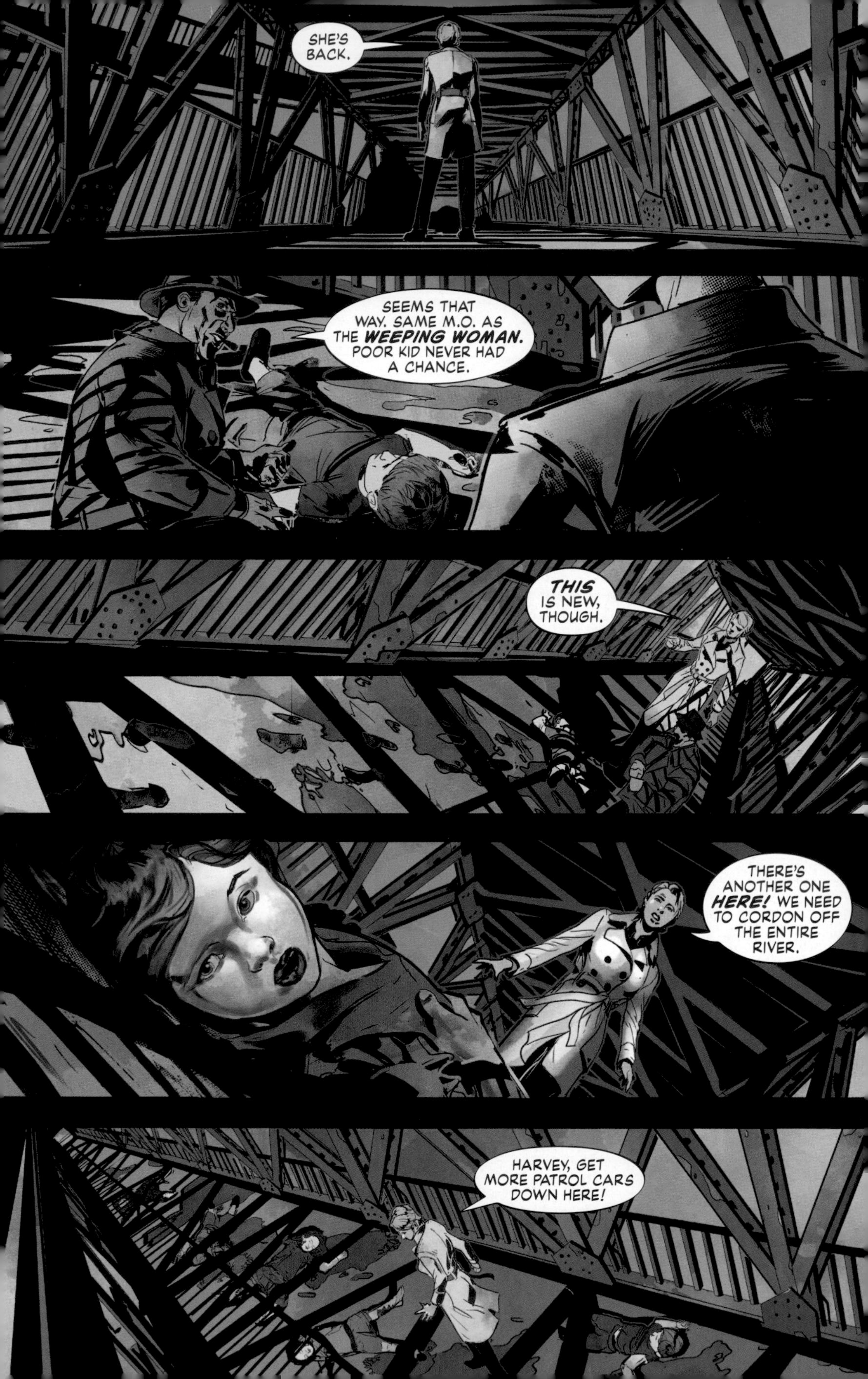
SHE'S BACK.
SEEMS THAT WAY. SAME M.O. AS THE WEEPING WOMAN. POOR KID NEVER HAD A CHANCE.
THIS IS NEW, THOUGH.
THERE'S ANOTHER ONE HERE! WE NEED TO CORDON OFF THE ENTIRE RIVER.
HARVEY, GET MORE PATROL CARS DOWN HERE!

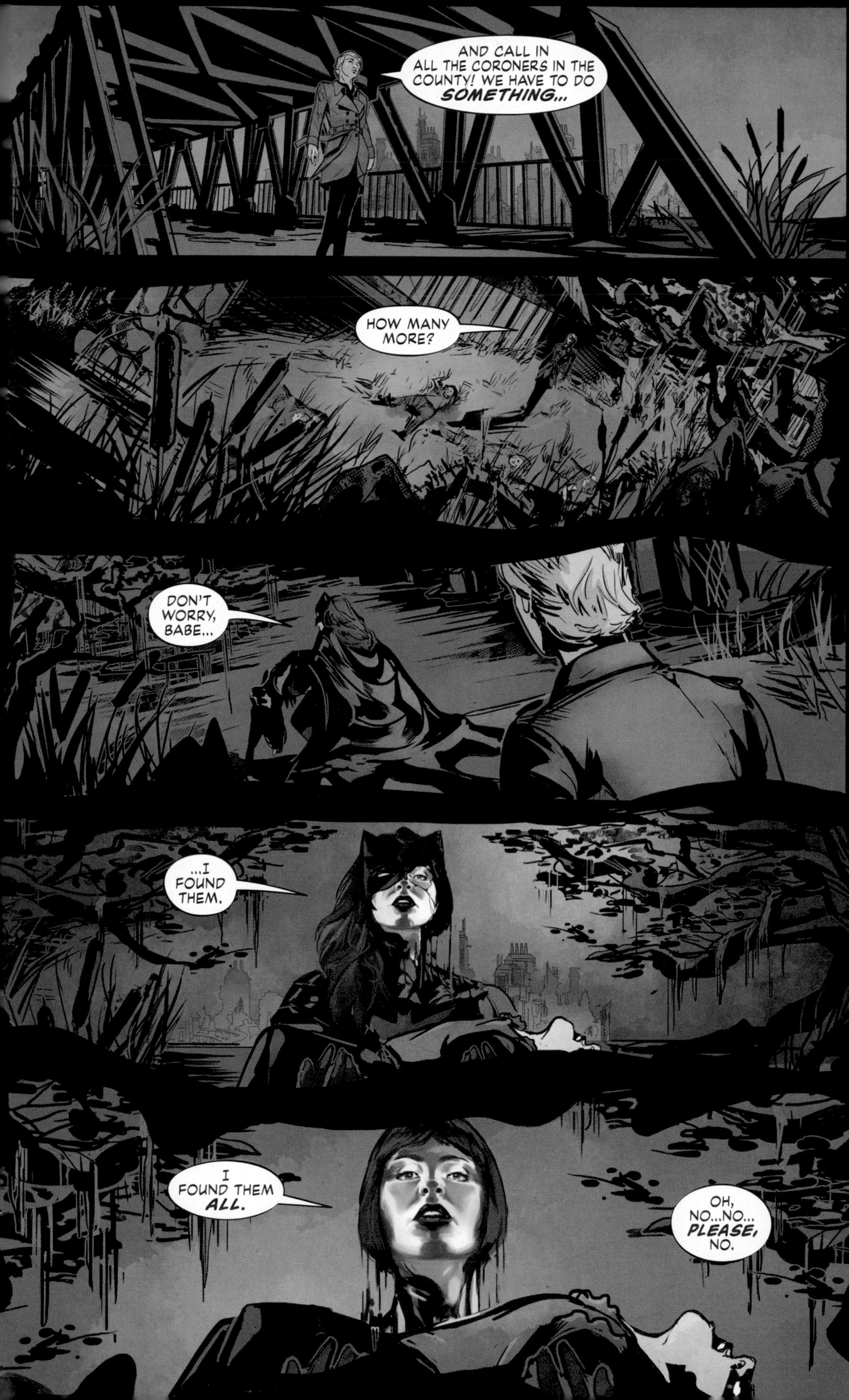
AND CALL IN ALL THE CORONERS IN THE COUNTY! WE HAVE TO DO **SOMETHING...**
HOW MANY MORE?
DON'T WORRY, BABE...
...I FOUND THEM.
I FOUND THEM **ALL.**
OH, NO...NO... **PLEASE,** NO.

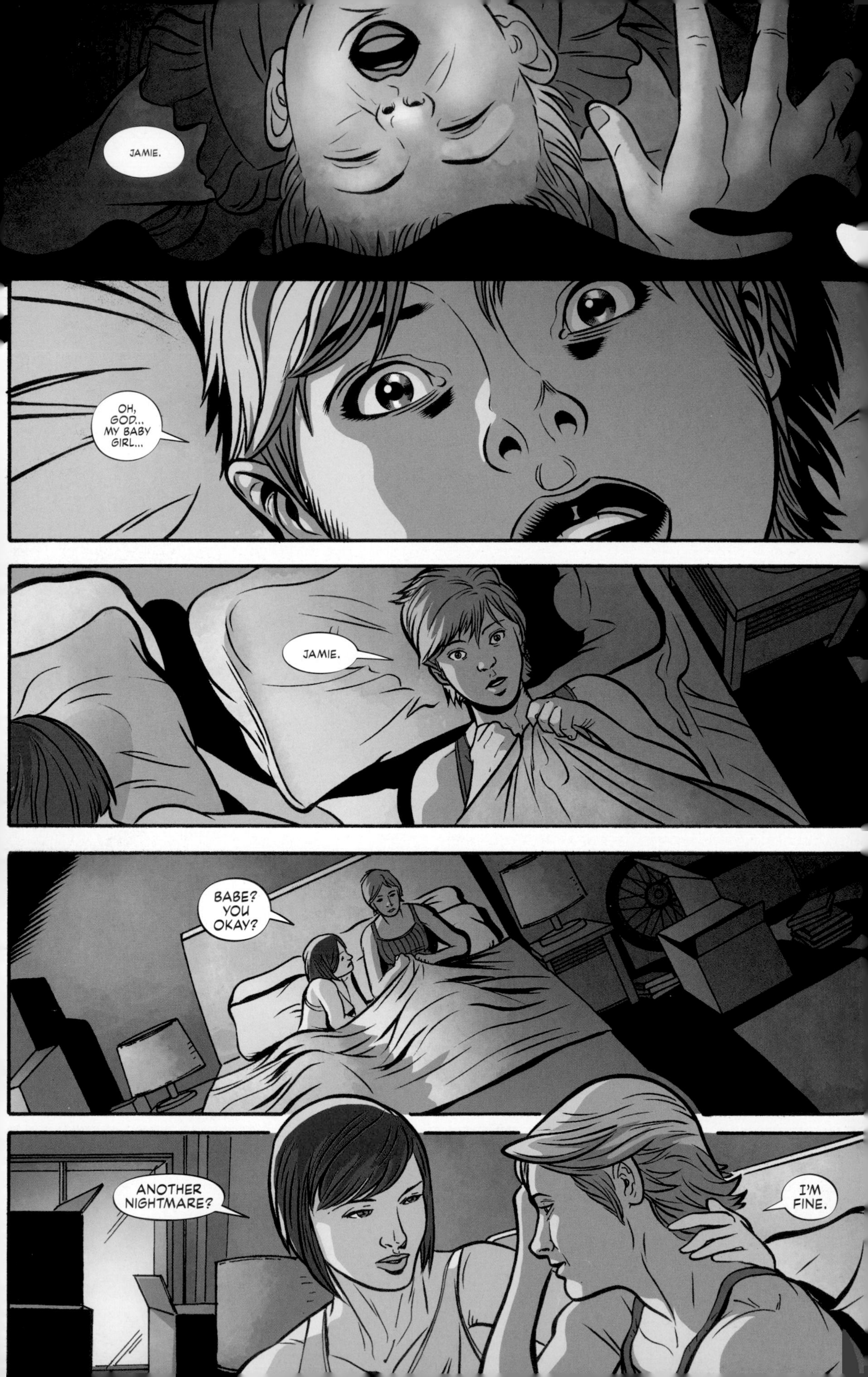
JAMIE.
OH, GOD... MY BABY GIRL...
JAMIE.
BABE? YOU OKAY?
ANOTHER NIGHTMARE?
I'M FINE.

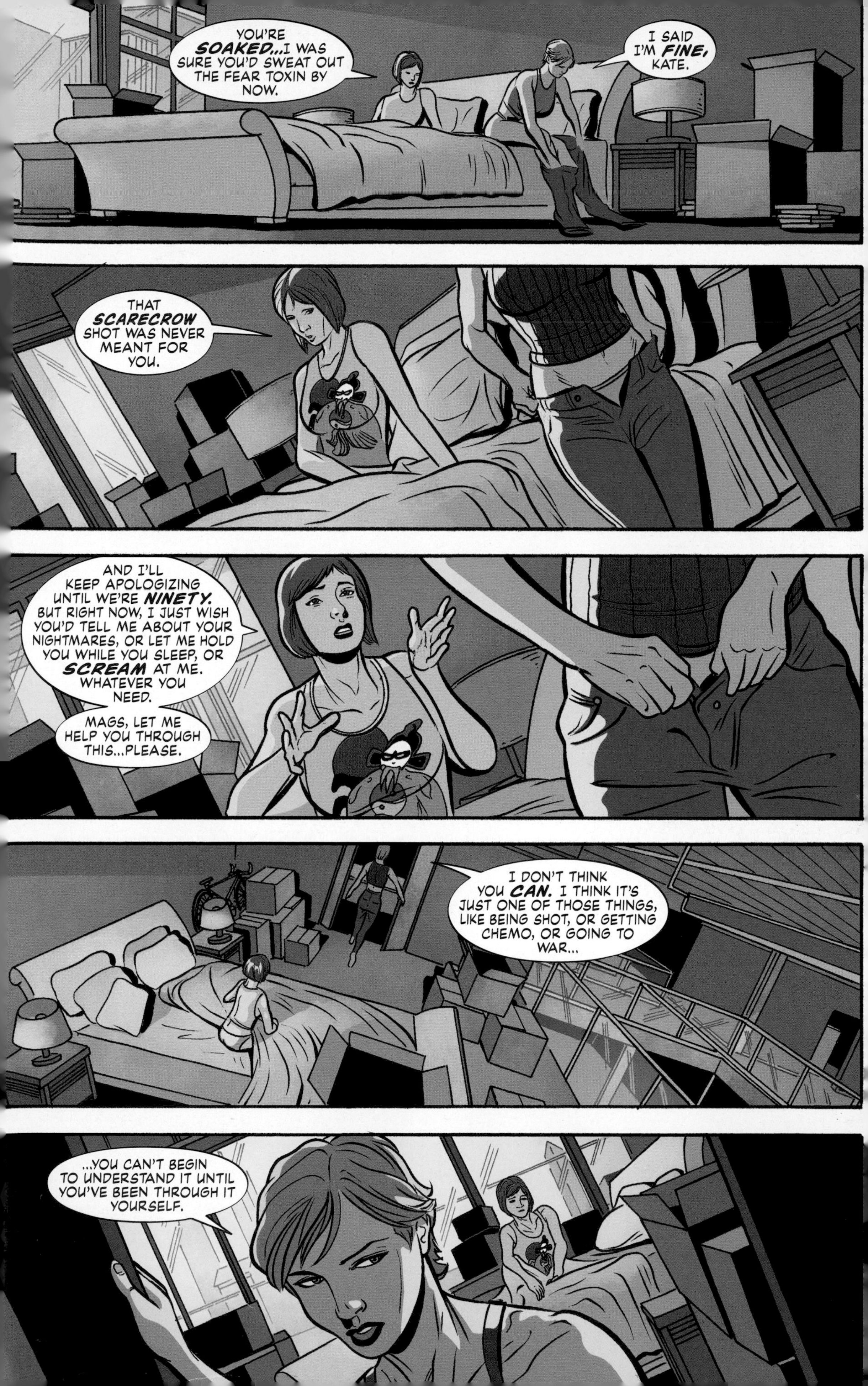
YOU'RE SOAKED...I WAS SURE YOU'D SWEAT OUT THE FEAR TOXIN BY NOW.
I SAID I'M FINE, KATE.
THAT SCARECROW SHOT WAS NEVER MEANT FOR YOU.
AND I'LL KEEP APOLOGIZING UNTIL WE'RE NINETY. BUT RIGHT NOW, I JUST WISH YOU'D TELL ME ABOUT YOUR NIGHTMARES, OR LET ME HOLD YOU WHILE YOU SLEEP, OR SCREAM AT ME. WHATEVER YOU NEED.
MAGS, LET ME HELP YOU THROUGH THIS...PLEASE.
I DON'T THINK YOU CAN. I THINK IT'S JUST ONE OF THOSE THINGS, LIKE BEING SHOT, OR GETTING CHEMO, OR GOING TO WAR...
...YOU CAN'T BEGIN TO UNDERSTAND IT UNTIL YOU'VE BEEN THROUGH IT YOURSELF.

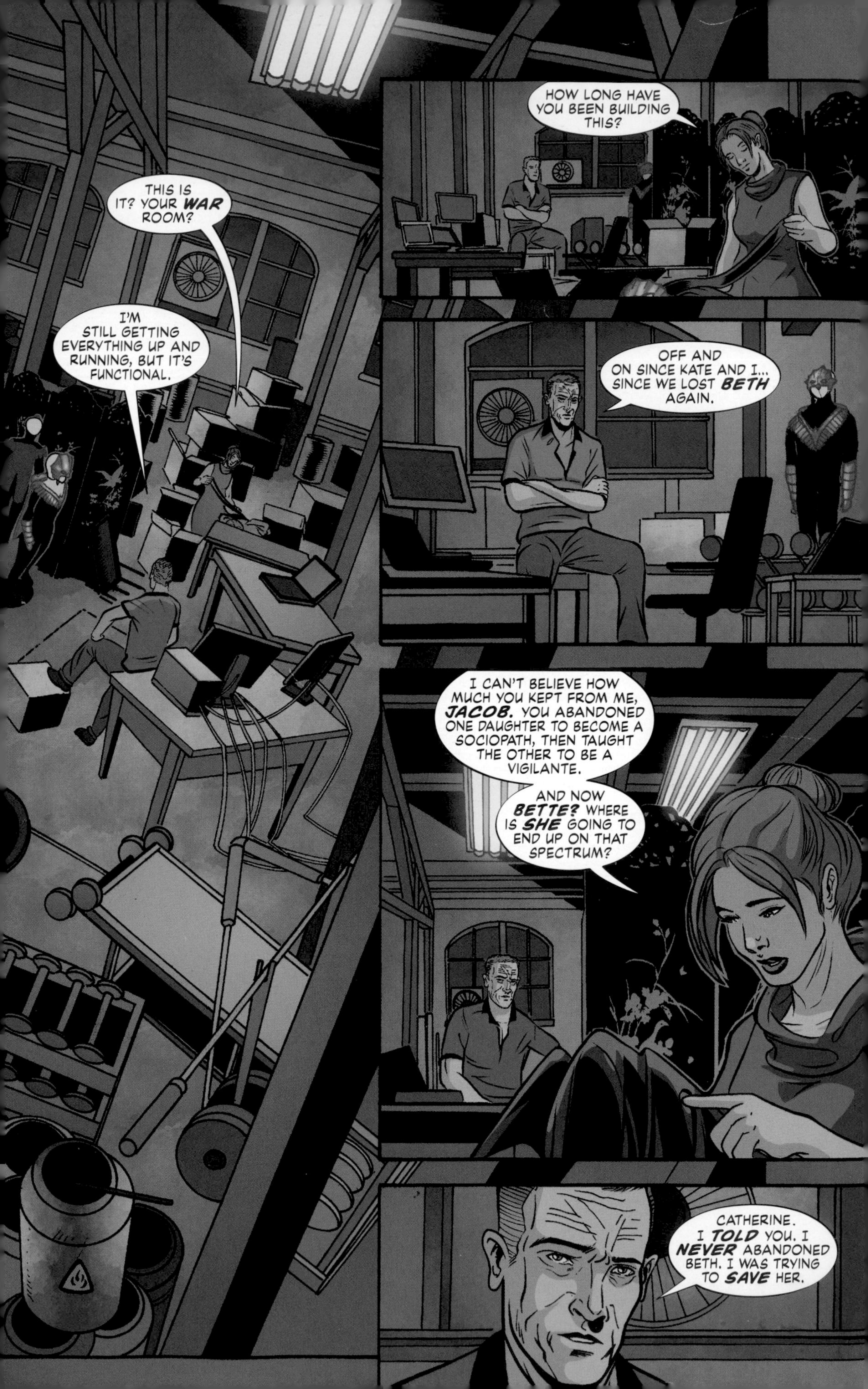
THIS IS IT? YOUR WAR ROOM?
I'M STILL GETTING EVERYTHING UP AND RUNNING, BUT IT'S FUNCTIONAL.
HOW LONG HAVE YOU BEEN BUILDING THIS?
OFF AND ON SINCE KATE AND I... SINCE WE LOST BETH AGAIN.
I CAN'T BELIEVE HOW MUCH YOU KEPT FROM ME, JACOB. YOU ABANDONED ONE DAUGHTER TO BECOME A SOCIOPATH, THEN TAUGHT THE OTHER TO BE A VIGILANTE.
AND NOW BETTE? WHERE IS SHE GOING TO END UP ON THAT SPECTRUM?
CATHERINE. I TOLD YOU. I NEVER ABANDONED BETH. I WAS TRYING TO SAVE HER.

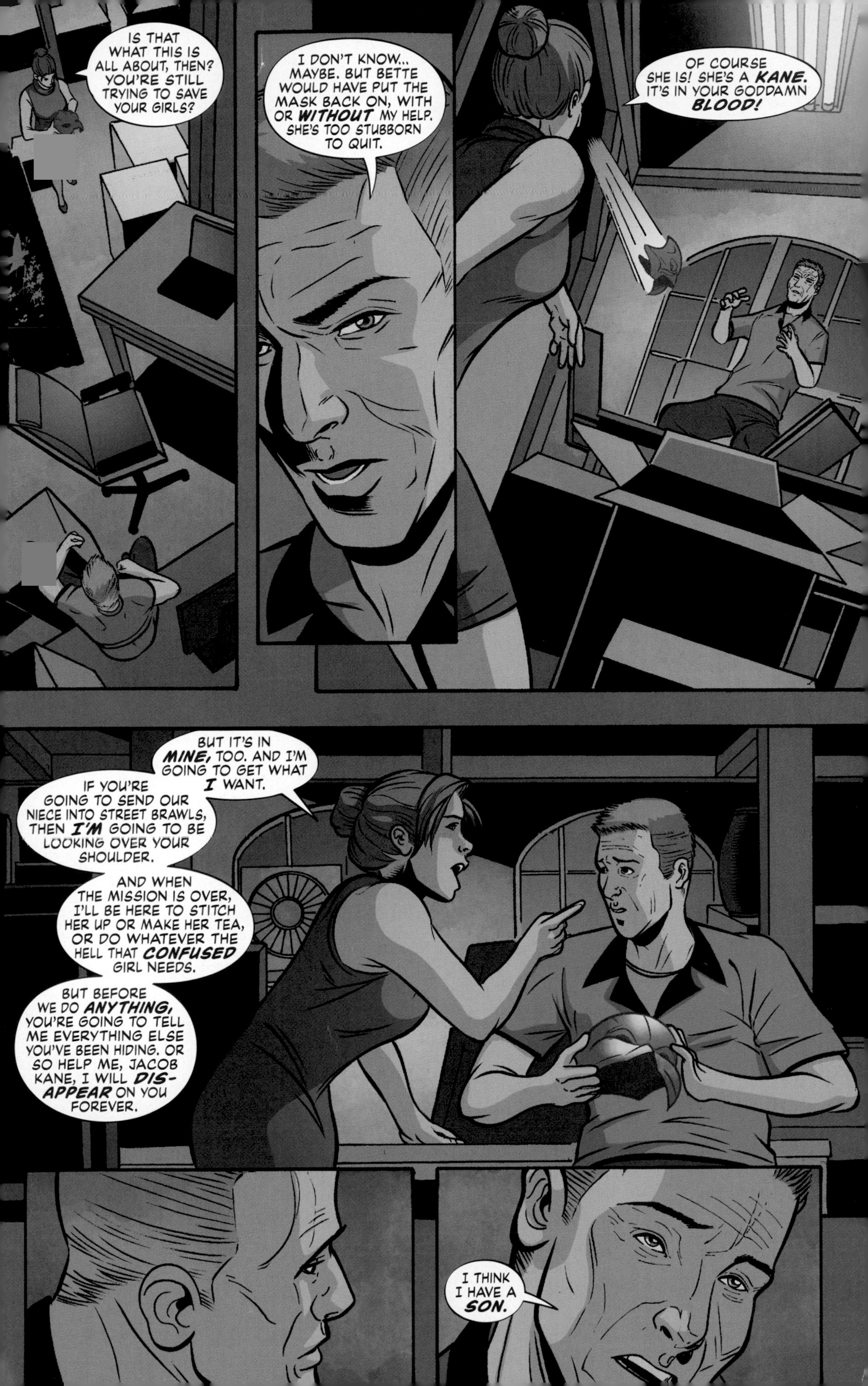
IS THAT WHAT THIS IS ALL ABOUT, THEN? YOU'RE STILL TRYING TO SAVE YOUR GIRLS?
I DON'T KNOW... MAYBE. BUT BETTE WOULD HAVE PUT THE MASK BACK ON, WITH OR WITHOUT MY HELP. SHE'S TOO STUBBORN TO QUIT.
OF COURSE SHE IS! SHE'S A KANE. IT'S IN YOUR GODDAMN BLOOD!
BUT IT'S IN MINE, TOO. AND I'M GOING TO GET WHAT I WANT.
IF YOU'RE GOING TO SEND OUR NIECE INTO STREET BRAWLS, THEN I'M GOING TO BE LOOKING OVER YOUR SHOULDER.
AND WHEN THE MISSION IS OVER, I'LL BE HERE TO STITCH HER UP OR MAKE HER TEA, OR DO WHATEVER THE HELL THAT CONFUSED GIRL NEEDS.
BUT BEFORE WE DO ANYTHING, YOU'RE GOING TO TELL ME EVERYTHING ELSE YOU'VE BEEN HIDING. OR SO HELP ME, JACOB KANE, I WILL DIS-APPEAR ON YOU FOREVER.
I THINK I HAVE A SON.

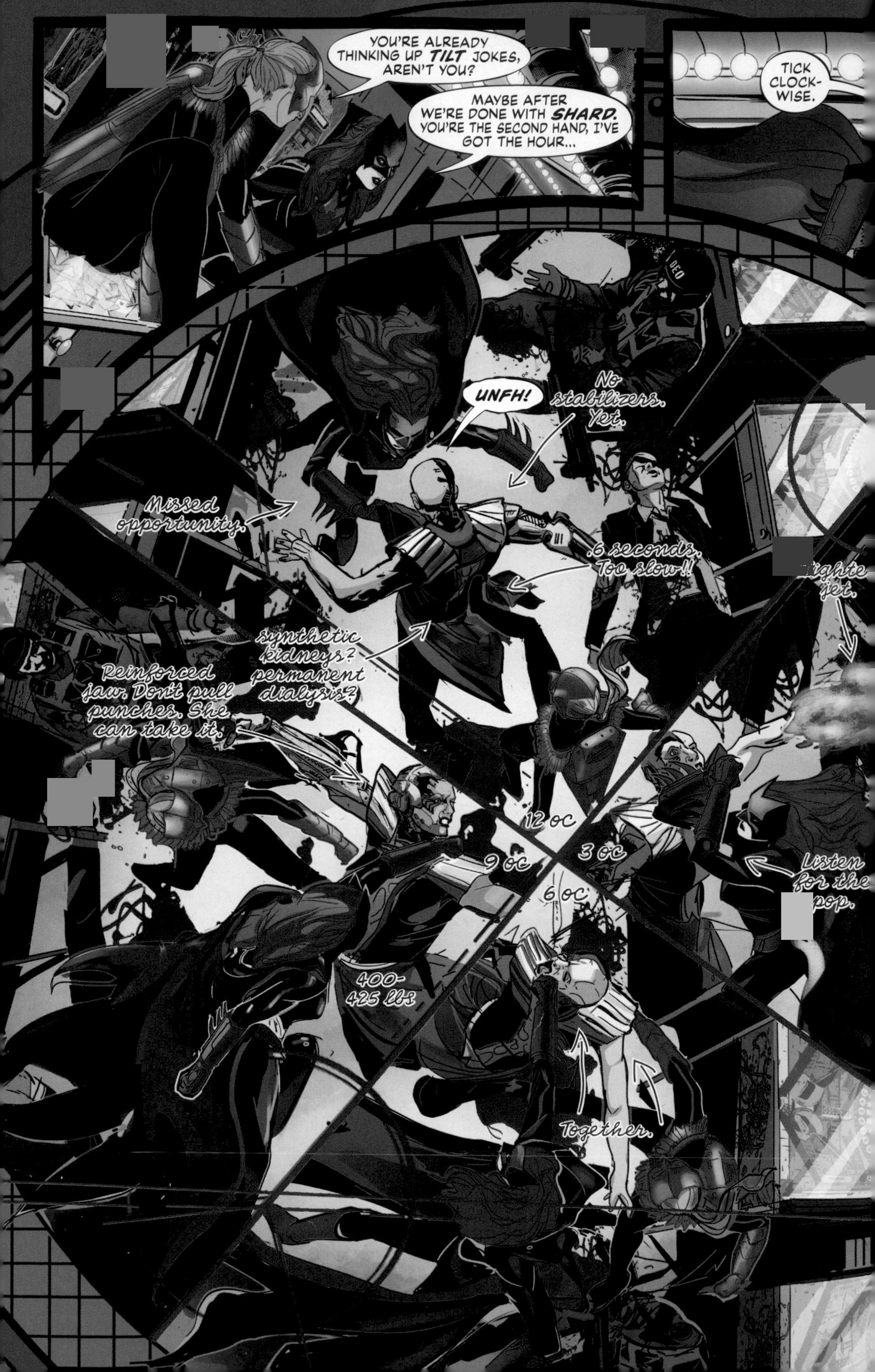

YOU'RE ALREADY THINKING UP TILT JOKES, AREN'T YOU?
MAYBE AFTER WE'RE DONE WITH SHARD. YOU'RE THE SECOND HAND, I'VE GOT THE HOUR...
TICK CLOCK-WISE.
UNFH!
No stabilizers. Yet.
Missed opportunity.
.6 seconds. Too slow!!
ighte jet.
synthetic kidneys? permanent dialysis?
Reinforced jaw. Don't pull punches. She can take it.
12 oc
9 oc
3 oc
6 oc
Listen for the pop.
400-425 lbs
Together.

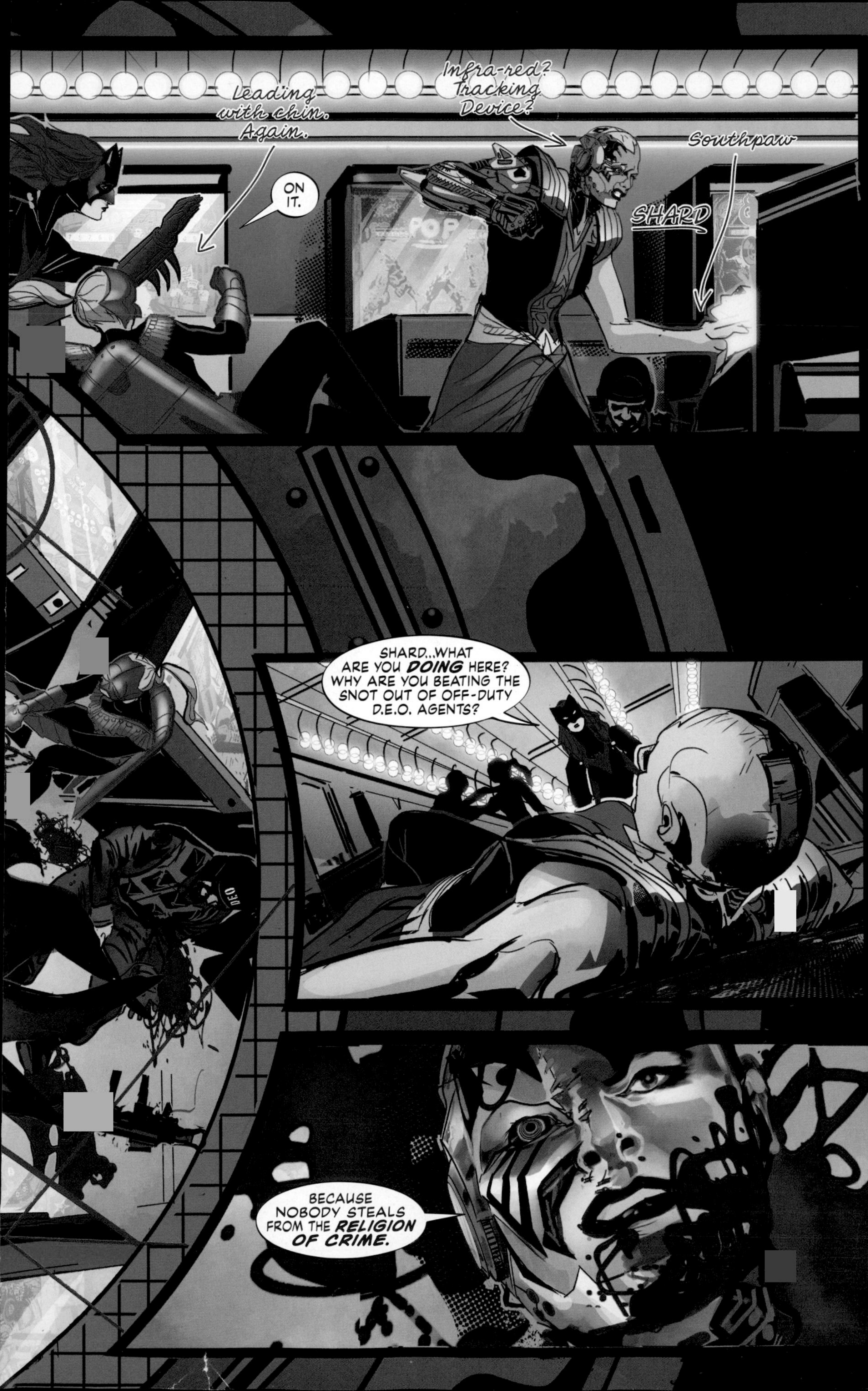
Leading with chin. Again.
ON IT.
Infra-red? Tracking Device?
Southpaw
SHARD
SHARD...WHAT ARE YOU DOING HERE? WHY ARE YOU BEATING THE SNOT OUT OF OFF-DUTY D.E.O. AGENTS?
BECAUSE NOBODY STEALS FROM THE RELIGION OF CRIME.

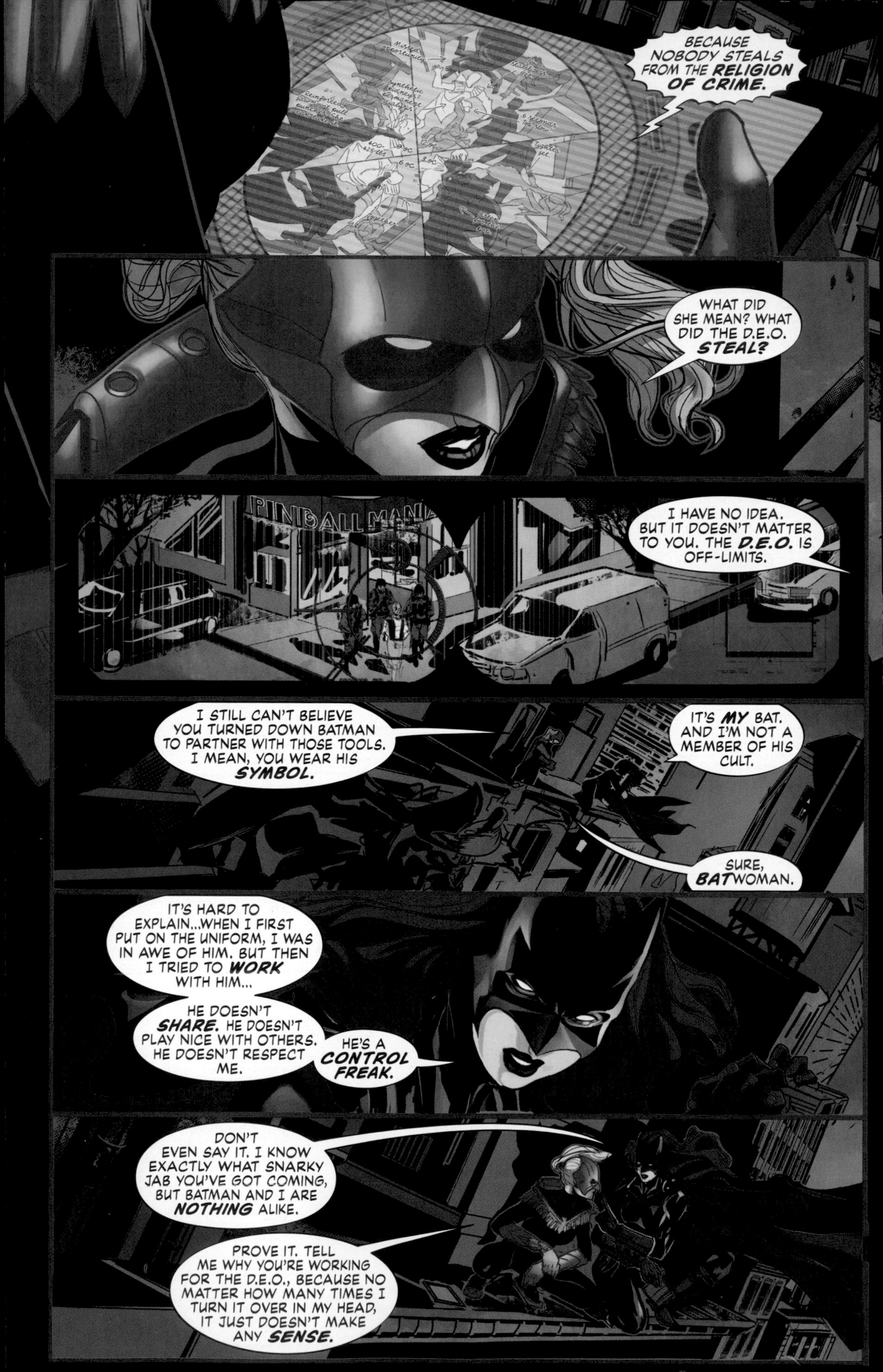
BECAUSE NOBODY STEALS FROM THE RELIGION OF CRIME.
WHAT DID SHE MEAN? WHAT DID THE D.E.O. STEAL?
PINBALL MANIA
I HAVE NO IDEA. BUT IT DOESN'T MATTER TO YOU. THE D.E.O. IS OFF-LIMITS.
I STILL CAN'T BELIEVE YOU TURNED DOWN BATMAN TO PARTNER WITH THOSE TOOLS. I MEAN, YOU WEAR HIS SYMBOL.
IT'S MY BAT. AND I'M NOT A MEMBER OF HIS CULT.
SURE, BATWOMAN.
IT'S HARD TO EXPLAIN...WHEN I FIRST PUT ON THE UNIFORM, I WAS IN AWE OF HIM. BUT THEN I TRIED TO WORK WITH HIM...
HE DOESN'T SHARE. HE DOESN'T PLAY NICE WITH OTHERS. HE DOESN'T RESPECT ME.
HE'S A CONTROL FREAK.
DON'T EVEN SAY IT. I KNOW EXACTLY WHAT SNARKY JAB YOU'VE GOT COMING, BUT BATMAN AND I ARE NOTHING ALIKE.
PROVE IT. TELL ME WHY YOU'RE WORKING FOR THE D.E.O., BECAUSE NO MATTER HOW MANY TIMES I TURN IT OVER IN MY HEAD, IT JUST DOESN'T MAKE ANY SENSE.

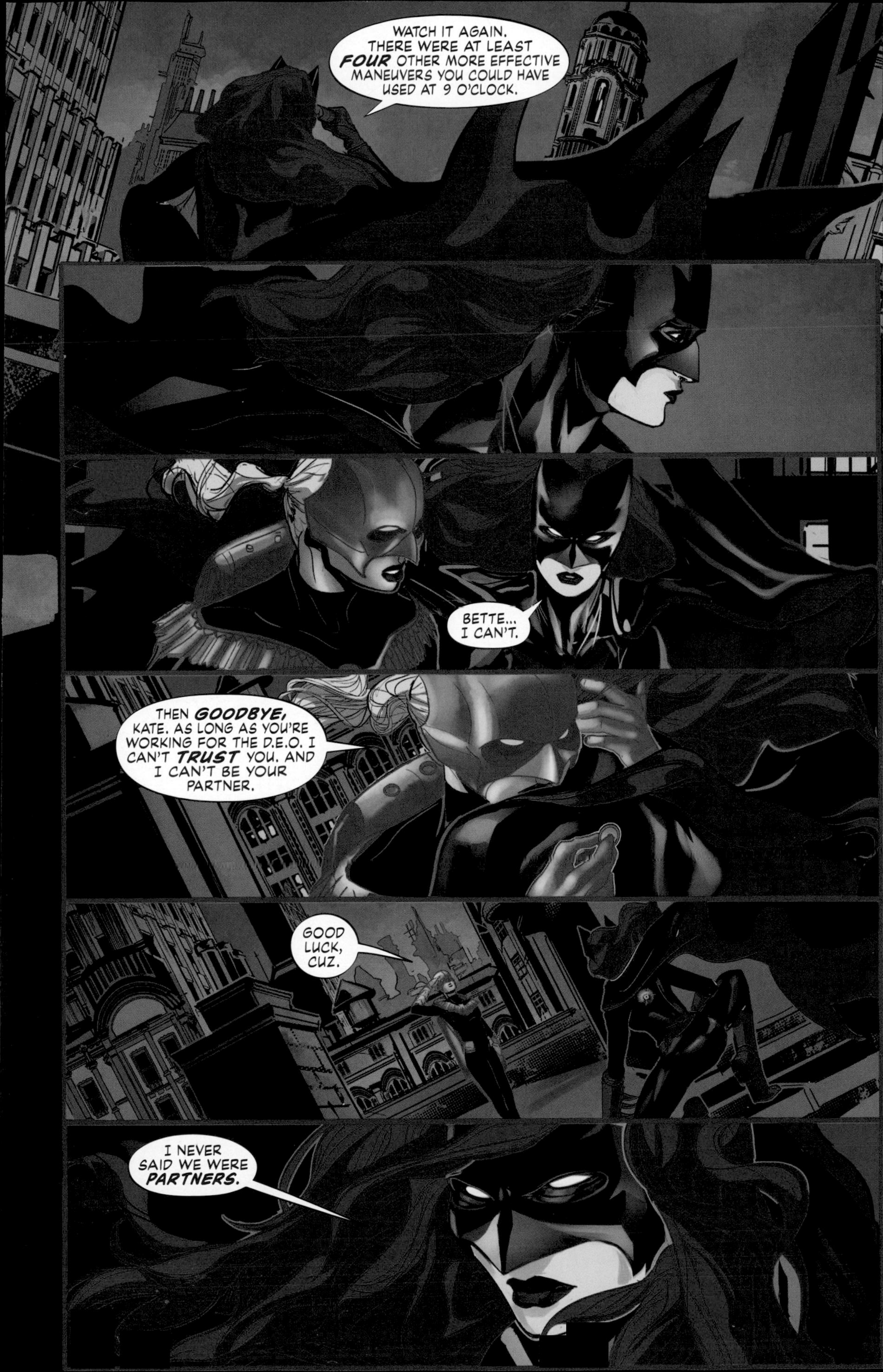

WATCH IT AGAIN. THERE WERE AT LEAST **FOUR** OTHER MORE EFFECTIVE MANEUVERS YOU COULD HAVE USED AT 9 O'CLOCK.
BETTE... I CAN'T.
THEN **GOODBYE,** KATE. AS LONG AS YOU'RE WORKING FOR THE D.E.O. I CAN'T **TRUST** YOU. AND I CAN'T BE YOUR PARTNER.
GOOD LUCK, CUZ.
I NEVER SAID WE WERE **PARTNERS.**

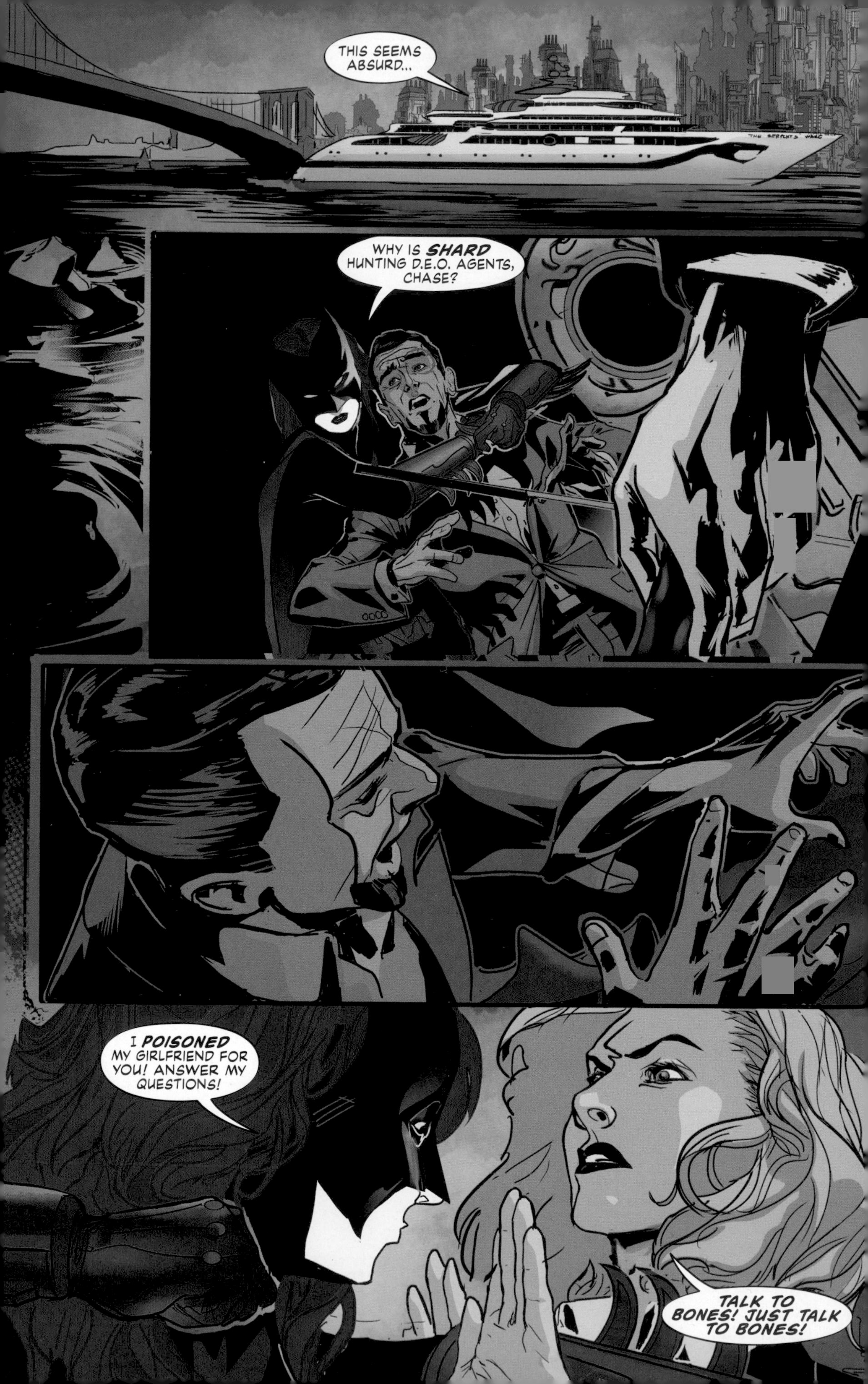
THIS SEEMS ABSURD...
WHY IS SHARD HUNTING D.E.O. AGENTS, CHASE?
I POISONED MY GIRLFRIEND FOR YOU! ANSWER MY QUESTIONS!
TALK TO BONES! JUST TALK TO BONES!

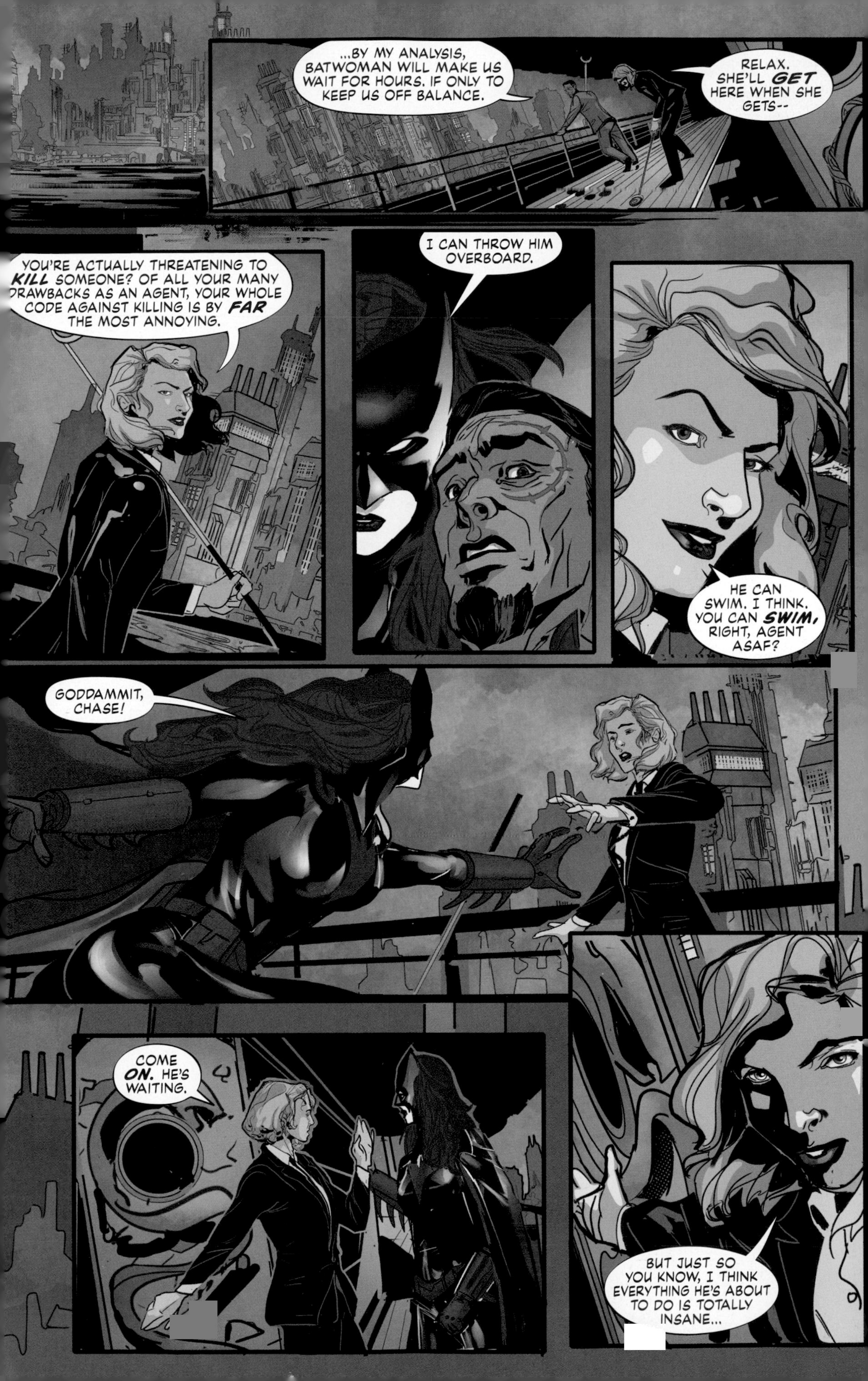
...BY MY ANALYSIS, BATWOMAN WILL MAKE US WAIT FOR HOURS, IF ONLY TO KEEP US OFF BALANCE.
RELAX. SHE'LL GET HERE WHEN SHE GETS--
YOU'RE ACTUALLY THREATENING TO KILL SOMEONE? OF ALL YOUR MANY DRAWBACKS AS AN AGENT, YOUR WHOLE CODE AGAINST KILLING IS BY FAR THE MOST ANNOYING.
I CAN THROW HIM OVERBOARD.
HE CAN SWIM. I THINK. YOU CAN SWIM, RIGHT, AGENT ASAF?
GODDAMMIT, CHASE!
COME ON. HE'S WAITING.
BUT JUST SO YOU KNOW, I THINK EVERYTHING HE'S ABOUT TO DO IS TOTALLY INSANE...

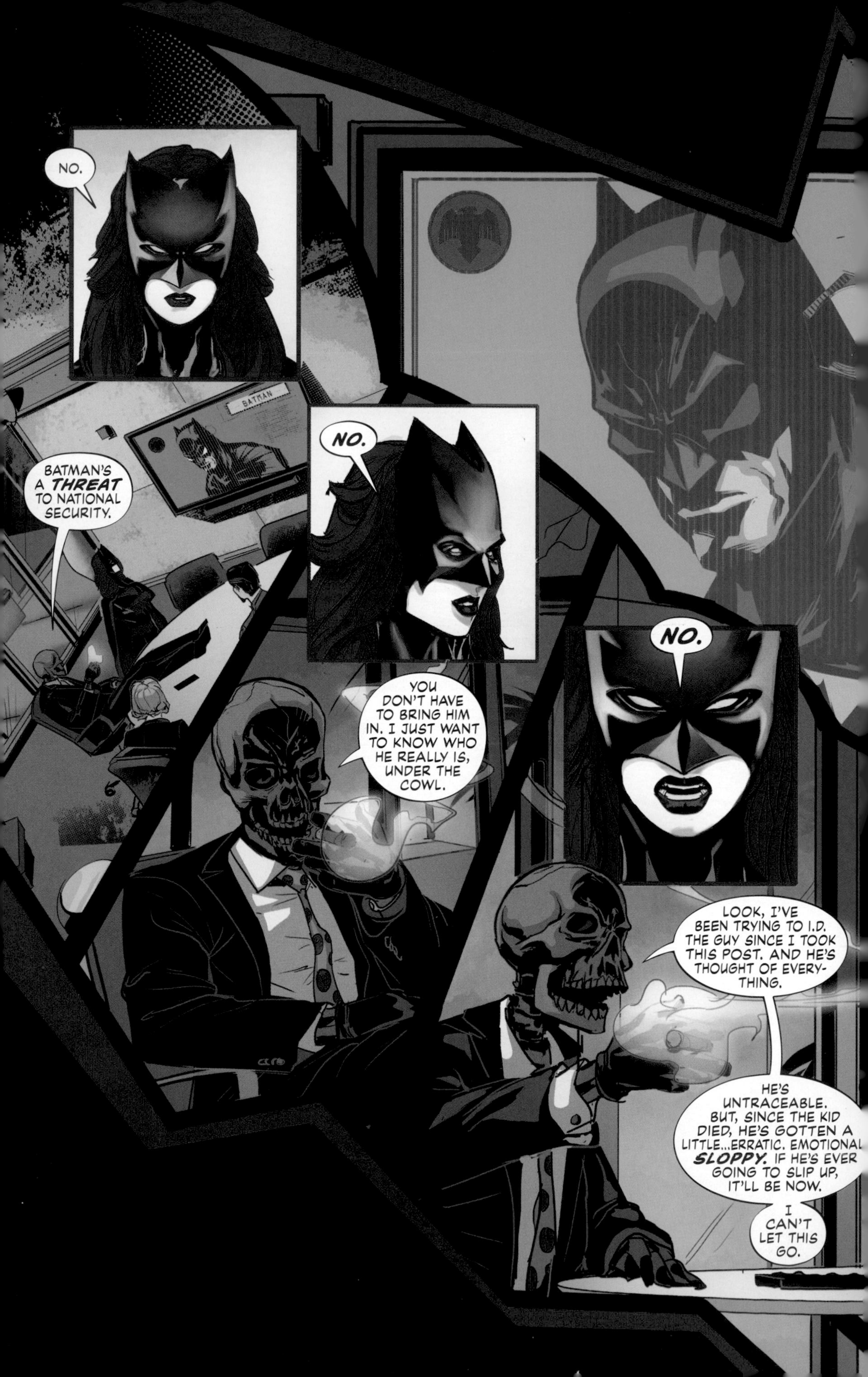
NO.
BATMAN'S A THREAT TO NATIONAL SECURITY.
NO.
YOU DON'T HAVE TO BRING HIM IN. I JUST WANT TO KNOW WHO HE REALLY IS, UNDER THE COWL.
NO.
LOOK, I'VE BEEN TRYING TO I.D. THE GUY SINCE I TOOK THIS POST. AND HE'S THOUGHT OF EVERY-THING.
HE'S UNTRACEABLE. BUT, SINCE THE KID DIED, HE'S GOTTEN A LITTLE...ERRATIC. EMOTIONAL. SLOPPY. IF HE'S EVER GOING TO SLIP UP, IT'LL BE NOW.
I CAN'T LET THIS GO.
BATMAN

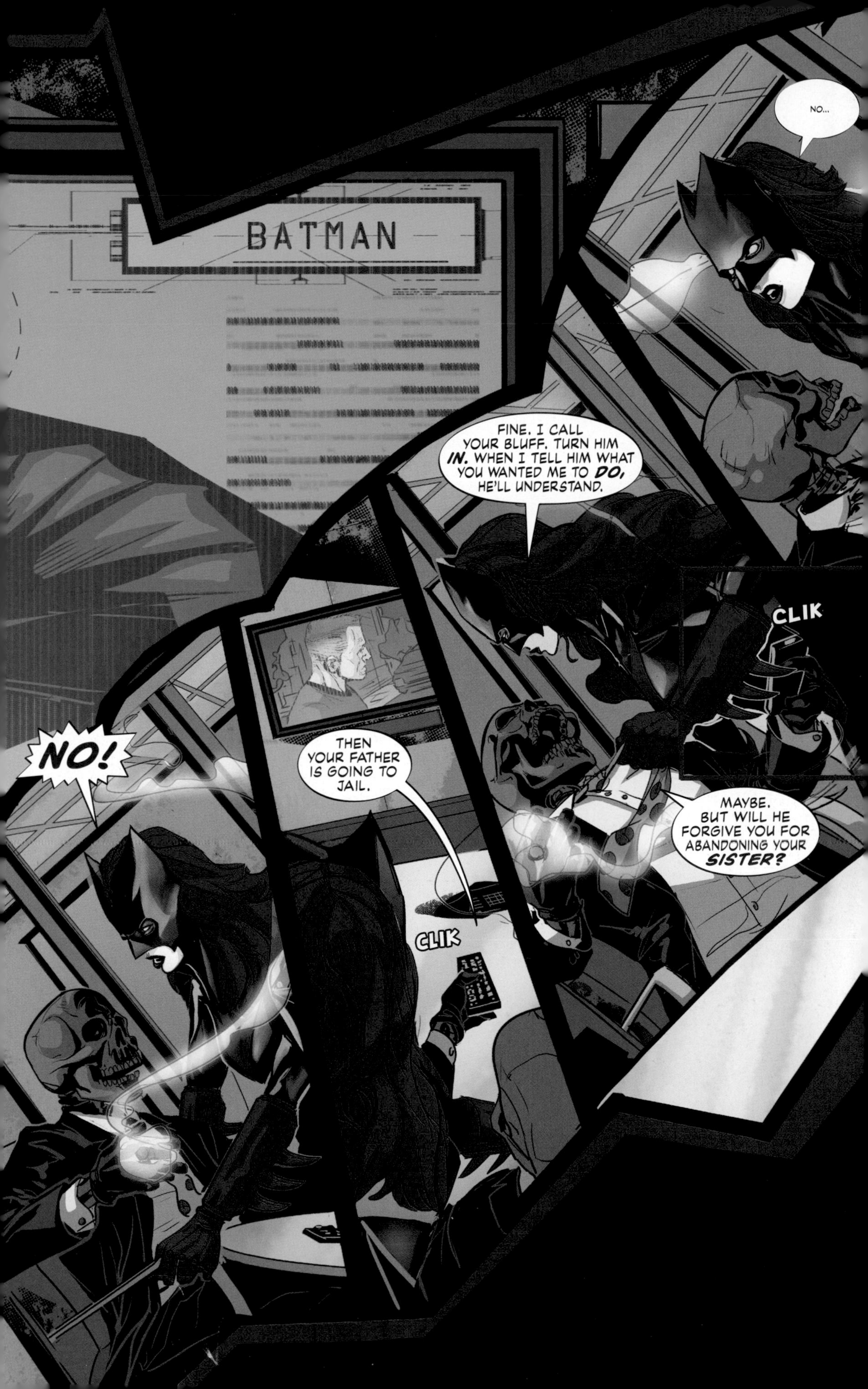

BATMAN
NO!
THEN YOUR FATHER IS GOING TO JAIL.
CLIK
FINE. I CALL YOUR BLUFF. TURN HIM IN. WHEN I TELL HIM WHAT YOU WANTED ME TO DO, HE'LL UNDERSTAND.
CLIK
MAYBE. BUT WILL HE FORGIVE YOU FOR ABANDONING YOUR SISTER?
NO...

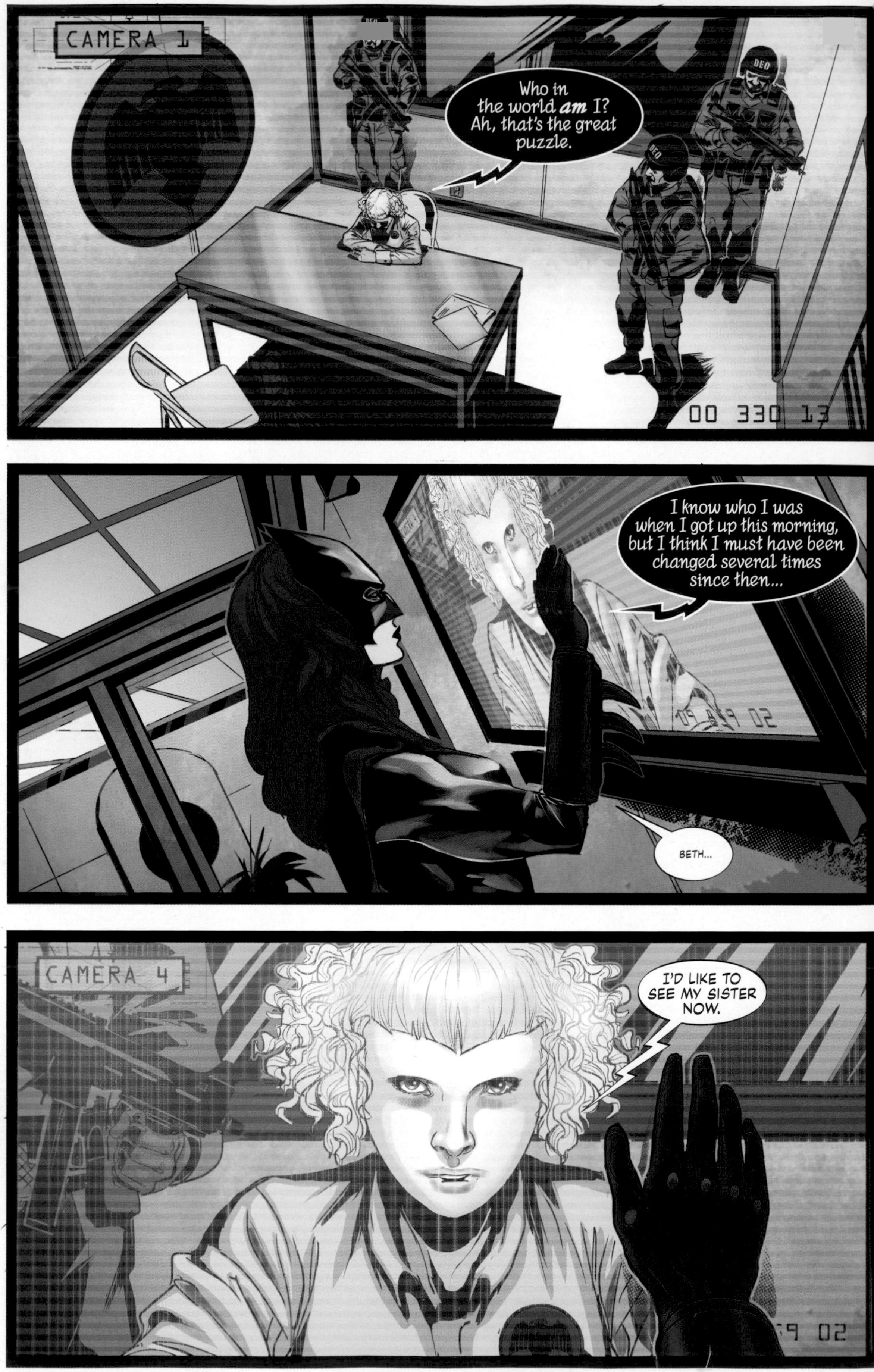
CAMERA 1
Who in the world *am* I? Ah, that's the great puzzle.
00 330 13
I know who I was when I got up this morning, but I think I must have been changed several times since then...
BETH...
CAMERA 4
I'D LIKE TO SEE MY SISTER NOW.

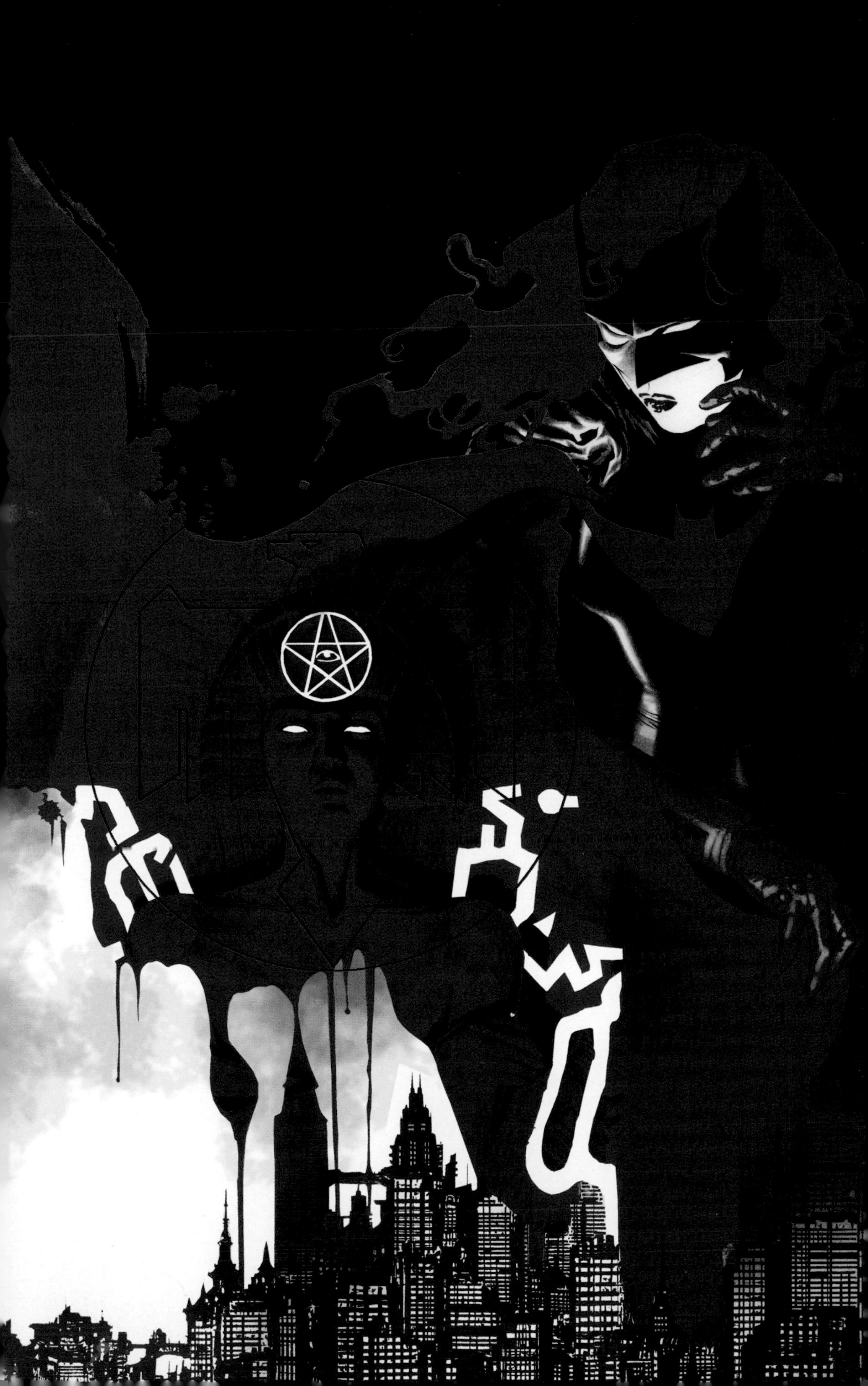

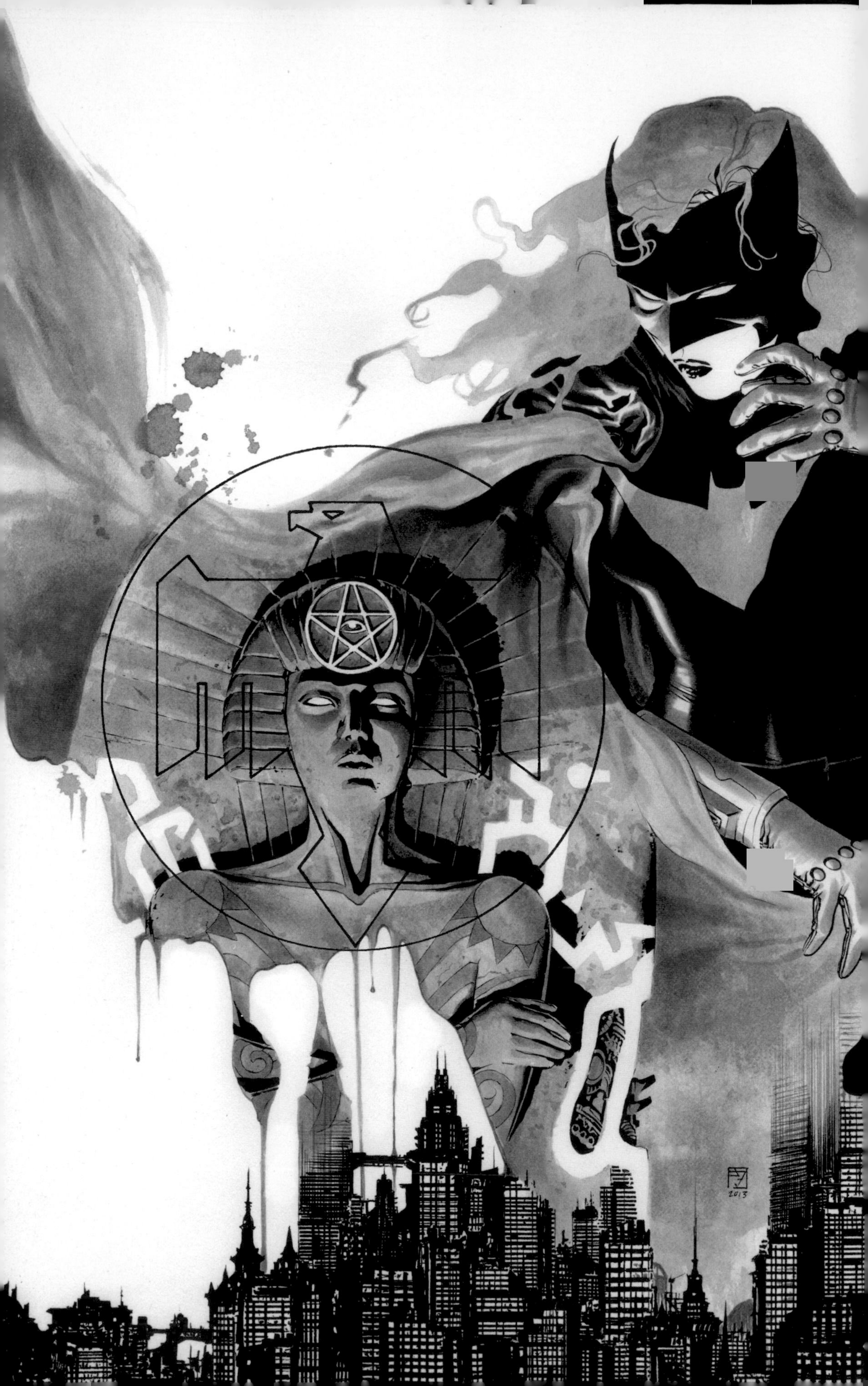

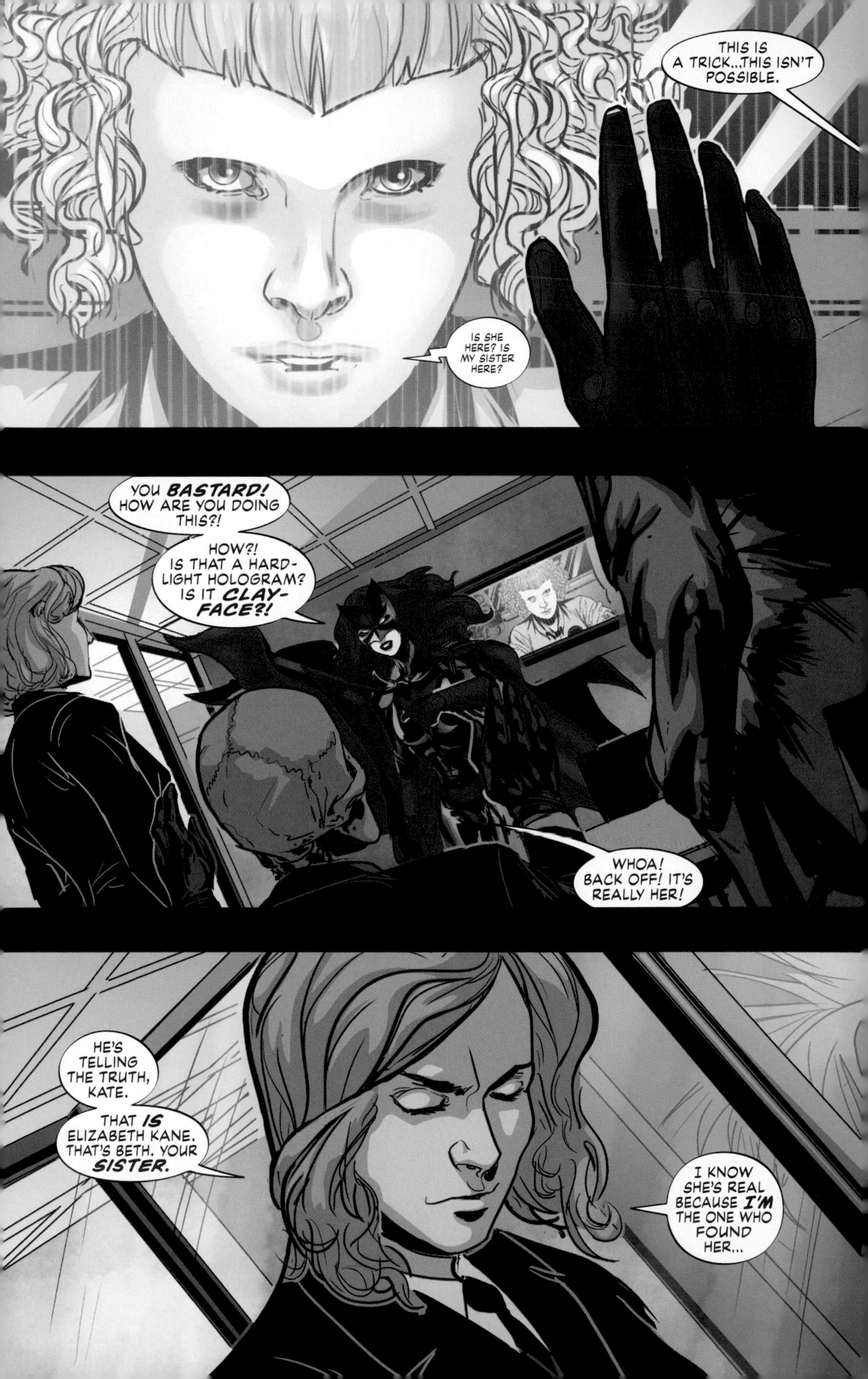
THIS IS A TRICK...THIS ISN'T POSSIBLE.
IS SHE HERE? IS MY SISTER HERE?
YOU BASTARD! HOW ARE YOU DOING THIS?!
HOW?! IS THAT A HARD-LIGHT HOLOGRAM? IS IT CLAY-FACE?!
WHOA! BACK OFF! IT'S REALLY HER!
HE'S TELLING THE TRUTH, KATE.
THAT IS ELIZABETH KANE. THAT'S BETH. YOUR SISTER.
I KNOW SHE'S REAL BECAUSE I'M THE ONE WHO FOUND HER...

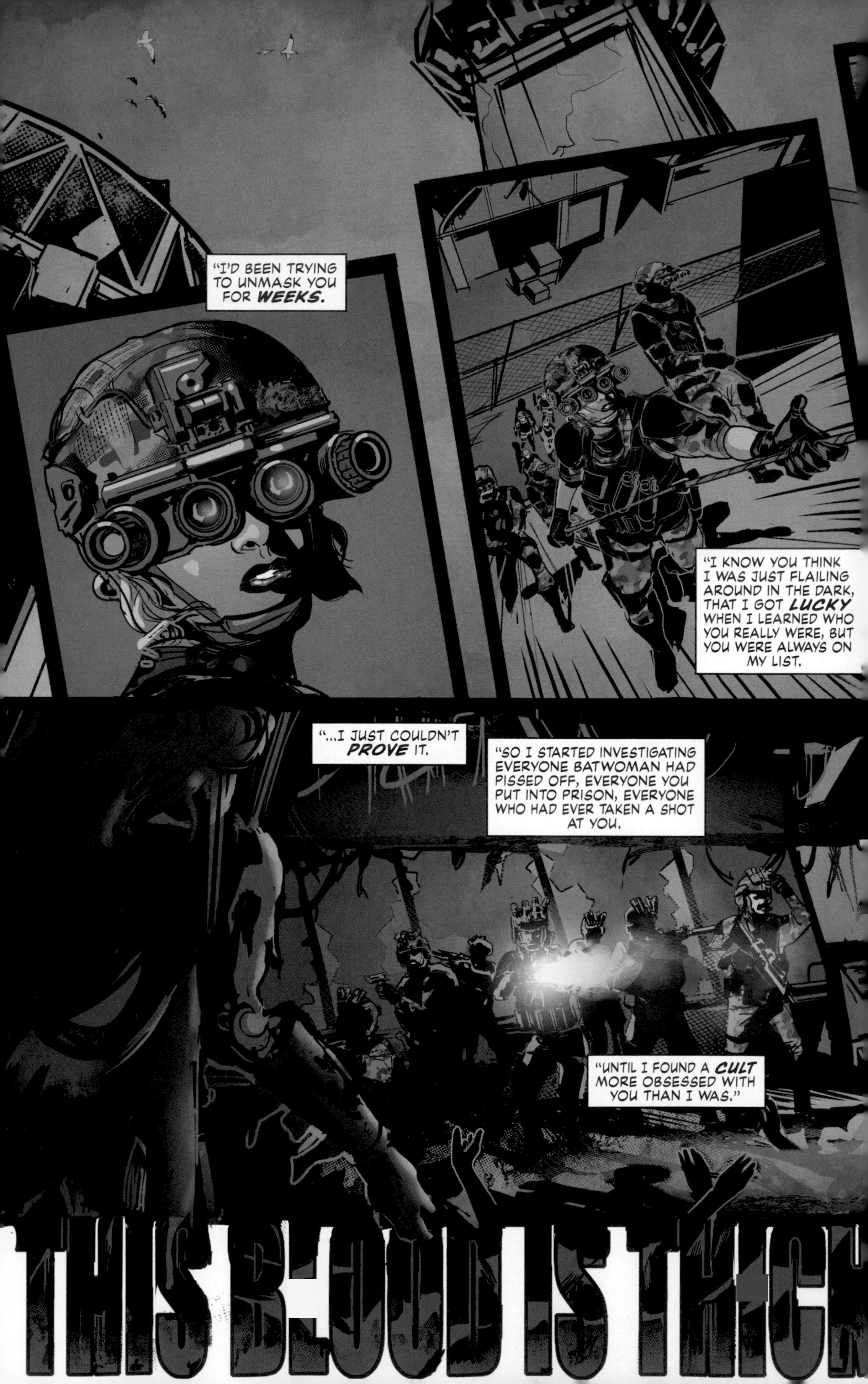
"I'D BEEN TRYING TO UNMASK YOU FOR WEEKS.
"I KNOW YOU THINK I WAS JUST FLAILING AROUND IN THE DARK, THAT I GOT LUCKY WHEN I LEARNED WHO YOU REALLY WERE, BUT YOU WERE ALWAYS ON MY LIST.
"...I JUST COULDN'T PROVE IT.
"SO I STARTED INVESTIGATING EVERYONE BATWOMAN HAD PISSED OFF, EVERYONE YOU PUT INTO PRISON, EVERYONE WHO HAD EVER TAKEN A SHOT AT YOU.
"UNTIL I FOUND A CULT MORE OBSESSED WITH YOU THAN I WAS."

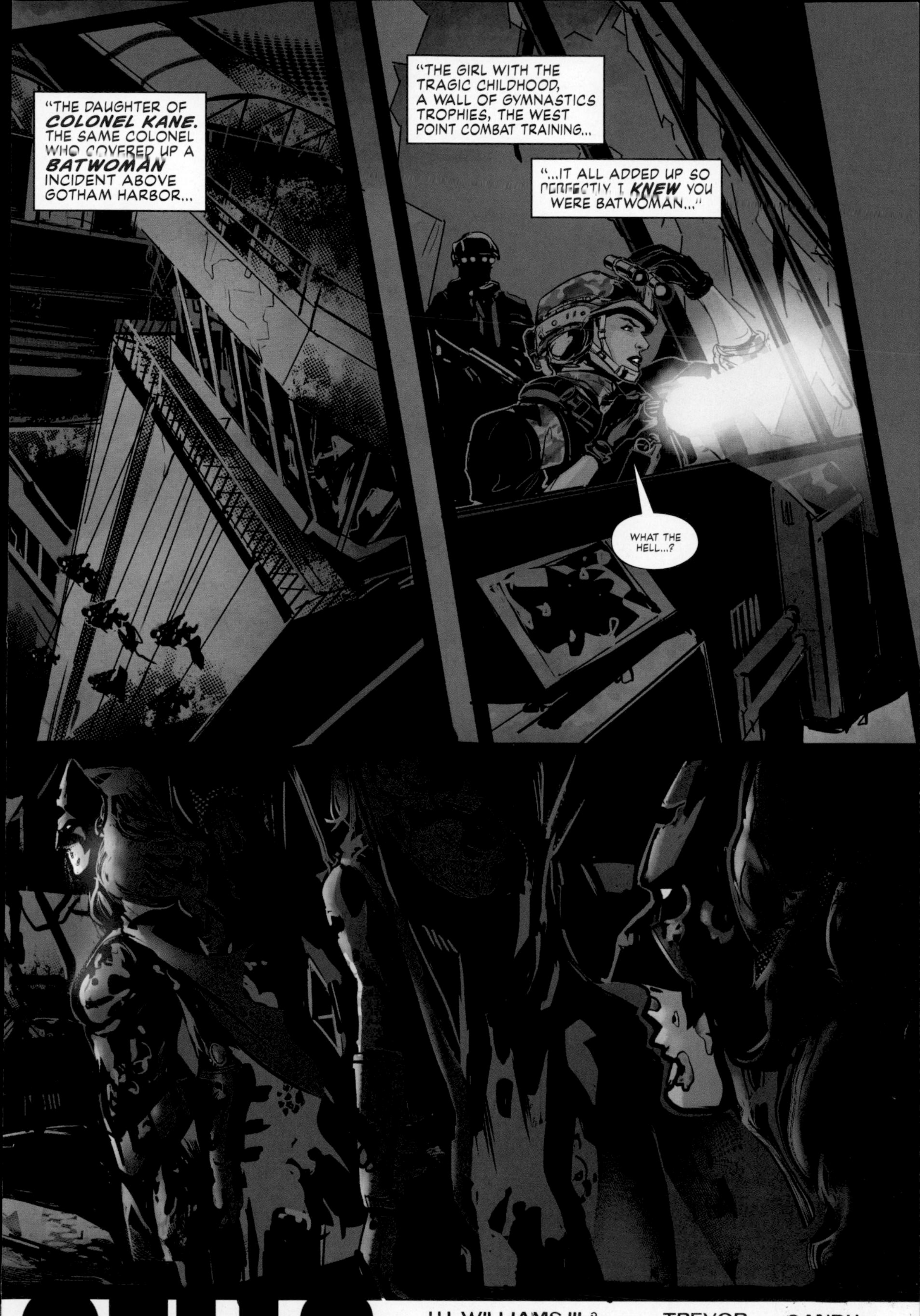
"THE DAUGHTER OF COLONEL KANE. THE SAME COLONEL WHO COVERED UP A BATWOMAN INCIDENT ABOVE GOTHAM HARBOR...
"THE GIRL WITH THE TRAGIC CHILDHOOD, A WALL OF GYMNASTICS TROPHIES, THE WEST POINT COMBAT TRAINING...
"...IT ALL ADDED UP SO PERFECTLY I KNEW YOU WERE BATWOMAN..."
WHAT THE HELL...?

CELLS

J.H. WILLIAMS III & W. HADEN BLACKMAN writers
TREVOR McCARTHY artist
SANDU FLOREA finishes pages 6, 10, 12-20
GUY MAJOR colorist
TODD KLEIN letterer
J.H. WILLIAMS III cover
DARREN SHAN asst. ed.
MIKE MARTS group editor

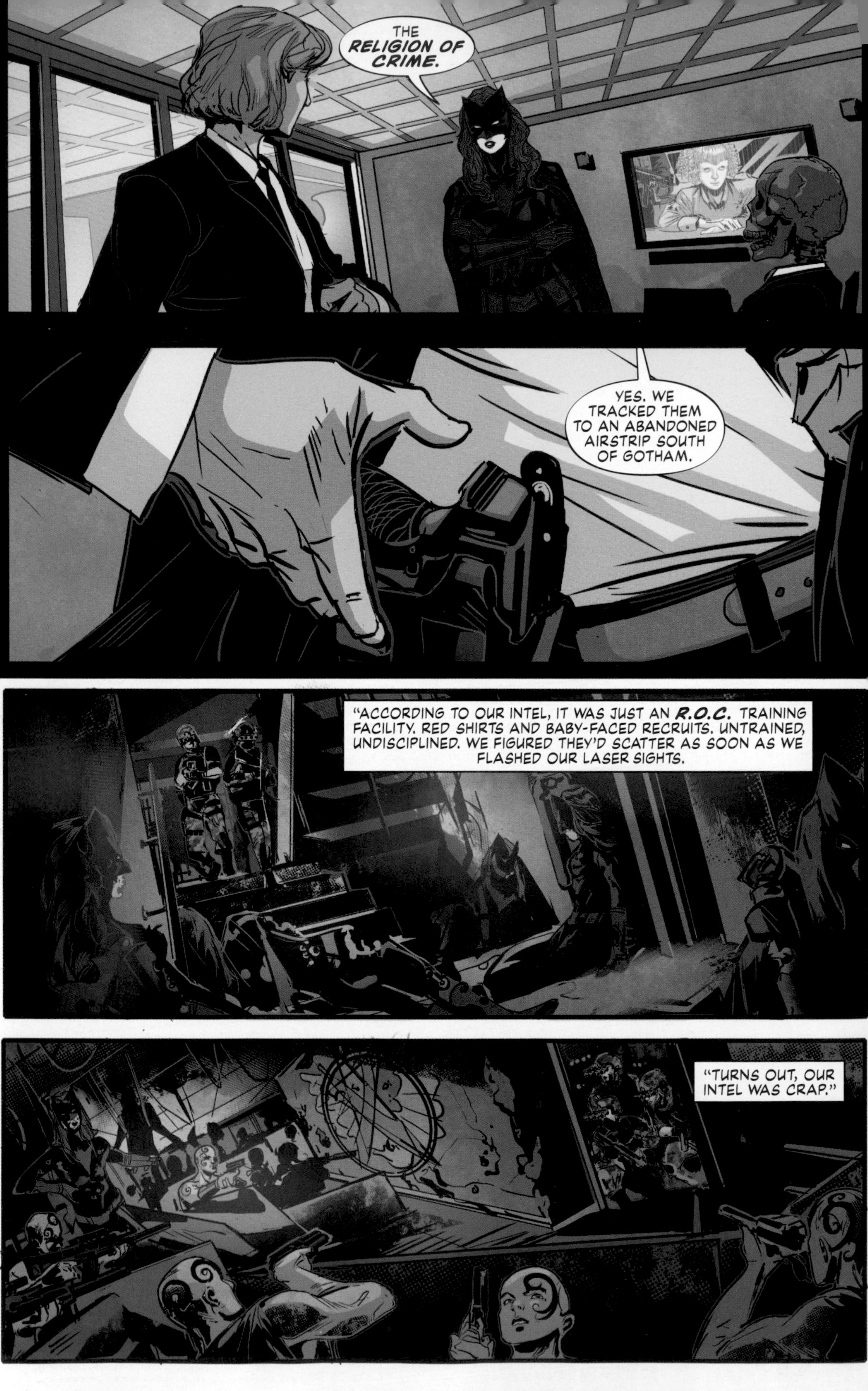
THE *RELIGION OF CRIME.*
YES. WE TRACKED THEM TO AN ABANDONED AIRSTRIP SOUTH OF GOTHAM.
"ACCORDING TO OUR INTEL, IT WAS JUST AN *R.O.C.* TRAINING FACILITY. RED SHIRTS AND BABY-FACED RECRUITS. UNTRAINED, UNDISCIPLINED. WE FIGURED THEY'D SCATTER AS SOON AS WE FLASHED OUR LASER SIGHTS.
"TURNS OUT, OUR INTEL WAS CRAP."

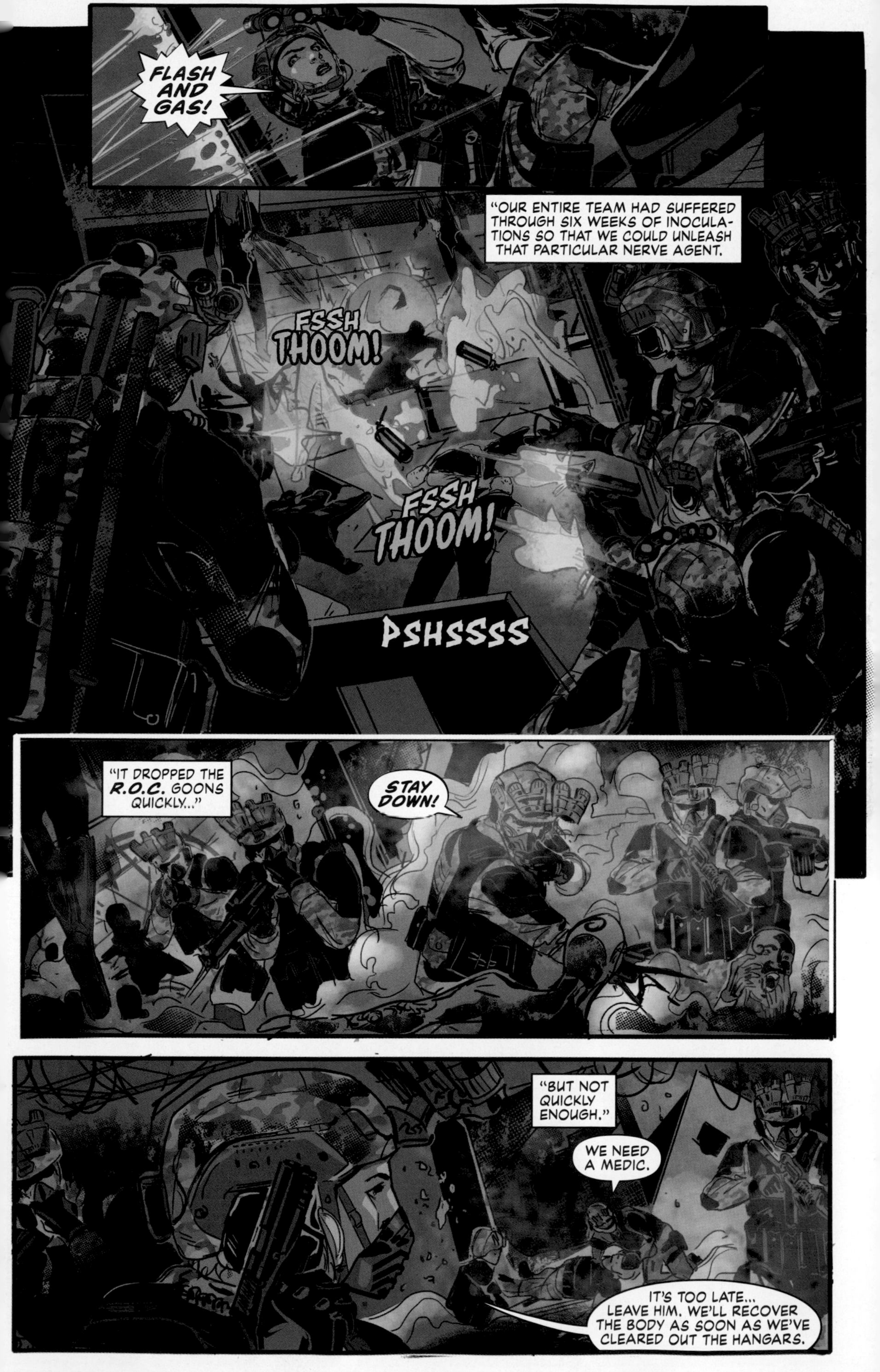
FLASH AND GAS!
"OUR ENTIRE TEAM HAD SUFFERED THROUGH SIX WEEKS OF INOCULATIONS SO THAT WE COULD UNLEASH THAT PARTICULAR NERVE AGENT.
FSSH THOOM!
FSSH THOOM!
PSHSSSS
"IT DROPPED THE R.O.C. GOONS QUICKLY..."
STAY DOWN!
"BUT NOT QUICKLY ENOUGH."
WE NEED A MEDIC.
IT'S TOO LATE... LEAVE HIM. WE'LL RECOVER THE BODY AS SOON AS WE'VE CLEARED OUT THE HANGARS.

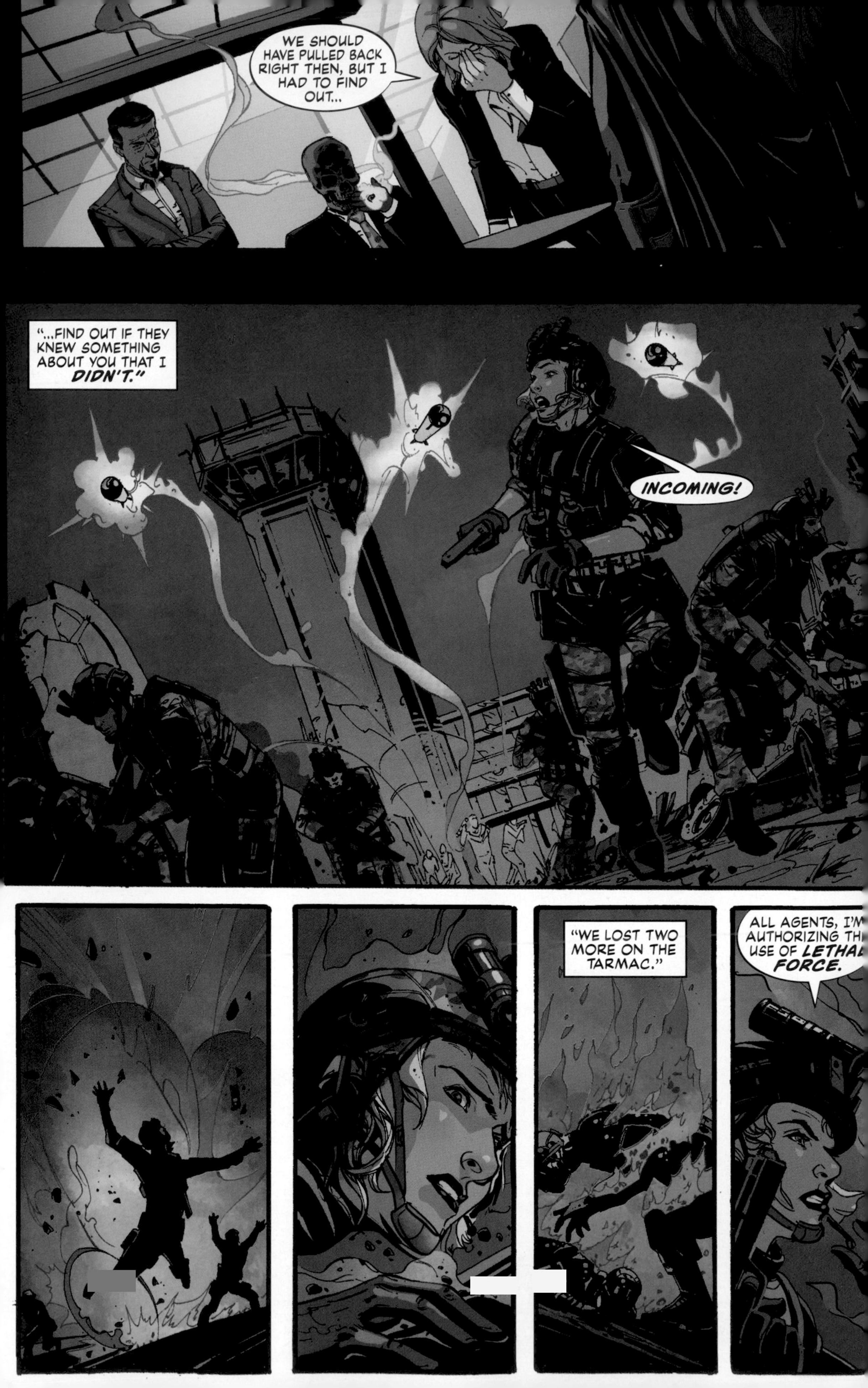
WE SHOULD HAVE PULLED BACK RIGHT THEN, BUT I HAD TO FIND OUT...
"...FIND OUT IF THEY KNEW SOMETHING ABOUT YOU THAT I DIDN'T."
INCOMING!
"WE LOST TWO MORE ON THE TARMAC."
ALL AGENTS, I'M AUTHORIZING TH USE OF LETHA FORCE.

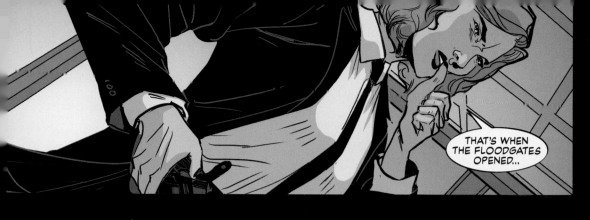

THAT'S WHEN THE FLOODGATES OPENED...

"...I DON'T KNOW WHAT COMPELS SOMEONE TO JOIN A *WAVE* OF HUMANITY...

"...THROW THEMSELVES AGAINST THE ROCKS...

"...DIE FOR *NOTHING.*"

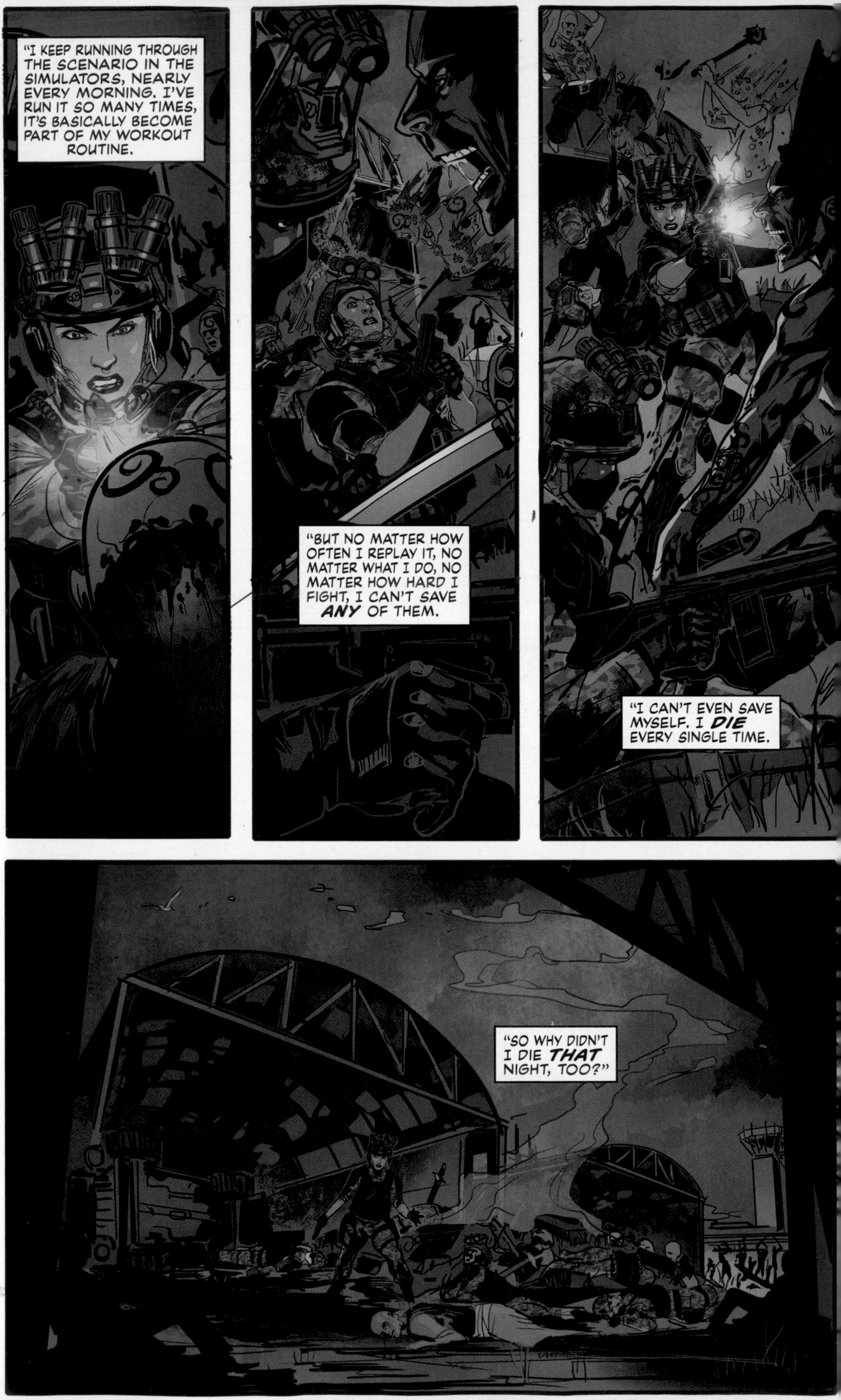
"I KEEP RUNNING THROUGH THE SCENARIO IN THE SIMULATORS, NEARLY EVERY MORNING. I'VE RUN IT SO MANY TIMES, IT'S BASICALLY BECOME PART OF MY WORKOUT ROUTINE.
"BUT NO MATTER HOW OFTEN I REPLAY IT, NO MATTER WHAT I DO, NO MATTER HOW HARD I FIGHT, I CAN'T SAVE ANY OF THEM.
"I CAN'T EVEN SAVE MYSELF. I DIE EVERY SINGLE TIME.
"SO WHY DIDN'T I DIE THAT NIGHT, TOO?"

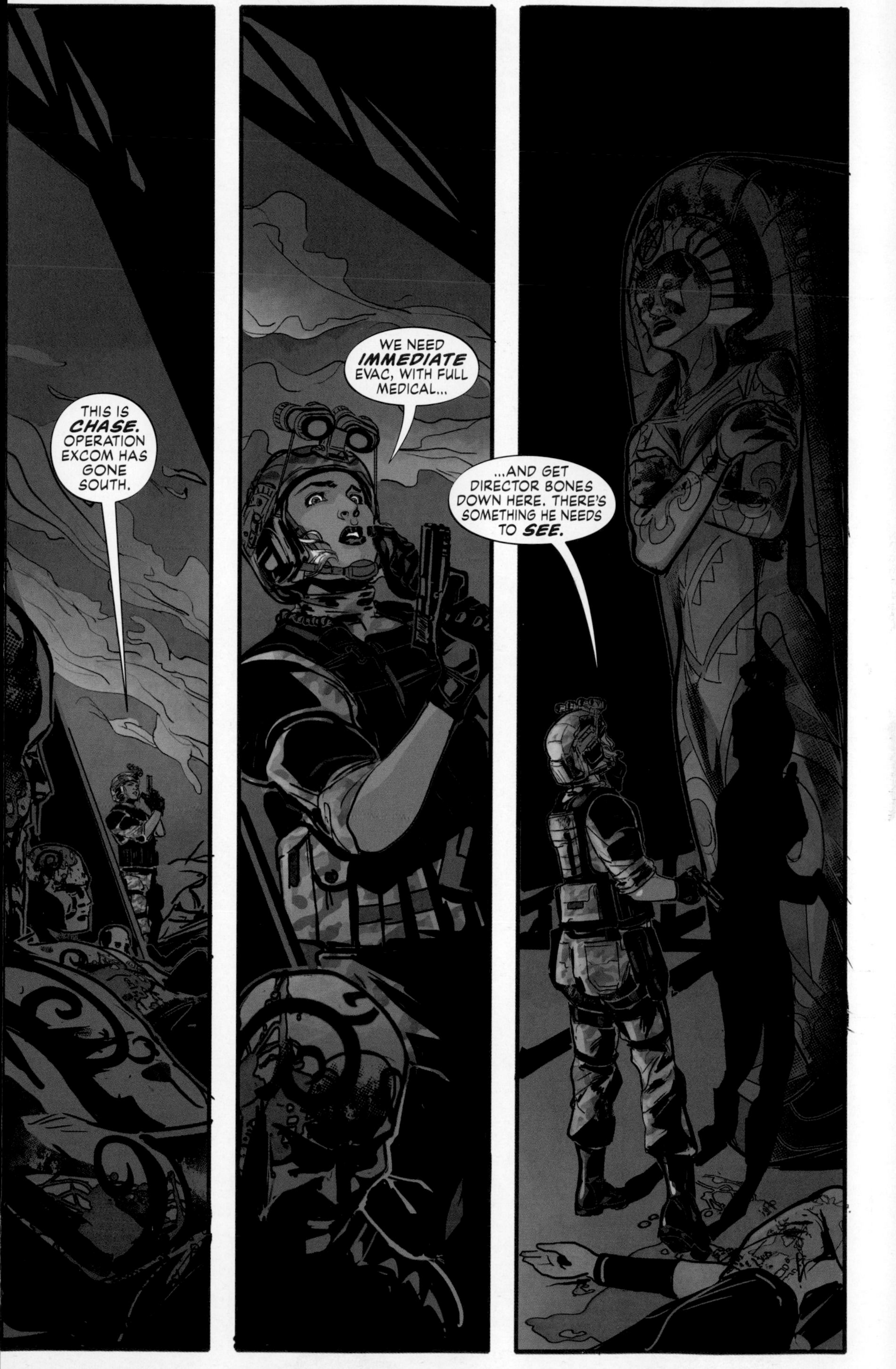
THIS IS CHASE. OPERATION EXCOM HAS GONE SOUTH.
WE NEED IMMEDIATE EVAC, WITH FULL MEDICAL...
...AND GET DIRECTOR BONES DOWN HERE. THERE'S SOMETHING HE NEEDS TO SEE.

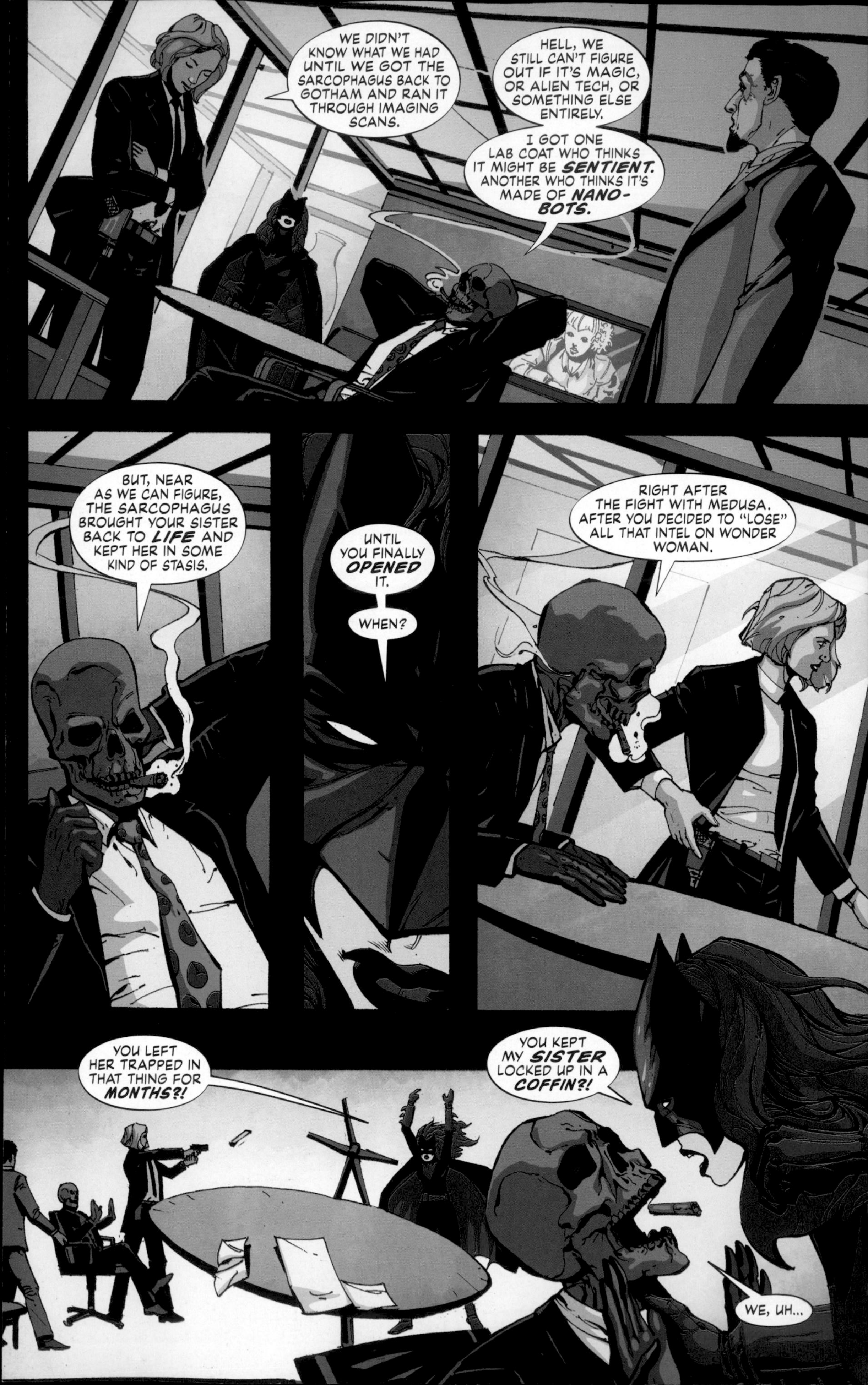
WE DIDN'T KNOW WHAT WE HAD UNTIL WE GOT THE SARCOPHAGUS BACK TO GOTHAM AND RAN IT THROUGH IMAGING SCANS.
HELL, WE STILL CAN'T FIGURE OUT IF IT'S MAGIC, OR ALIEN TECH, OR SOMETHING ELSE ENTIRELY.
I GOT ONE LAB COAT WHO THINKS IT MIGHT BE SENTIENT. ANOTHER WHO THINKS IT'S MADE OF NANO-BOTS.
BUT, NEAR AS WE CAN FIGURE, THE SARCOPHAGUS BROUGHT YOUR SISTER BACK TO LIFE AND KEPT HER IN SOME KIND OF STASIS.
UNTIL YOU FINALLY OPENED IT.
WHEN?
RIGHT AFTER THE FIGHT WITH MEDUSA. AFTER YOU DECIDED TO "LOSE" ALL THAT INTEL ON WONDER WOMAN.
YOU LEFT HER TRAPPED IN THAT THING FOR MONTHS?!
YOU KEPT MY SISTER LOCKED UP IN A COFFIN?!
WE, UH...

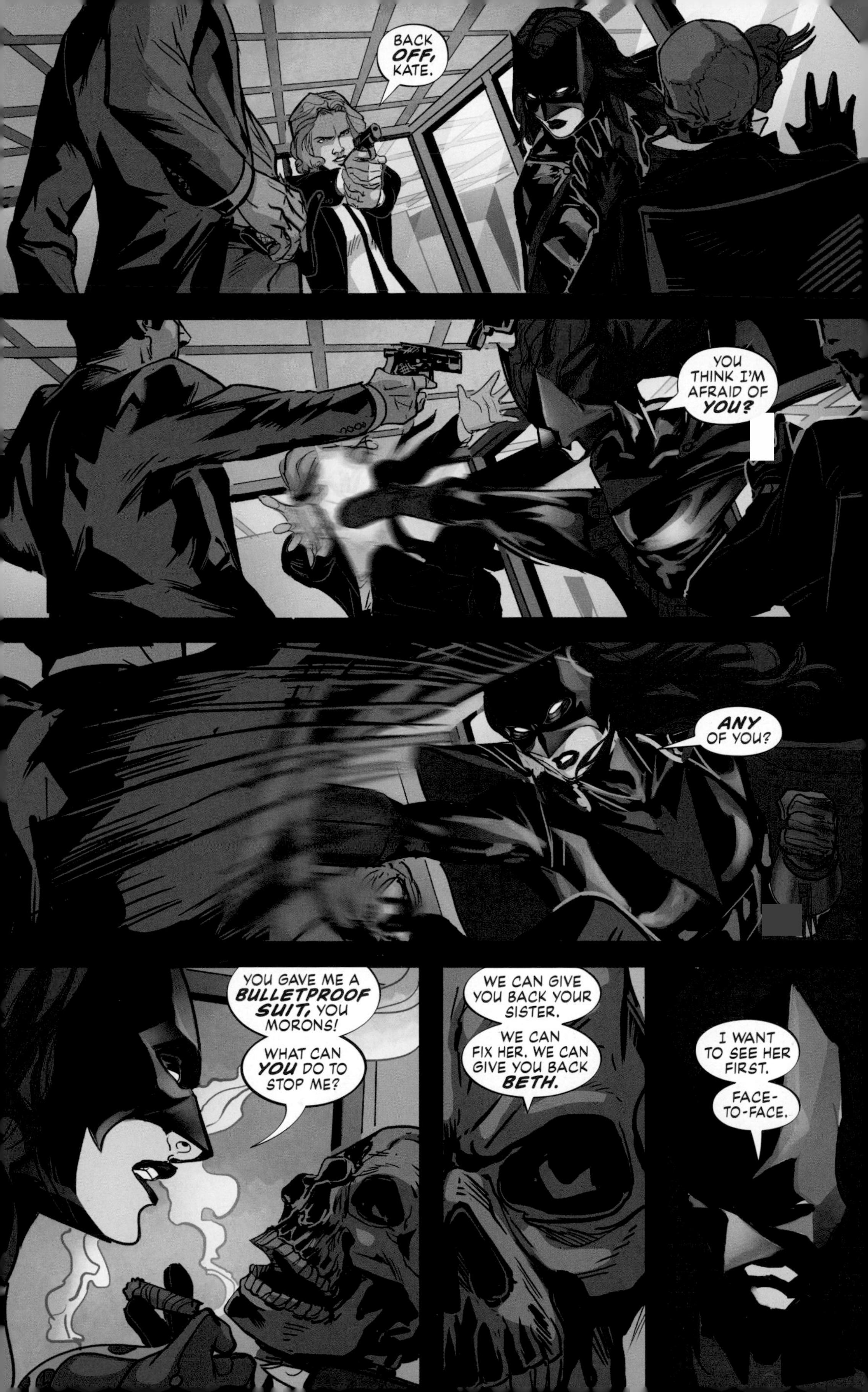
BACK OFF, KATE.
YOU THINK I'M AFRAID OF YOU?
ANY OF YOU?
YOU GAVE ME A BULLETPROOF SUIT, YOU MORONS!
WHAT CAN YOU DO TO STOP ME?
WE CAN GIVE YOU BACK YOUR SISTER.
WE CAN FIX HER. WE CAN GIVE YOU BACK BETH.
I WANT TO SEE HER FIRST.
FACE-TO-FACE.

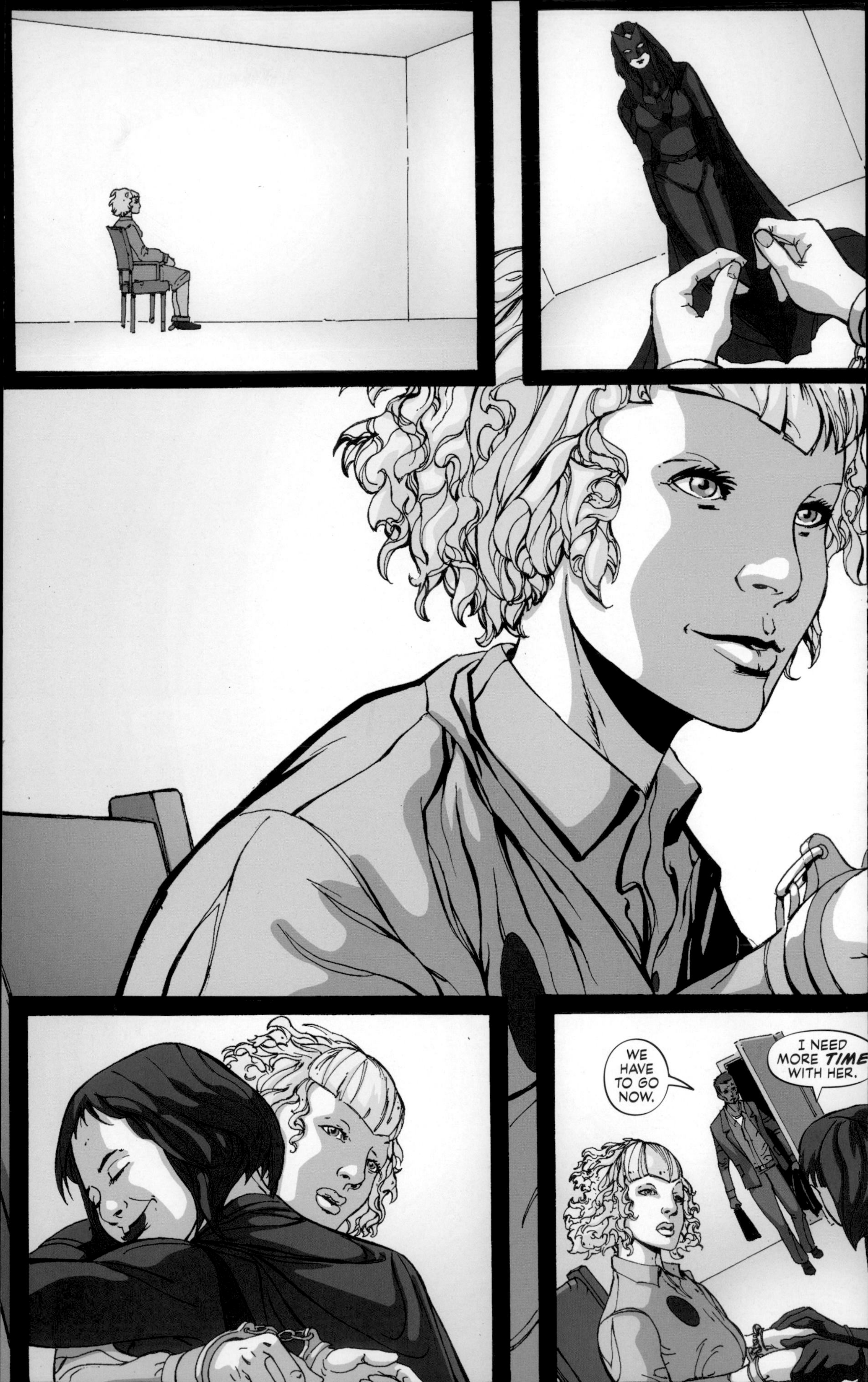
WE HAVE TO GO NOW.
I NEED MORE TIME WITH HER.

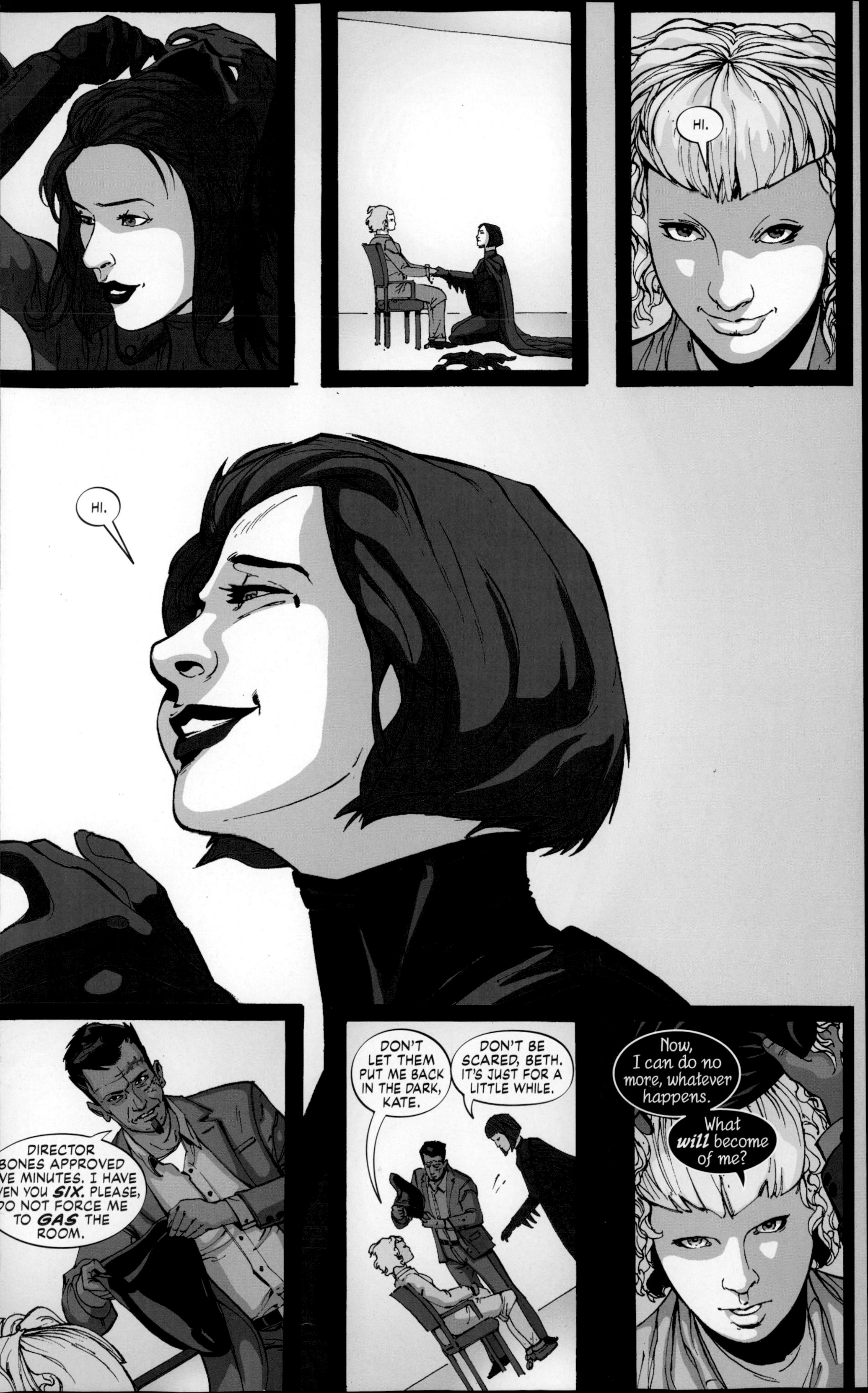
HI.
HI.
DIRECTOR BONES APPROVED FIVE MINUTES. I HAVE GIVEN YOU SIX. PLEASE, DO NOT FORCE ME TO GAS THE ROOM.
DON'T LET THEM PUT ME BACK IN THE DARK, KATE.
DON'T BE SCARED, BETH. IT'S JUST FOR A LITTLE WHILE.
Now, I can do no more, whatever happens.
What will become of me?

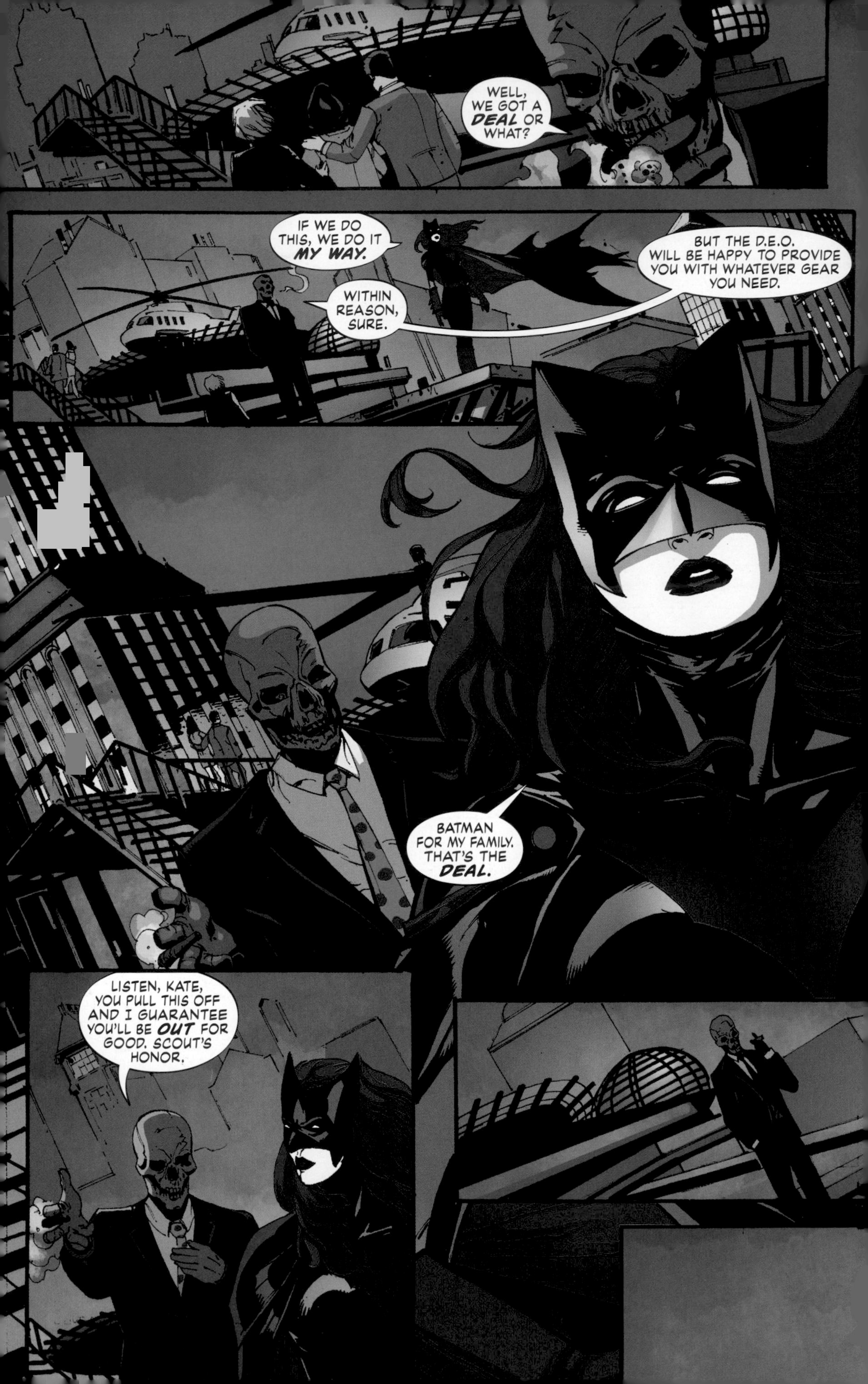
WELL, WE GOT A DEAL OR WHAT?
IF WE DO THIS, WE DO IT MY WAY.
WITHIN REASON, SURE.
BUT THE D.E.O. WILL BE HAPPY TO PROVIDE YOU WITH WHATEVER GEAR YOU NEED.
BATMAN FOR MY FAMILY. THAT'S THE DEAL.
LISTEN, KATE, YOU PULL THIS OFF AND I GUARANTEE YOU'LL BE OUT FOR GOOD. SCOUT'S HONOR.

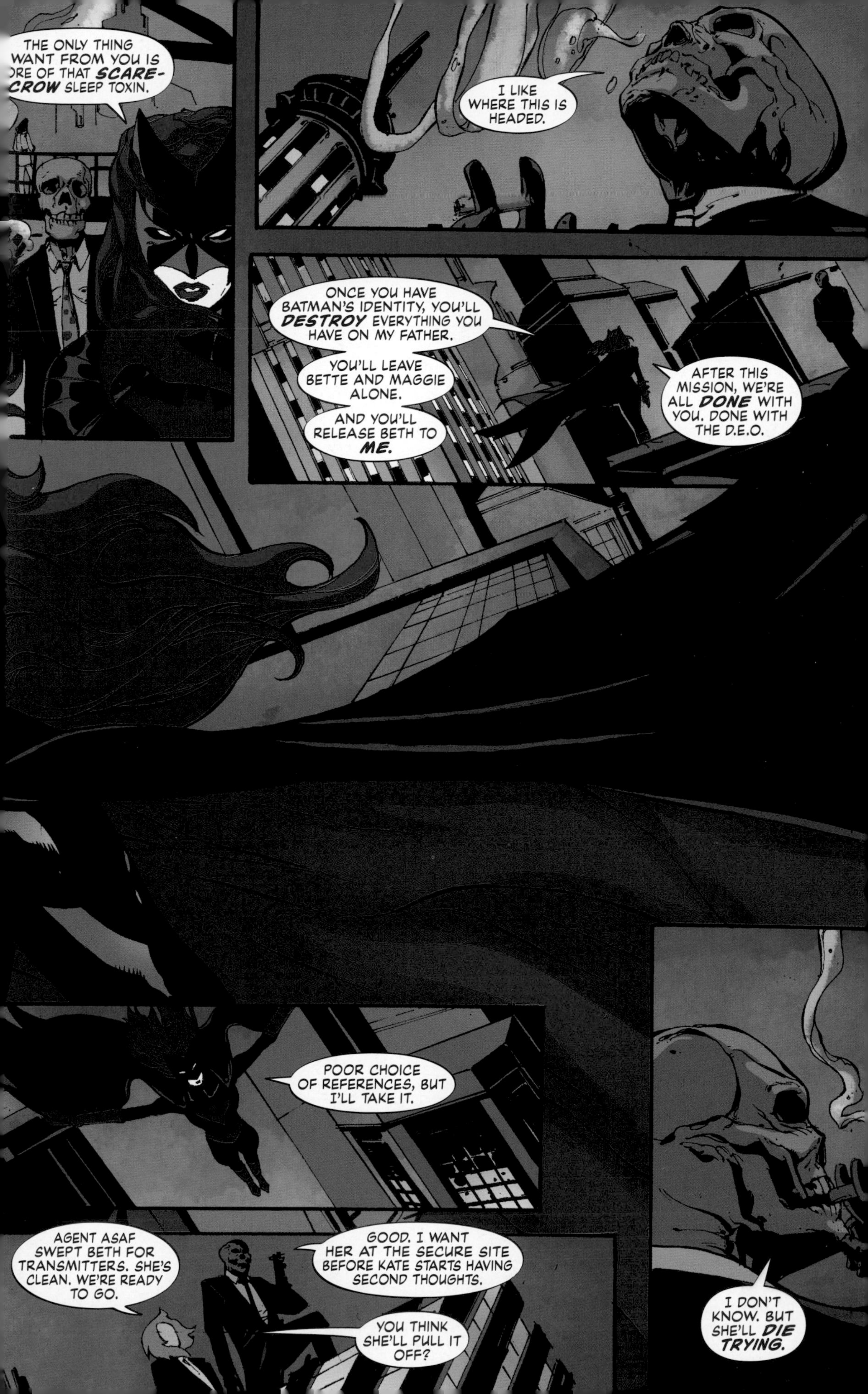
THE ONLY THING
WANT FROM YOU IS
ORE OF THAT SCARE-
CROW SLEEP TOXIN.
I LIKE WHERE THIS IS HEADED.
ONCE YOU HAVE BATMAN'S IDENTITY, YOU'LL DESTROY EVERYTHING YOU HAVE ON MY FATHER.
YOU'LL LEAVE BETTE AND MAGGIE ALONE.
AND YOU'LL RELEASE BETH TO ME.
AFTER THIS MISSION, WE'RE ALL DONE WITH YOU. DONE WITH THE D.E.O.
POOR CHOICE OF REFERENCES, BUT I'LL TAKE IT.
AGENT ASAF SWEPT BETH FOR TRANSMITTERS. SHE'S CLEAN. WE'RE READY TO GO.
GOOD. I WANT HER AT THE SECURE SITE BEFORE KATE STARTS HAVING SECOND THOUGHTS.
YOU THINK SHE'LL PULL IT OFF?
I DON'T KNOW. BUT SHE'LL DIE TRYING.

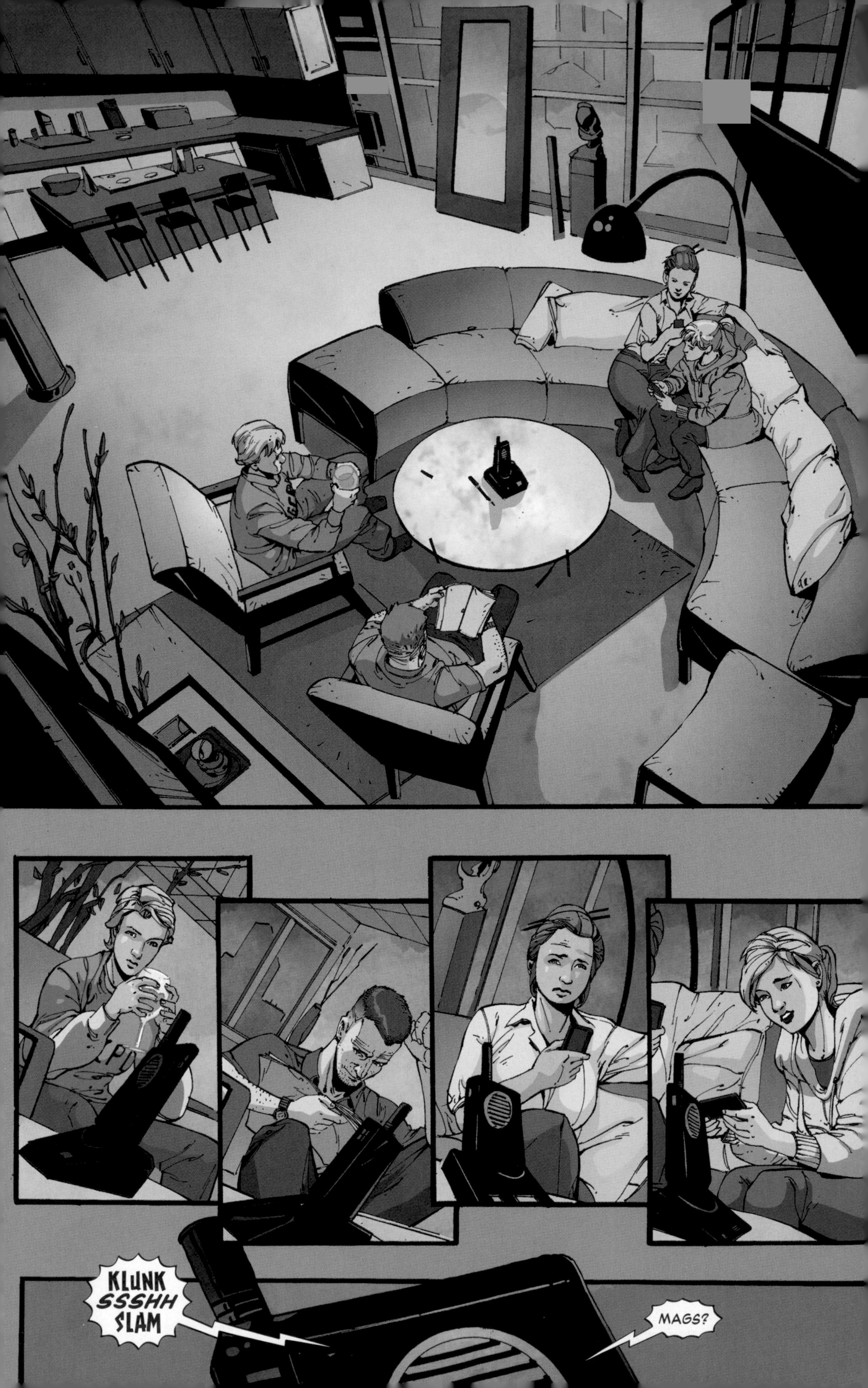
KLUNK
SSSHH
SLAM
MAGS?

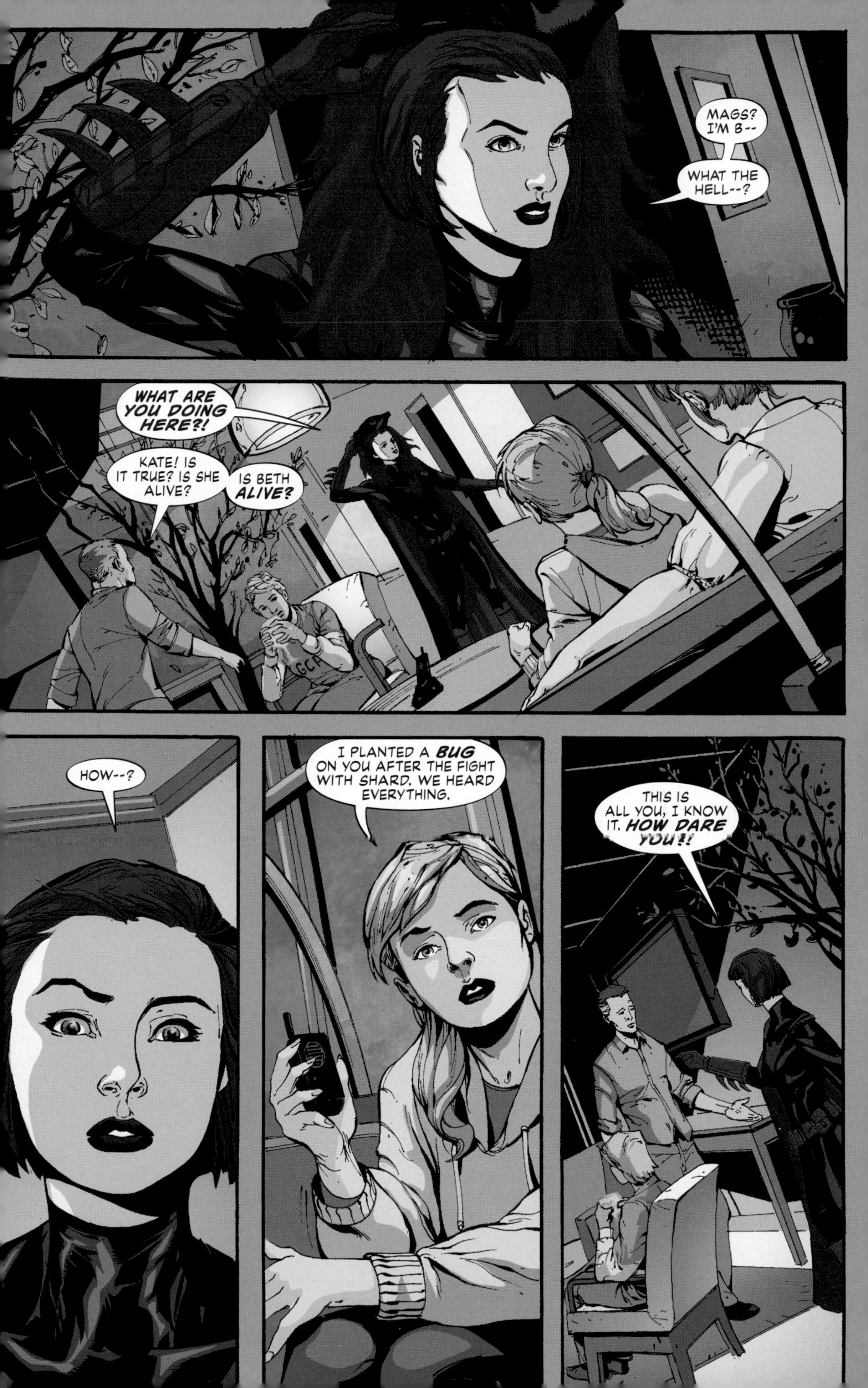
MAGS? I'M B--
WHAT THE HELL--?
WHAT ARE YOU DOING HERE?!
KATE! IS IT TRUE? IS SHE ALIVE?
IS BETH ALIVE?
HOW--?
I PLANTED A BUG ON YOU AFTER THE FIGHT WITH SHARD. WE HEARD EVERYTHING.
THIS IS ALL YOU, I KNOW IT. HOW DARE YOU!!

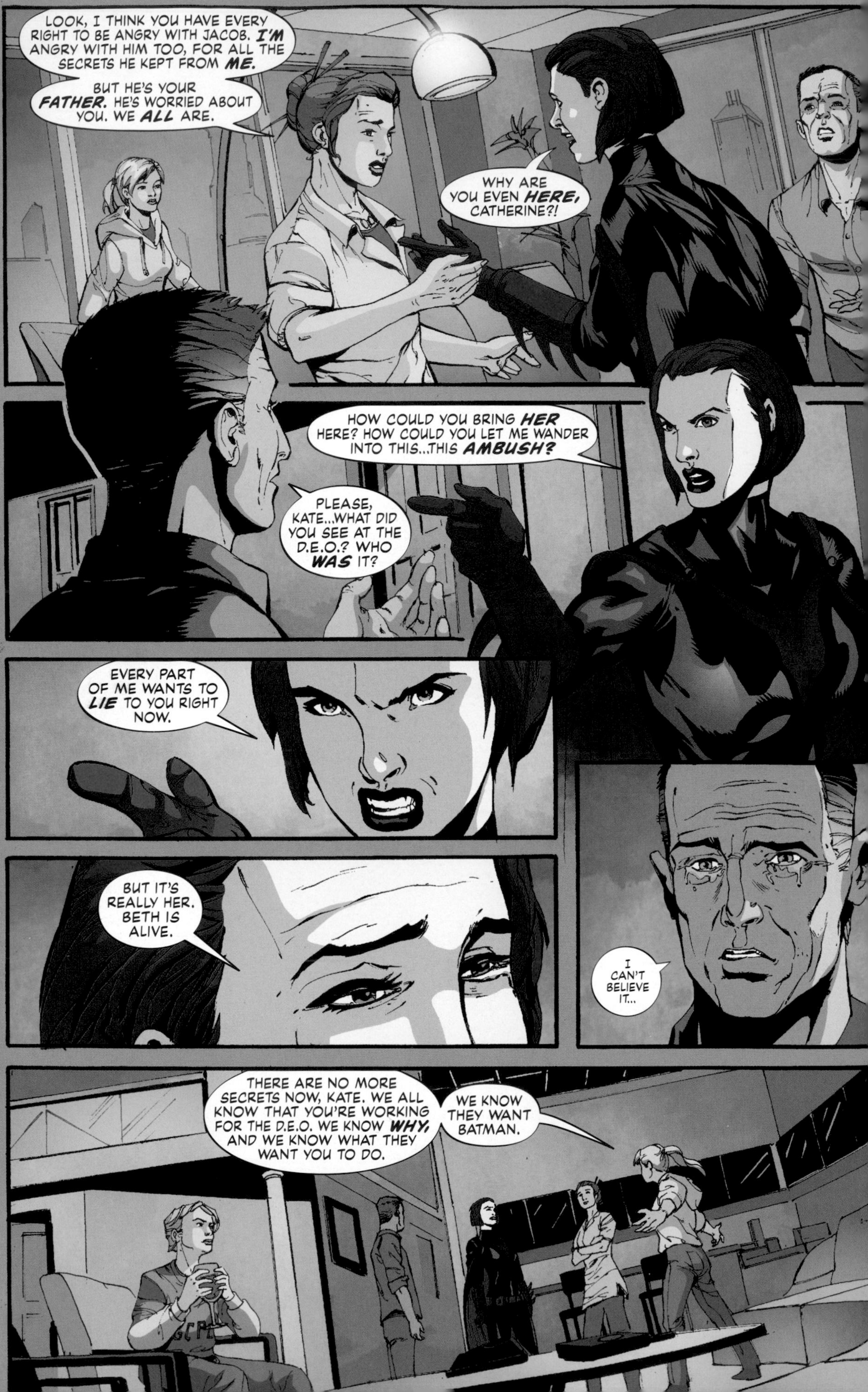
LOOK, I THINK YOU HAVE EVERY RIGHT TO BE ANGRY WITH JACOB. I'M ANGRY WITH HIM TOO, FOR ALL THE SECRETS HE KEPT FROM ME.
BUT HE'S YOUR FATHER. HE'S WORRIED ABOUT YOU. WE ALL ARE.
WHY ARE YOU EVEN HERE, CATHERINE?!
HOW COULD YOU BRING HER HERE? HOW COULD YOU LET ME WANDER INTO THIS...THIS AMBUSH?
PLEASE, KATE...WHAT DID YOU SEE AT THE D.E.O.? WHO WAS IT?
EVERY PART OF ME WANTS TO LIE TO YOU RIGHT NOW.
BUT IT'S REALLY HER. BETH IS ALIVE.
I CAN'T BELIEVE IT...
THERE ARE NO MORE SECRETS NOW, KATE. WE ALL KNOW THAT YOU'RE WORKING FOR THE D.E.O. WE KNOW WHY, AND WE KNOW WHAT THEY WANT YOU TO DO.
WE KNOW THEY WANT BATMAN.

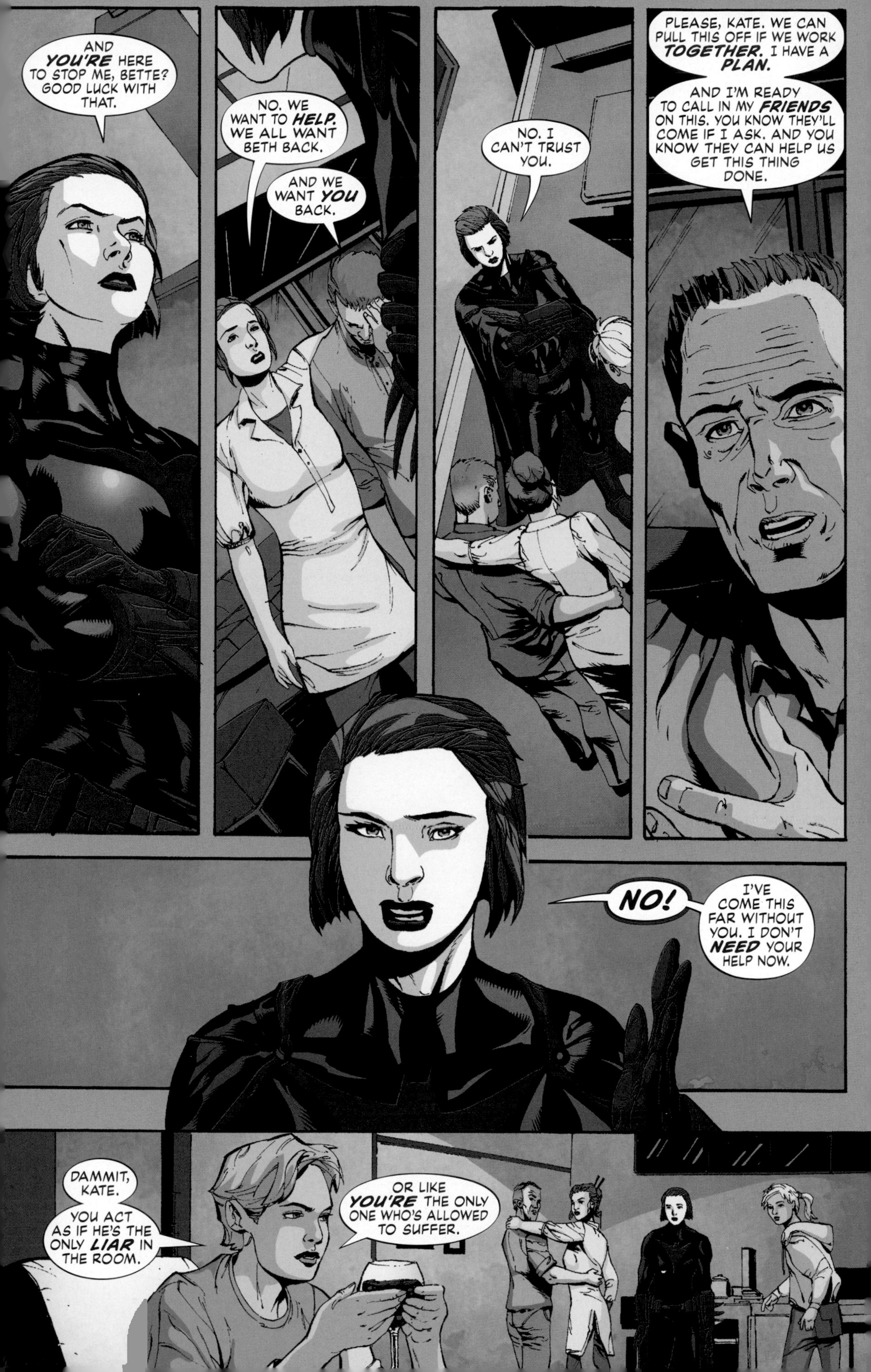
AND *YOU'RE* HERE TO STOP ME, BETTE? GOOD LUCK WITH THAT.
NO. WE WANT TO *HELP.* WE ALL WANT BETH BACK.
AND WE WANT *YOU* BACK.
NO. I CAN'T TRUST YOU.
PLEASE, KATE. WE CAN PULL THIS OFF IF WE WORK *TOGETHER.* I HAVE A *PLAN.*
AND I'M READY TO CALL IN MY *FRIENDS* ON THIS. YOU KNOW THEY'LL COME IF I ASK. AND YOU KNOW THEY CAN HELP US GET THIS THING DONE.
NO!
I'VE COME THIS FAR WITHOUT YOU. I DON'T *NEED* YOUR HELP NOW.
DAMMIT, KATE.
YOU ACT AS IF HE'S THE ONLY *LIAR* IN THE ROOM.
OR LIKE *YOU'RE* THE ONLY ONE WHO'S ALLOWED TO SUFFER.

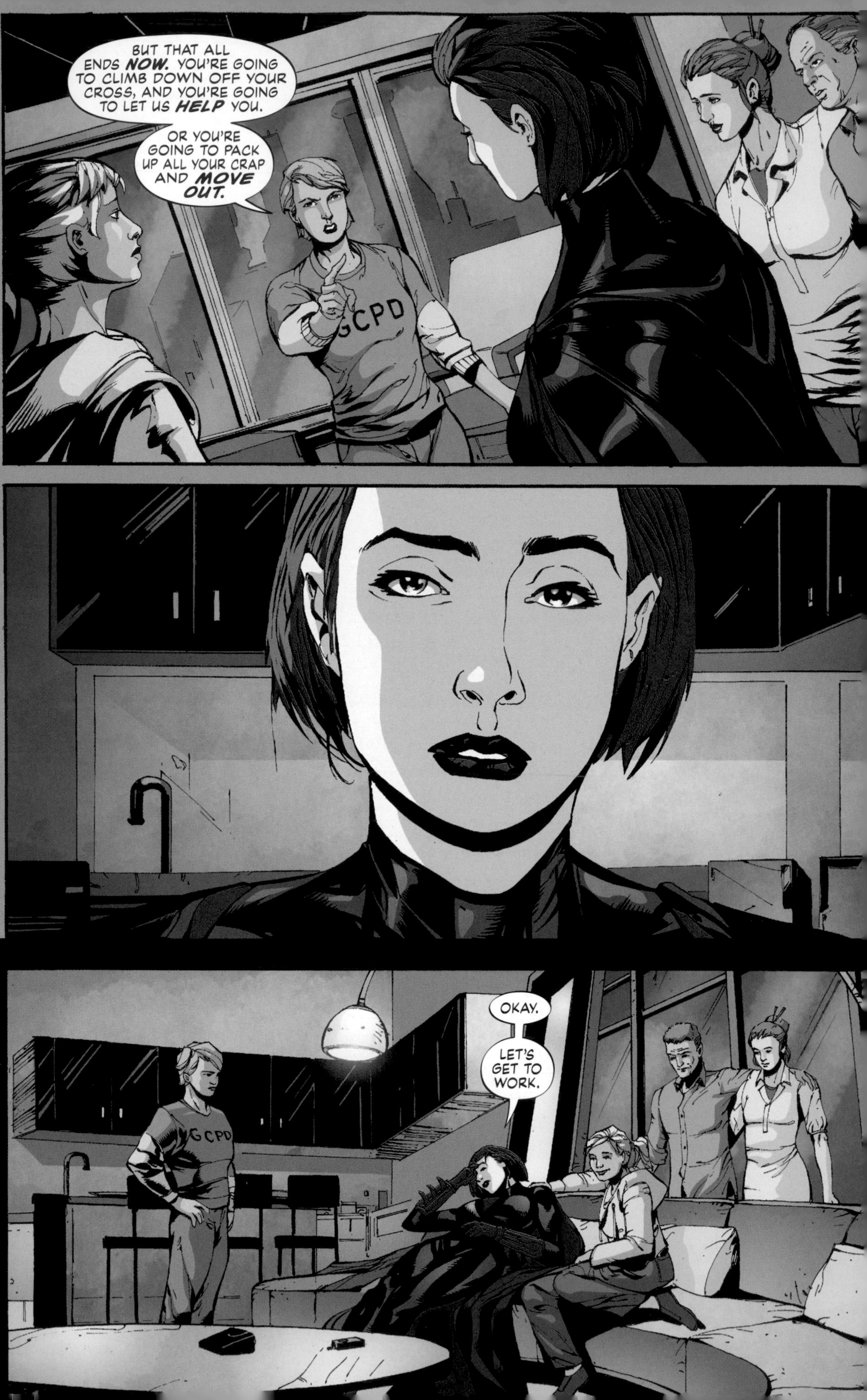
BUT THAT ALL ENDS **NOW.** YOU'RE GOING TO CLIMB DOWN OFF YOUR CROSS, AND YOU'RE GOING TO LET US **HELP** YOU.
OR YOU'RE GOING TO PACK UP ALL YOUR CRAP AND **MOVE OUT.**
GCPD
GCPD
OKAY.
LET'S GET TO WORK.

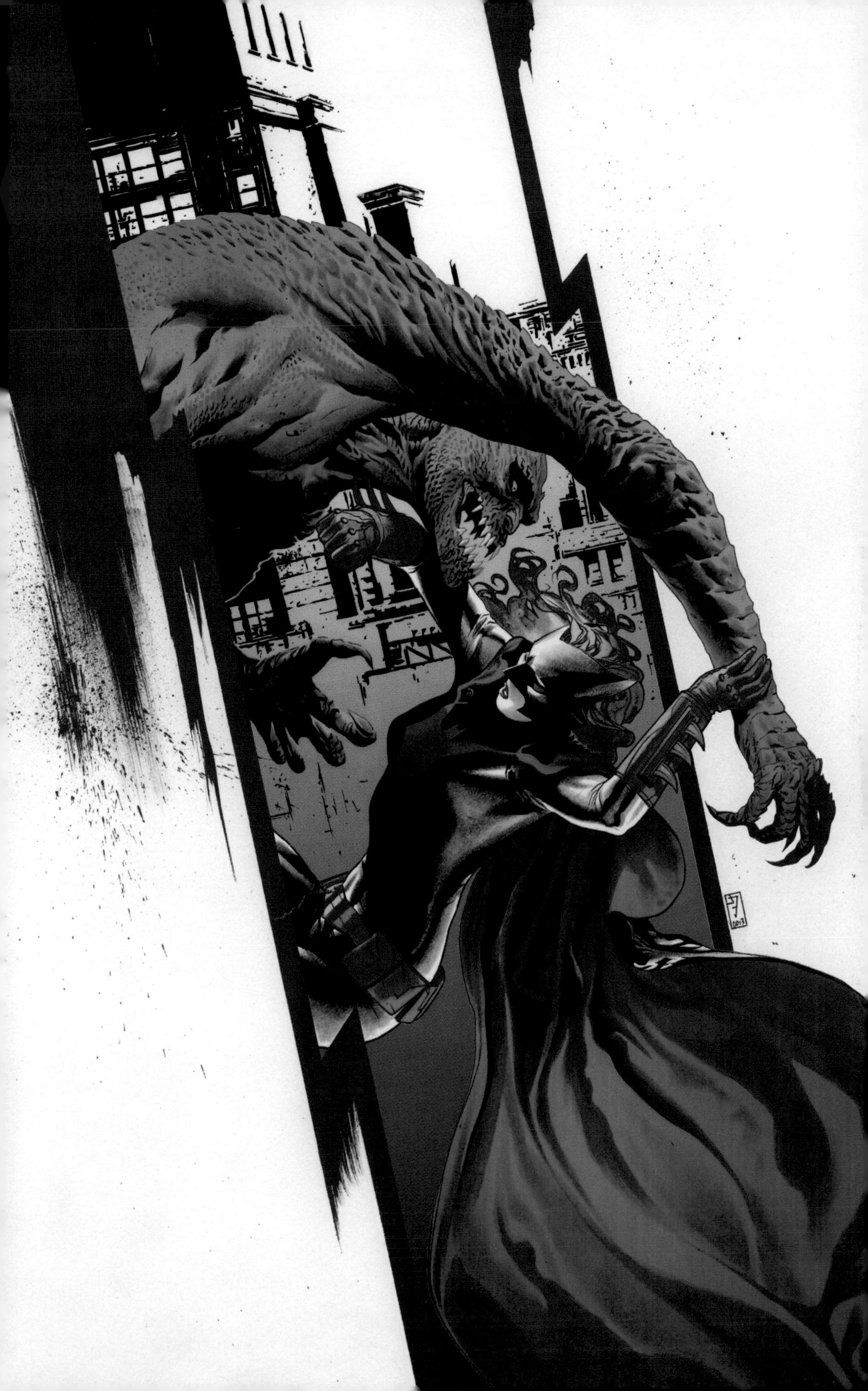

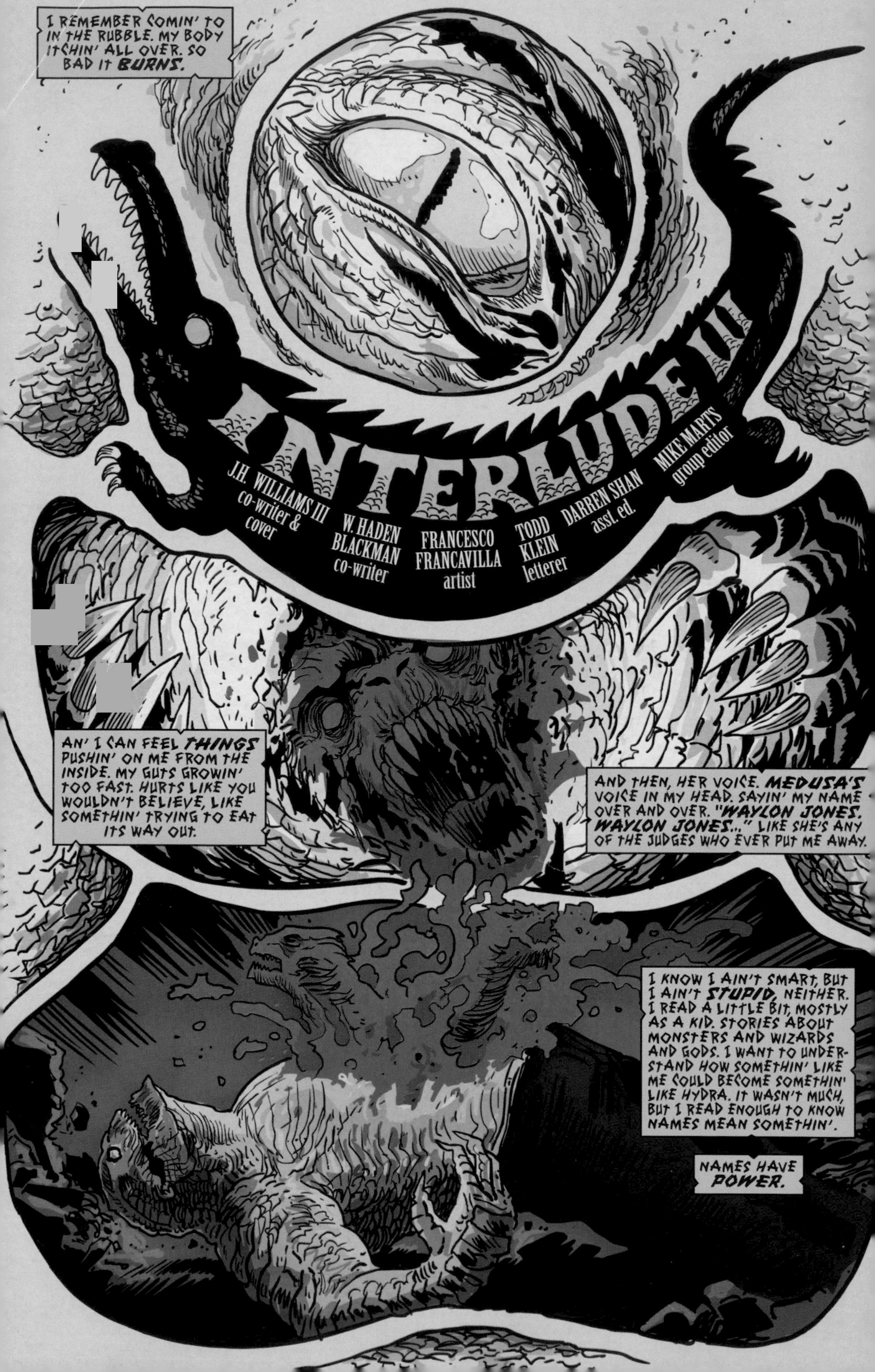
I REMEMBER COMIN' TO IN THE RUBBLE. MY BODY ITCHIN' ALL OVER. SO BAD IT BURNS.
INTERLUDE II
J.H. WILLIAMS III co-writer & cover
W. HADEN BLACKMAN co-writer
FRANCESCO FRANCAVILLA artist
TODD KLEIN letterer
DARREN SHAN asst. ed.
MIKE MARTS group editor
AN' I CAN FEEL THINGS PUSHIN' ON ME FROM THE INSIDE. MY GUTS GROWIN' TOO FAST. HURTS LIKE YOU WOULDN'T BELIEVE, LIKE SOMETHIN' TRYING TO EAT ITS WAY OUT.
AND THEN, HER VOICE. MEDUSA'S VOICE IN MY HEAD. SAYIN' MY NAME OVER AND OVER. "WAYLON JONES. WAYLON JONES..." LIKE SHE'S ANY OF THE JUDGES WHO EVER PUT ME AWAY.
I KNOW I AIN'T SMART, BUT I AIN'T STUPID, NEITHER. I READ A LITTLE BIT, MOSTLY AS A KID. STORIES ABOUT MONSTERS AND WIZARDS AND GODS. I WANT TO UNDERSTAND HOW SOMETHIN' LIKE ME COULD BECOME SOMETHIN' LIKE HYDRA. IT WASN'T MUCH, BUT I READ ENOUGH TO KNOW NAMES MEAN SOMETHIN'.
NAMES HAVE POWER.

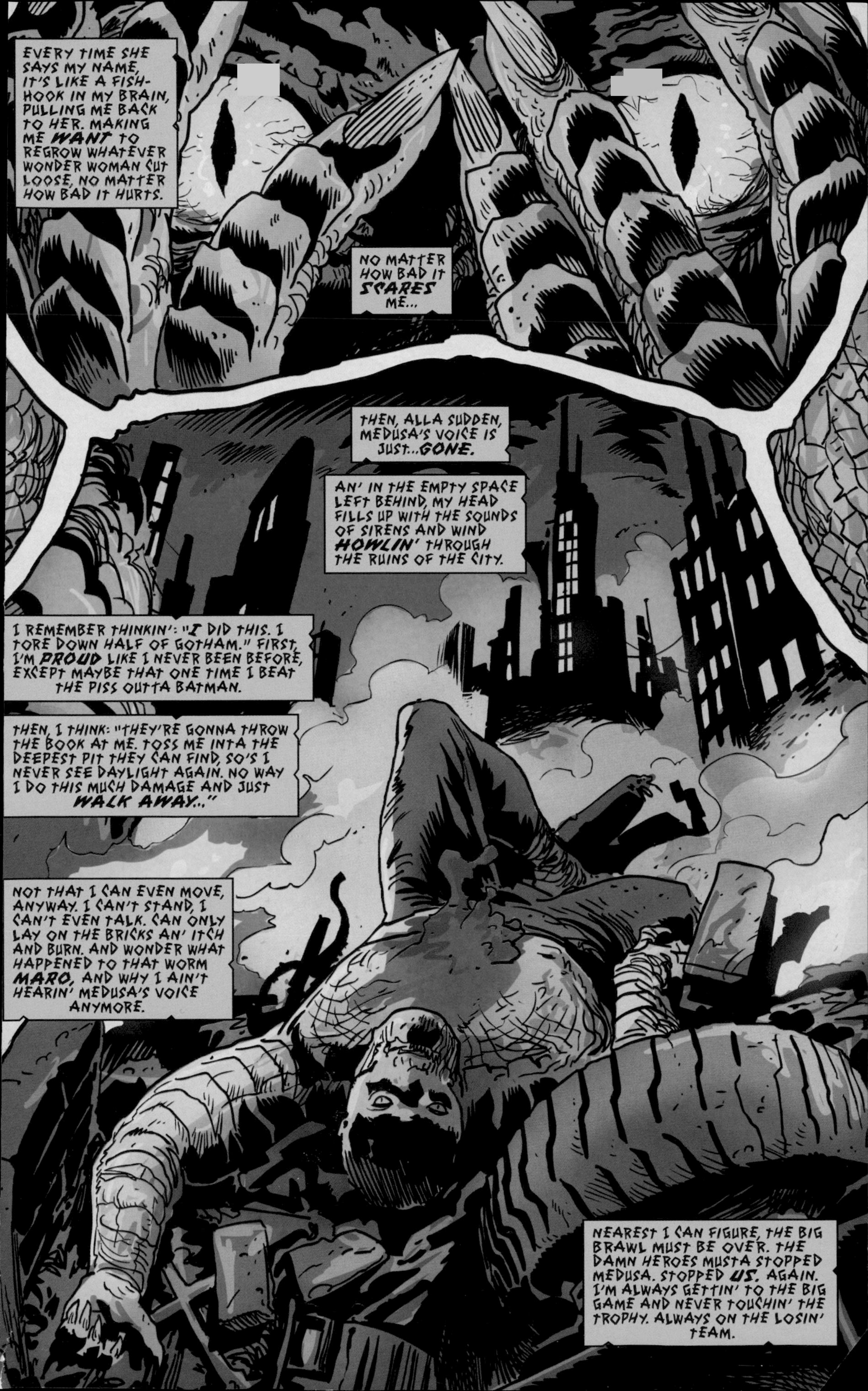
EVERY TIME SHE SAYS MY NAME, IT'S LIKE A FISH-HOOK IN MY BRAIN, PULLING ME BACK TO HER. MAKING ME WANT TO REGROW WHATEVER WONDER WOMAN CUT LOOSE, NO MATTER HOW BAD IT HURTS.
NO MATTER HOW BAD IT SCARES ME...
THEN, ALLA SUDDEN, MEDUSA'S VOICE IS JUST...GONE.
AN' IN THE EMPTY SPACE LEFT BEHIND, MY HEAD FILLS UP WITH THE SOUNDS OF SIRENS AND WIND HOWLIN' THROUGH THE RUINS OF THE CITY.
I REMEMBER THINKIN': "I DID THIS. I TORE DOWN HALF OF GOTHAM." FIRST, I'M PROUD LIKE I NEVER BEEN BEFORE, EXCEPT MAYBE THAT ONE TIME I BEAT THE PISS OUTTA BATMAN.
THEN, I THINK: "THEY'RE GONNA THROW THE BOOK AT ME. TOSS ME INTA THE DEEPEST PIT THEY CAN FIND, SO'S I NEVER SEE DAYLIGHT AGAIN. NO WAY I DO THIS MUCH DAMAGE AND JUST WALK AWAY..."
NOT THAT I CAN EVEN MOVE, ANYWAY. I CAN'T STAND, I CAN'T EVEN TALK. CAN ONLY LAY ON THE BRICKS AN' ITCH AND BURN. AND WONDER WHAT HAPPENED TO THAT WORM MARO, AND WHY I AIN'T HEARIN' MEDUSA'S VOICE ANYMORE.
NEAREST I CAN FIGURE, THE BIG BRAWL MUST BE OVER. THE DAMN HEROES MUSTA STOPPED MEDUSA. STOPPED US. AGAIN. I'M ALWAYS GETTIN' TO THE BIG GAME AND NEVER TOUCHIN' THE TROPHY. ALWAYS ON THE LOSIN' TEAM.

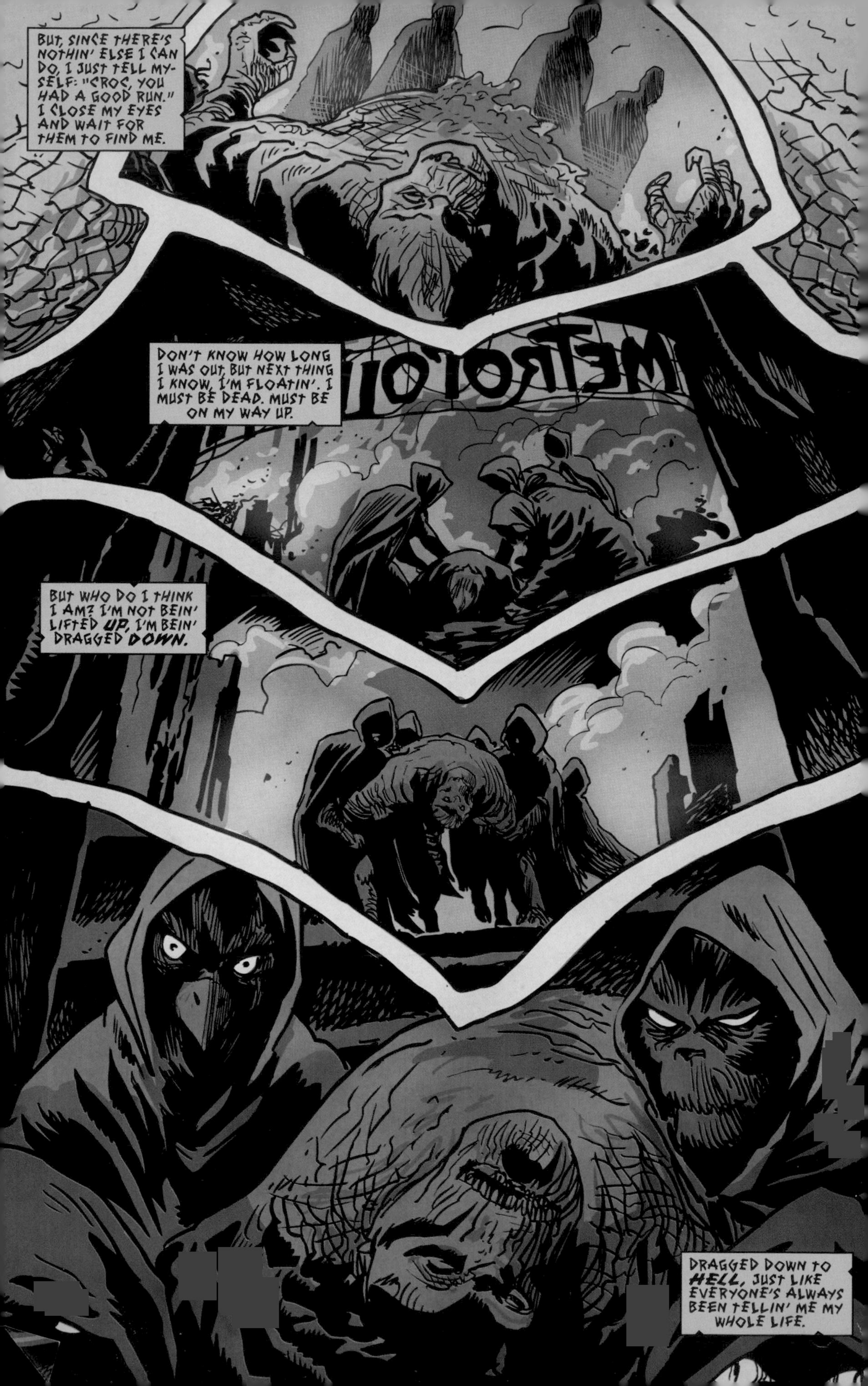
BUT, SINCE THERE'S NOTHIN' ELSE I CAN DO, I JUST TELL MYSELF: "CROC, YOU HAD A GOOD RUN." I CLOSE MY EYES AND WAIT FOR THEM TO FIND ME.
DON'T KNOW HOW LONG I WAS OUT, BUT NEXT THING I KNOW, I'M FLOATIN'. I MUST BE DEAD. MUST BE ON MY WAY UP.
BUT WHO DO I THINK I AM? I'M NOT BEIN' LIFTED UP, I'M BEIN' DRAGGED DOWN.
DRAGGED DOWN TO HELL, JUST LIKE EVERYONE'S ALWAYS BEEN TELLIN' ME MY WHOLE LIFE.

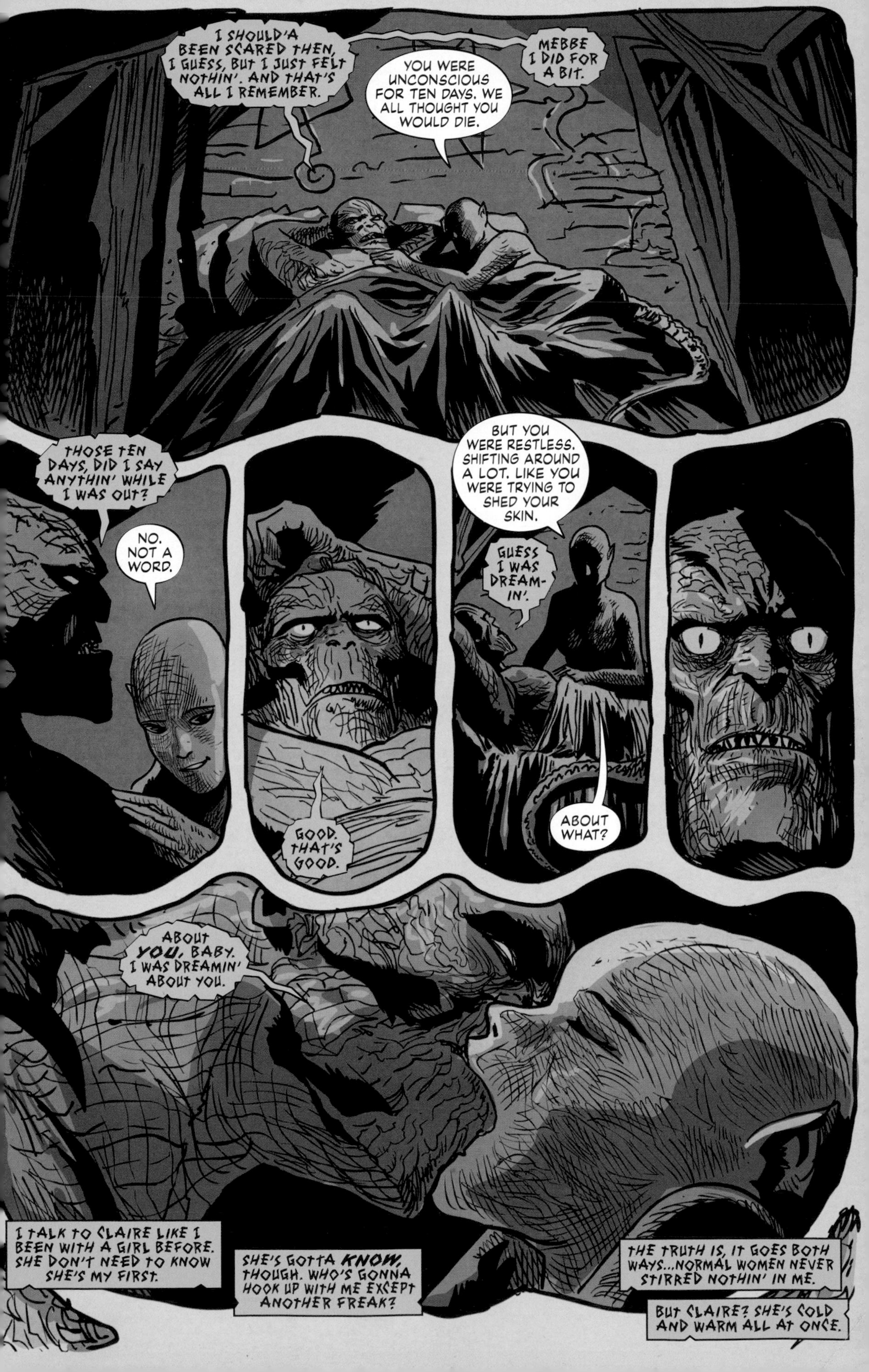
I SHOULD'A BEEN SCARED THEN, I GUESS, BUT I JUST FELT NOTHIN'. AND THAT'S ALL I REMEMBER.
YOU WERE UNCONSCIOUS FOR TEN DAYS. WE ALL THOUGHT YOU WOULD DIE.
MEBBE I DID FOR A BIT.
THOSE TEN DAYS, DID I SAY ANYTHIN' WHILE I WAS OUT?
NO. NOT A WORD.
GOOD. THAT'S GOOD.
BUT YOU WERE RESTLESS. SHIFTING AROUND A LOT. LIKE YOU WERE TRYING TO SHED YOUR SKIN.
GUESS I WAS DREAMIN'.
ABOUT WHAT?
ABOUT YOU, BABY. I WAS DREAMIN' ABOUT YOU.
I TALK TO CLAIRE LIKE I BEEN WITH A GIRL BEFORE. SHE DON'T NEED TO KNOW SHE'S MY FIRST.
SHE'S GOTTA KNOW, THOUGH. WHO'S GONNA HOOK UP WITH ME EXCEPT ANOTHER FREAK?
THE TRUTH IS, IT GOES BOTH WAYS...NORMAL WOMEN NEVER STIRRED NOTHIN' IN ME.
BUT CLAIRE? SHE'S COLD AND WARM ALL AT ONCE.

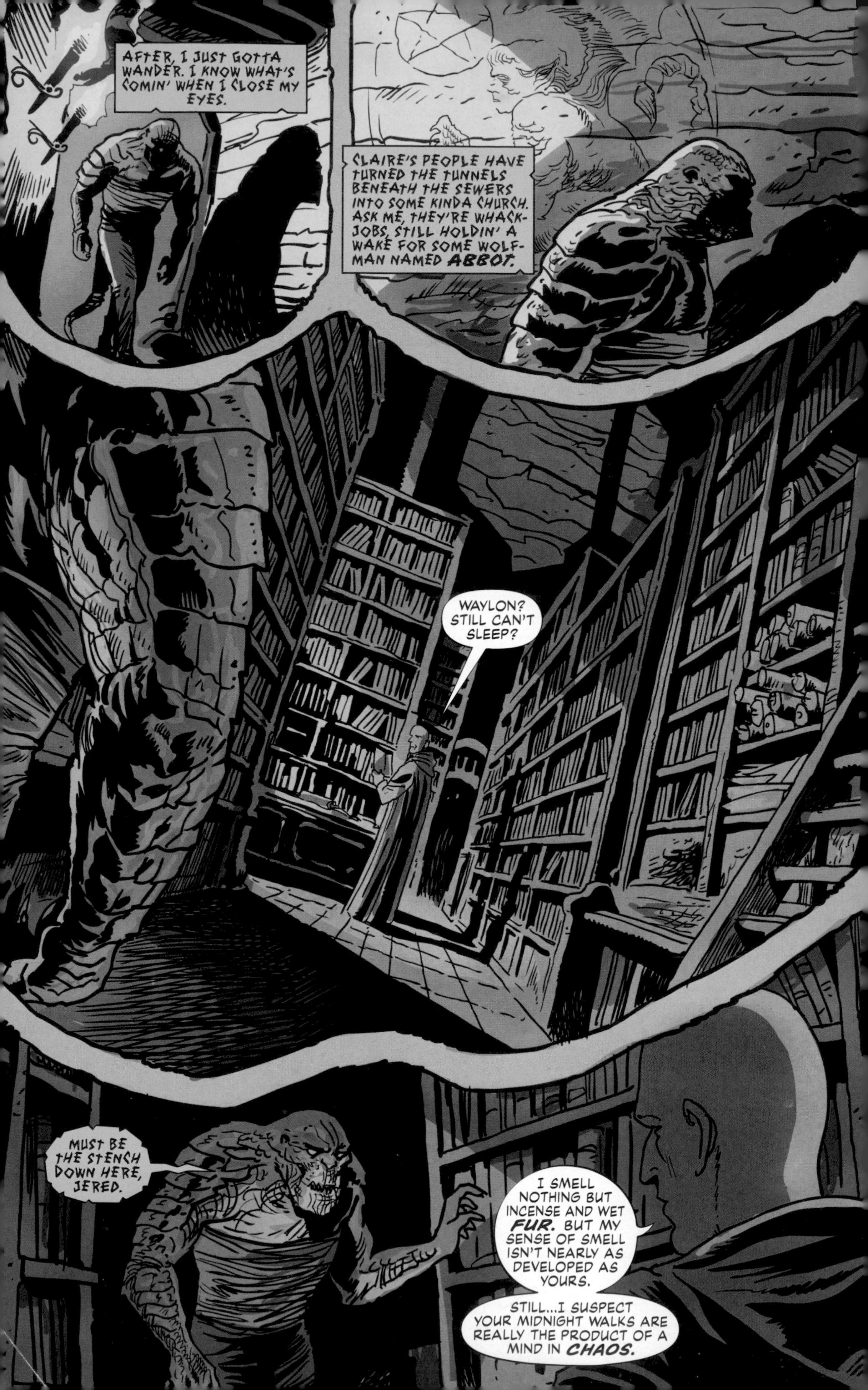
AFTER, I JUST GOTTA WANDER. I KNOW WHAT'S COMIN' WHEN I CLOSE MY EYES.
CLAIRE'S PEOPLE HAVE TURNED THE TUNNELS BENEATH THE SEWERS INTO SOME KINDA CHURCH. ASK ME, THEY'RE WHACK-JOBS, STILL HOLDIN' A WAKE FOR SOME WOLF-MAN NAMED ABBOT.
WAYLON? STILL CAN'T SLEEP?
MUST BE THE STENCH DOWN HERE, JERED.
I SMELL NOTHING BUT INCENSE AND WET FUR. BUT MY SENSE OF SMELL ISN'T NEARLY AS DEVELOPED AS YOURS.
STILL...I SUSPECT YOUR MIDNIGHT WALKS ARE REALLY THE PRODUCT OF A MIND IN CHAOS.

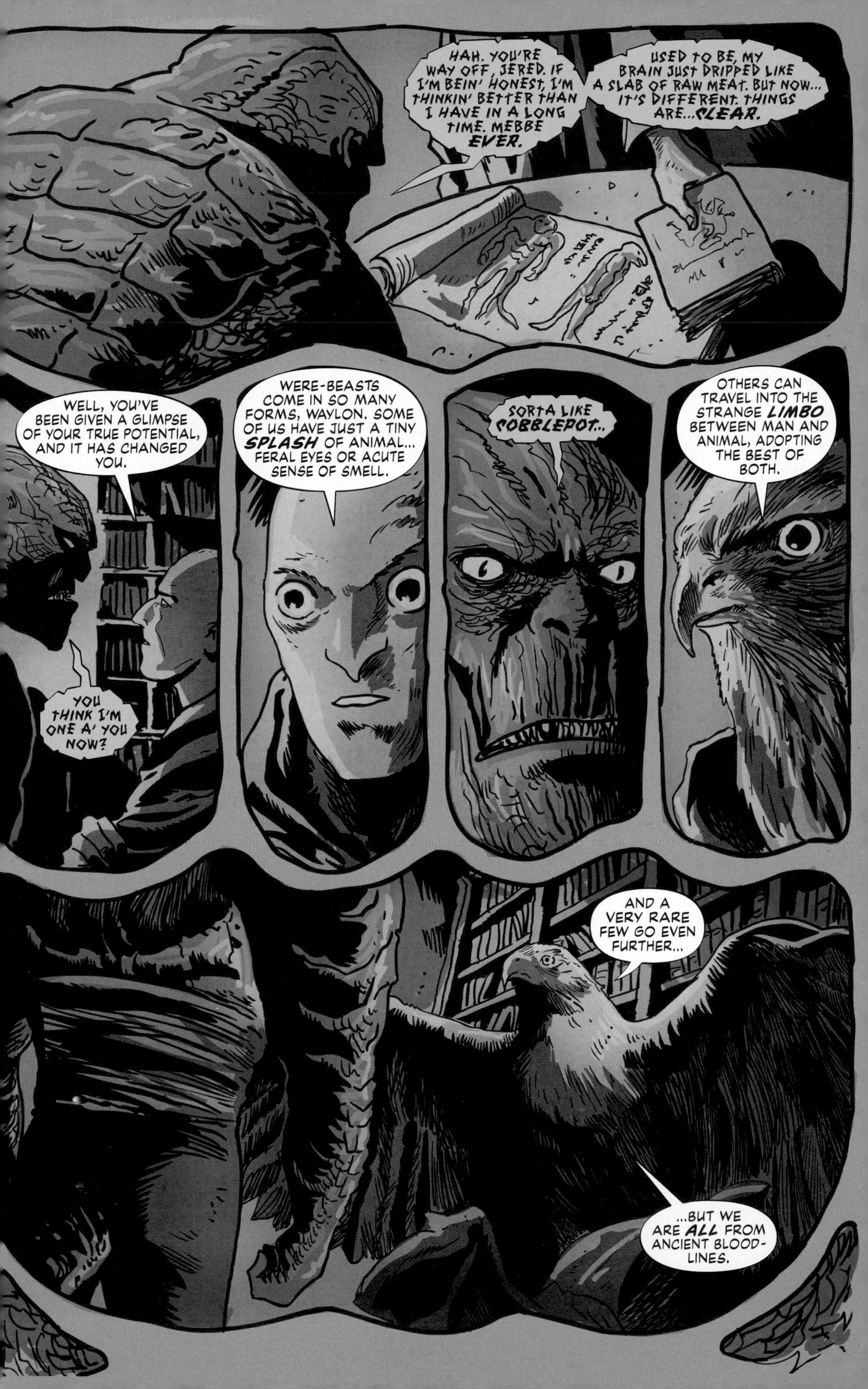
HAH. YOU'RE WAY OFF, JERED. IF I'M BEIN' HONEST, I'M THINKIN' BETTER THAN I HAVE IN A LONG TIME. MEBBE EVER.
USED TO BE, MY BRAIN JUST DRIPPED LIKE A SLAB OF RAW MEAT. BUT NOW... IT'S DIFFERENT. THINGS ARE...CLEAR.
WELL, YOU'VE BEEN GIVEN A GLIMPSE OF YOUR TRUE POTENTIAL, AND IT HAS CHANGED YOU.
YOU THINK I'M ONE A' YOU NOW?
WERE-BEASTS COME IN SO MANY FORMS, WAYLON. SOME OF US HAVE JUST A TINY SPLASH OF ANIMAL... FERAL EYES OR ACUTE SENSE OF SMELL.
SORTA LIKE COBBLEPOT...
OTHERS CAN TRAVEL INTO THE STRANGE LIMBO BETWEEN MAN AND ANIMAL, ADOPTING THE BEST OF BOTH.
AND A VERY RARE FEW GO EVEN FURTHER...
...BUT WE ARE ALL FROM ANCIENT BLOOD-LINES.

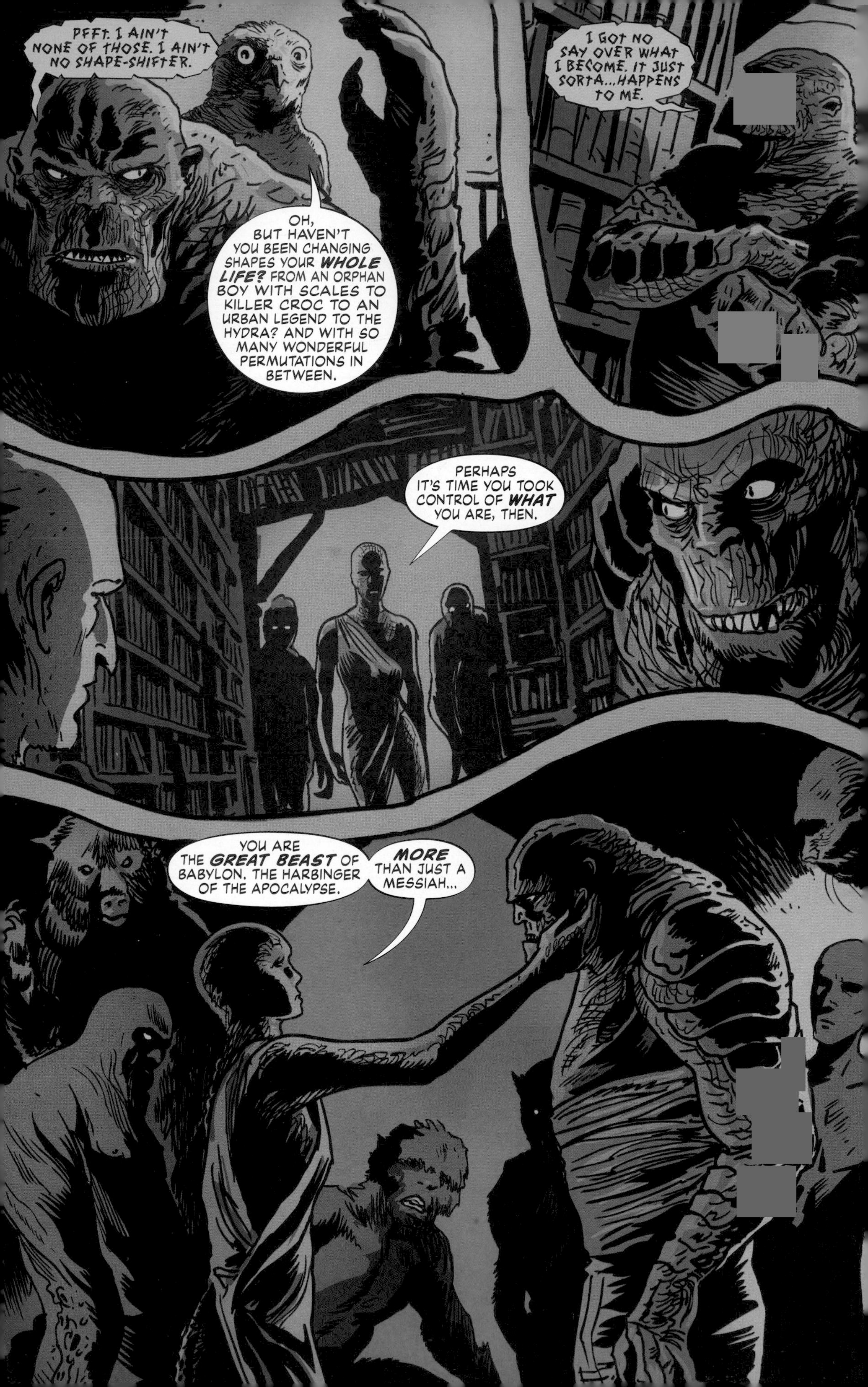
PFFT. I AIN'T NONE OF THOSE. I AIN'T NO SHAPE-SHIFTER.
I GOT NO SAY OVER WHAT I BECOME. IT JUST SORTA...HAPPENS TO ME.
OH, BUT HAVEN'T YOU BEEN CHANGING SHAPES YOUR *WHOLE LIFE?* FROM AN ORPHAN BOY WITH SCALES TO KILLER CROC TO AN URBAN LEGEND TO THE HYDRA? AND WITH SO MANY WONDERFUL PERMUTATIONS IN BETWEEN.
PERHAPS IT'S TIME YOU TOOK CONTROL OF *WHAT* YOU ARE, THEN.
YOU ARE THE *GREAT BEAST* OF BABYLON. THE HARBINGER OF THE APOCALYPSE.
MORE THAN JUST A MESSIAH...

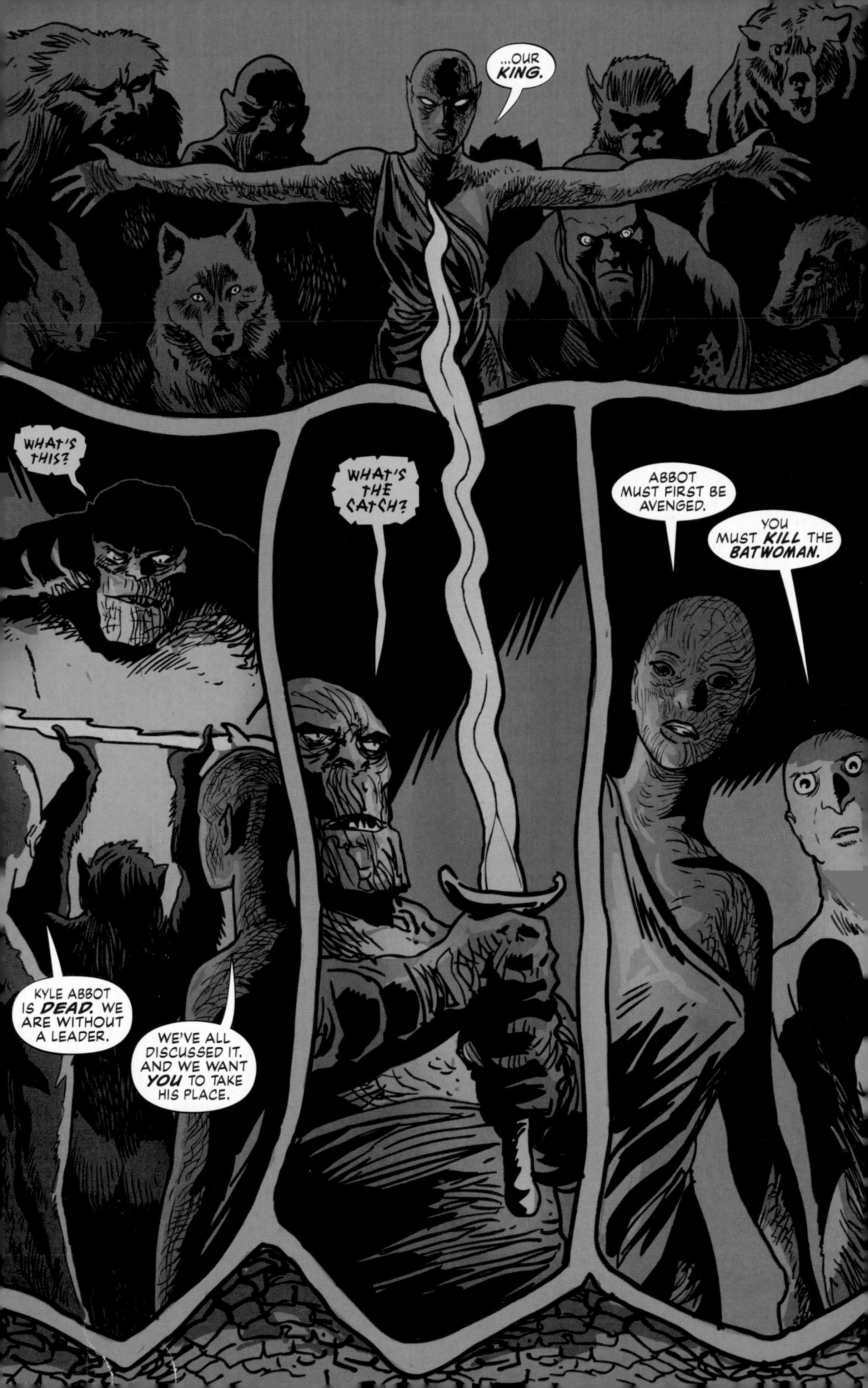
...OUR KING.
WHAT'S THIS?
KYLE ABBOT IS DEAD. WE ARE WITHOUT A LEADER.
WE'VE ALL DISCUSSED IT. AND WE WANT YOU TO TAKE HIS PLACE.
WHAT'S THE CATCH?
ABBOT MUST FIRST BE AVENGED.
YOU MUST KILL THE BATWOMAN.

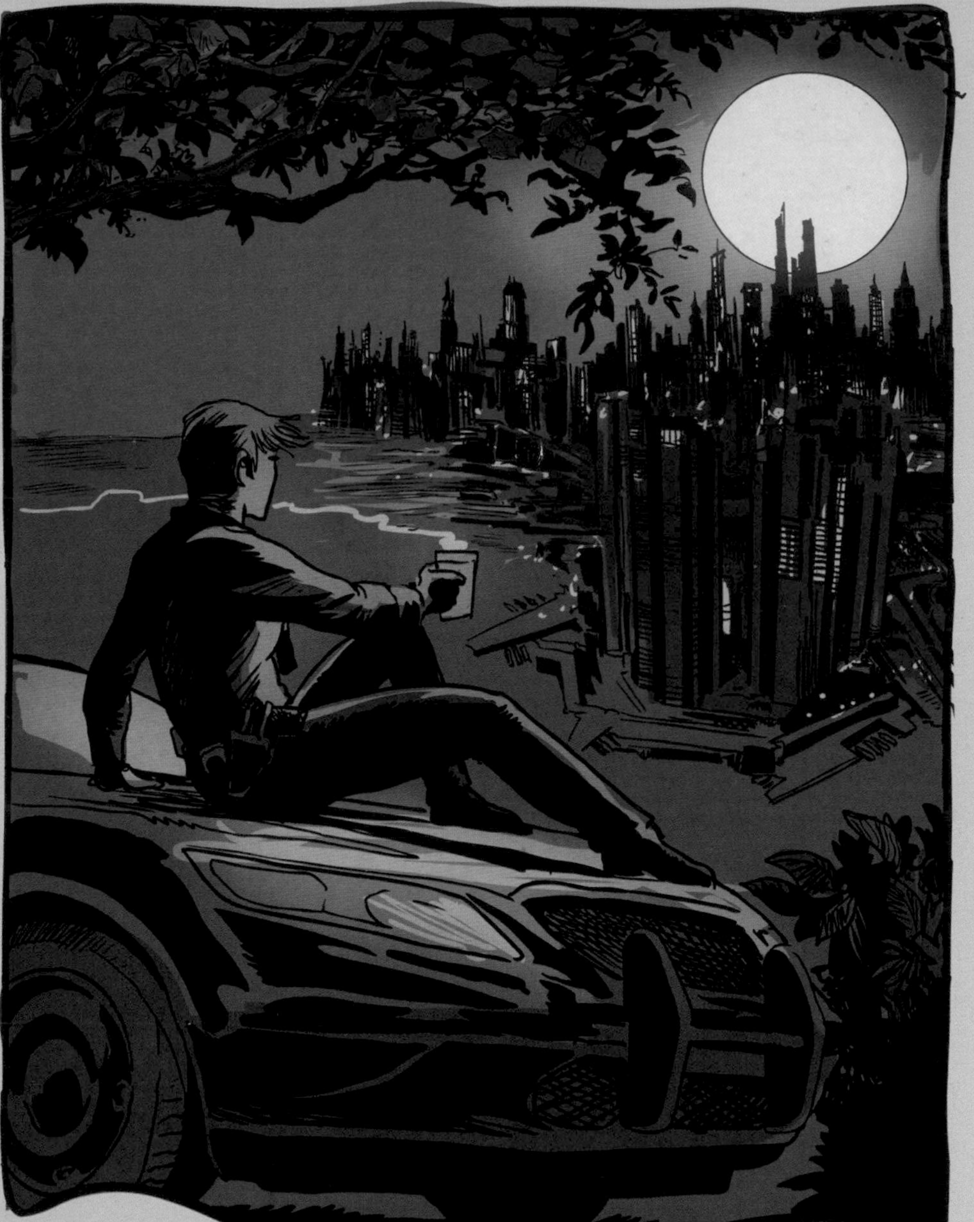

'COURSE I GOTTA SAY YES. WHERE ELSE AM I GONNA GO? WITH THE WERES, I GOT A BED AND THREE SQUARES.

AND CLAIRE.

TAKES A WHILE TO FIGGER OUT THE ***HOW*** OF IT ALL, THOUGH. NOT LIKE I CAN JUST GO INTO GOTHAM AND STIR UP TROUBLE AND HOPE IT'LL BE BATWOMAN WHO SHOWS.

KNOWIN' MY LUCK, I'D JUST GET NIGHTWING TRYIN' TO CLUB IN MY SKULL.

BUT JERED TELLS ME THE WERES GOT EYES AND EARS AND ***SNOUTS*** EVERYWHERE.

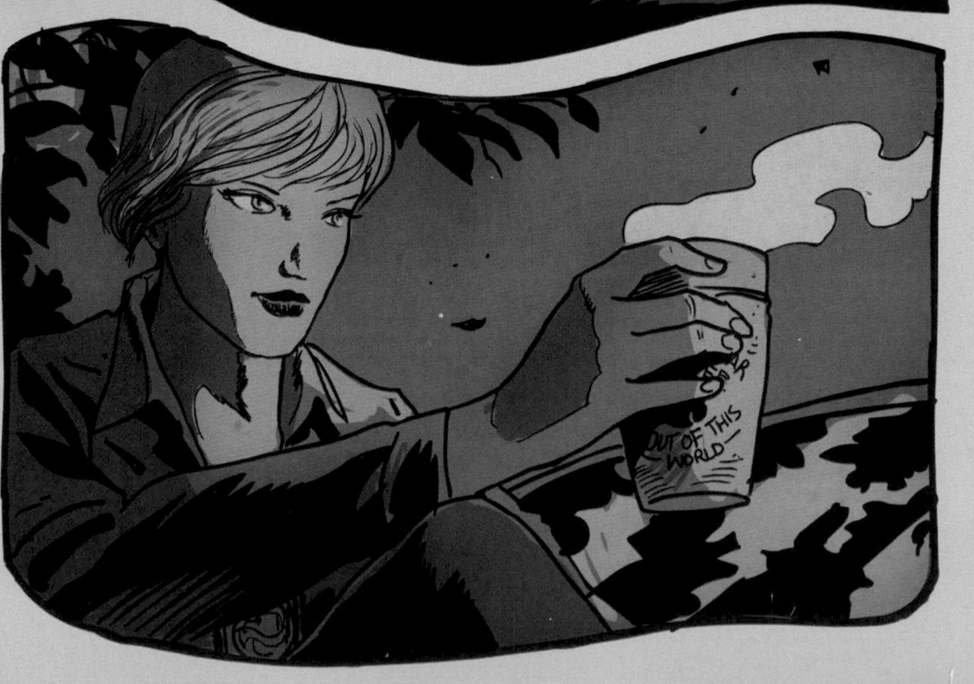
OUT OF THIS WORLD

THIS COP, THIS ***MAGGIE SAWYER,*** JERED SAYS SHE'S GOT BATWOMAN'S SCENT ALL OVER HER. SO, I'M THINKIN' MEBBE THEY'RE THE SAME CHICK.

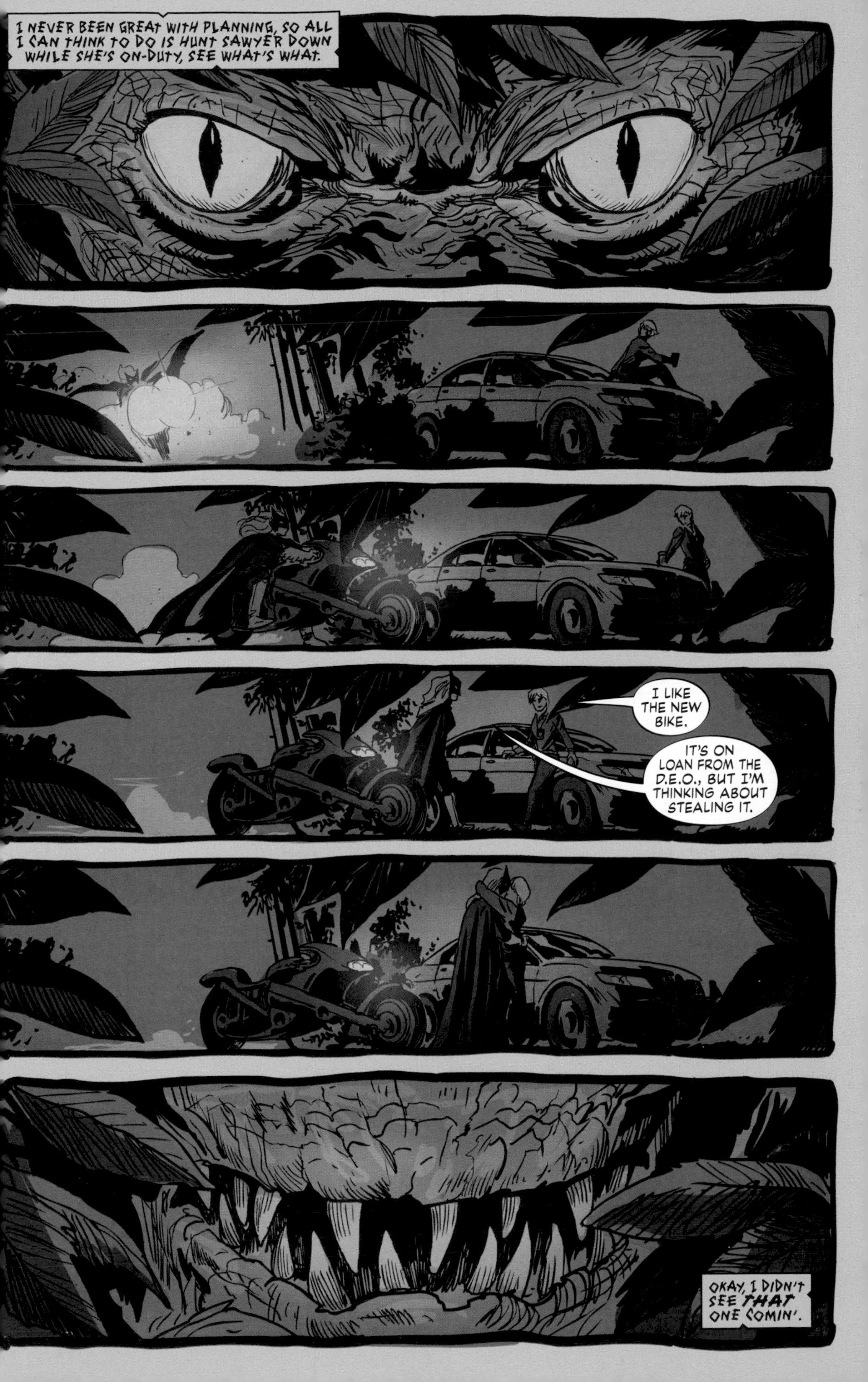
I NEVER BEEN GREAT WITH PLANNING, SO ALL I CAN THINK TO DO IS HUNT SAWYER DOWN WHILE SHE'S ON-DUTY, SEE WHAT'S WHAT.
I LIKE THE NEW BIKE.
IT'S ON LOAN FROM THE D.E.O., BUT I'M THINKING ABOUT STEALING IT.
OKAY, I DIDN'T SEE *THAT* ONE COMIN'.

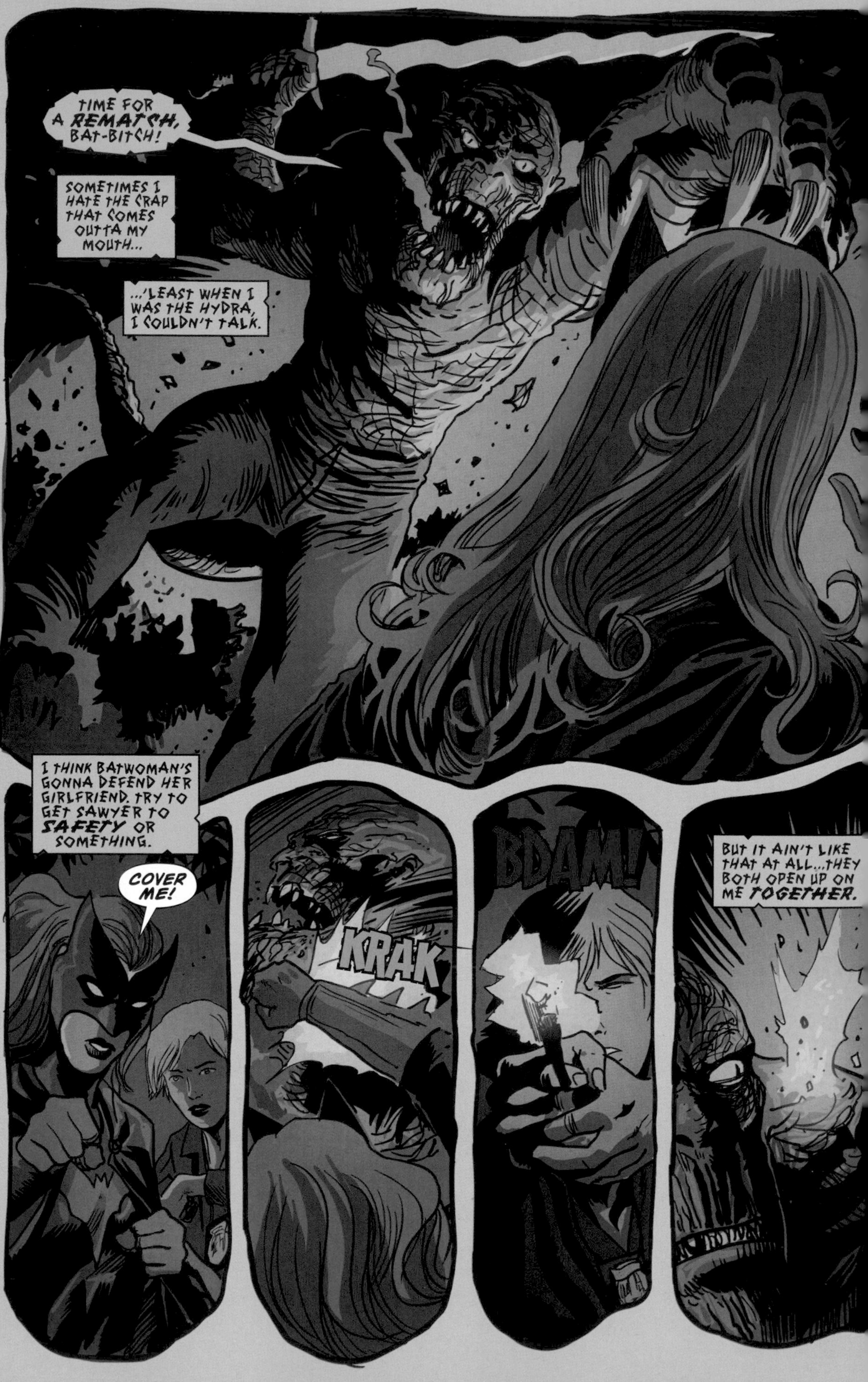
TIME FOR A REMATCH, BAT-BITCH!
SOMETIMES I HATE THE CRAP THAT COMES OUTTA MY MOUTH...
...'LEAST WHEN I WAS THE HYDRA, I COULDN'T TALK.
I THINK BATWOMAN'S GONNA DEFEND HER GIRLFRIEND. TRY TO GET SAWYER TO SAFETY OR SOMETHING.
COVER ME!
KRAK
BDAM!
BUT IT AIN'T LIKE THAT AT ALL...THEY BOTH OPEN UP ON ME TOGETHER.

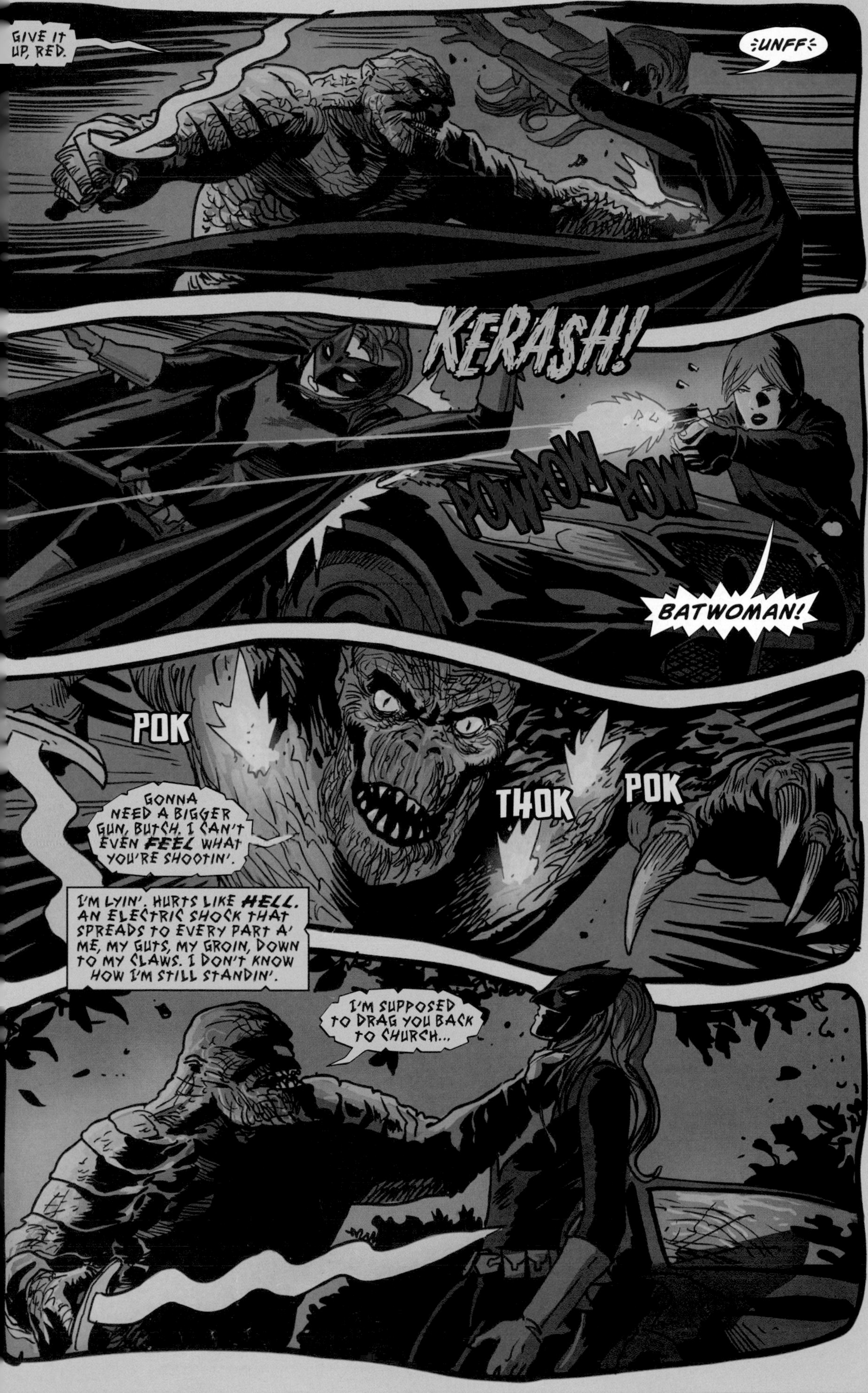
GIVE IT UP, RED.
UNFF
KERASH!
POWPOW POW
BATWOMAN!
POK
THOK
POK
GONNA NEED A BIGGER GUN, BUTCH. I CAN'T EVEN FEEL WHAT YOU'RE SHOOTIN'.
I'M LYIN'. HURTS LIKE HELL. AN ELECTRIC SHOCK THAT SPREADS TO EVERY PART A' ME, MY GUTS, MY GROIN, DOWN TO MY CLAWS. I DON'T KNOW HOW I'M STILL STANDIN'.
I'M SUPPOSED TO DRAG YOU BACK TO CHURCH...

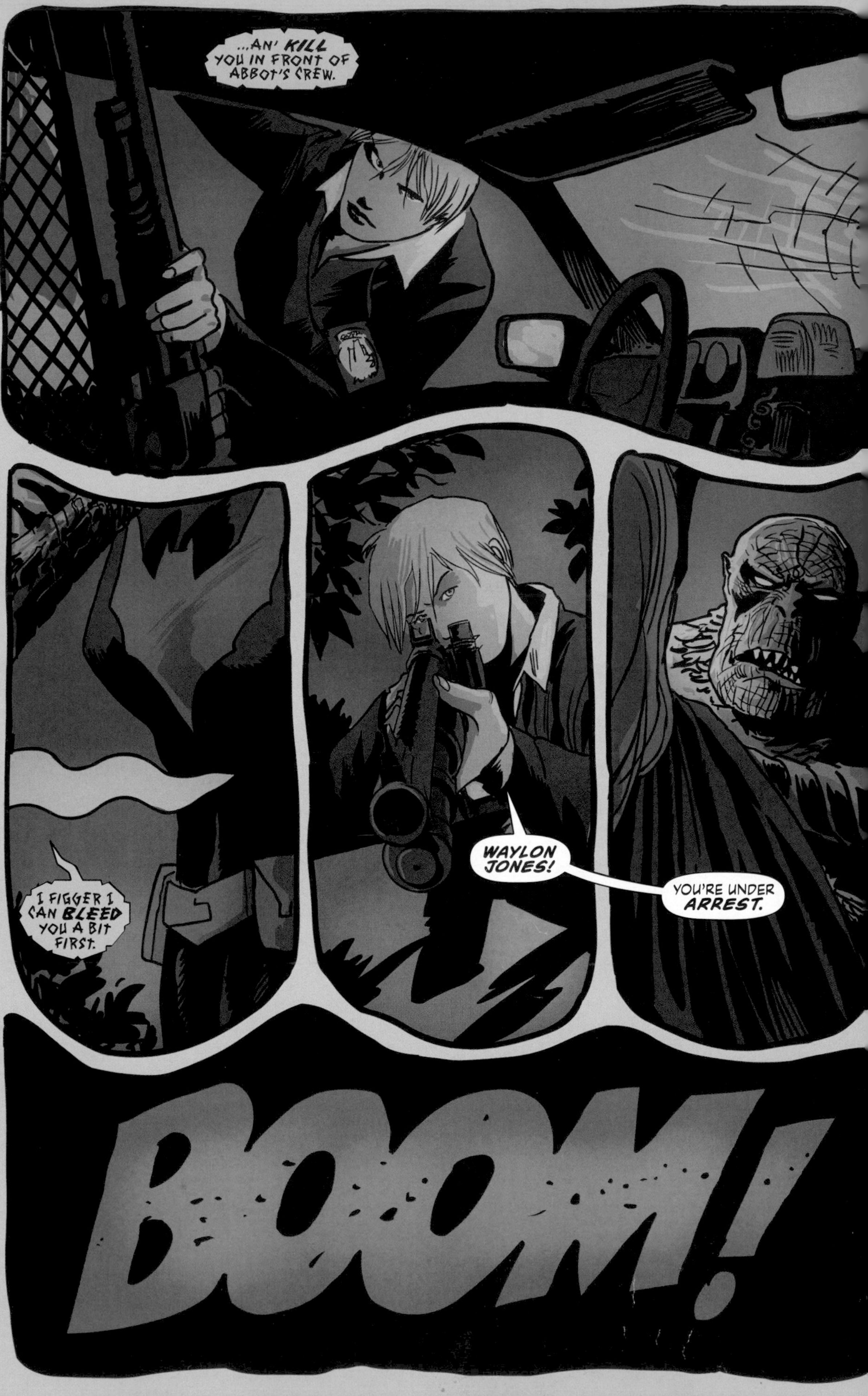
...AN' KILL YOU IN FRONT OF ABBOT'S CREW.
I FIGGER I CAN BLEED YOU A BIT FIRST.
WAYLON JONES!
YOU'RE UNDER ARREST.
BOOM!

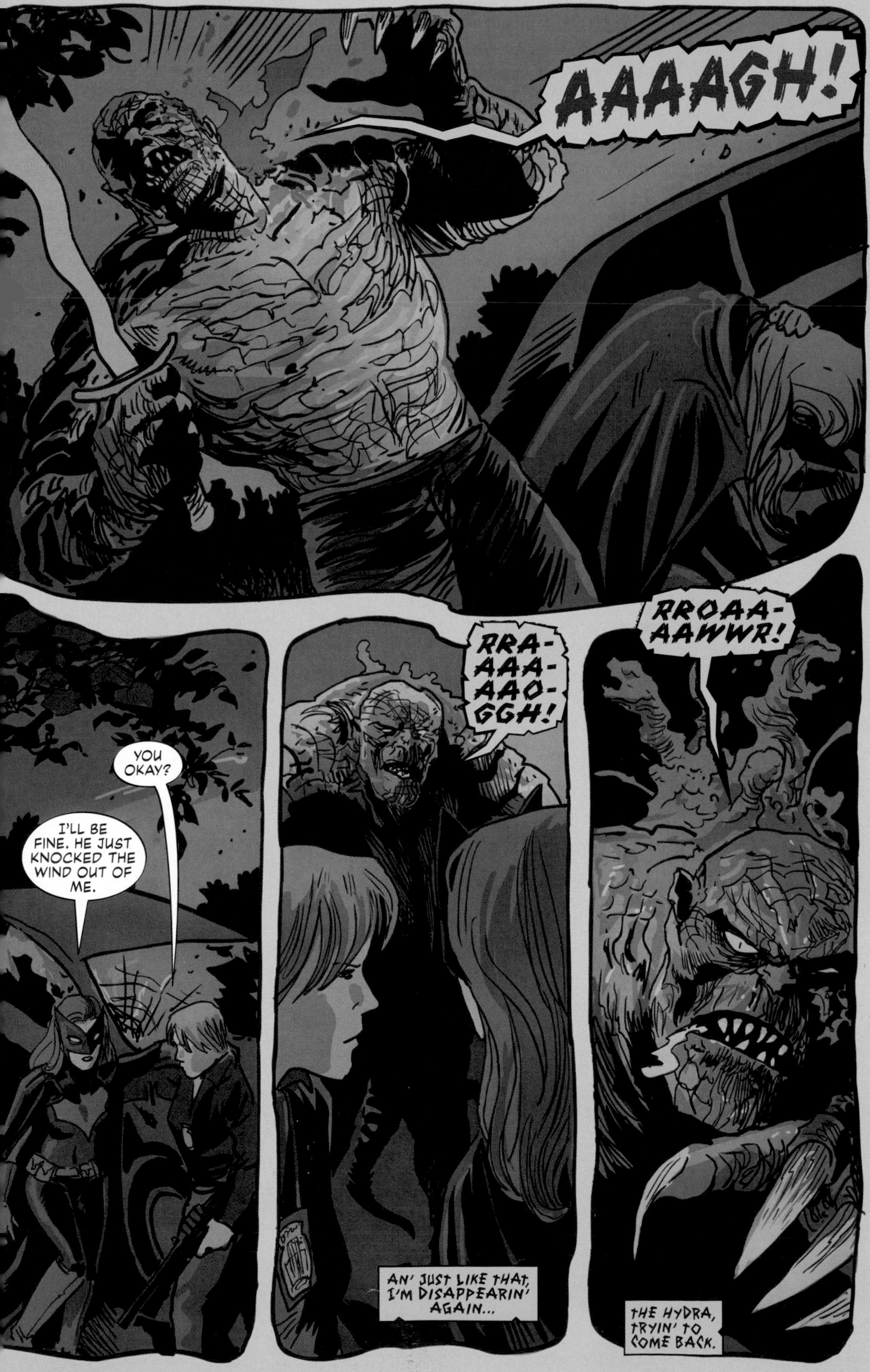
AAAAGH!
YOU OKAY?
I'LL BE FINE. HE JUST KNOCKED THE WIND OUT OF ME.
RRA-AAA-AAO-GGH!
AN' JUST LIKE THAT, I'M DISAPPEARIN' AGAIN...
RROAA-AAWWR!
THE HYDRA, TRYIN' TO COME BACK.

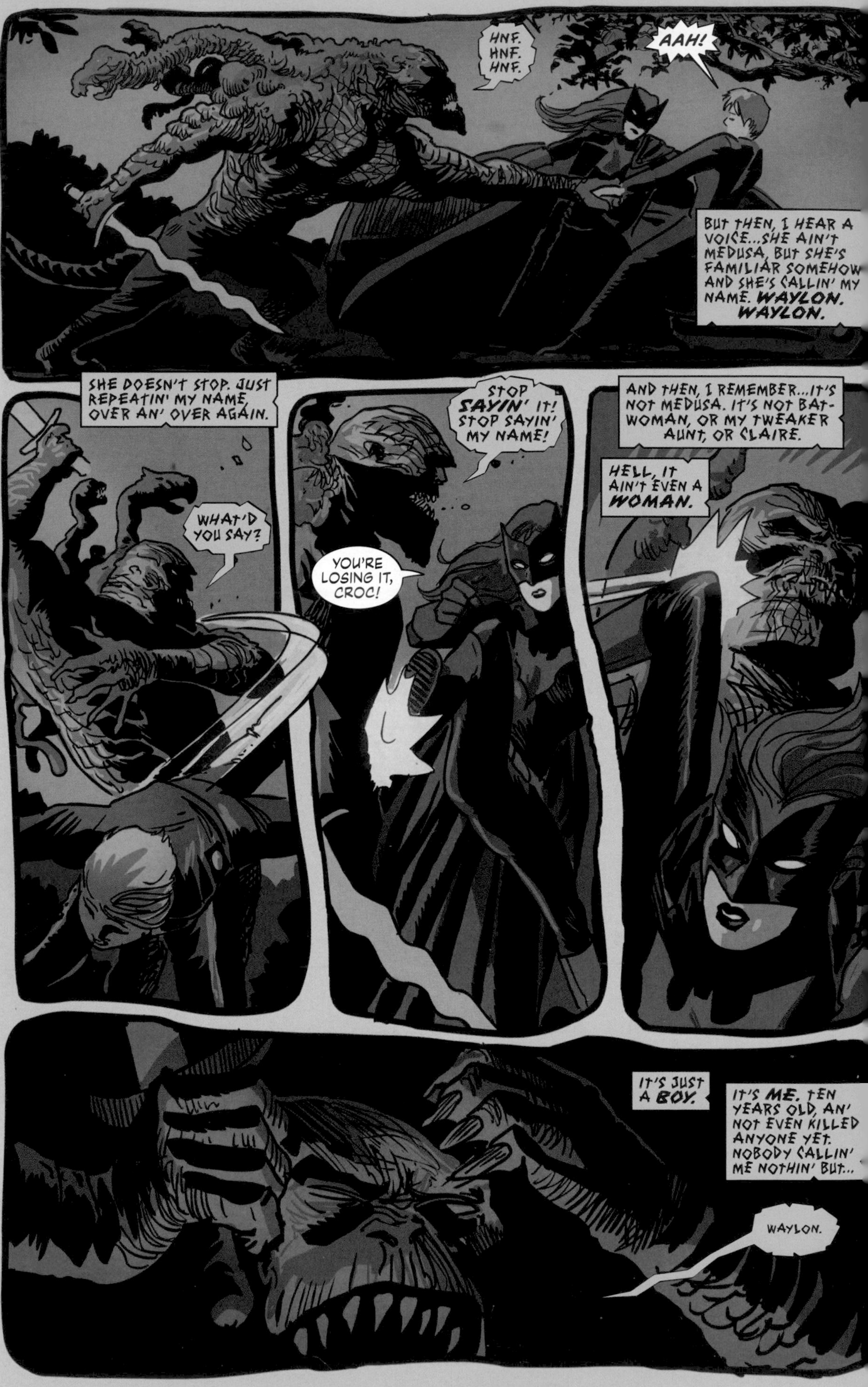
HNF. HNF. HNF.
AAH!
BUT THEN, I HEAR A VOICE...SHE AIN'T MEDUSA, BUT SHE'S FAMILIAR SOMEHOW AND SHE'S CALLIN' MY NAME. WAYLON. WAYLON.
SHE DOESN'T STOP. JUST REPEATIN' MY NAME, OVER AN' OVER AGAIN.
WHAT'D YOU SAY?
STOP SAYIN' IT! STOP SAYIN' MY NAME!
YOU'RE LOSING IT, CROC!
AND THEN, I REMEMBER...IT'S NOT MEDUSA. IT'S NOT BAT-WOMAN, OR MY TWEAKER AUNT, OR CLAIRE.
HELL, IT AIN'T EVEN A WOMAN.
IT'S JUST A BOY.
IT'S ME. TEN YEARS OLD, AN' NOT EVEN KILLED ANYONE YET. NOBODY CALLIN' ME NOTHIN' BUT...
WAYLON.

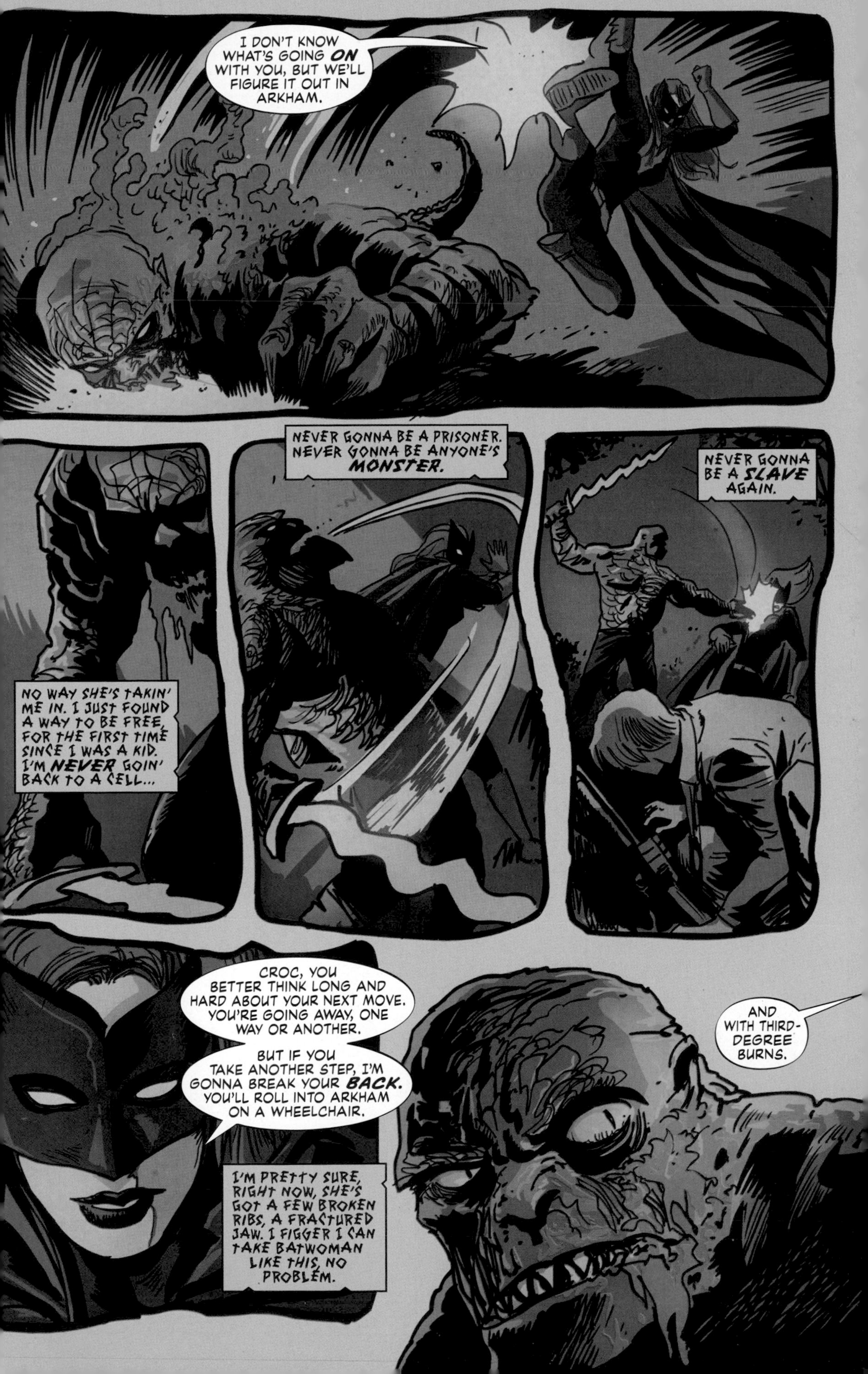
I DON'T KNOW WHAT'S GOING ON WITH YOU, BUT WE'LL FIGURE IT OUT IN ARKHAM.
NO WAY SHE'S TAKIN' ME IN. I JUST FOUND A WAY TO BE FREE, FOR THE FIRST TIME SINCE I WAS A KID. I'M NEVER GOIN' BACK TO A CELL...
NEVER GONNA BE A PRISONER. NEVER GONNA BE ANYONE'S MONSTER.
NEVER GONNA BE A SLAVE AGAIN.
CROC, YOU BETTER THINK LONG AND HARD ABOUT YOUR NEXT MOVE. YOU'RE GOING AWAY, ONE WAY OR ANOTHER.
BUT IF YOU TAKE ANOTHER STEP, I'M GONNA BREAK YOUR BACK. YOU'LL ROLL INTO ARKHAM ON A WHEELCHAIR.
AND WITH THIRD-DEGREE BURNS.
I'M PRETTY SURE, RIGHT NOW, SHE'S GOT A FEW BROKEN RIBS, A FRACTURED JAW. I FIGGER I CAN TAKE BATWOMAN LIKE THIS, NO PROBLEM.

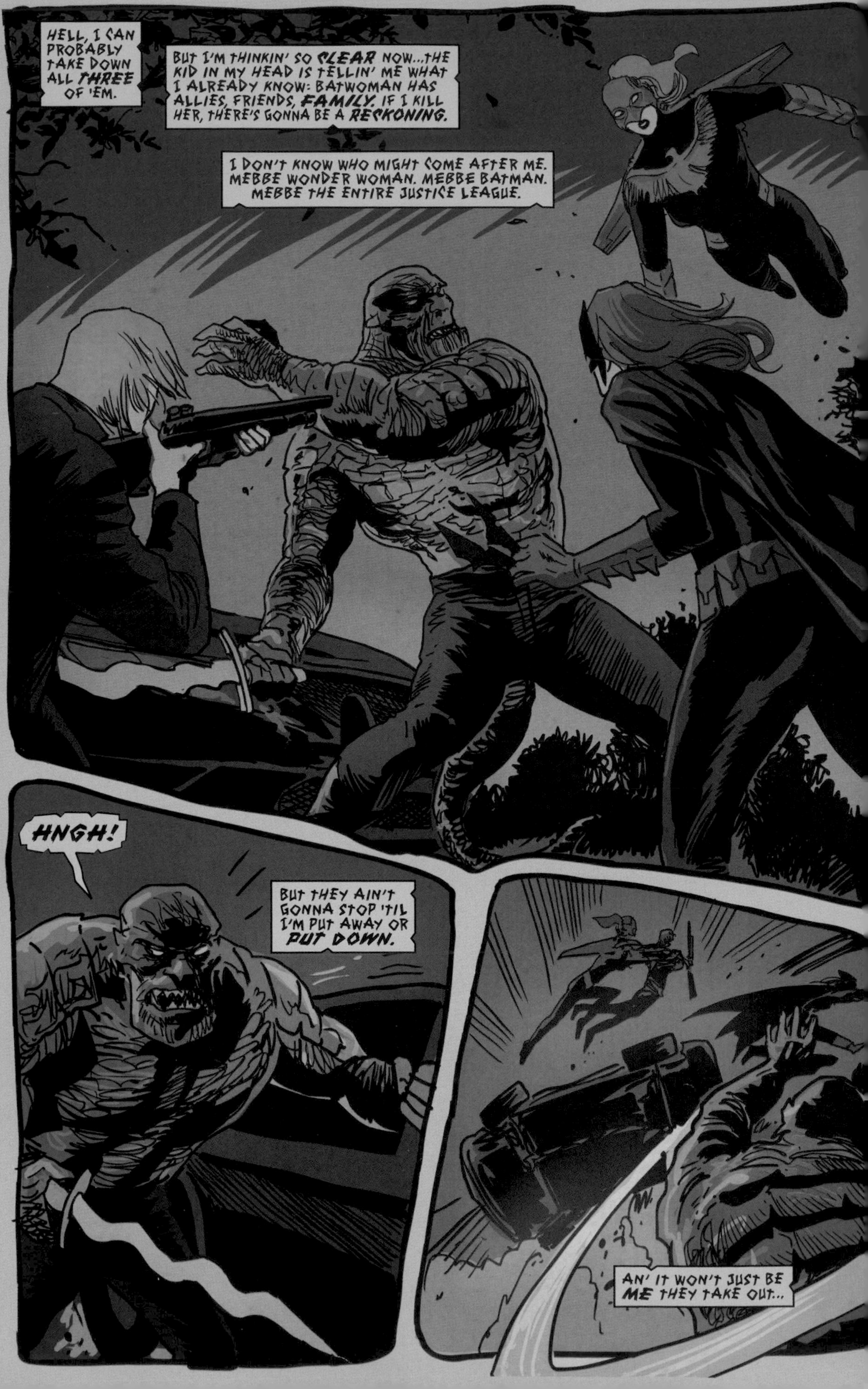
HELL, I CAN PROBABLY TAKE DOWN ALL THREE OF 'EM.
BUT I'M THINKIN' SO CLEAR NOW...THE KID IN MY HEAD IS TELLIN' ME WHAT I ALREADY KNOW: BATWOMAN HAS ALLIES, FRIENDS, FAMILY. IF I KILL HER, THERE'S GONNA BE A RECKONING.
I DON'T KNOW WHO MIGHT COME AFTER ME. MEBBE WONDER WOMAN. MEBBE BATMAN. MEBBE THE ENTIRE JUSTICE LEAGUE.
HNGH!
BUT THEY AIN'T GONNA STOP 'TIL I'M PUT AWAY OR PUT DOWN.
AN' IT WON'T JUST BE ME THEY TAKE OUT...

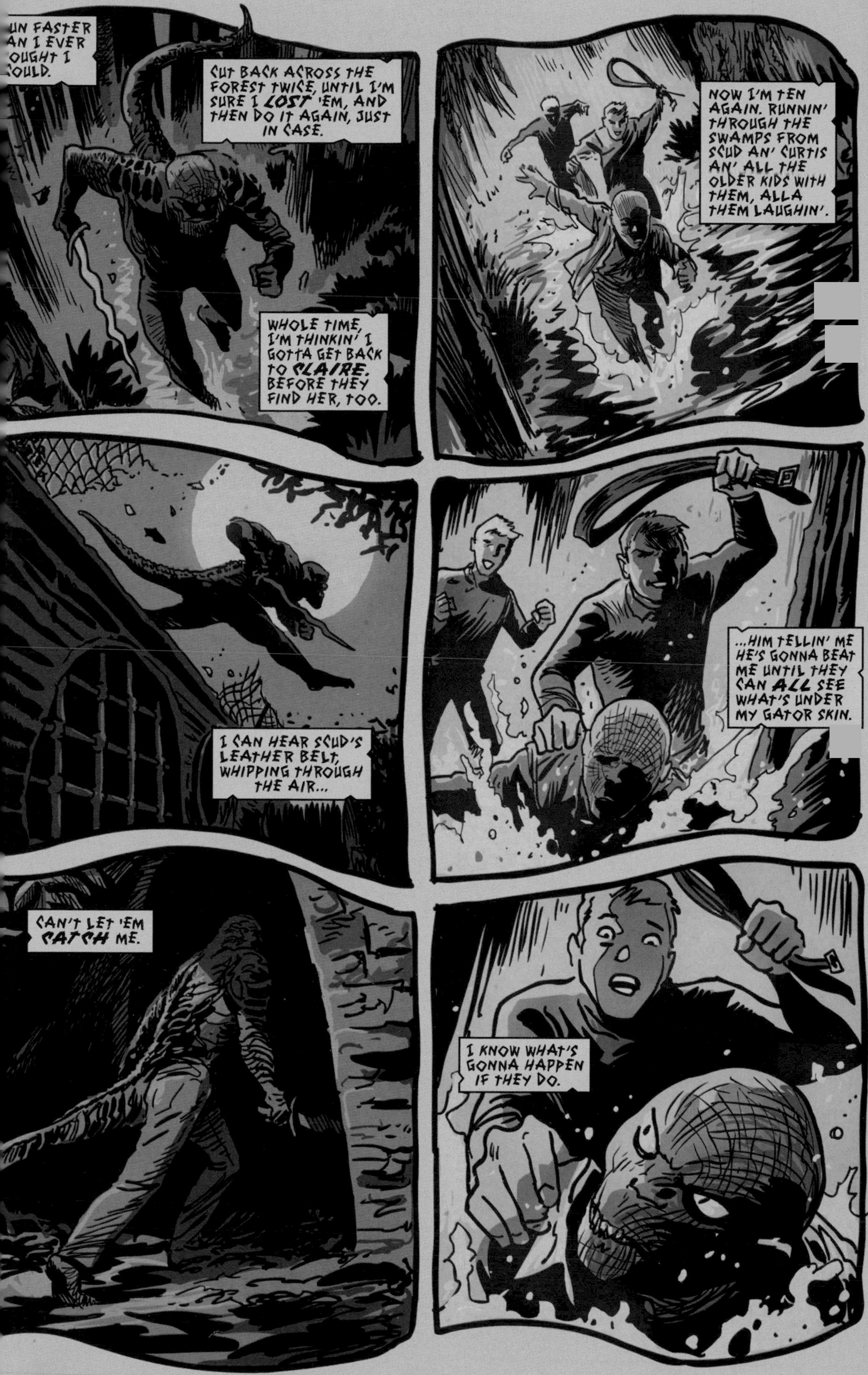
UN FASTER
AN I EVER
OUGHT I
COULD.
CUT BACK ACROSS THE FOREST TWICE, UNTIL I'M SURE I LOST 'EM, AND THEN DO IT AGAIN, JUST IN CASE.
WHOLE TIME, I'M THINKIN' I GOTTA GET BACK TO CLAIRE. BEFORE THEY FIND HER, TOO.
NOW I'M TEN AGAIN. RUNNIN' THROUGH THE SWAMPS FROM SCUD AN' CURTIS AN' ALL THE OLDER KIDS WITH THEM, ALLA THEM LAUGHIN'.
I CAN HEAR SCUD'S LEATHER BELT, WHIPPING THROUGH THE AIR...
...HIM TELLIN' ME HE'S GONNA BEAT ME UNTIL THEY CAN ALL SEE WHAT'S UNDER MY GATOR SKIN.
CAN'T LET 'EM CATCH ME.
I KNOW WHAT'S GONNA HAPPEN IF THEY DO.

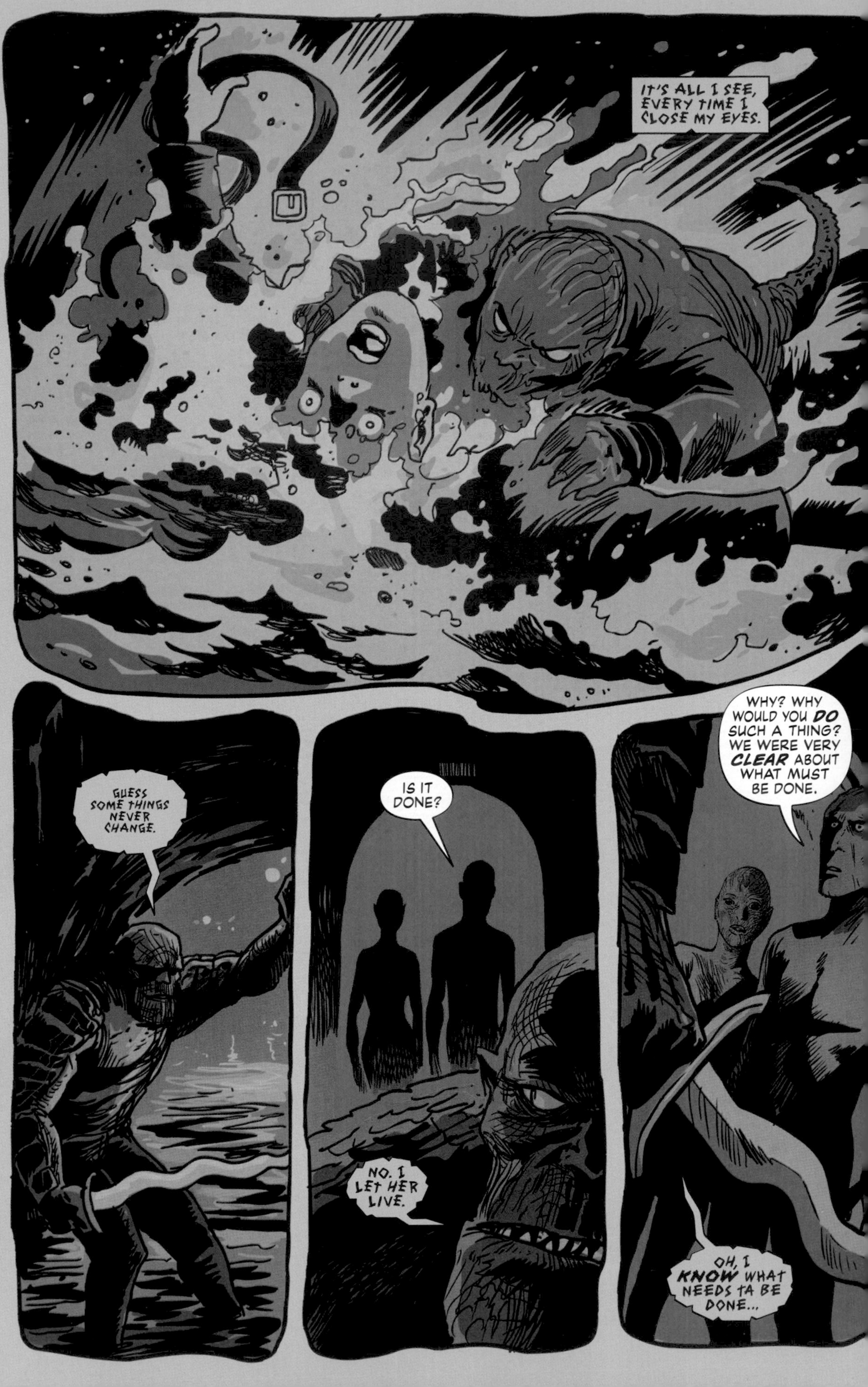
IT'S ALL I SEE, EVERY TIME I CLOSE MY EYES.
GUESS SOME THINGS NEVER CHANGE.
IS IT DONE?
NO. I LET HER LIVE.
WHY? WHY WOULD YOU DO SUCH A THING? WE WERE VERY CLEAR ABOUT WHAT MUST BE DONE.
OH, I KNOW WHAT NEEDS TA BE DONE...

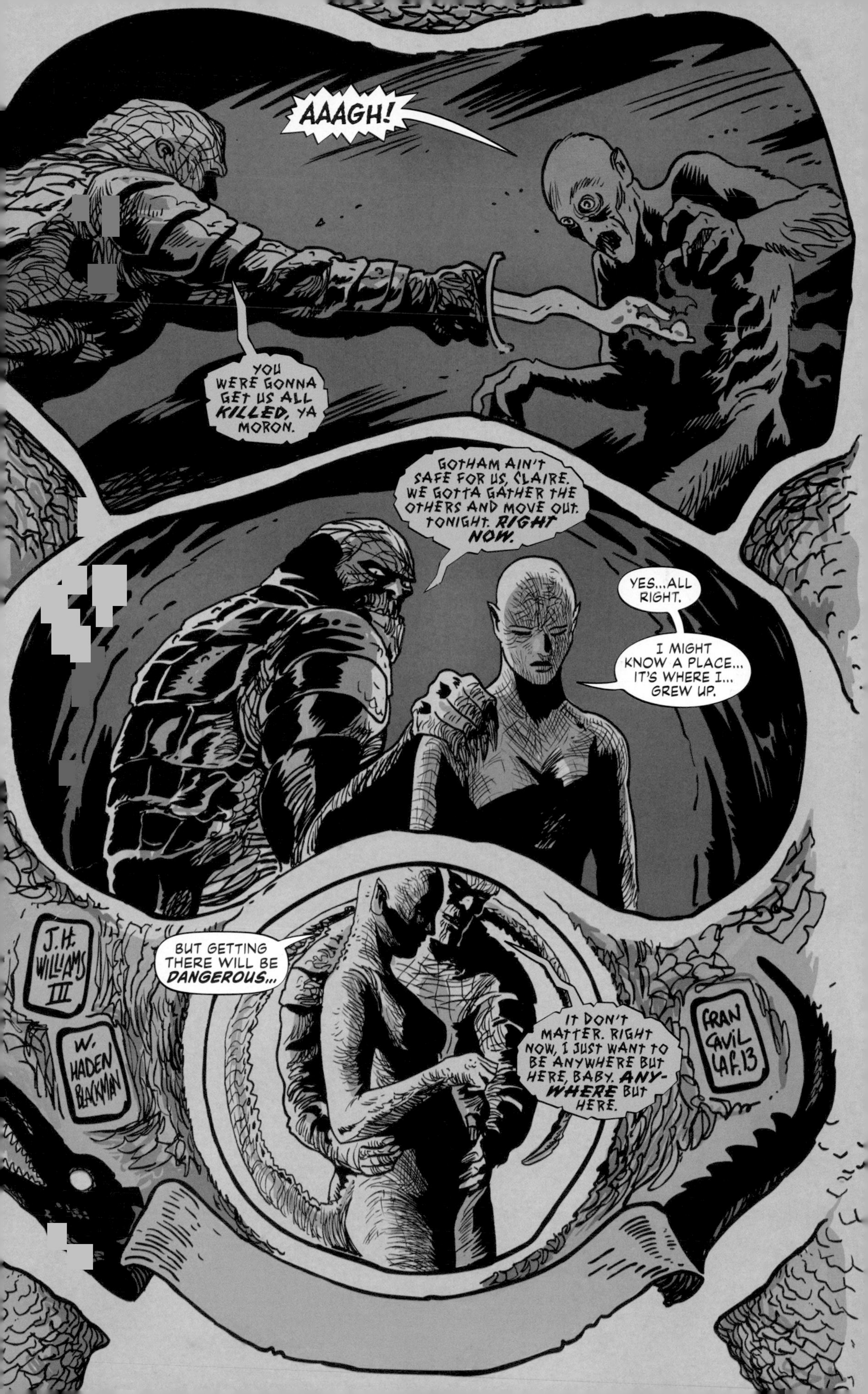
AAAGH!
YOU WERE GONNA GET US ALL KILLED, YA MORON.
GOTHAM AIN'T SAFE FOR US, CLAIRE. WE GOTTA GATHER THE OTHERS AND MOVE OUT. TONIGHT. RIGHT NOW.
YES...ALL RIGHT.
I MIGHT KNOW A PLACE... IT'S WHERE I... GREW UP.
J.H. WILLIAMS III
W. HADEN BLACKMAN
BUT GETTING THERE WILL BE DANGEROUS...
IT DON'T MATTER. RIGHT NOW, I JUST WANT TO BE ANYWHERE BUT HERE, BABY. ANY-WHERE BUT HERE.
FRAN CAVIL LAF.13

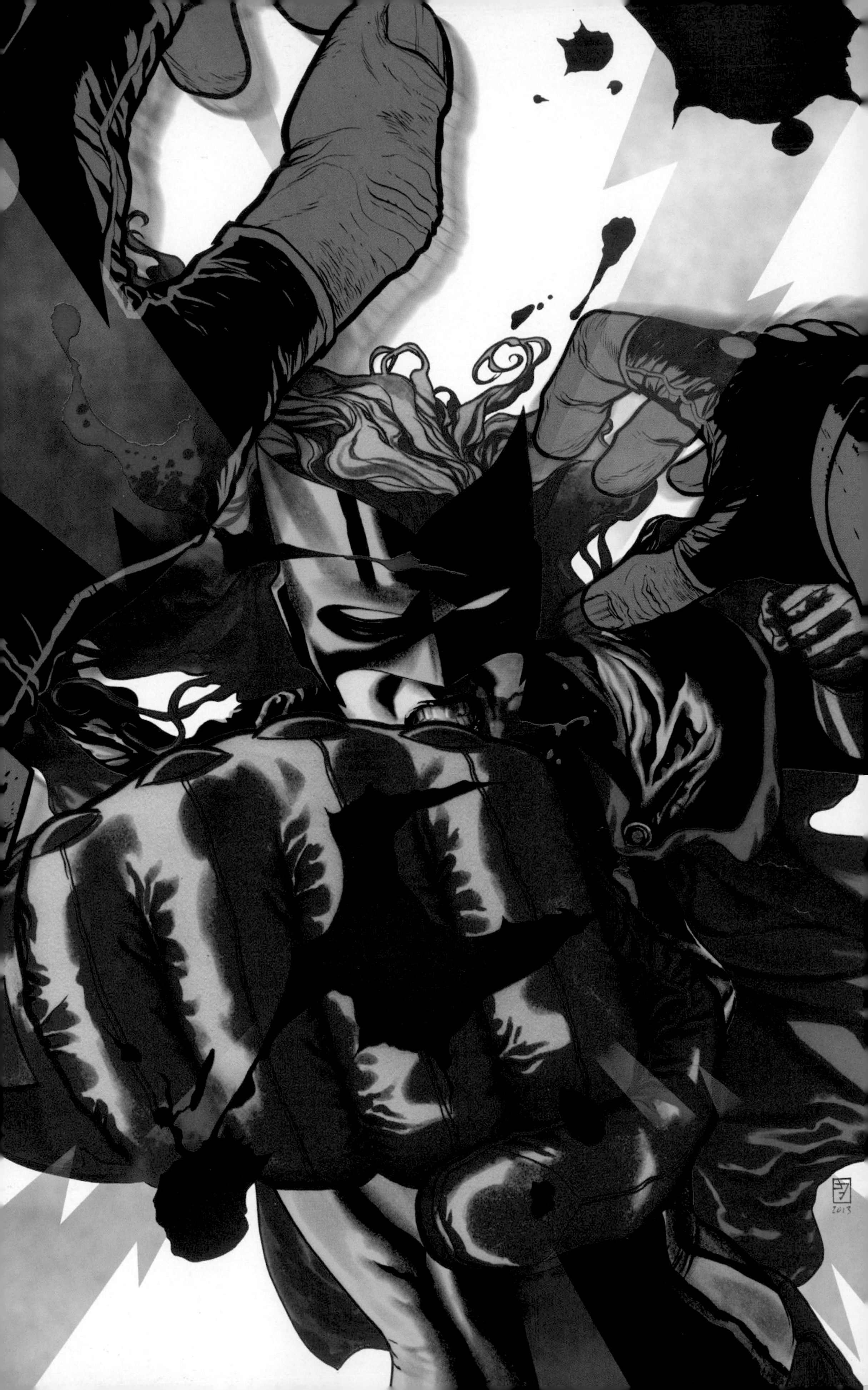

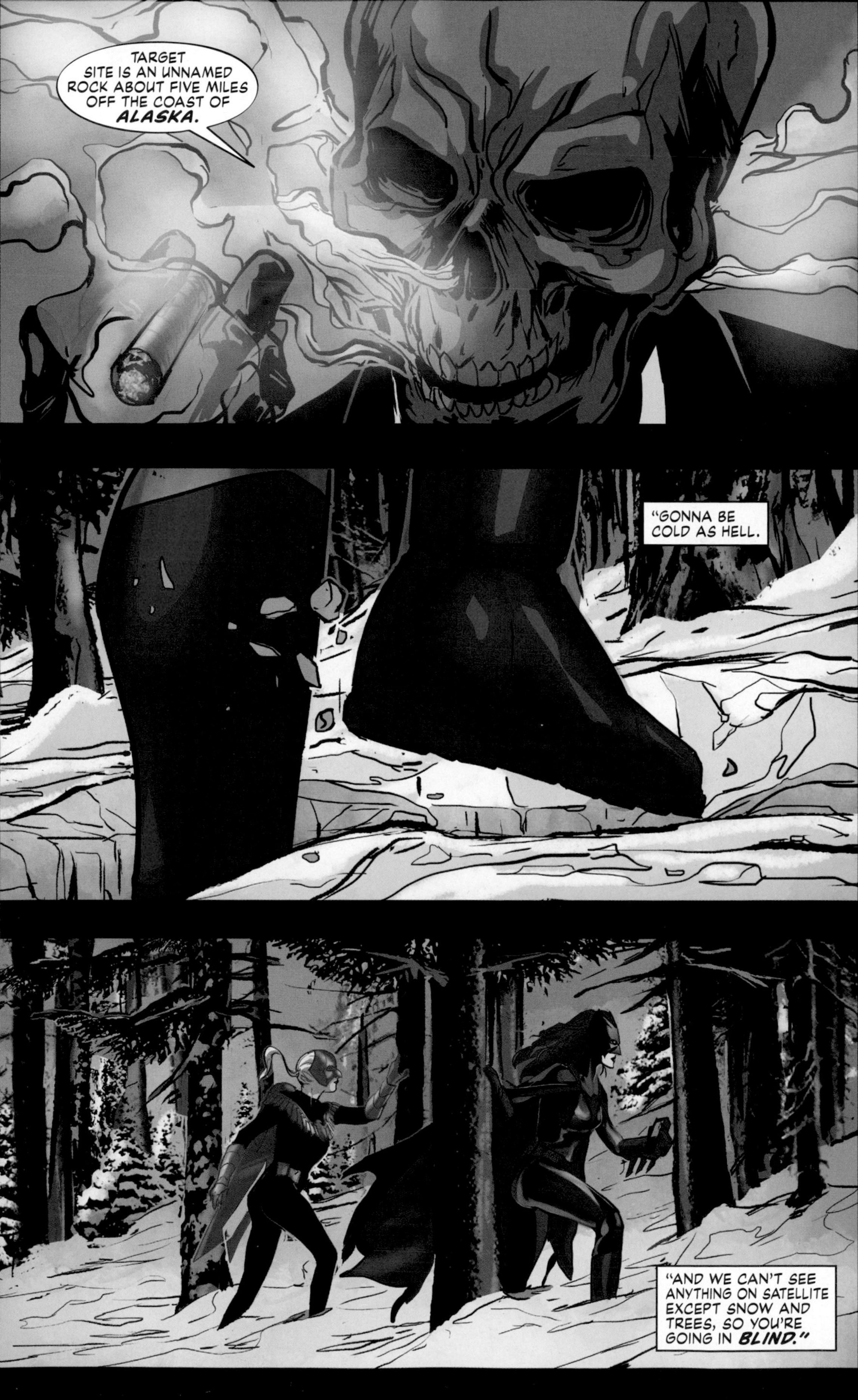
TARGET SITE IS AN UNNAMED ROCK ABOUT FIVE MILES OFF THE COAST OF ALASKA.
"GONNA BE COLD AS HELL.
"AND WE CAN'T SEE ANYTHING ON SATELLITE EXCEPT SNOW AND TREES, SO YOU'RE GOING IN BLIND."

"YOUR TARGET HAS BEEN OUT THERE FOR OVER A WEEK."

WE'VE GOT HIM HEADING DUE WEST.

WE'RE GETTING CLOSE. BE READY.

FLAME-THROWERS ARE PRIMED. I'M GOOD TO GO.

"JUST WATCH YOUR BACK."

"HE'S *SMARTER* THAN HE LOOKS."

HOLD UP...

...THE DRONE LOST HIM. HE'S EITHER CRAWLED INTO A CAVE OR IS MASKING HIS HEAT SIGNATURE SOMEHOW.

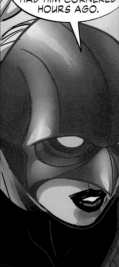

THAT SUCKS. WE'RE ON AN *ISLAND*...WHER THE HELL IS HE GOING T GO? WE SHOULD HAV HAD HIM CORNERED HOURS AGO.

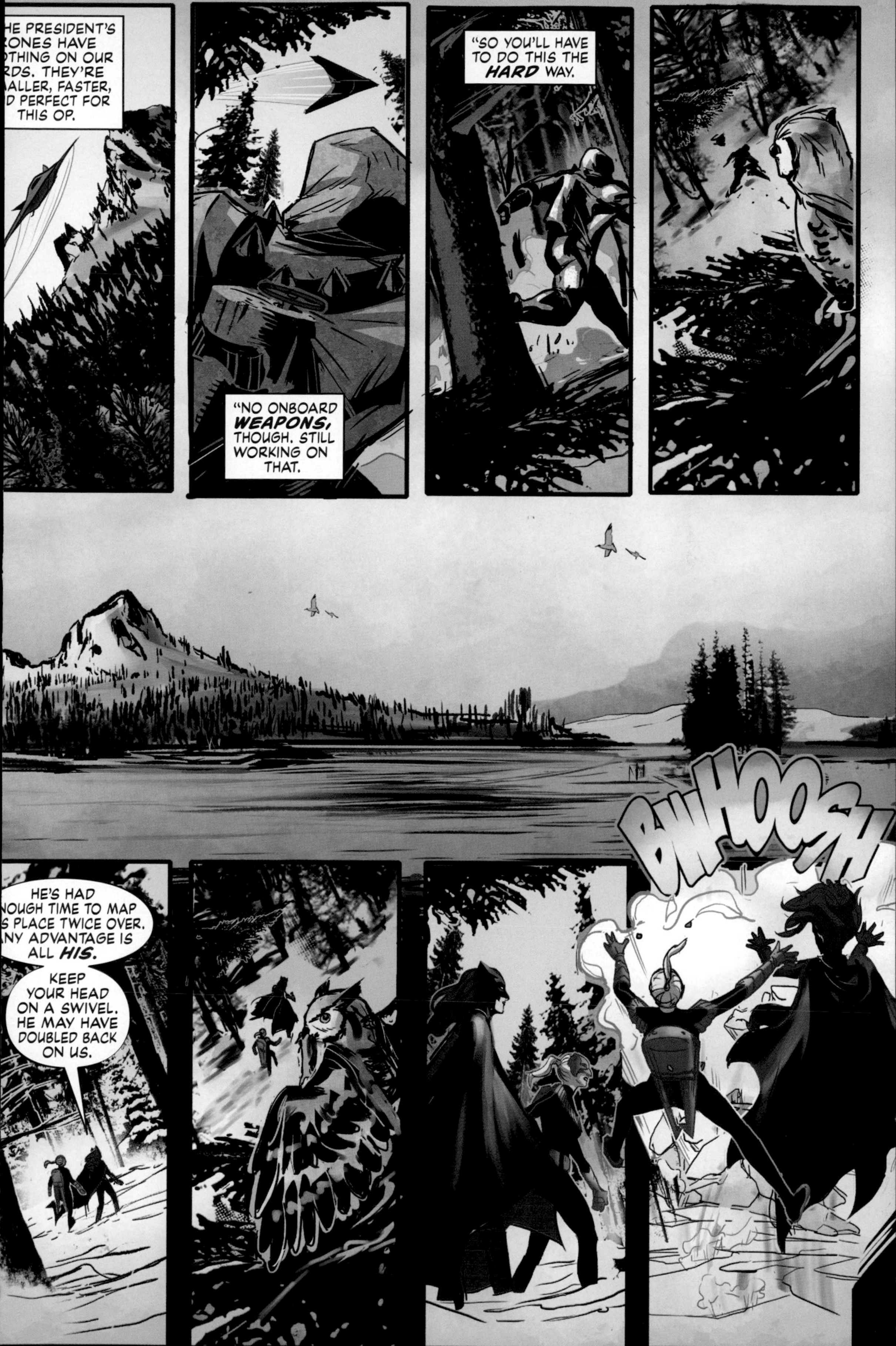
HE PRESIDENT'S
RONES HAVE
OTHING ON OUR
RDS. THEY'RE
ALLER, FASTER,
D PERFECT FOR
THIS OP.
"NO ONBOARD WEAPONS, THOUGH. STILL WORKING ON THAT.
"SO YOU'LL HAVE TO DO THIS THE HARD WAY.
HE'S HAD
NOUGH TIME TO MAP
S PLACE TWICE OVER.
NY ADVANTAGE IS
ALL HIS.
KEEP YOUR HEAD ON A SWIVEL. HE MAY HAVE DOUBLED BACK ON US.
BWHOOSH

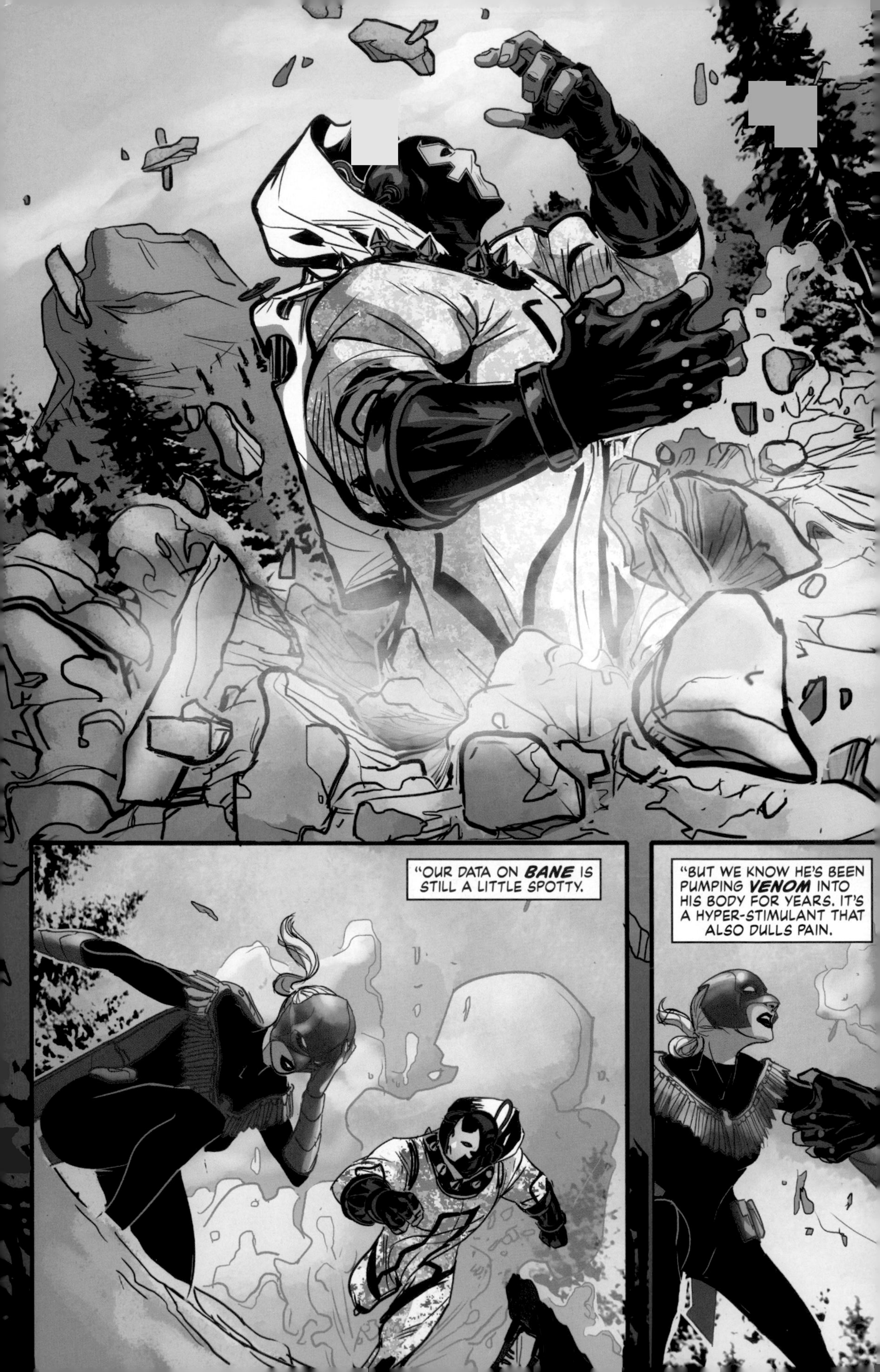
"OUR DATA ON BANE IS STILL A LITTLE SPOTTY.
"BUT WE KNOW HE'S BEEN PUMPING VENOM INTO HIS BODY FOR YEARS. IT'S A HYPER-STIMULANT THAT ALSO DULLS PAIN.

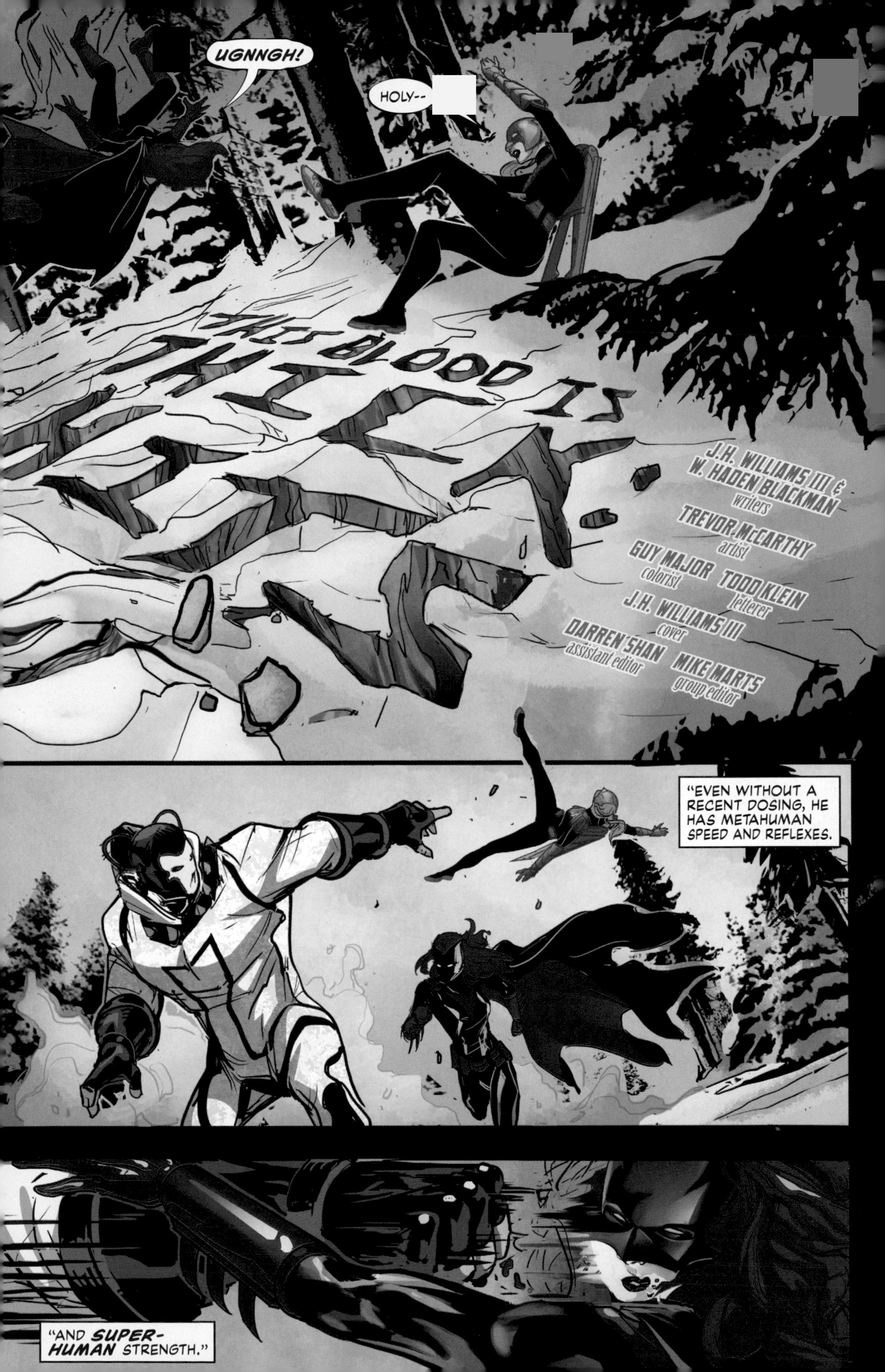
UGNNGH!
HOLY--
THIS BLOOD IS THICK.
J.H. WILLIAMS III & W. HADEN BLACKMAN writers
TREVOR McCARTHY artist
GUY MAJOR colorist
TODD KLEIN letterer
J.H. WILLIAMS III cover
DARREN SHAN assistant editor
MIKE MARTS group editor
"EVEN WITHOUT A RECENT DOSING, HE HAS METAHUMAN SPEED AND REFLEXES.
"AND SUPER-HUMAN STRENGTH."

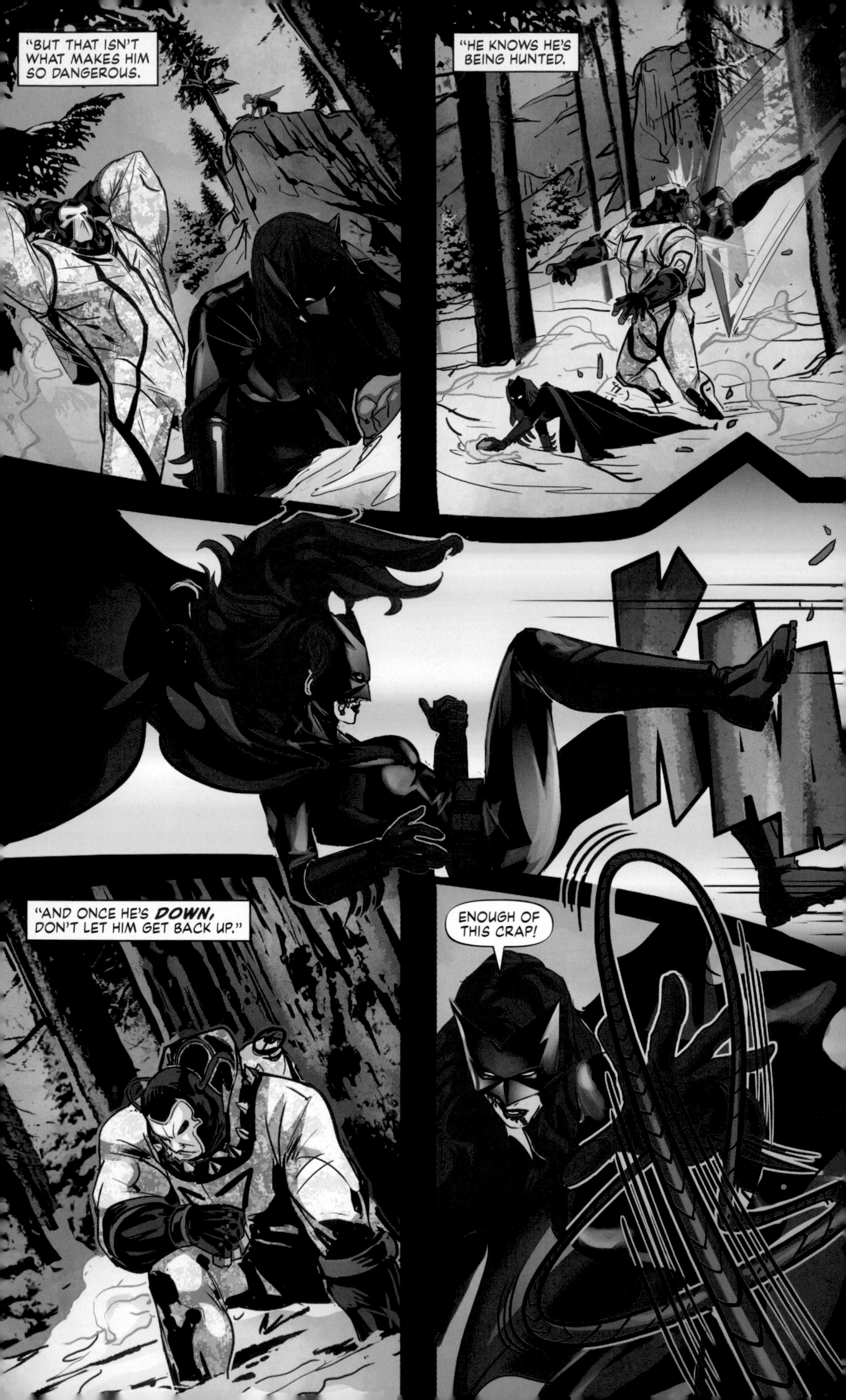
"BUT THAT ISN'T WHAT MAKES HIM SO DANGEROUS.
"HE KNOWS HE'S BEING HUNTED.
"AND ONCE HE'S *DOWN,* DON'T LET HIM GET BACK UP."
ENOUGH OF THIS CRAP!

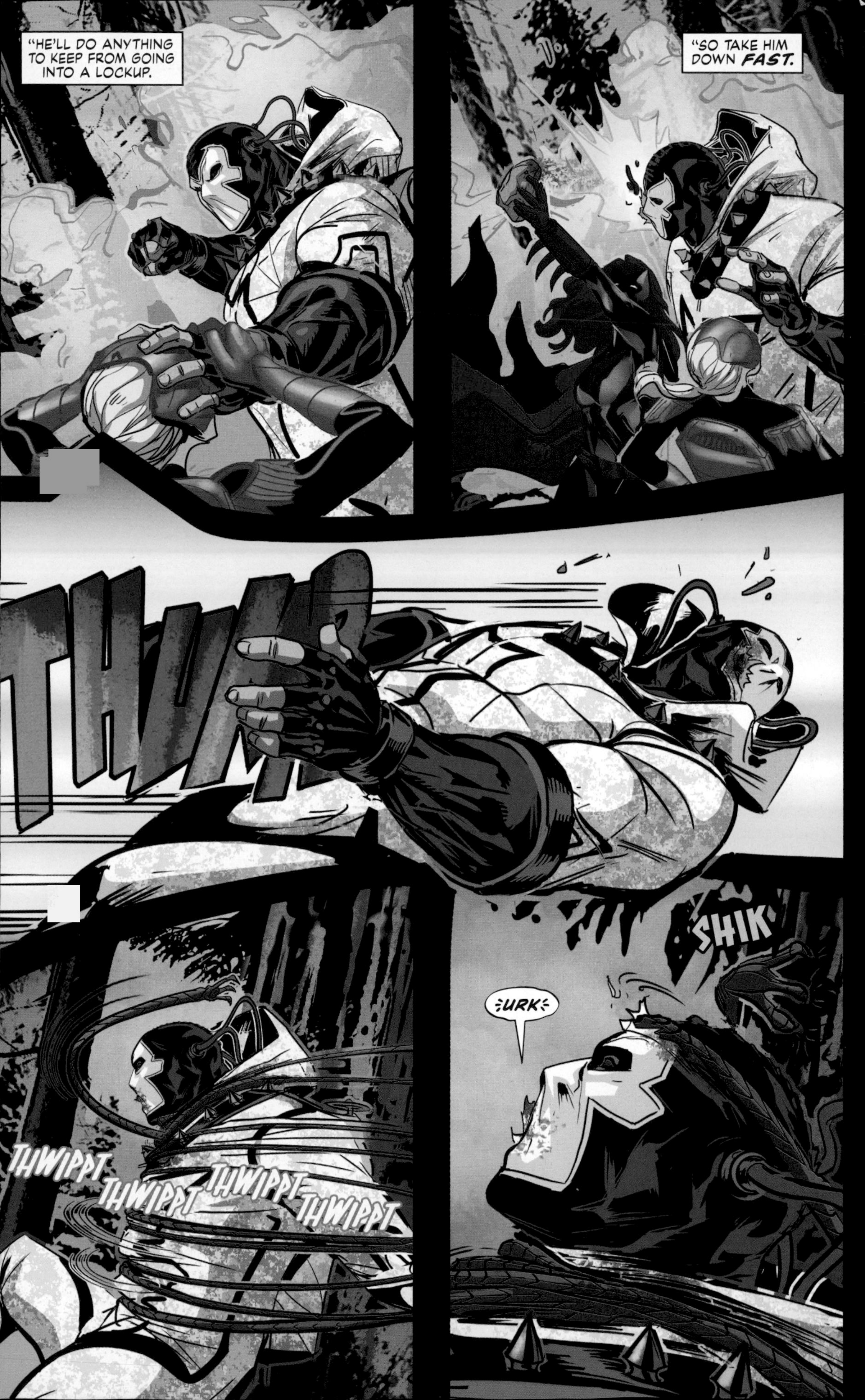
"HE'LL DO ANYTHING TO KEEP FROM GOING INTO A LOCKUP.
"SO TAKE HIM DOWN FAST.
THWAM
THWIPPT
THWIPPT
THWIPPT
THWIPPT
SHIK
URK

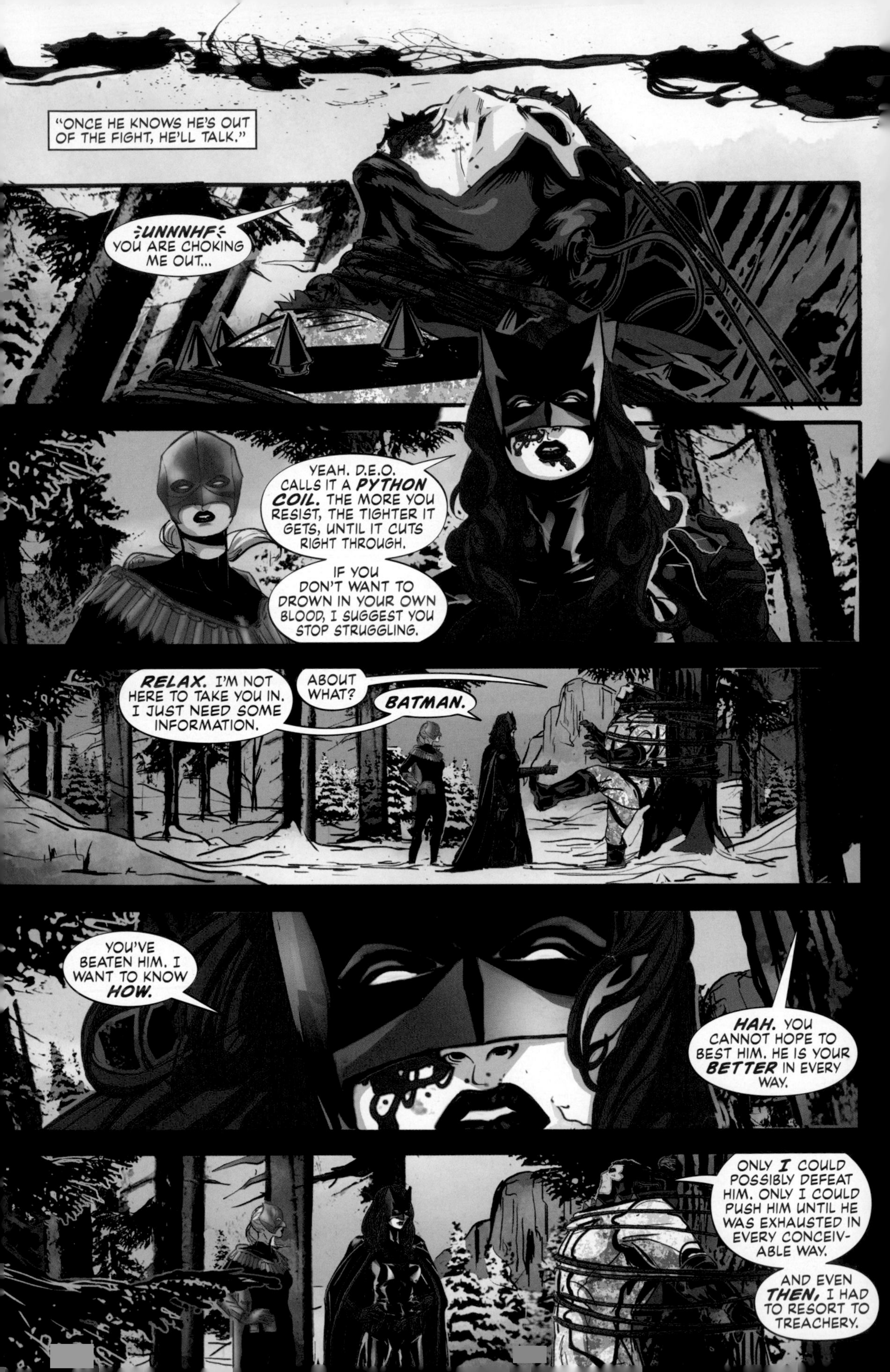
"ONCE HE KNOWS HE'S OUT OF THE FIGHT, HE'LL TALK."
UNNNHF YOU ARE CHOKING ME OUT...
YEAH. D.E.O. CALLS IT A PYTHON COIL. THE MORE YOU RESIST, THE TIGHTER IT GETS, UNTIL IT CUTS RIGHT THROUGH.
IF YOU DON'T WANT TO DROWN IN YOUR OWN BLOOD, I SUGGEST YOU STOP STRUGGLING.
RELAX. I'M NOT HERE TO TAKE YOU IN. I JUST NEED SOME INFORMATION.
ABOUT WHAT?
BATMAN.
YOU'VE BEATEN HIM. I WANT TO KNOW HOW.
HAH. YOU CANNOT HOPE TO BEST HIM. HE IS YOUR BETTER IN EVERY WAY.
ONLY I COULD POSSIBLY DEFEAT HIM. ONLY I COULD PUSH HIM UNTIL HE WAS EXHAUSTED IN EVERY CONCEIV-ABLE WAY.
AND EVEN THEN, I HAD TO RESORT TO TREACHERY.

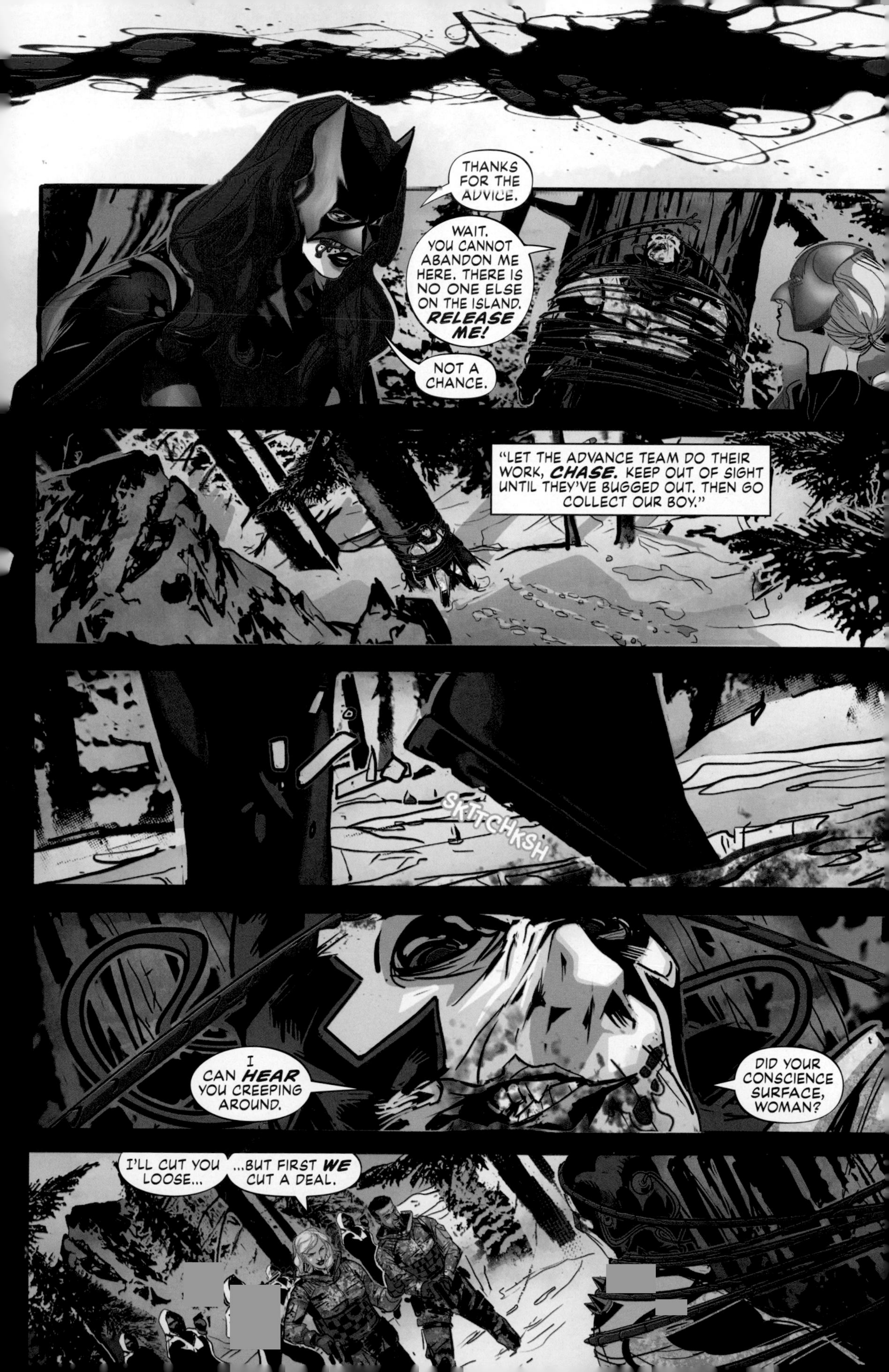

THANKS FOR THE ADVICE.
WAIT. YOU CANNOT ABANDON ME HERE. THERE IS NO ONE ELSE ON THE ISLAND. RELEASE ME!
NOT A CHANCE.
"LET THE ADVANCE TEAM DO THEIR WORK, CHASE. KEEP OUT OF SIGHT UNTIL THEY'VE BUGGED OUT. THEN GO COLLECT OUR BOY."
SKTTCHKSH
I CAN HEAR YOU CREEPING AROUND.
DID YOUR CONSCIENCE SURFACE, WOMAN?
I'LL CUT YOU LOOSE...
...BUT FIRST WE CUT A DEAL.

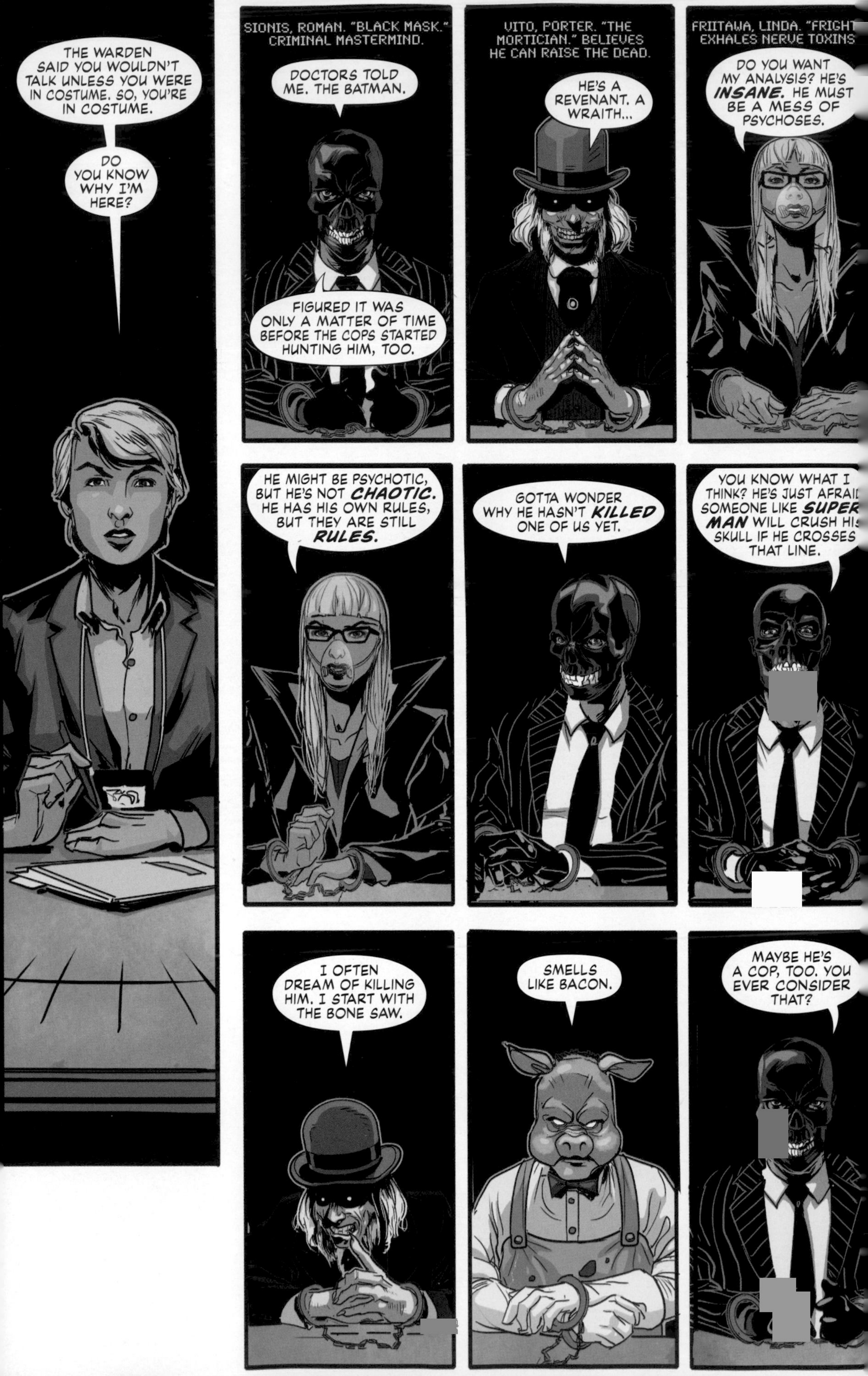
THE WARDEN SAID YOU WOULDN'T TALK UNLESS YOU WERE IN COSTUME. SO, YOU'RE IN COSTUME.
DO YOU KNOW WHY I'M HERE?
SIONIS, ROMAN. "BLACK MASK." CRIMINAL MASTERMIND.
DOCTORS TOLD ME. THE BATMAN.
FIGURED IT WAS ONLY A MATTER OF TIME BEFORE THE COPS STARTED HUNTING HIM, TOO.
VITO, PORTER. "THE MORTICIAN." BELIEVES HE CAN RAISE THE DEAD.
HE'S A REVENANT. A WRAITH...
FRIITAWA, LINDA. "FRIGHT
EXHALES NERVE TOXINS
DO YOU WANT MY ANALYSIS? HE'S *INSANE.* HE MUST BE A MESS OF PSYCHOSES.
HE MIGHT BE PSYCHOTIC, BUT HE'S NOT *CHAOTIC.* HE HAS HIS OWN RULES, BUT THEY ARE STILL *RULES.*
GOTTA WONDER WHY HE HASN'T *KILLED* ONE OF US YET.
YOU KNOW WHAT I THINK? HE'S JUST AFRAI SOMEONE LIKE *SUPER MAN* WILL CRUSH HI SKULL IF HE CROSSES THAT LINE.
I OFTEN DREAM OF KILLING HIM. I START WITH THE BONE SAW.
SMELLS LIKE BACON.
MAYBE HE'S A COP, TOO. YOU EVER CONSIDER THAT?

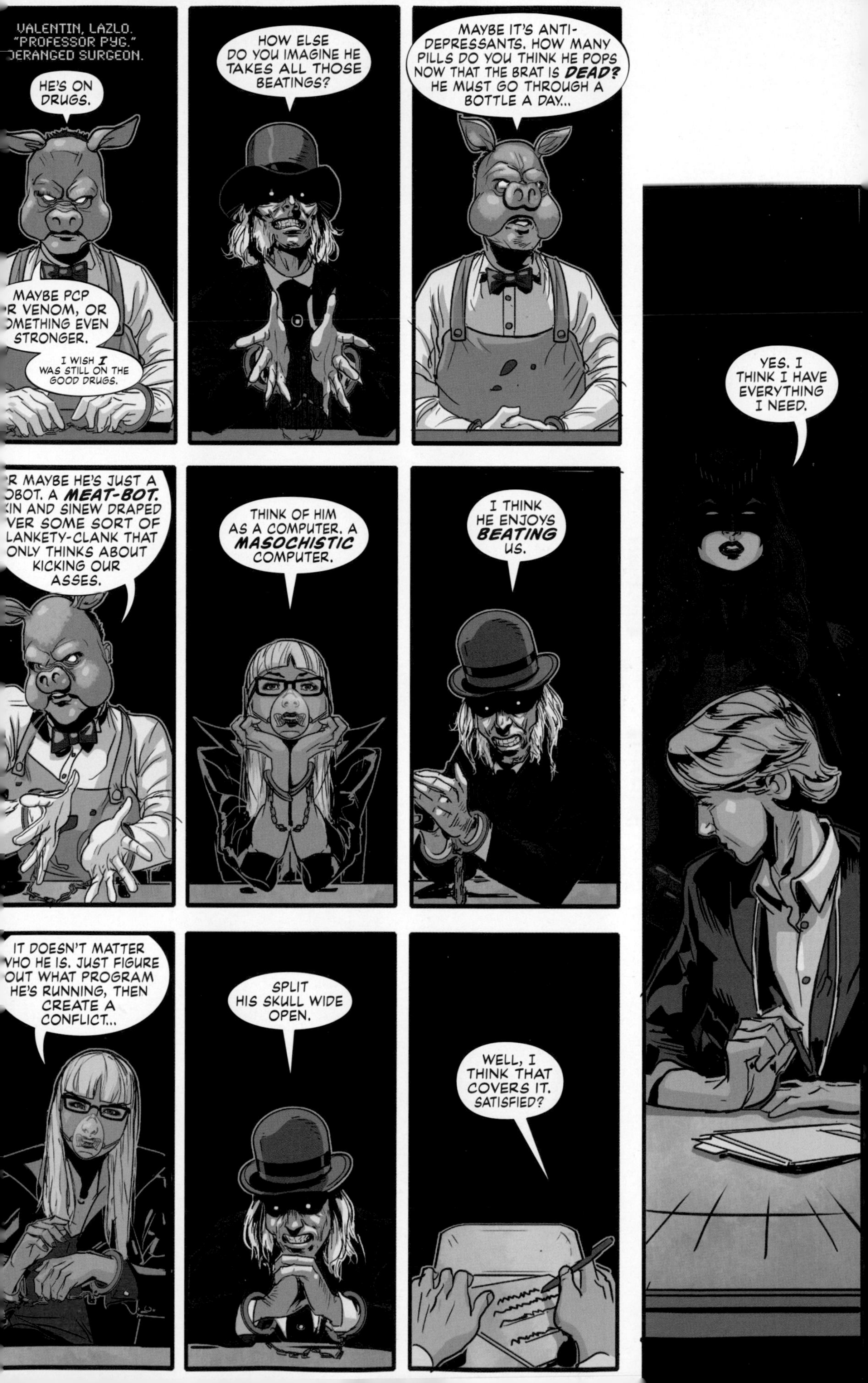

VALENTIN, LAZLO. "PROFESSOR PYG." DERANGED SURGEON.
HE'S ON DRUGS.
MAYBE PCP R VENOM, OR OMETHING EVEN STRONGER.
I WISH I WAS STILL ON THE GOOD DRUGS.
HOW ELSE DO YOU IMAGINE HE TAKES ALL THOSE BEATINGS?
MAYBE IT'S ANTI-DEPRESSANTS. HOW MANY PILLS DO YOU THINK HE POPS NOW THAT THE BRAT IS DEAD? HE MUST GO THROUGH A BOTTLE A DAY...
R MAYBE HE'S JUST A OBOT. A MEAT-BOT. KIN AND SINEW DRAPED VER SOME SORT OF LANKETY-CLANK THAT ONLY THINKS ABOUT KICKING OUR ASSES.
THINK OF HIM AS A COMPUTER. A MASOCHISTIC COMPUTER.
I THINK HE ENJOYS BEATING US.
IT DOESN'T MATTER VHO HE IS. JUST FIGURE OUT WHAT PROGRAM HE'S RUNNING, THEN CREATE A CONFLICT...
SPLIT HIS SKULL WIDE OPEN.
WELL, I THINK THAT COVERS IT. SATISFIED?
YES. I THINK I HAVE EVERYTHING I NEED.

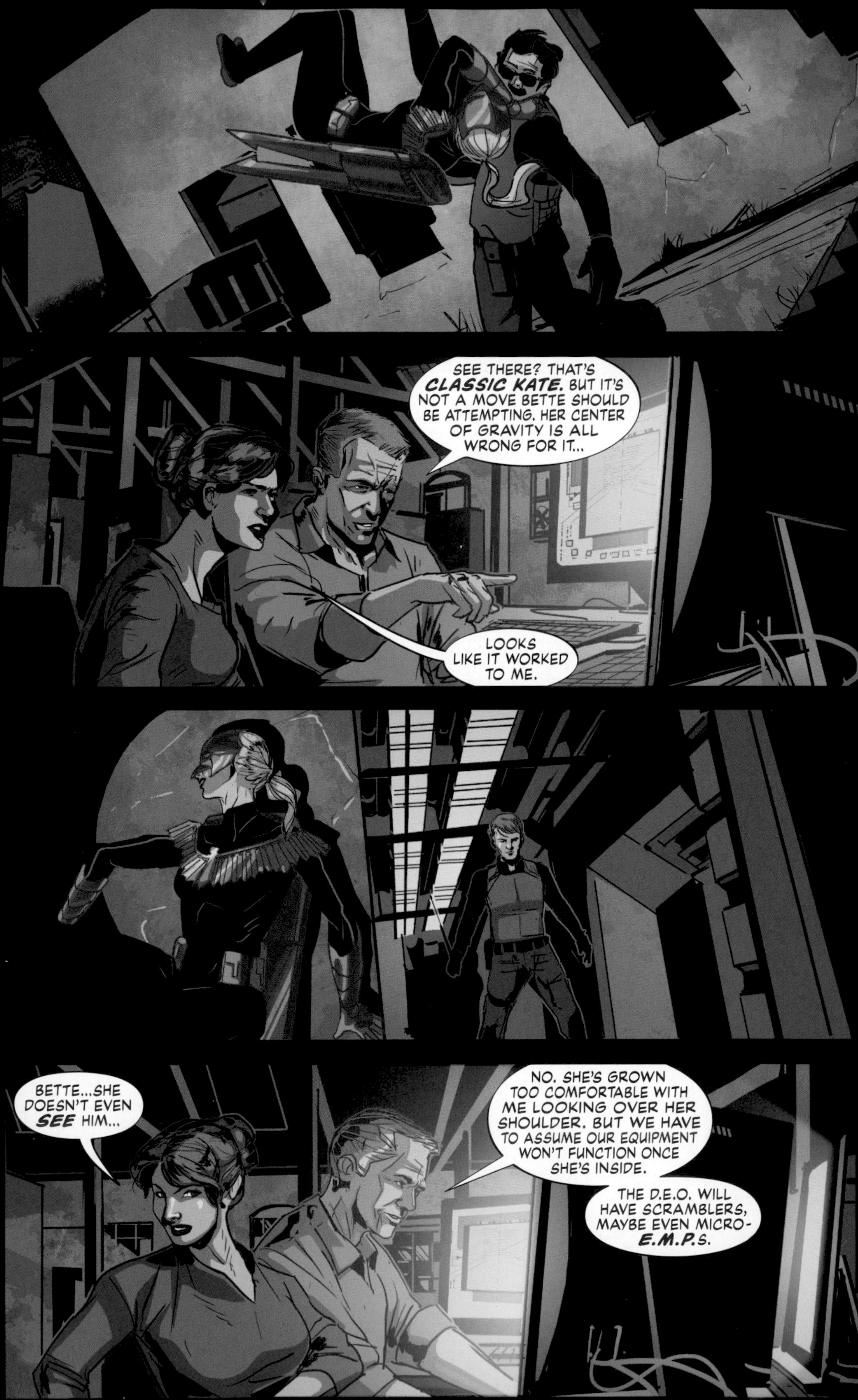
SEE THERE? THAT'S *CLASSIC KATE.* BUT IT'S NOT A MOVE BETTE SHOULD BE ATTEMPTING. HER CENTER OF GRAVITY IS ALL WRONG FOR IT...
LOOKS LIKE IT WORKED TO ME.
BETTE...SHE DOESN'T EVEN *SEE* HIM...
NO. SHE'S GROWN TOO COMFORTABLE WITH ME LOOKING OVER HER SHOULDER. BUT WE HAVE TO ASSUME OUR EQUIPMENT WON'T FUNCTION ONCE SHE'S INSIDE.
THE D.E.O. WILL HAVE SCRAMBLERS, MAYBE EVEN MICRO-*E.M.P.*S.

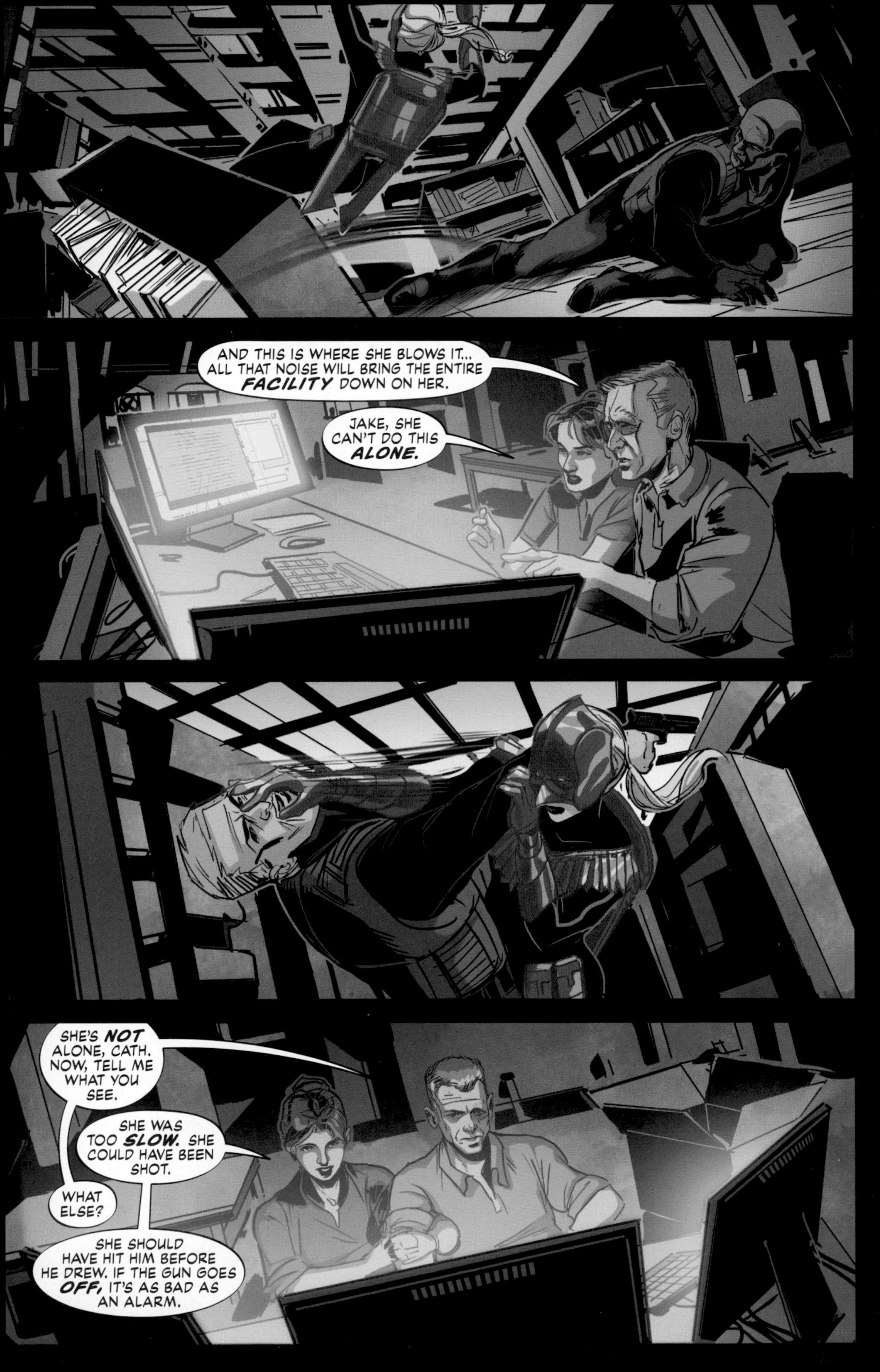
AND THIS IS WHERE SHE BLOWS IT... ALL THAT NOISE WILL BRING THE ENTIRE FACILITY DOWN ON HER.
JAKE, SHE CAN'T DO THIS ALONE.
SHE'S NOT ALONE, CATH. NOW, TELL ME WHAT YOU SEE.
SHE WAS TOO SLOW. SHE COULD HAVE BEEN SHOT.
WHAT ELSE?
SHE SHOULD HAVE HIT HIM BEFORE HE DREW. IF THE GUN GOES OFF, IT'S AS BAD AS AN ALARM.

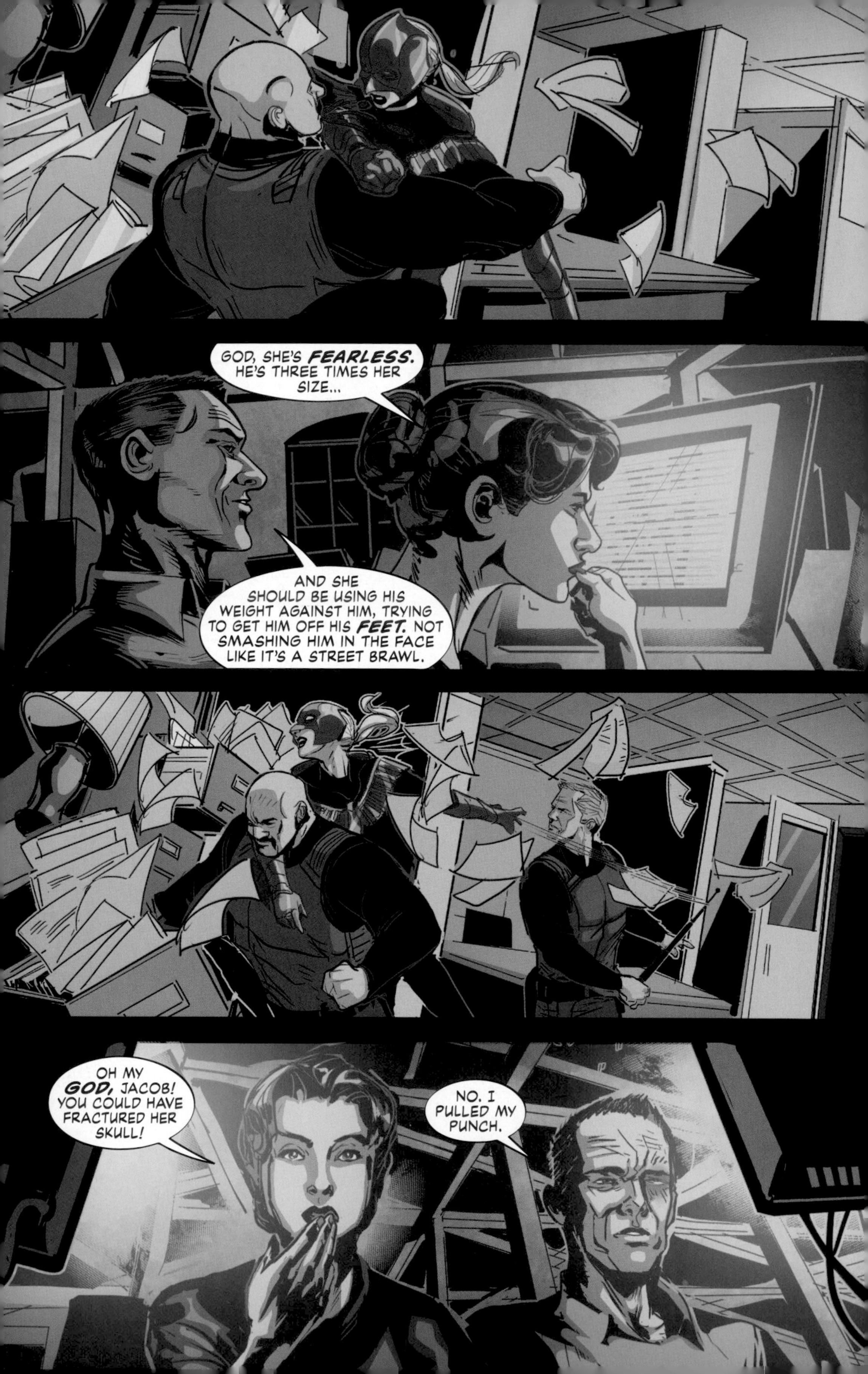
GOD, SHE'S FEARLESS. HE'S THREE TIMES HER SIZE...
AND SHE SHOULD BE USING HIS WEIGHT AGAINST HIM, TRYING TO GET HIM OFF HIS FEET. NOT SMASHING HIM IN THE FACE LIKE IT'S A STREET BRAWL.
OH MY GOD, JACOB! YOU COULD HAVE FRACTURED HER SKULL!
NO. I PULLED MY PUNCH.

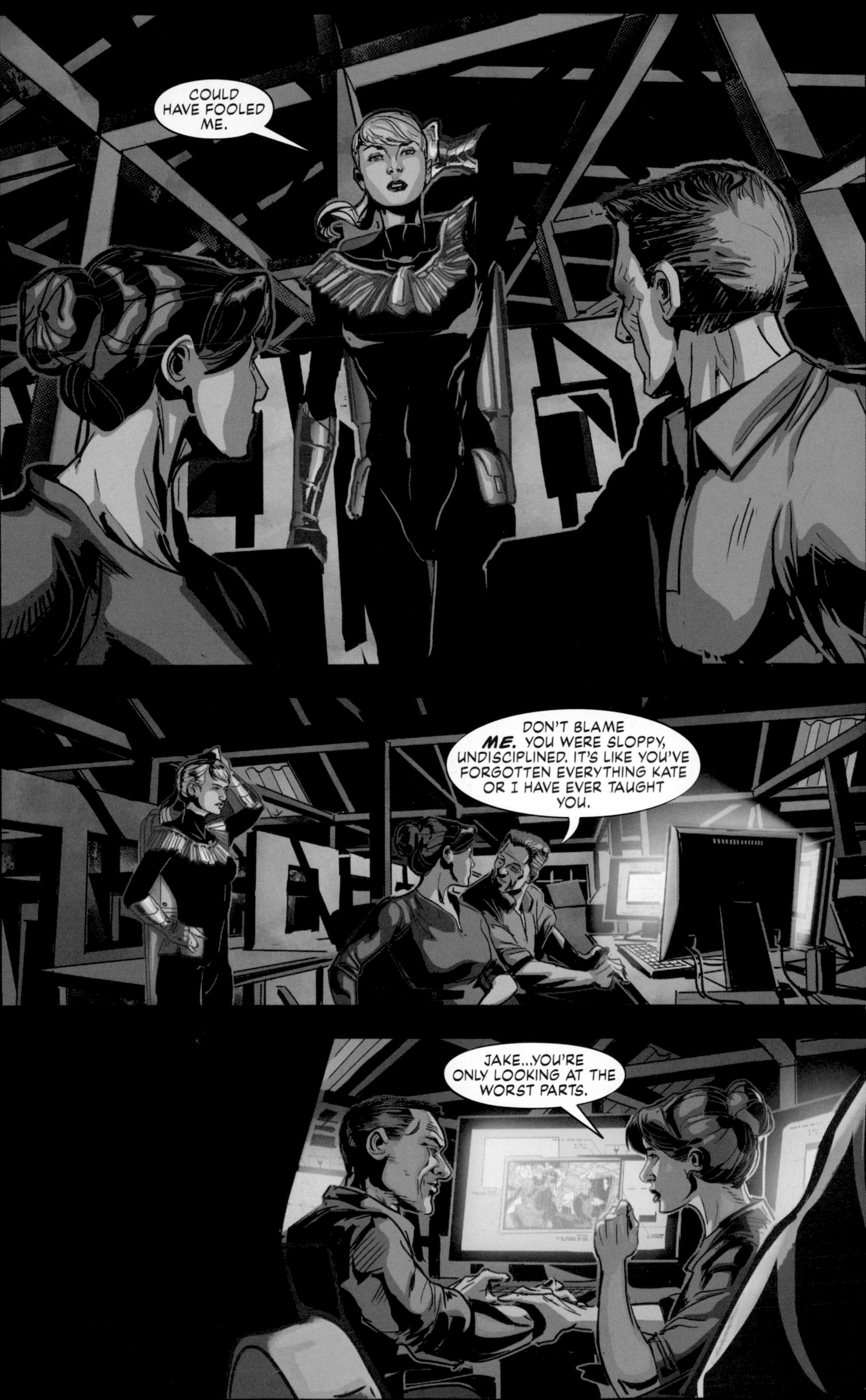
COULD HAVE FOOLED ME.
DON'T BLAME *ME.* YOU WERE SLOPPY, UNDISCIPLINED. IT'S LIKE YOU'VE FORGOTTEN EVERYTHING KATE OR I HAVE EVER TAUGHT YOU.
JAKE...YOU'RE ONLY LOOKING AT THE WORST PARTS.

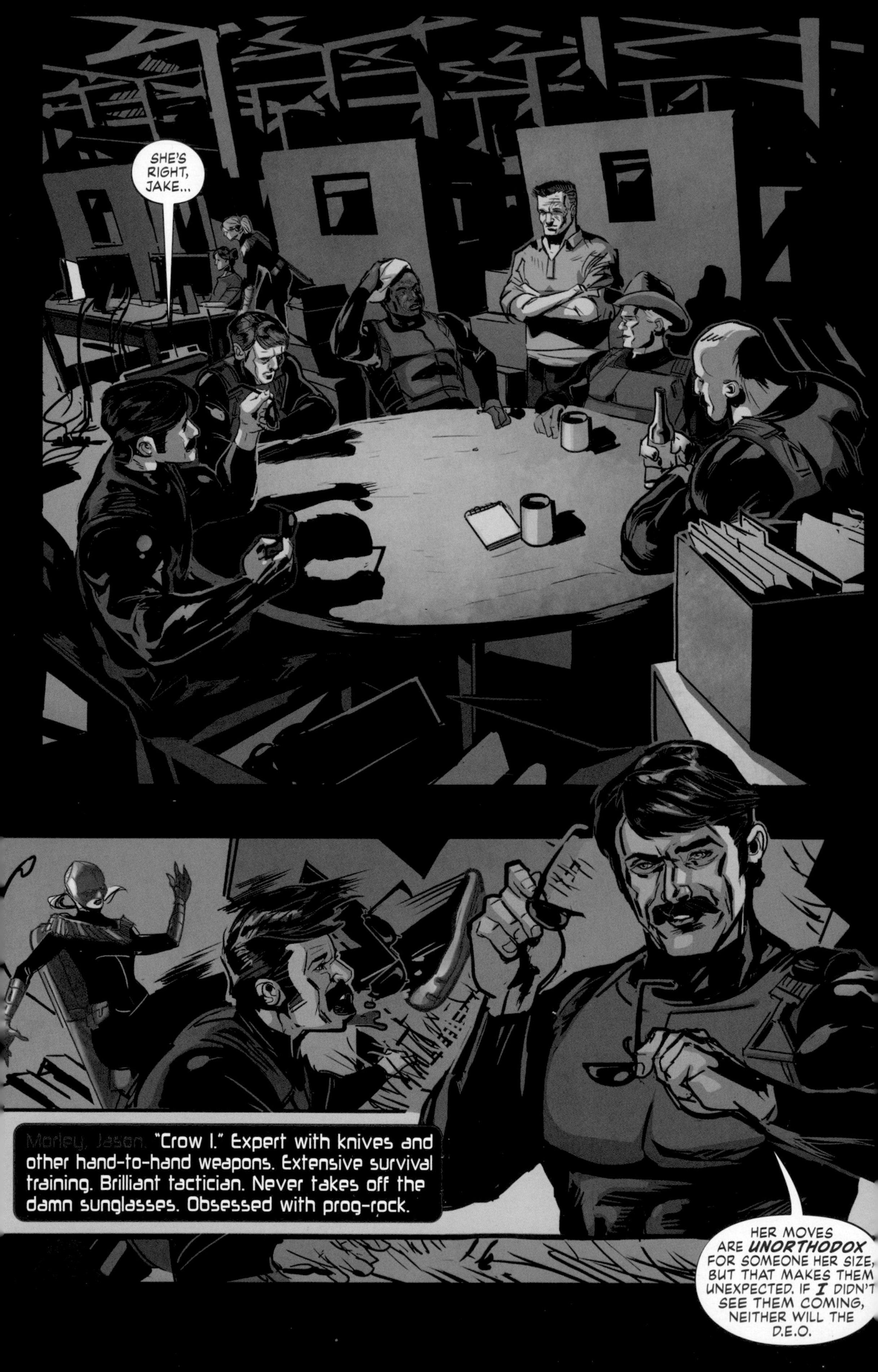
SHE'S RIGHT, JAKE...
Morley, Jason. "Crow I." Expert with knives and other hand-to-hand weapons. Extensive survival training. Brilliant tactician. Never takes off the damn sunglasses. Obsessed with prog-rock.
HER MOVES ARE ***UNORTHODOX*** FOR SOMEONE HER SIZE, BUT THAT MAKES THEM UNEXPECTED. IF ***I*** DIDN'T SEE THEM COMING, NEITHER WILL THE D.E.O.

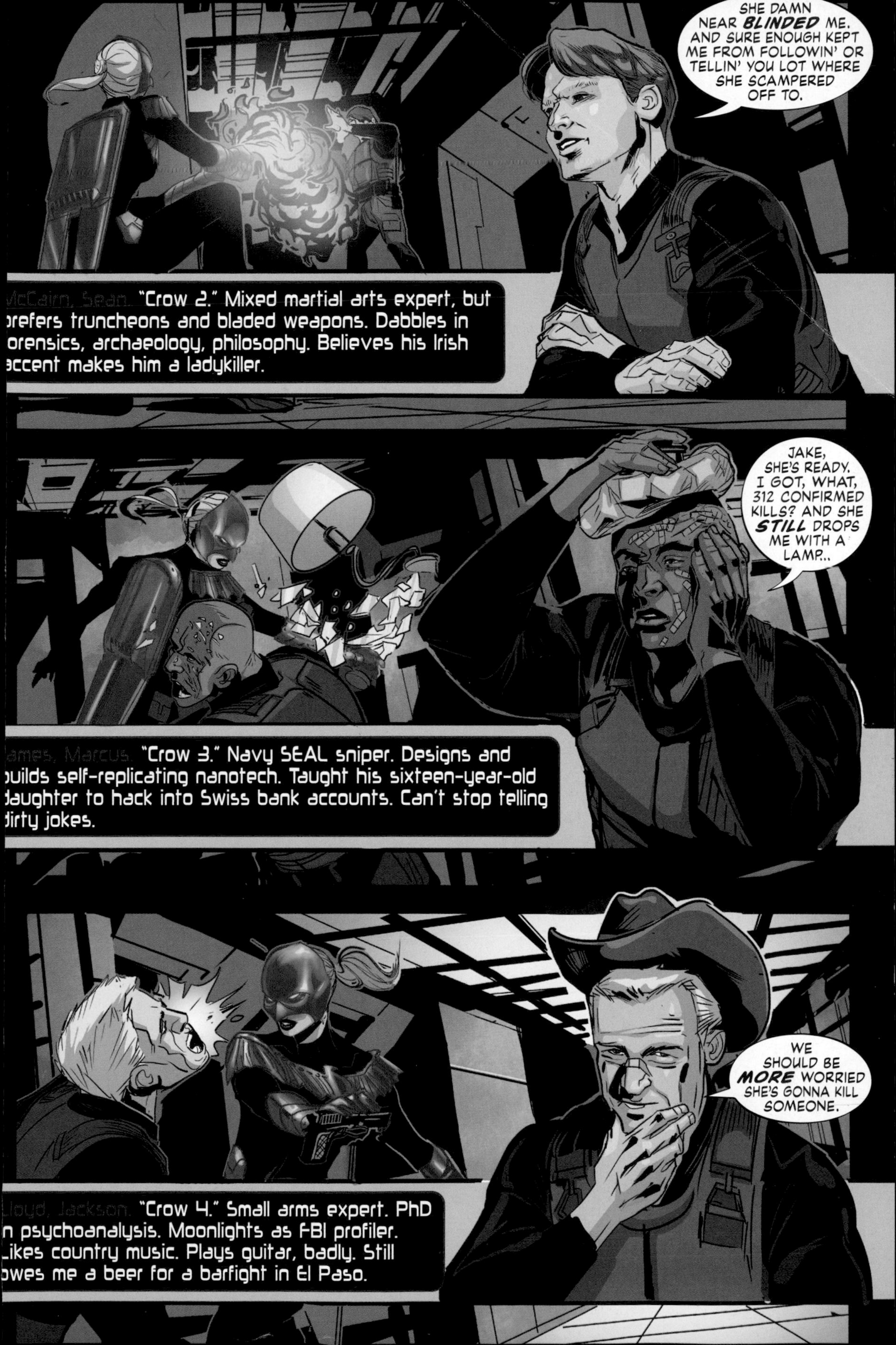

SHE DAMN NEAR **BLINDED** ME. AND SURE ENOUGH KEPT ME FROM FOLLOWIN' OR TELLIN' YOU LOT WHERE SHE SCAMPERED OFF TO.
McCairn, Sean. "Crow 2." Mixed martial arts expert, but prefers truncheons and bladed weapons. Dabbles in forensics, archaeology, philosophy. Believes his Irish accent makes him a ladykiller.
JAKE, SHE'S READY. I GOT, WHAT, 312 CONFIRMED KILLS? AND SHE **STILL** DROPS ME WITH A LAMP...
James, Marcus. "Crow 3." Navy SEAL sniper. Designs and builds self-replicating nanotech. Taught his sixteen-year-old daughter to hack into Swiss bank accounts. Can't stop telling dirty jokes.
WE SHOULD BE **MORE** WORRIED SHE'S GONNA KILL SOMEONE.
Lloyd, Jackson. "Crow 4." Small arms expert. PhD in psychoanalysis. Moonlights as FBI profiler. Likes country music. Plays guitar, badly. Still owes me a beer for a barfight in El Paso.

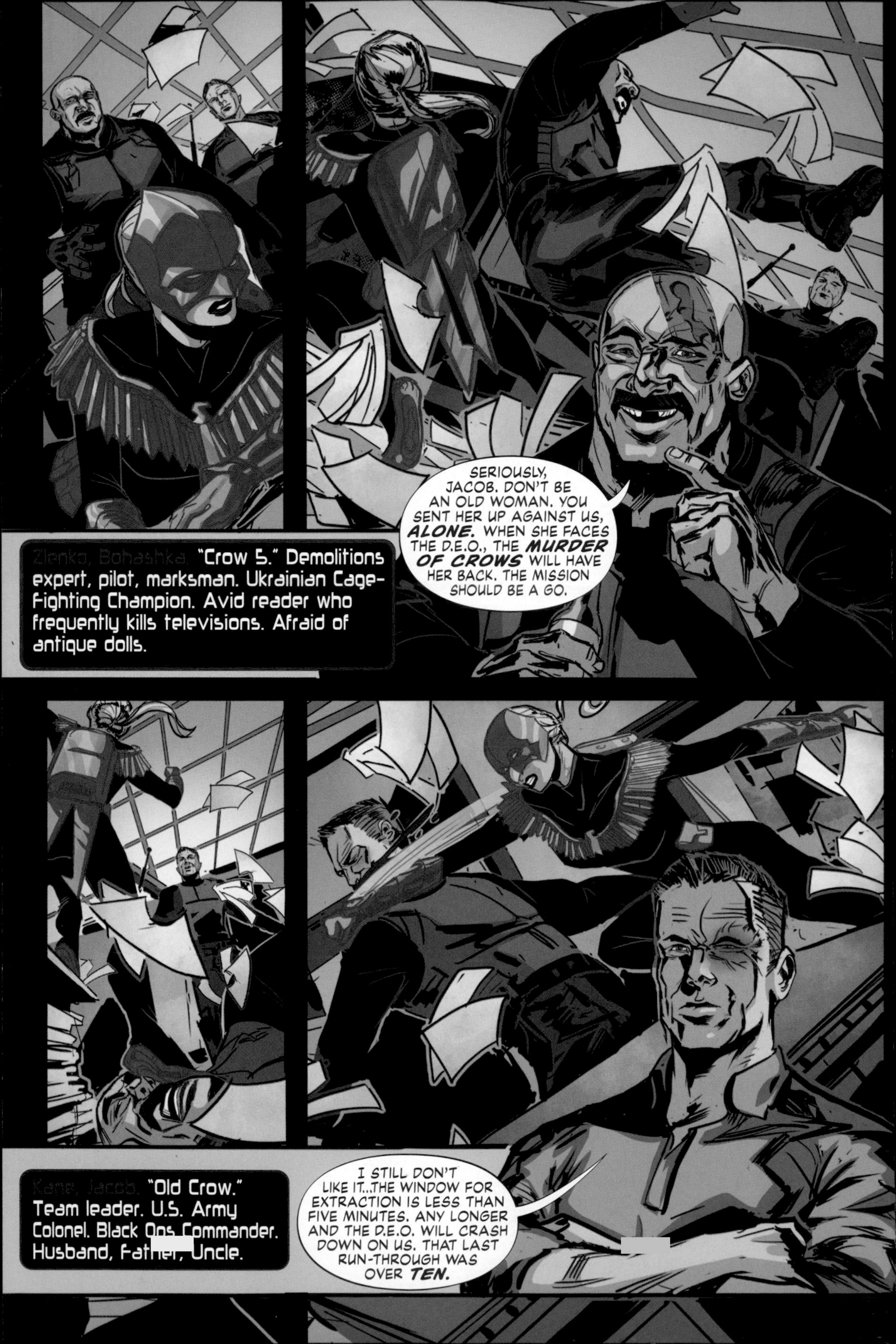
Zlenko, Bohashka. "Crow 5." Demolitions expert, pilot, marksman. Ukrainian Cage-Fighting Champion. Avid reader who frequently kills televisions. Afraid of antique dolls.
SERIOUSLY, JACOB. DON'T BE AN OLD WOMAN. YOU SENT HER UP AGAINST US, ALONE. WHEN SHE FACES THE D.E.O., THE MURDER OF CROWS WILL HAVE HER BACK. THE MISSION SHOULD BE A GO.
Kane, Jacob. "Old Crow." Team leader. U.S. Army Colonel. Black Ops Commander. Husband, Father, Uncle.
I STILL DON'T LIKE IT...THE WINDOW FOR EXTRACTION IS LESS THAN FIVE MINUTES. ANY LONGER AND THE D.E.O. WILL CRASH DOWN ON US. THAT LAST RUN-THROUGH WAS OVER TEN.

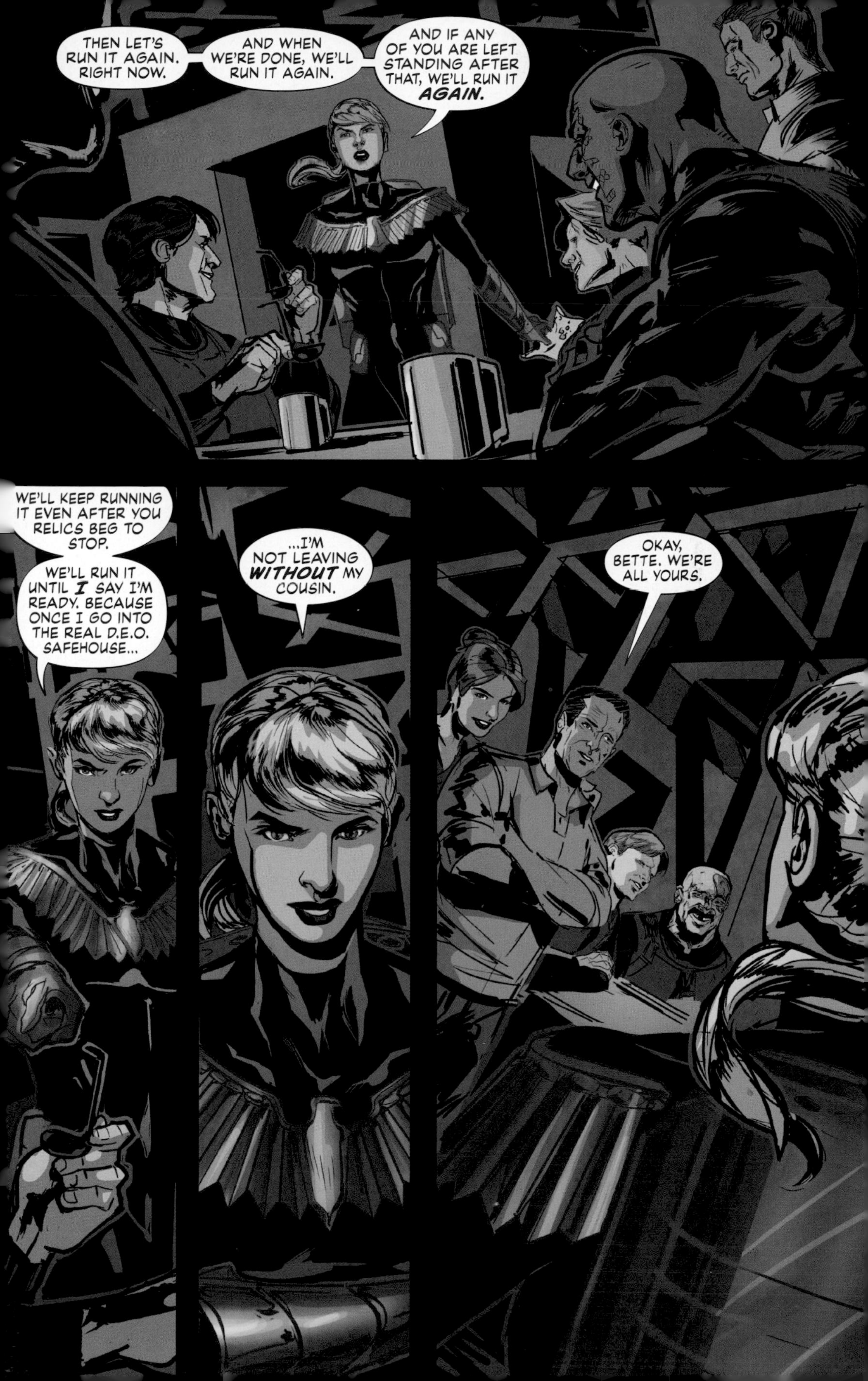
THEN LET'S RUN IT AGAIN. RIGHT NOW.
AND WHEN WE'RE DONE, WE'LL RUN IT AGAIN.
AND IF ANY OF YOU ARE LEFT STANDING AFTER THAT, WE'LL RUN IT AGAIN.
WE'LL KEEP RUNNING IT EVEN AFTER YOU RELICS BEG TO STOP.
WE'LL RUN IT UNTIL I SAY I'M READY. BECAUSE ONCE I GO INTO THE REAL D.E.O. SAFEHOUSE...
...I'M NOT LEAVING WITHOUT MY COUSIN.
OKAY, BETTE. WE'RE ALL YOURS.

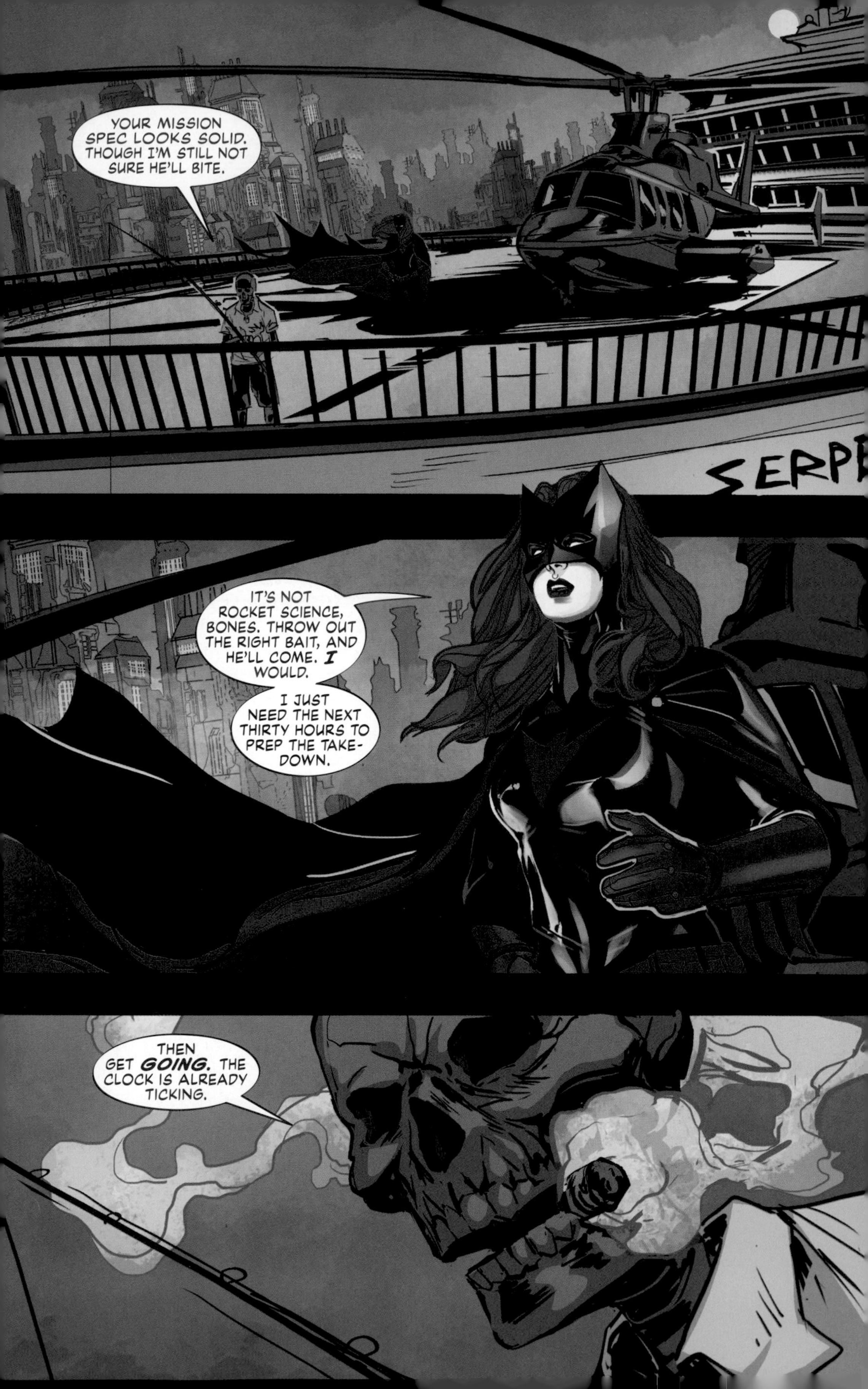
YOUR MISSION SPEC LOOKS SOLID. THOUGH I'M STILL NOT SURE HE'LL BITE.
SERPE
IT'S NOT ROCKET SCIENCE, BONES. THROW OUT THE RIGHT BAIT, AND HE'LL COME. I WOULD.
I JUST NEED THE NEXT THIRTY HOURS TO PREP THE TAKE-DOWN.
THEN GET GOING. THE CLOCK IS ALREADY TICKING.

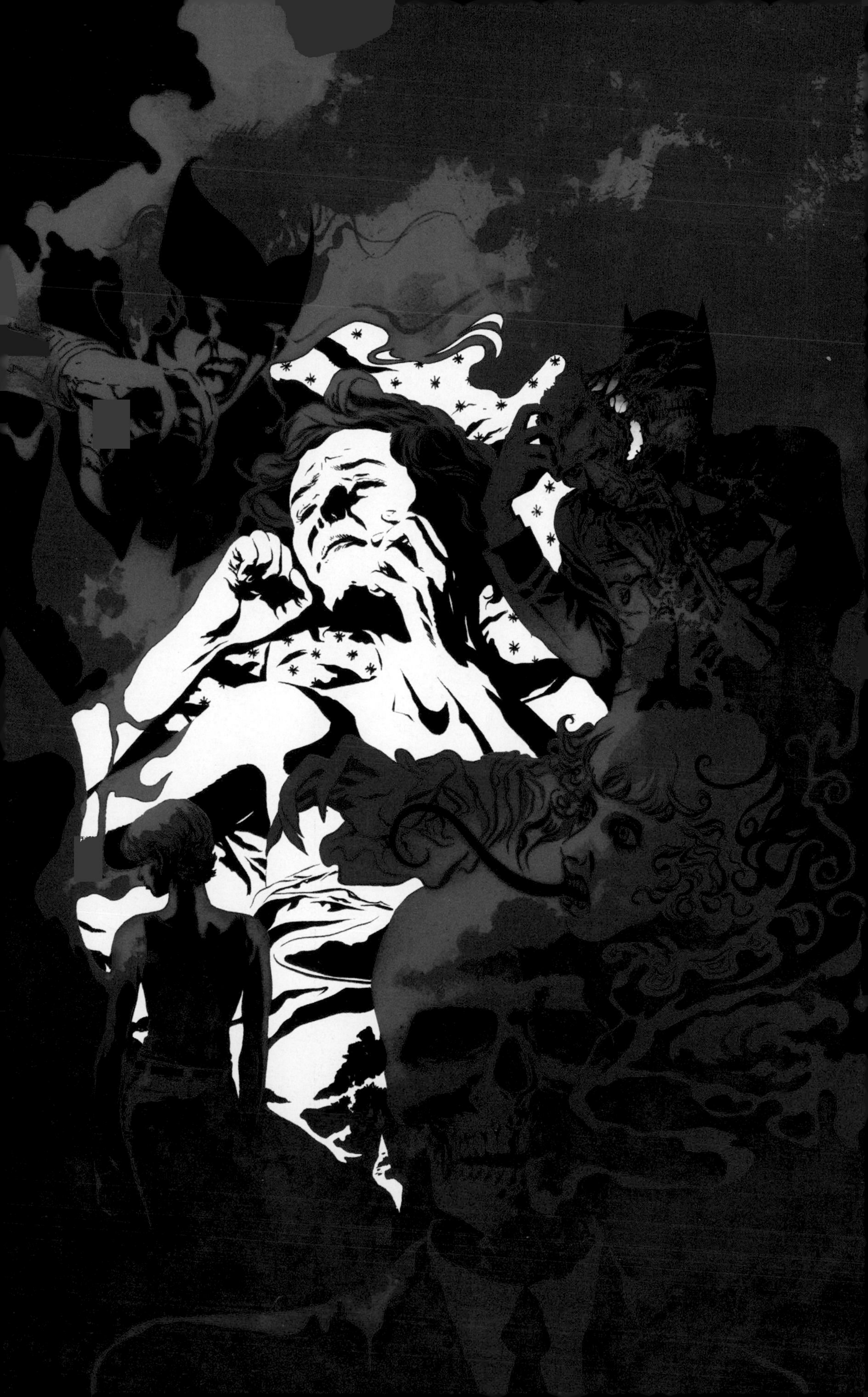

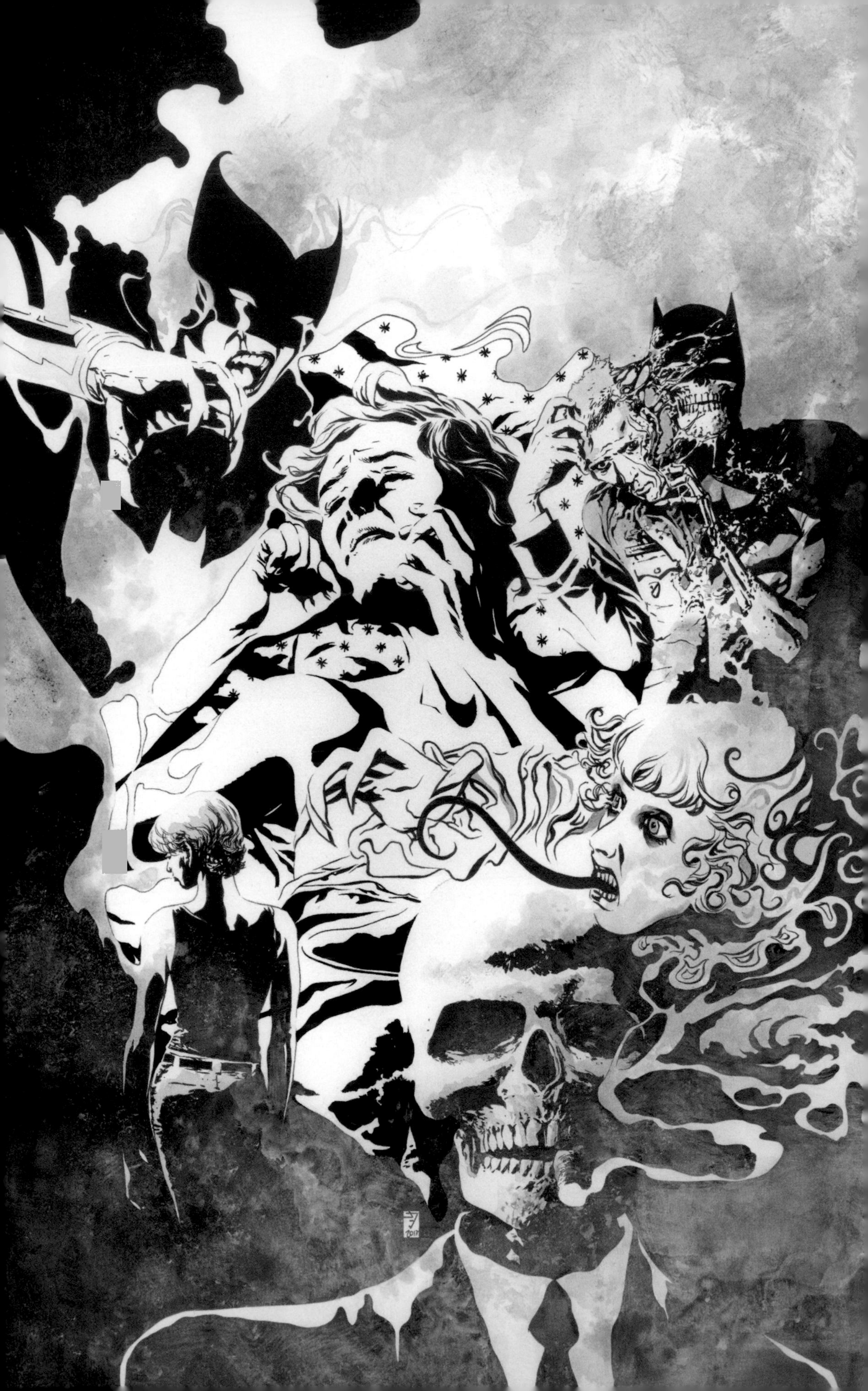

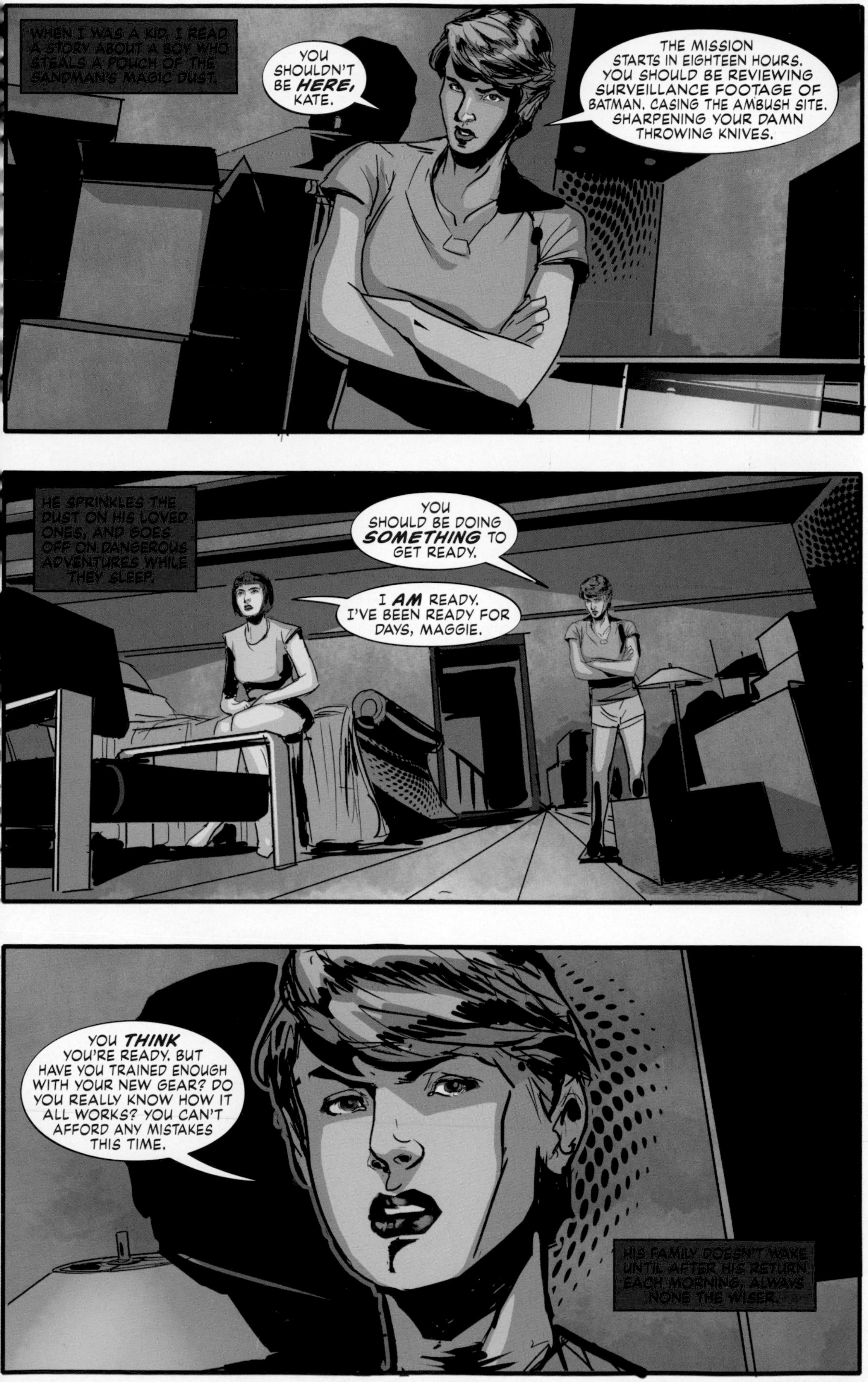
WHEN I WAS A KID, I READ A STORY ABOUT A BOY WHO STEALS A POUCH OF THE SANDMAN'S MAGIC DUST.
YOU SHOULDN'T BE HERE, KATE.
THE MISSION STARTS IN EIGHTEEN HOURS. YOU SHOULD BE REVIEWING SURVEILLANCE FOOTAGE OF BATMAN. CASING THE AMBUSH SITE. SHARPENING YOUR DAMN THROWING KNIVES.
HE SPRINKLES THE DUST ON HIS LOVED ONES, AND GOES OFF ON DANGEROUS ADVENTURES WHILE THEY SLEEP.
YOU SHOULD BE DOING SOMETHING TO GET READY.
I AM READY. I'VE BEEN READY FOR DAYS, MAGGIE.
YOU THINK YOU'RE READY. BUT HAVE YOU TRAINED ENOUGH WITH YOUR NEW GEAR? DO YOU REALLY KNOW HOW IT ALL WORKS? YOU CAN'T AFFORD ANY MISTAKES THIS TIME.
HIS FAMILY DOESN'T WAKE UNTIL AFTER HIS RETURN EACH MORNING, ALWAYS NONE THE WISER.

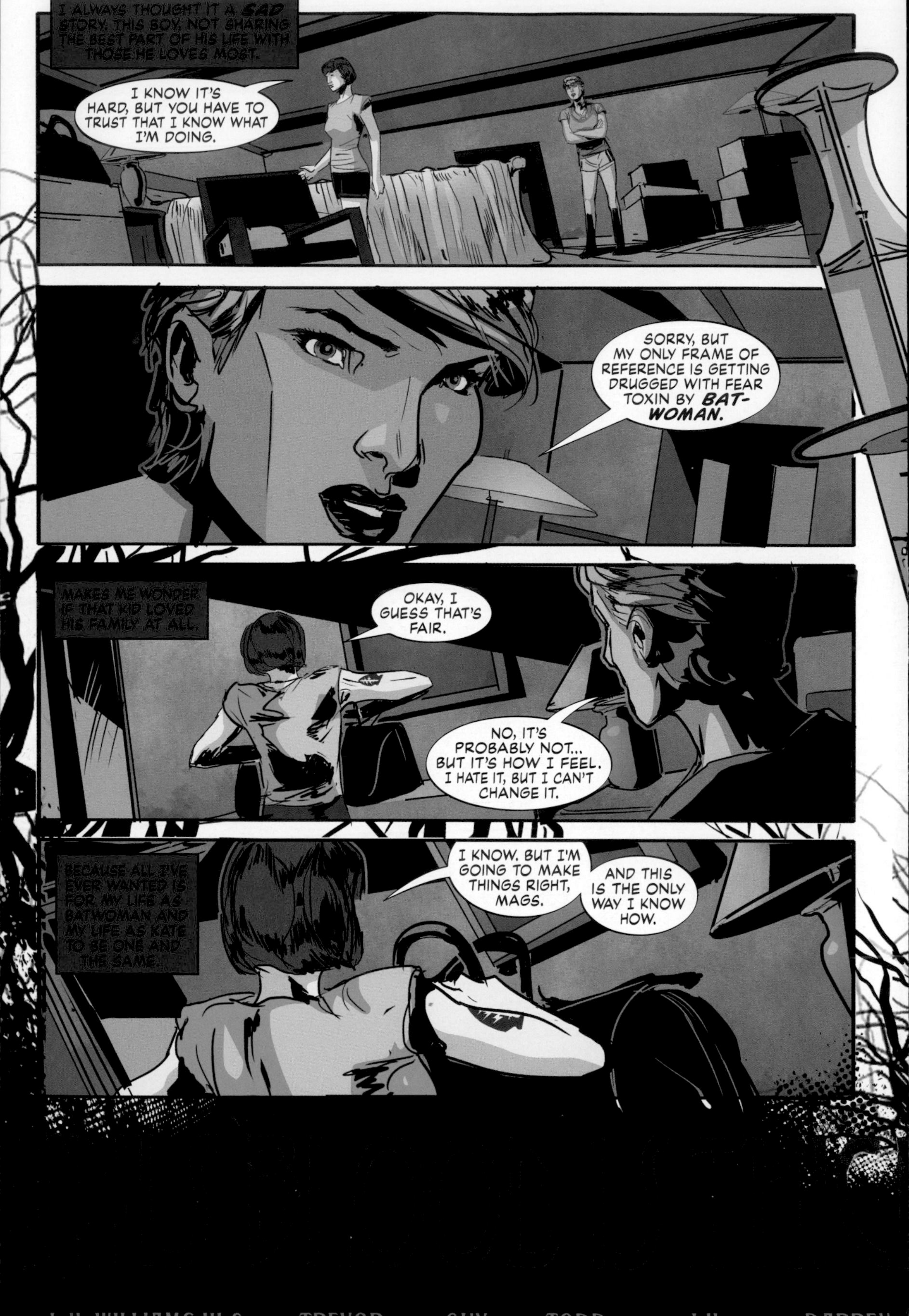
I ALWAYS THOUGHT IT A SAD STORY. THIS BOY, NOT SHARING THE BEST PART OF HIS LIFE WITH THOSE HE LOVES MOST.
I KNOW IT'S HARD, BUT YOU HAVE TO TRUST THAT I KNOW WHAT I'M DOING.
SORRY, BUT MY ONLY FRAME OF REFERENCE IS GETTING DRUGGED WITH FEAR TOXIN BY BAT-WOMAN.
MAKES ME WONDER IF THAT KID LOVED HIS FAMILY AT ALL.
OKAY, I GUESS THAT'S FAIR.
NO, IT'S PROBABLY NOT... BUT IT'S HOW I FEEL. I HATE IT, BUT I CAN'T CHANGE IT.
BECAUSE ALL I'VE EVER WANTED IS FOR MY LIFE AS BATWOMAN AND MY LIFE AS KATE TO BE ONE AND THE SAME.
I KNOW. BUT I'M GOING TO MAKE THINGS RIGHT, MAGS.
AND THIS IS THE ONLY WAY I KNOW HOW.

J. H. WILLIAMS III & W. HADEN BLACKMAN writers
TREVOR McGARTHY artist
GUY MAJOR colorist
TODD KLEIN letterer
J.H. WILLIAMS III cover
DARREN SHAN asst. editor

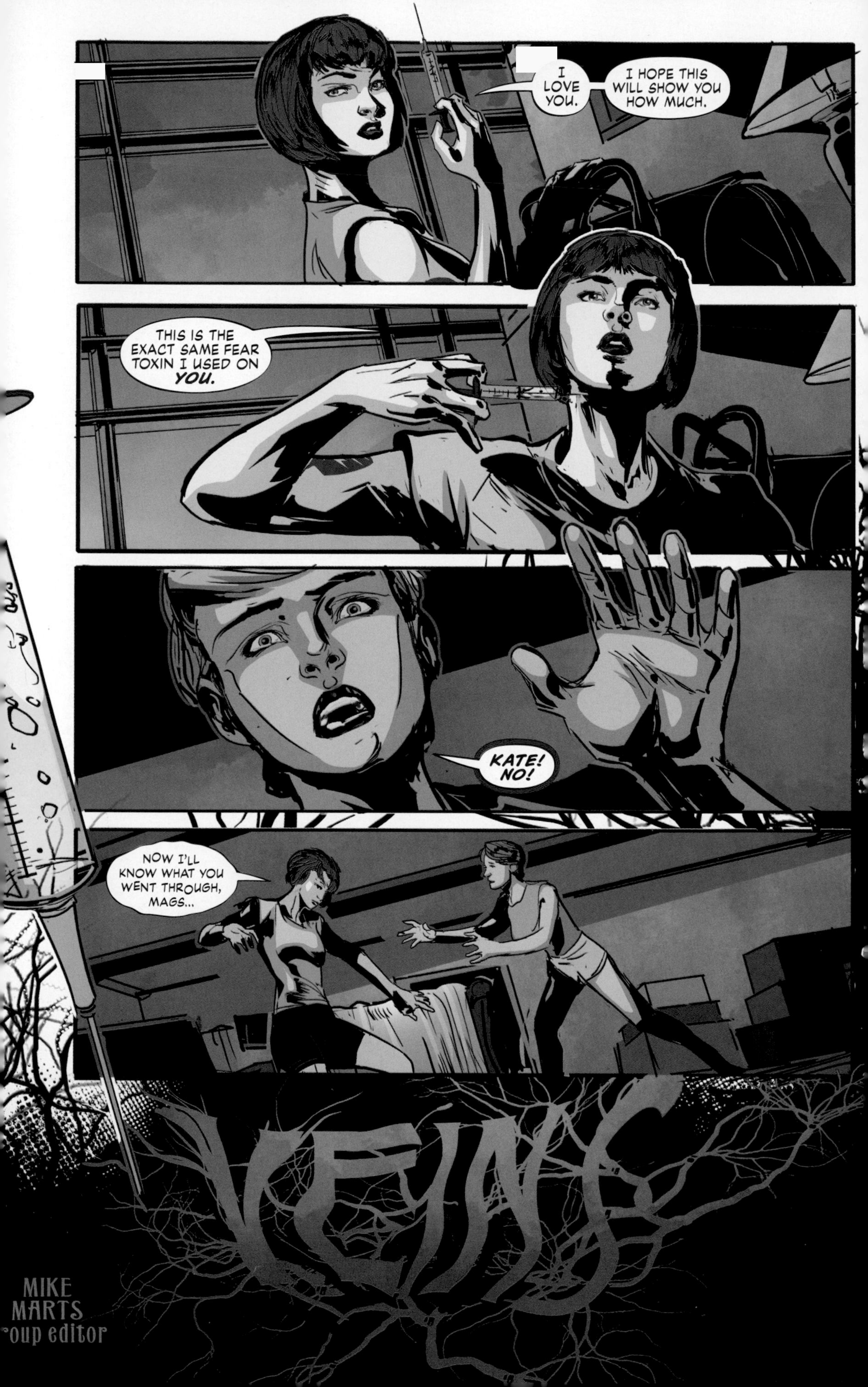
I LOVE YOU.
I HOPE THIS WILL SHOW YOU HOW MUCH.
THIS IS THE EXACT SAME FEAR TOXIN I USED ON YOU.
KATE! NO!
NOW I'LL KNOW WHAT YOU WENT THROUGH, MAGS...
VEINS
MIKE MARTS
oup editor

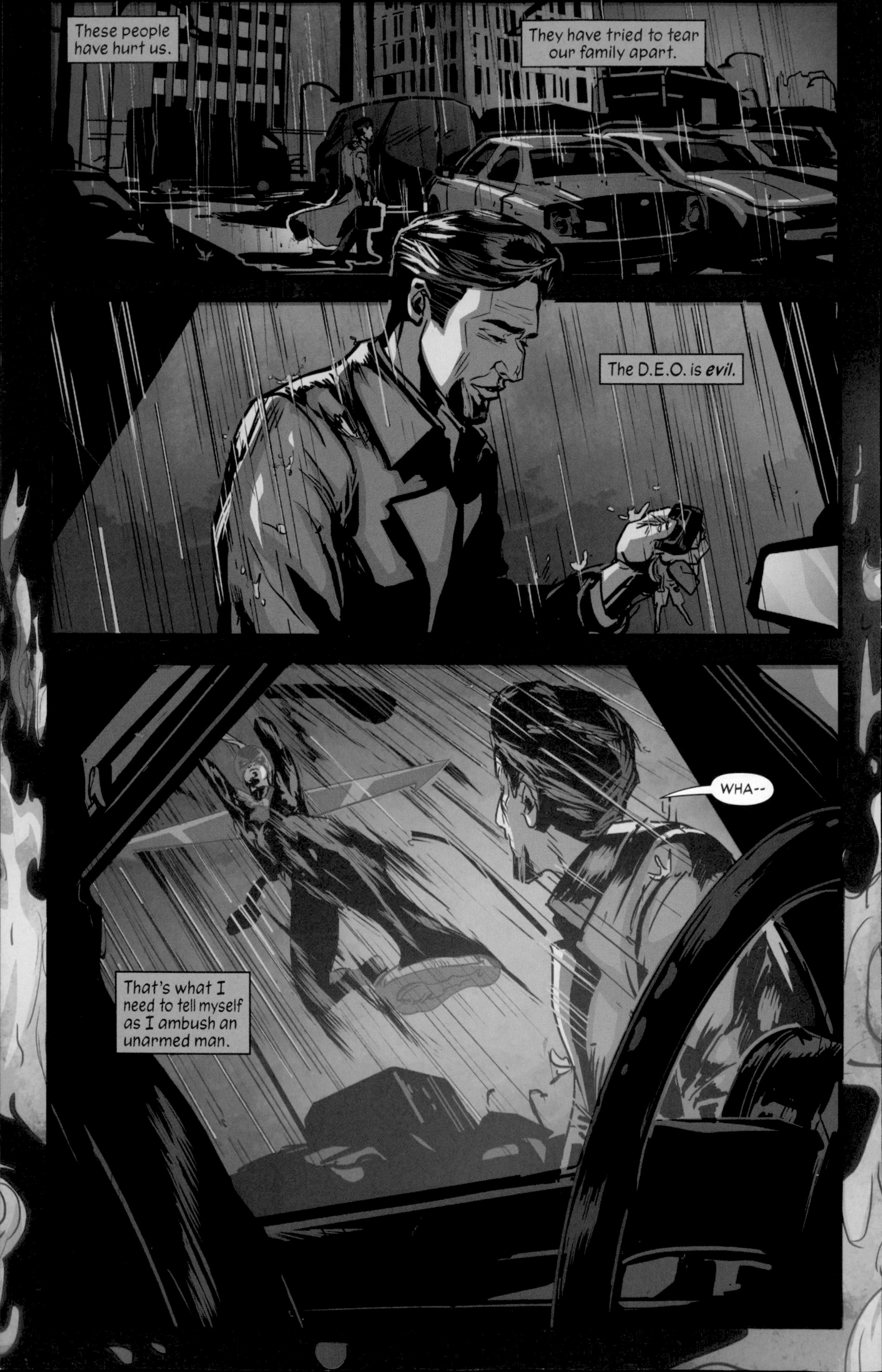
These people have hurt us.
They have tried to tear our family apart.
The D.E.O. is *evil*.
WHA--
That's what I need to tell myself as I ambush an unarmed man.

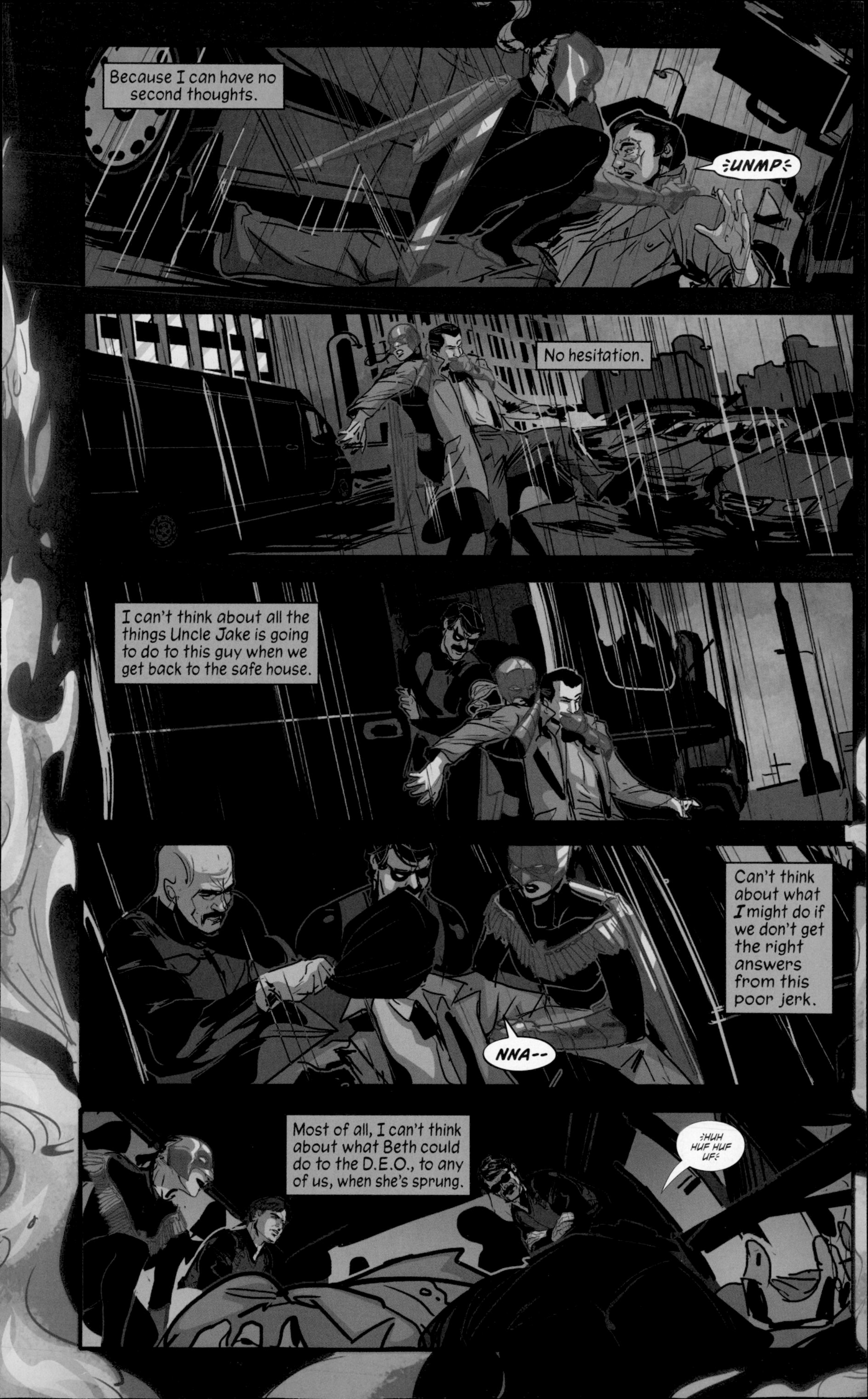
Because I can have no second thoughts.
UNMP
No hesitation.
I can't think about all the things Uncle Jake is going to do to this guy when we get back to the safe house.
Can't think about what I might do if we don't get the right answers from this poor jerk.
NNA--
Most of all, I can't think about what Beth could do to the D.E.O., to any of us, when she's sprung.
HUH HUF HUF UF

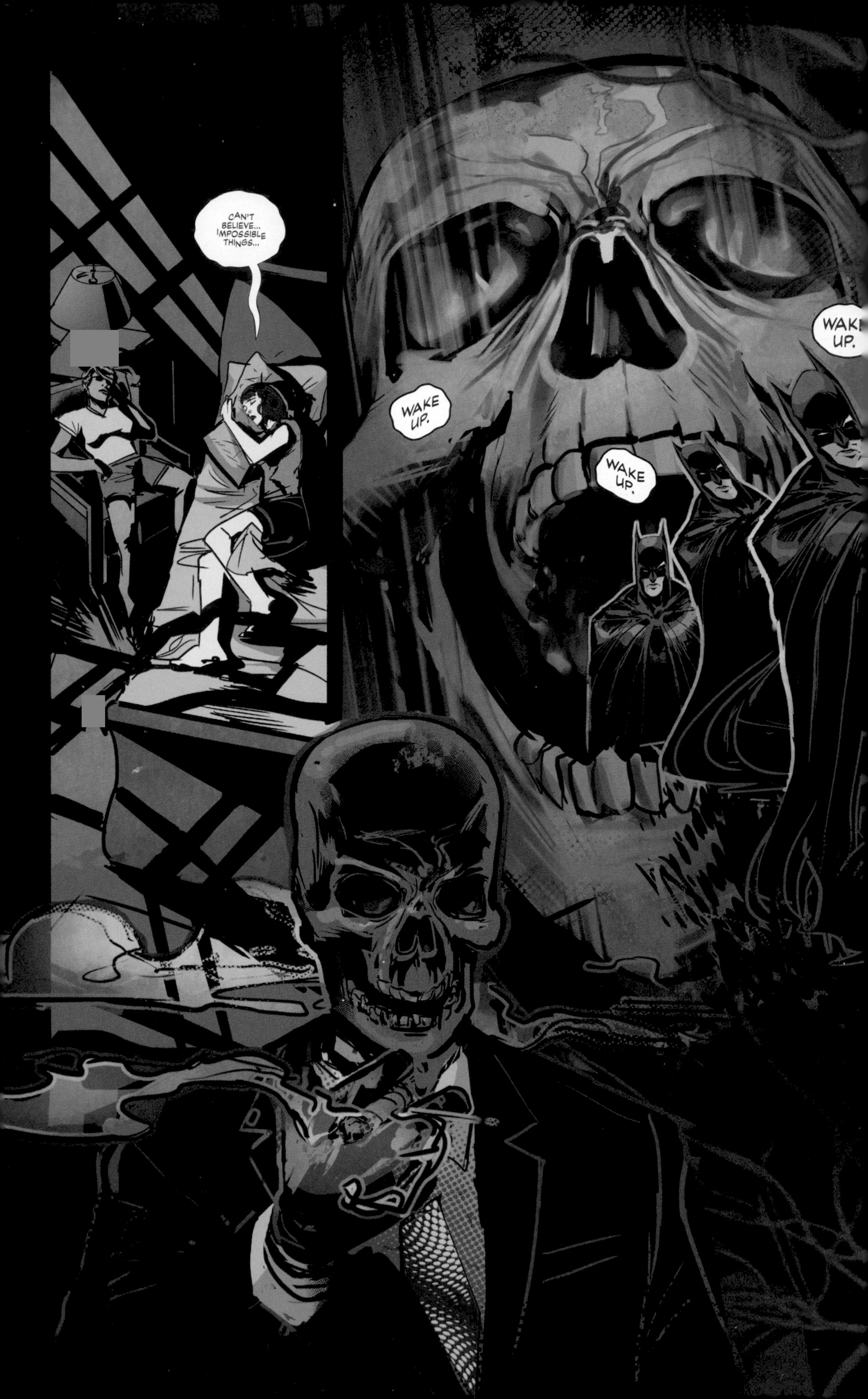
CAN'T BELIEVE... IMPOSSIBLE THINGS...
WAKE UP.
WAKE UP.
WAKE UP.

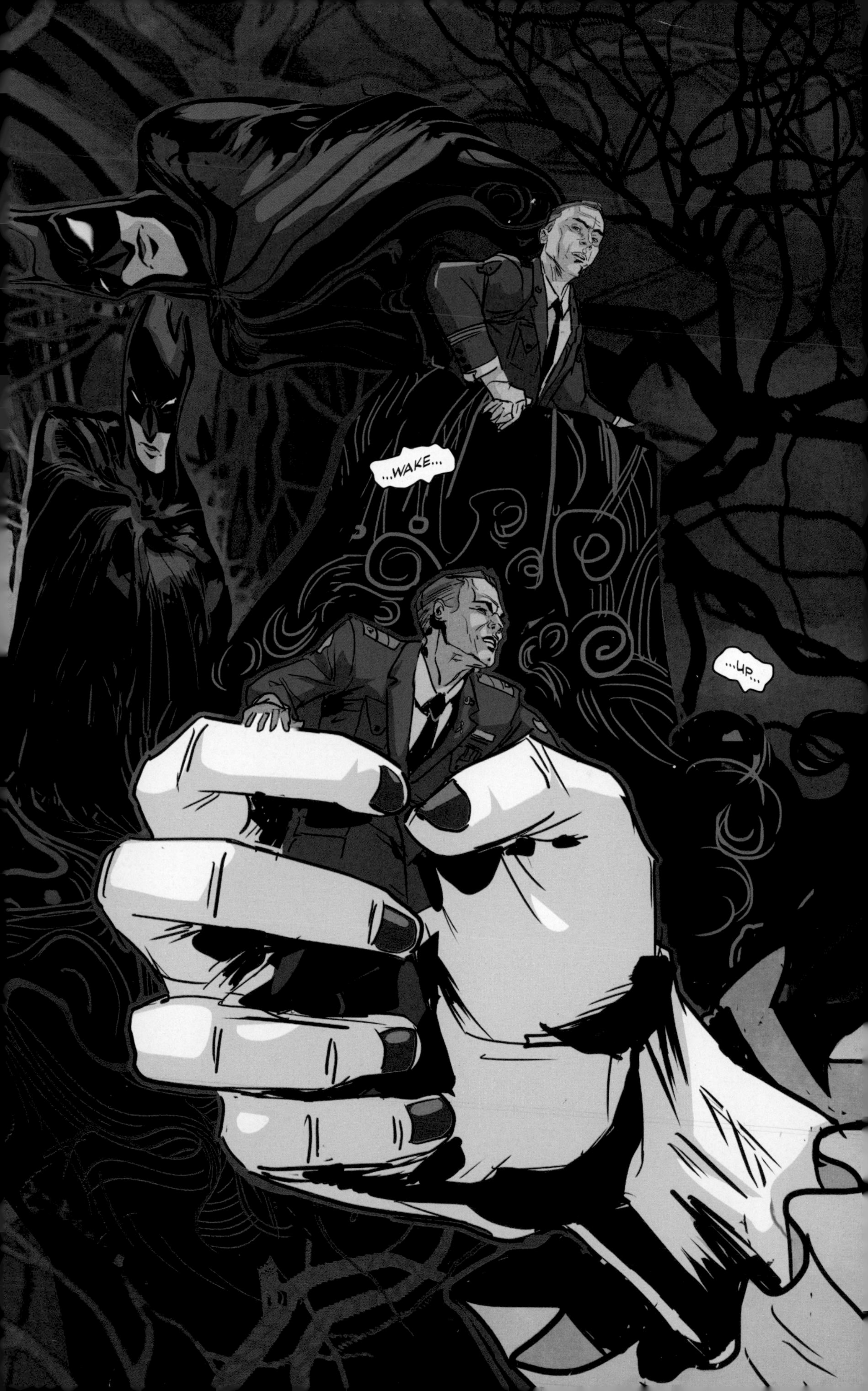
...WAKE...
...UP...

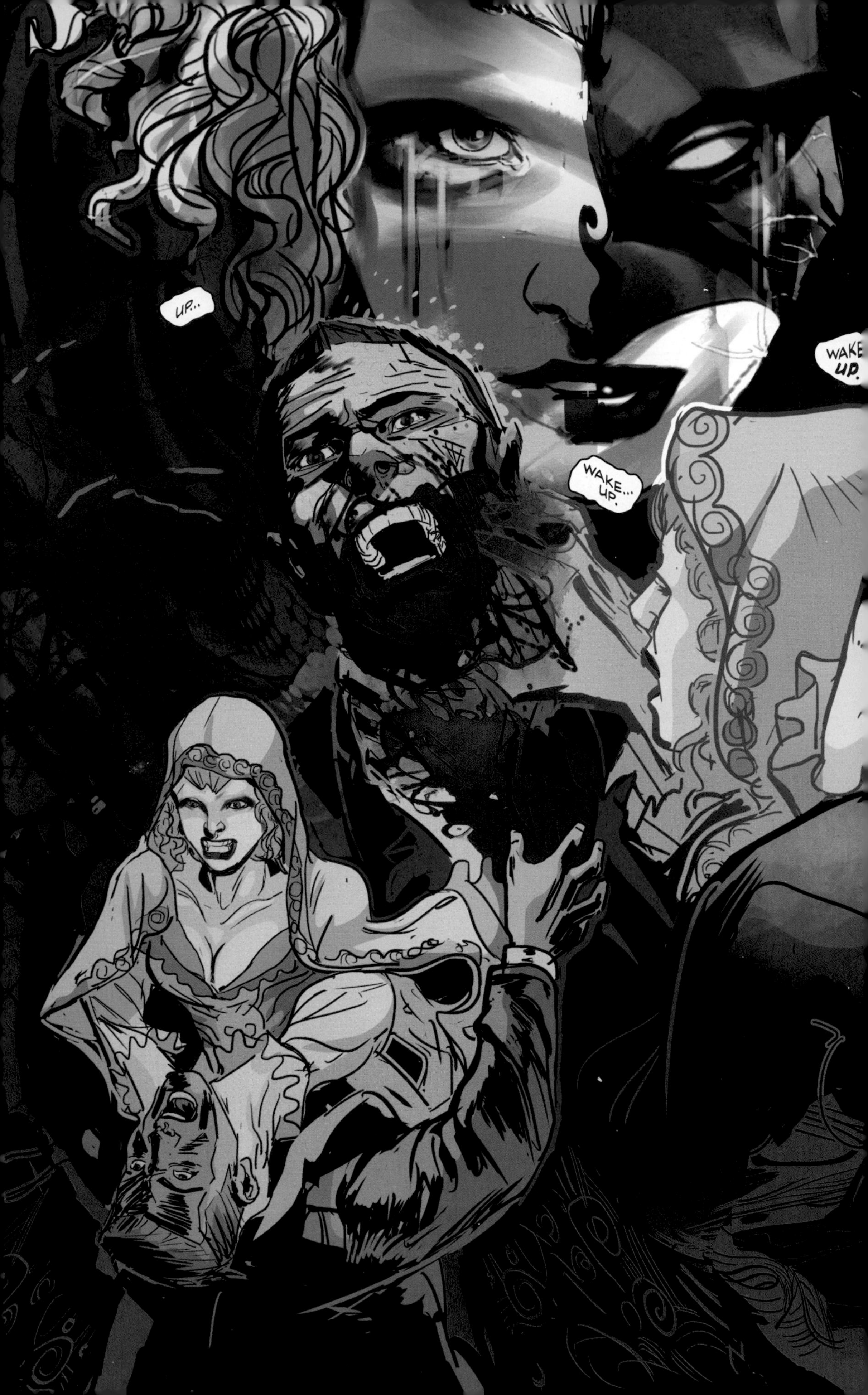
UP...
WAKE UP.
WAKE... UP.

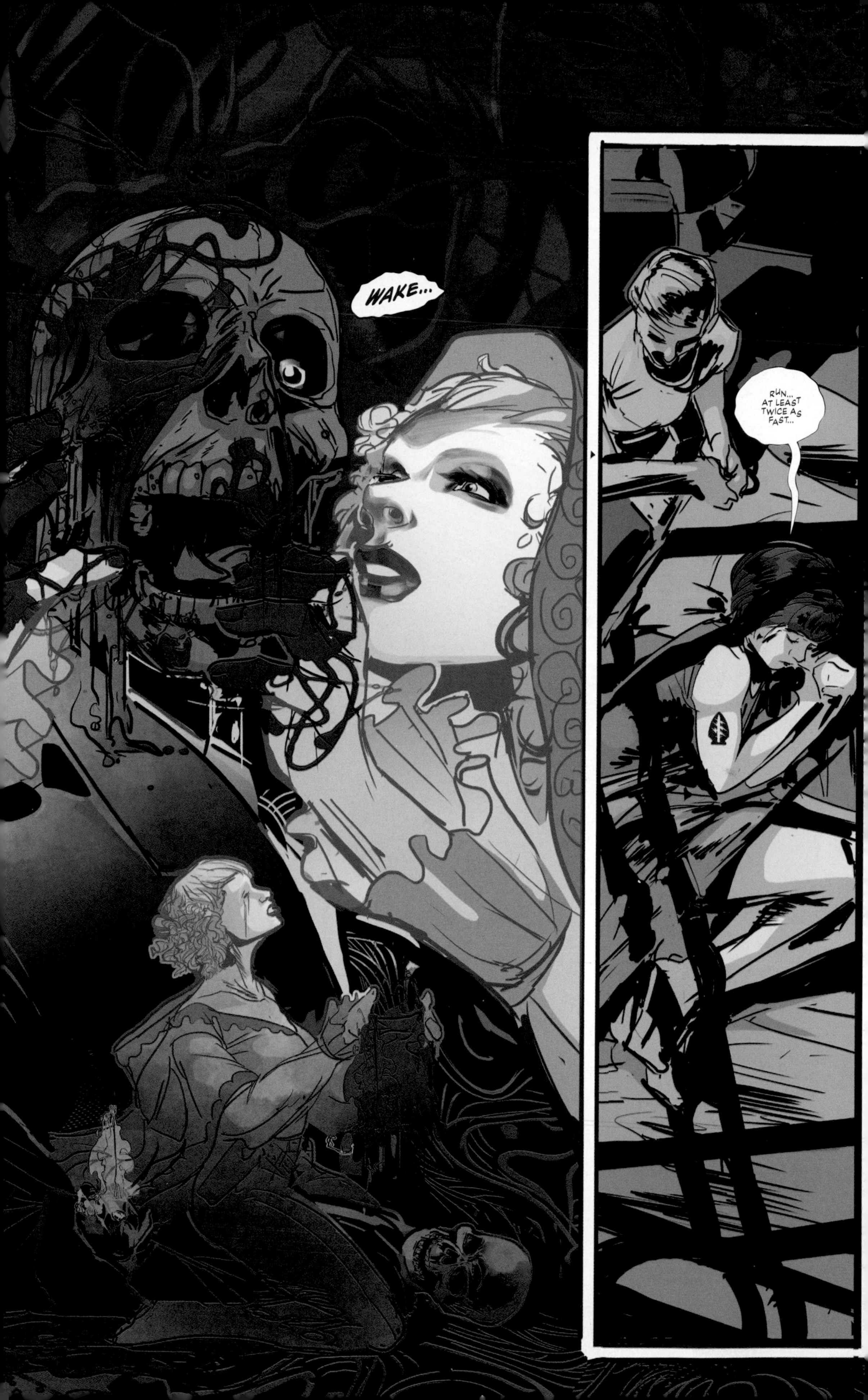
WAKE...
RUN... AT LEAST TWICE AS FAST...

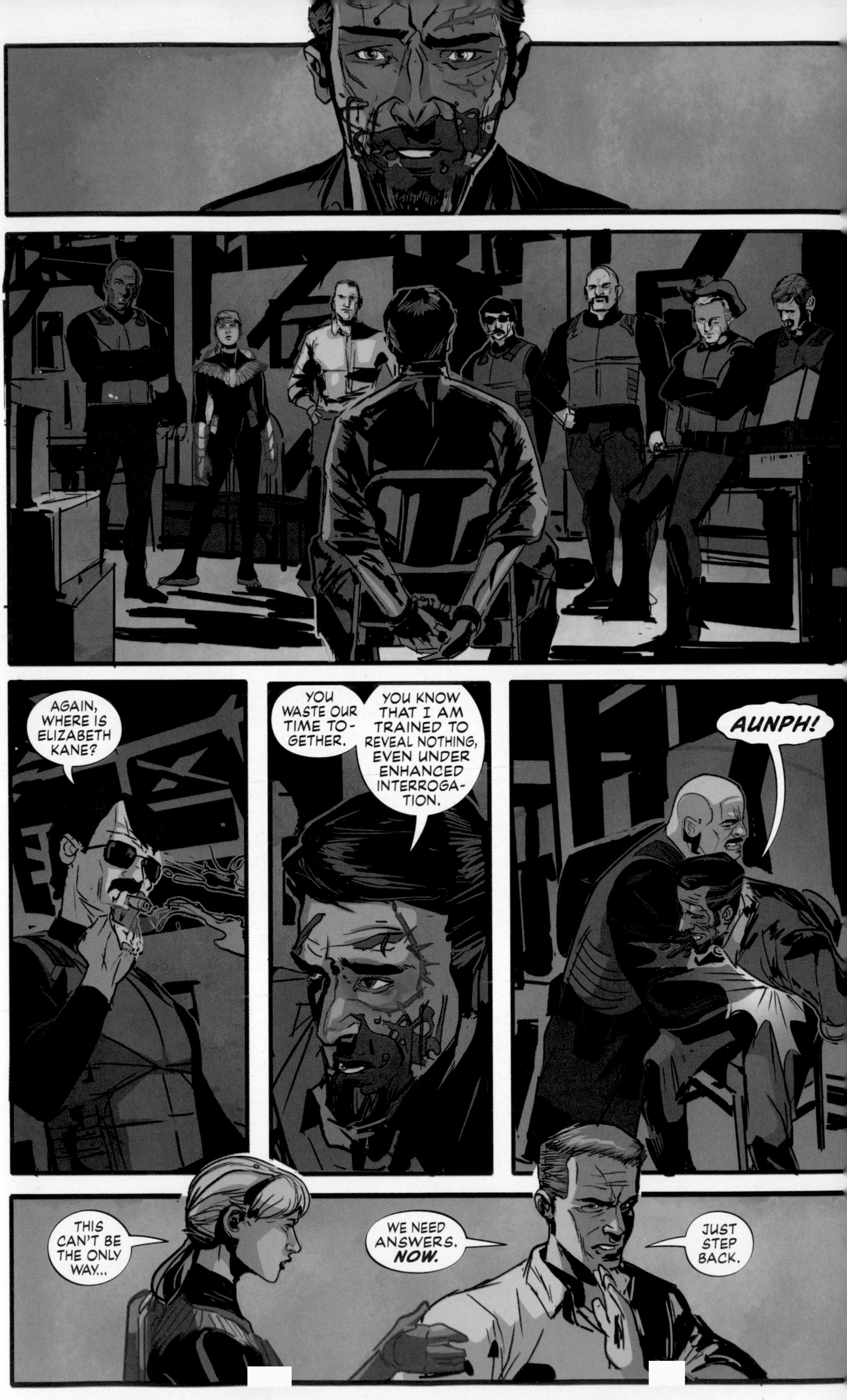
AGAIN, WHERE IS ELIZABETH KANE?
YOU WASTE OUR TIME TO-GETHER.
YOU KNOW THAT I AM TRAINED TO REVEAL NOTHING, EVEN UNDER ENHANCED INTERROGA-TION.
AUNPH!
THIS CAN'T BE THE ONLY WAY...
WE NEED ANSWERS. NOW.
JUST STEP BACK.

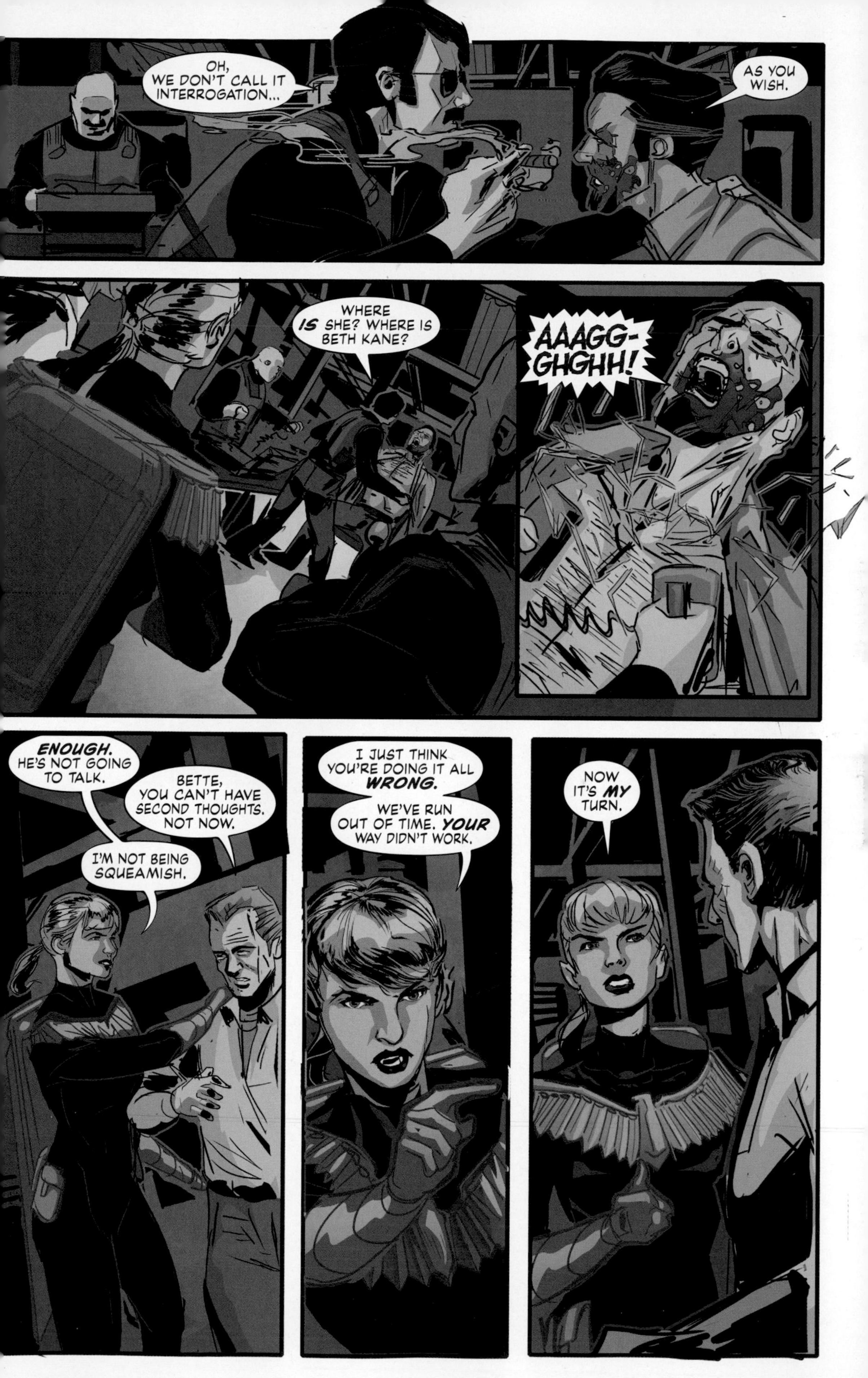
OH, WE DON'T CALL IT INTERROGATION...
AS YOU WISH.
WHERE *IS* SHE? WHERE IS BETH KANE?
AAAGG-GHGHH!
ENOUGH. HE'S NOT GOING TO TALK.
BETTE, YOU CAN'T HAVE SECOND THOUGHTS. NOT NOW.
I'M NOT BEING SQUEAMISH.
I JUST THINK YOU'RE DOING IT ALL *WRONG.*
WE'VE RUN OUT OF TIME. *YOUR* WAY DIDN'T WORK.
NOW IT'S *MY* TURN.

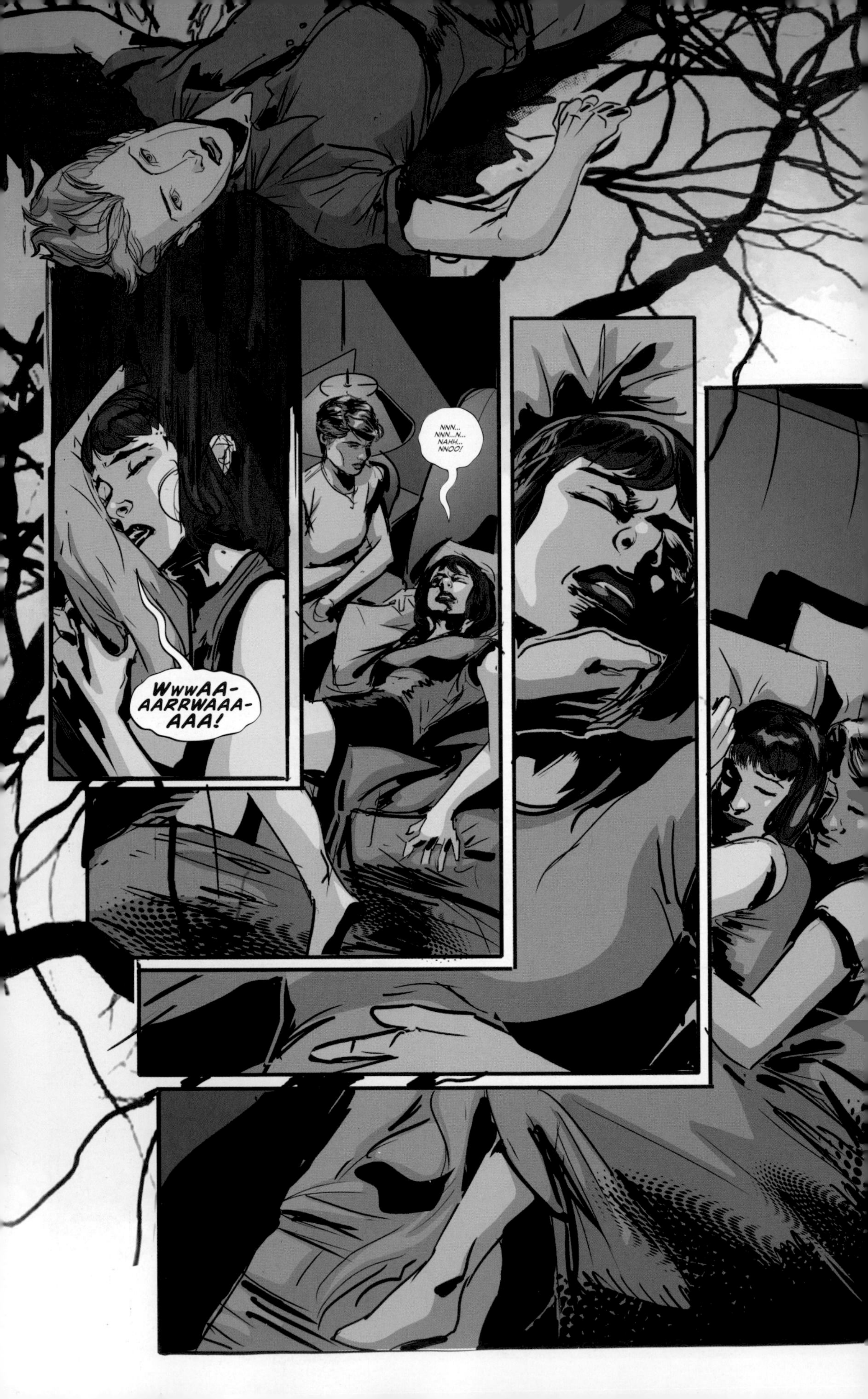
WwwAA-AARRWAAA-AAA!
NNN... NNN...N... NAHH... NNOO!

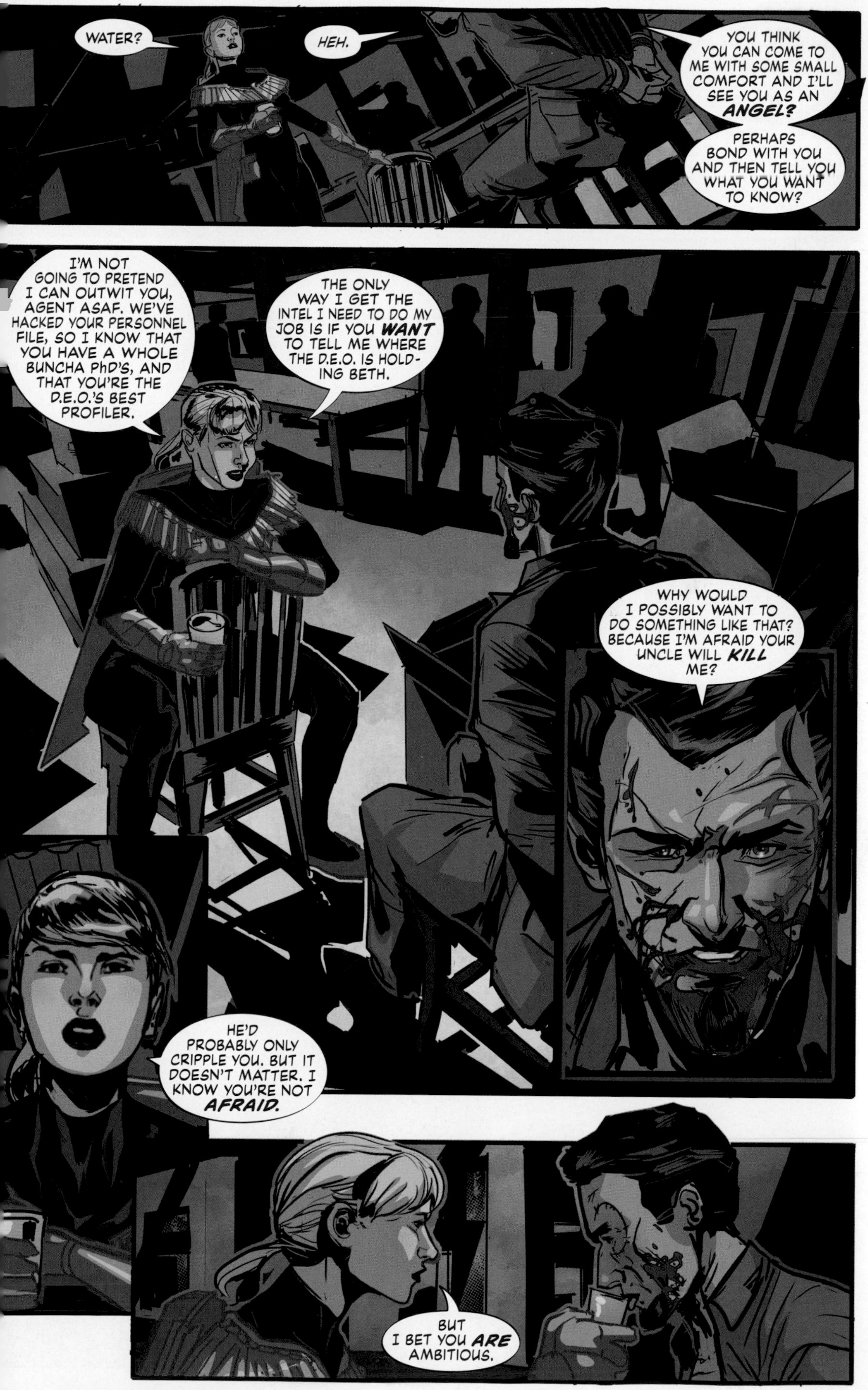
WATER?
HEH.
YOU THINK YOU CAN COME TO ME WITH SOME SMALL COMFORT AND I'LL SEE YOU AS AN ANGEL?
PERHAPS BOND WITH YOU AND THEN TELL YOU WHAT YOU WANT TO KNOW?
I'M NOT GOING TO PRETEND I CAN OUTWIT YOU, AGENT ASAF. WE'VE HACKED YOUR PERSONNEL FILE, SO I KNOW THAT YOU HAVE A WHOLE BUNCHA PhD'S, AND THAT YOU'RE THE D.E.O.'S BEST PROFILER.
THE ONLY WAY I GET THE INTEL I NEED TO DO MY JOB IS IF YOU WANT TO TELL ME WHERE THE D.E.O. IS HOLDING BETH.
WHY WOULD I POSSIBLY WANT TO DO SOMETHING LIKE THAT? BECAUSE I'M AFRAID YOUR UNCLE WILL KILL ME?
HE'D PROBABLY ONLY CRIPPLE YOU. BUT IT DOESN'T MATTER. I KNOW YOU'RE NOT AFRAID.
BUT I BET YOU ARE AMBITIOUS.

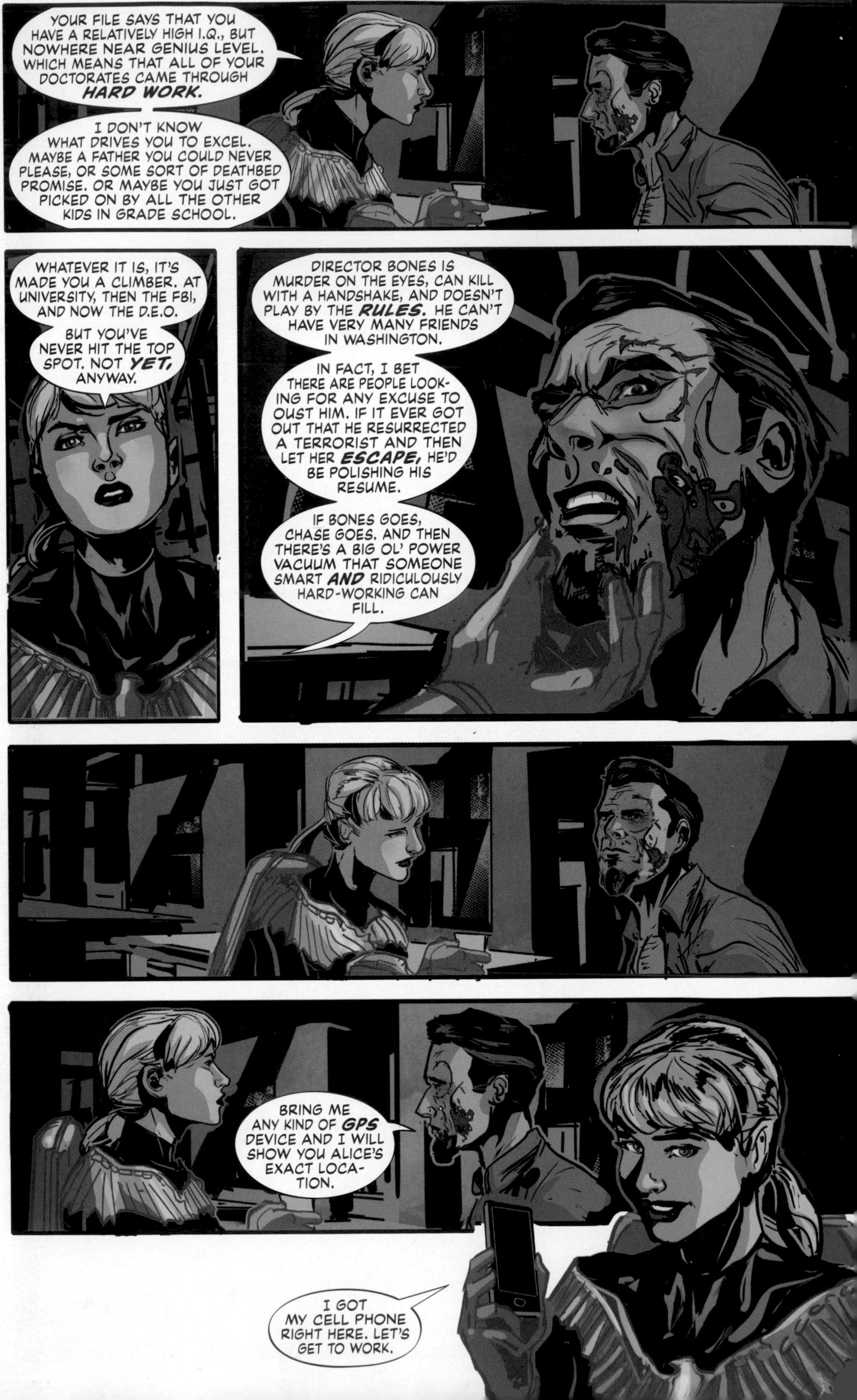
YOUR FILE SAYS THAT YOU HAVE A RELATIVELY HIGH I.Q., BUT NOWHERE NEAR GENIUS LEVEL. WHICH MEANS THAT ALL OF YOUR DOCTORATES CAME THROUGH HARD WORK.
I DON'T KNOW WHAT DRIVES YOU TO EXCEL. MAYBE A FATHER YOU COULD NEVER PLEASE, OR SOME SORT OF DEATHBED PROMISE. OR MAYBE YOU JUST GOT PICKED ON BY ALL THE OTHER KIDS IN GRADE SCHOOL.
WHATEVER IT IS, IT'S MADE YOU A CLIMBER. AT UNIVERSITY, THEN THE FBI, AND NOW THE D.E.O.
BUT YOU'VE NEVER HIT THE TOP SPOT. NOT YET, ANYWAY.
DIRECTOR BONES IS MURDER ON THE EYES, CAN KILL WITH A HANDSHAKE, AND DOESN'T PLAY BY THE RULES. HE CAN'T HAVE VERY MANY FRIENDS IN WASHINGTON.
IN FACT, I BET THERE ARE PEOPLE LOOKING FOR ANY EXCUSE TO OUST HIM. IF IT EVER GOT OUT THAT HE RESURRECTED A TERRORIST AND THEN LET HER ESCAPE, HE'D BE POLISHING HIS RESUME.
IF BONES GOES, CHASE GOES. AND THEN THERE'S A BIG OL' POWER VACUUM THAT SOMEONE SMART AND RIDICULOUSLY HARD-WORKING CAN FILL.
BRING ME ANY KIND OF GPS DEVICE AND I WILL SHOW YOU ALICE'S EXACT LOCATION.
I GOT MY CELL PHONE RIGHT HERE. LET'S GET TO WORK.

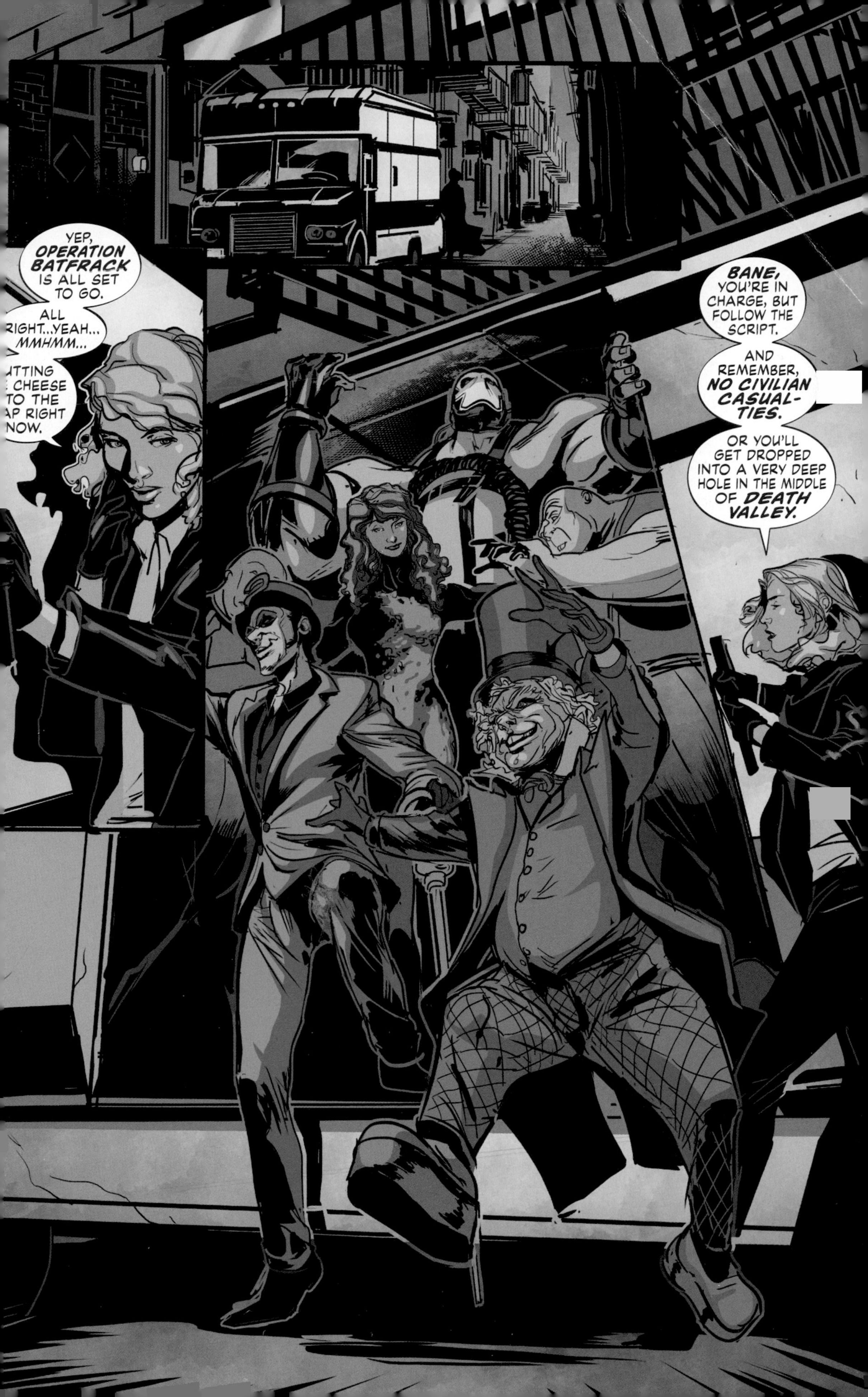

YEP, OPERATION BATFRACK IS ALL SET TO GO.
ALL RIGHT...YEAH... MMHMM...
UTTING CHEESE TO THE AP RIGHT NOW.
BANE, YOU'RE IN CHARGE, BUT FOLLOW THE SCRIPT.
AND REMEMBER, NO CIVILIAN CASUALTIES.
OR YOU'LL GET DROPPED INTO A VERY DEEP HOLE IN THE MIDDLE OF DEATH VALLEY.

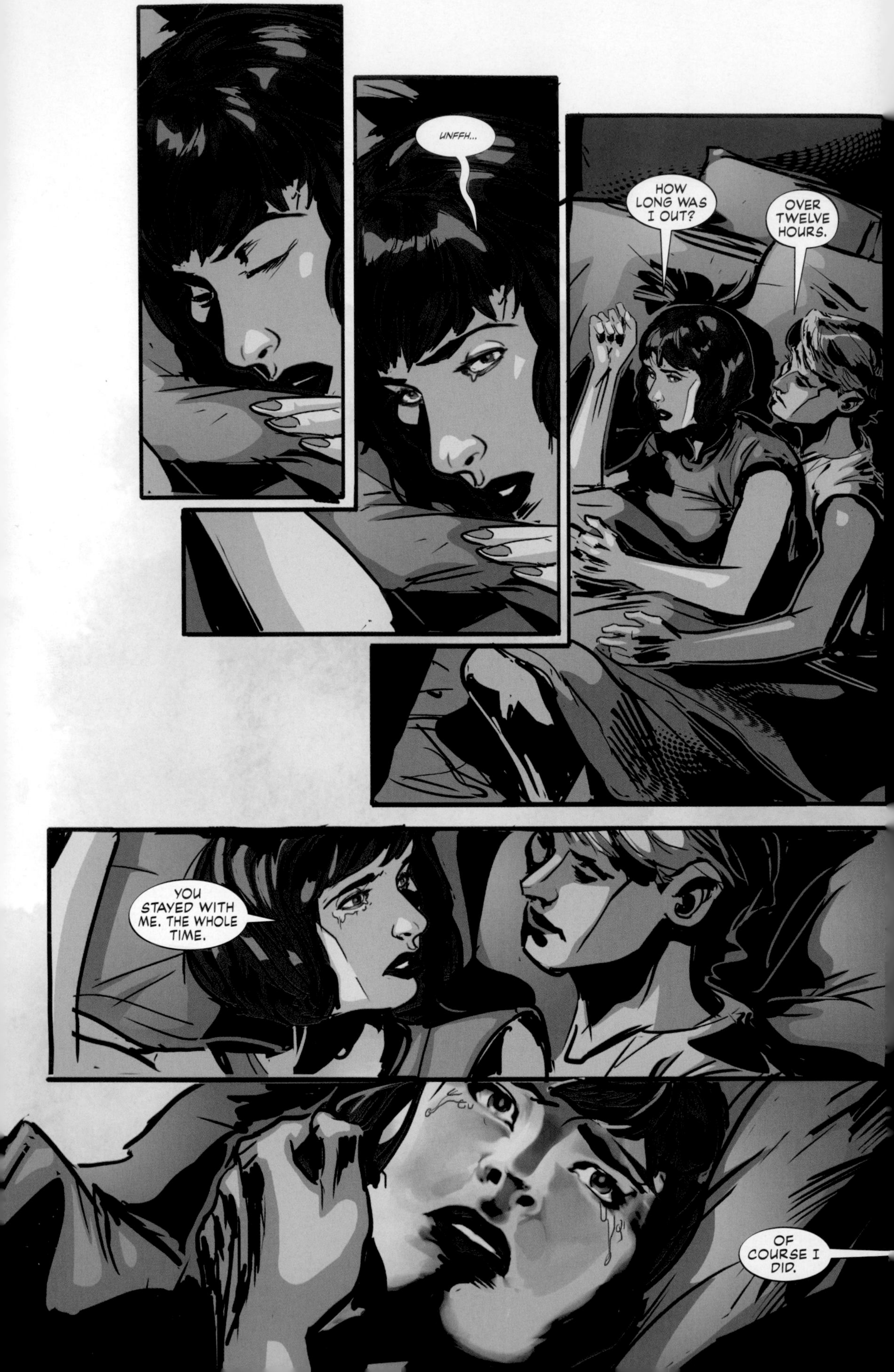
UNFFH...
HOW LONG WAS I OUT?
OVER TWELVE HOURS.
YOU STAYED WITH ME. THE WHOLE TIME.
OF COURSE I DID.

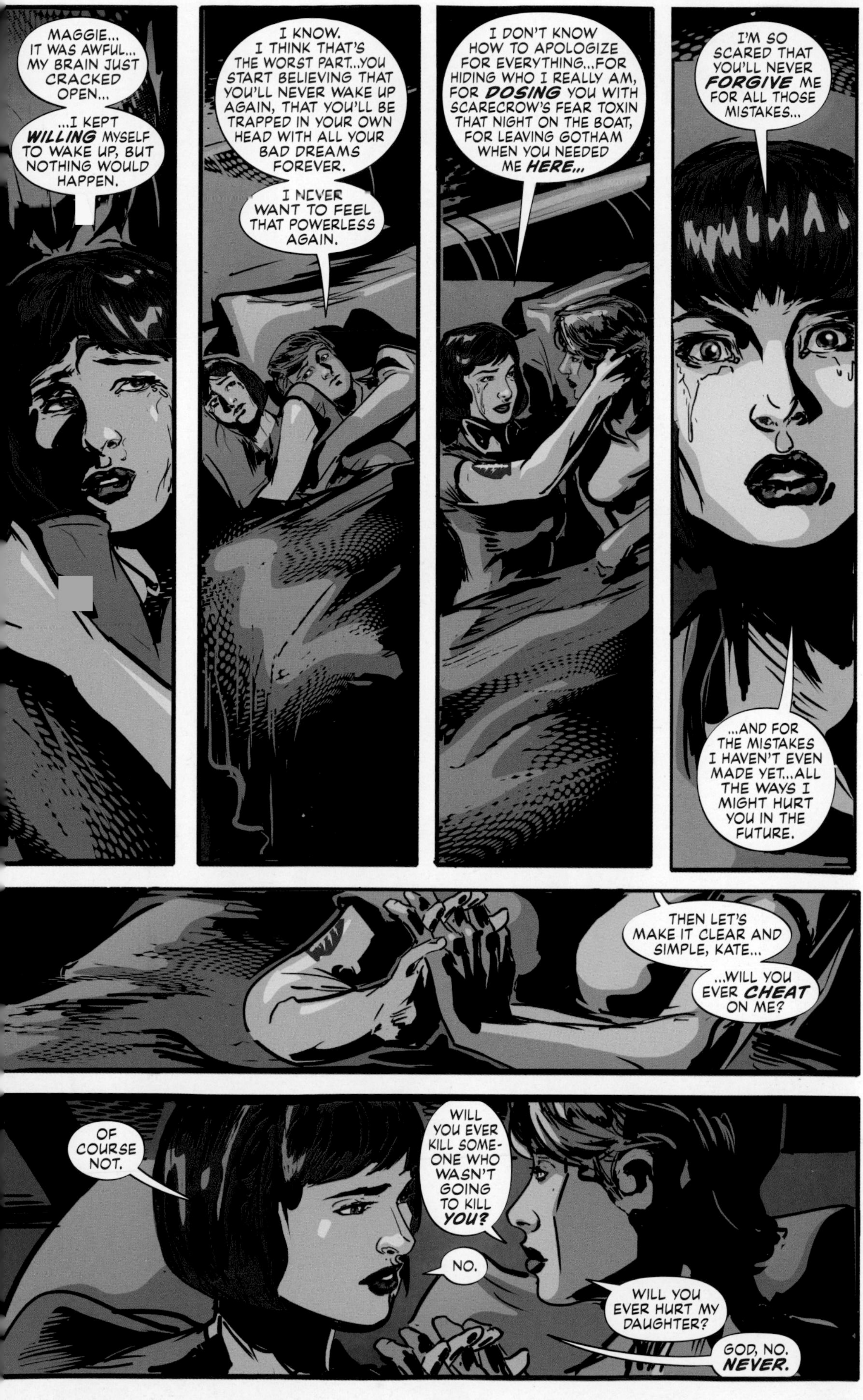
MAGGIE... IT WAS AWFUL... MY BRAIN JUST CRACKED OPEN...
...I KEPT WILLING MYSELF TO WAKE UP, BUT NOTHING WOULD HAPPEN.
I KNOW. I THINK THAT'S THE WORST PART...YOU START BELIEVING THAT YOU'LL NEVER WAKE UP AGAIN, THAT YOU'LL BE TRAPPED IN YOUR OWN HEAD WITH ALL YOUR BAD DREAMS FOREVER.
I NEVER WANT TO FEEL THAT POWERLESS AGAIN.
I DON'T KNOW HOW TO APOLOGIZE FOR EVERYTHING...FOR HIDING WHO I REALLY AM, FOR DOSING YOU WITH SCARECROW'S FEAR TOXIN THAT NIGHT ON THE BOAT, FOR LEAVING GOTHAM WHEN YOU NEEDED ME HERE...
I'M SO SCARED THAT YOU'LL NEVER FORGIVE ME FOR ALL THOSE MISTAKES...
...AND FOR THE MISTAKES I HAVEN'T EVEN MADE YET...ALL THE WAYS I MIGHT HURT YOU IN THE FUTURE.
THEN LET'S MAKE IT CLEAR AND SIMPLE, KATE...
...WILL YOU EVER CHEAT ON ME?
OF COURSE NOT.
WILL YOU EVER KILL SOME-ONE WHO WASN'T GOING TO KILL YOU?
NO.
WILL YOU EVER HURT MY DAUGHTER?
GOD, NO. NEVER.

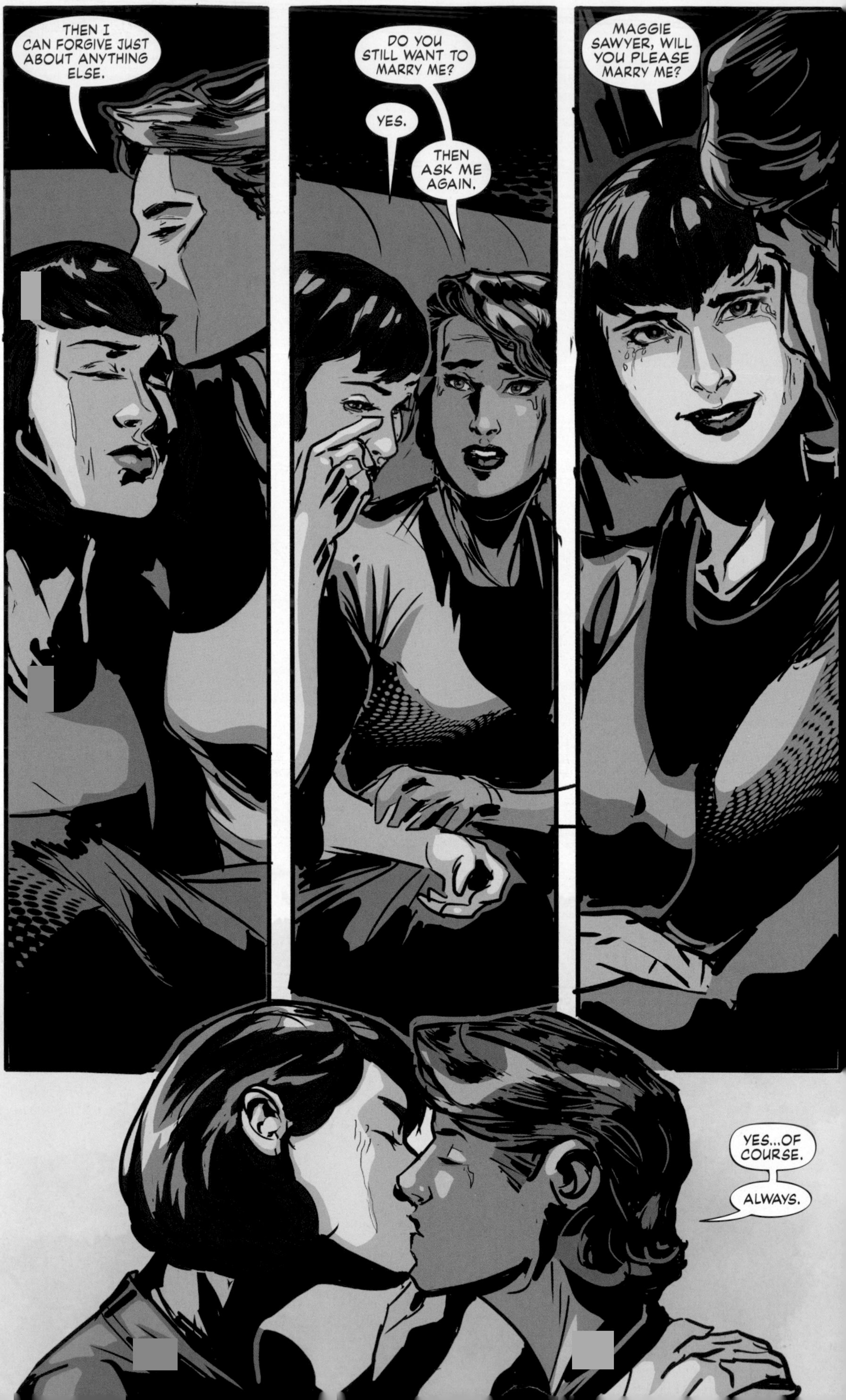
THEN I CAN FORGIVE JUST ABOUT ANYTHING ELSE.
DO YOU STILL WANT TO MARRY ME?
YES.
THEN ASK ME AGAIN.
MAGGIE SAWYER, WILL YOU PLEASE MARRY ME?
YES...OF COURSE.
ALWAYS.

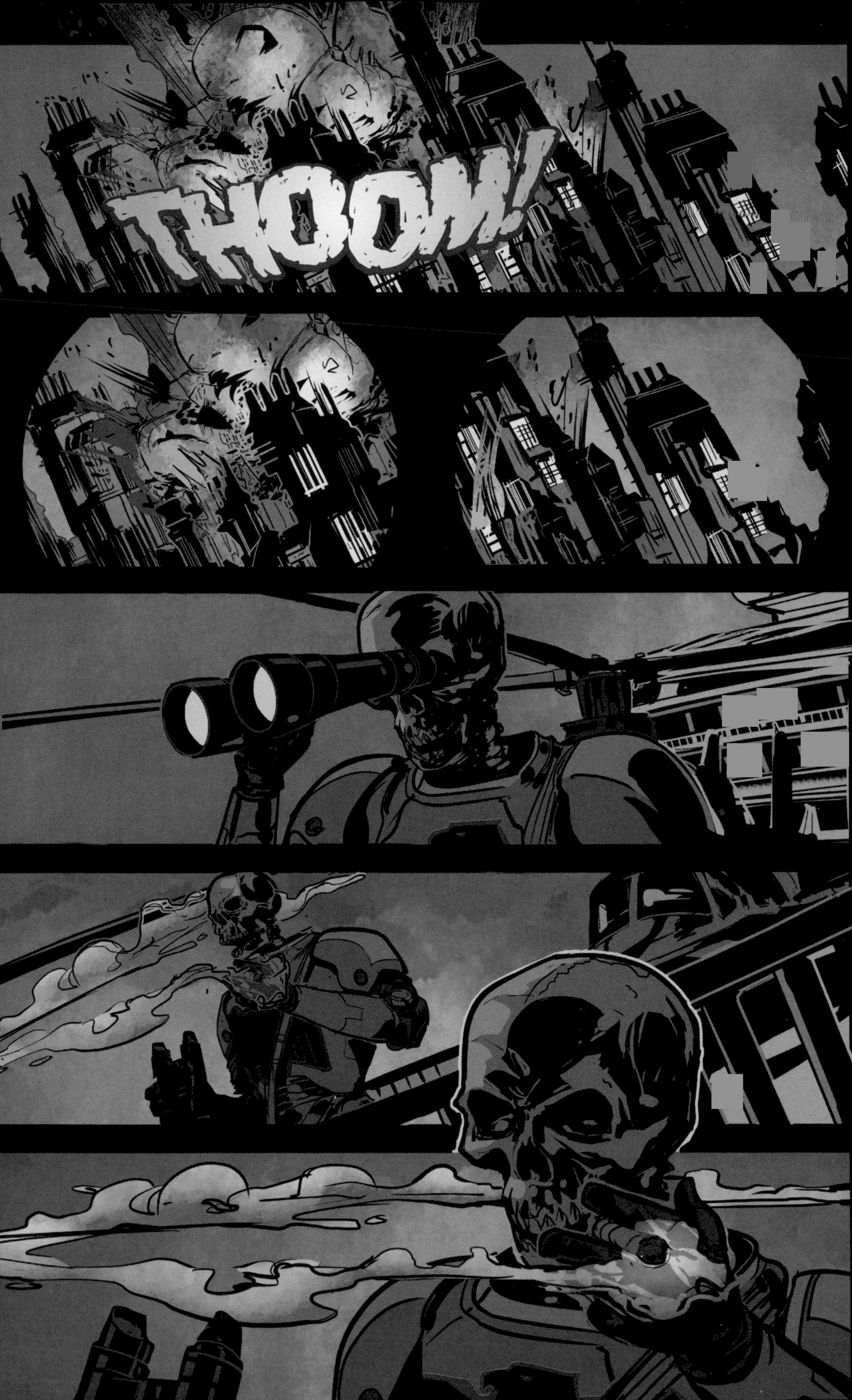
THOOM!

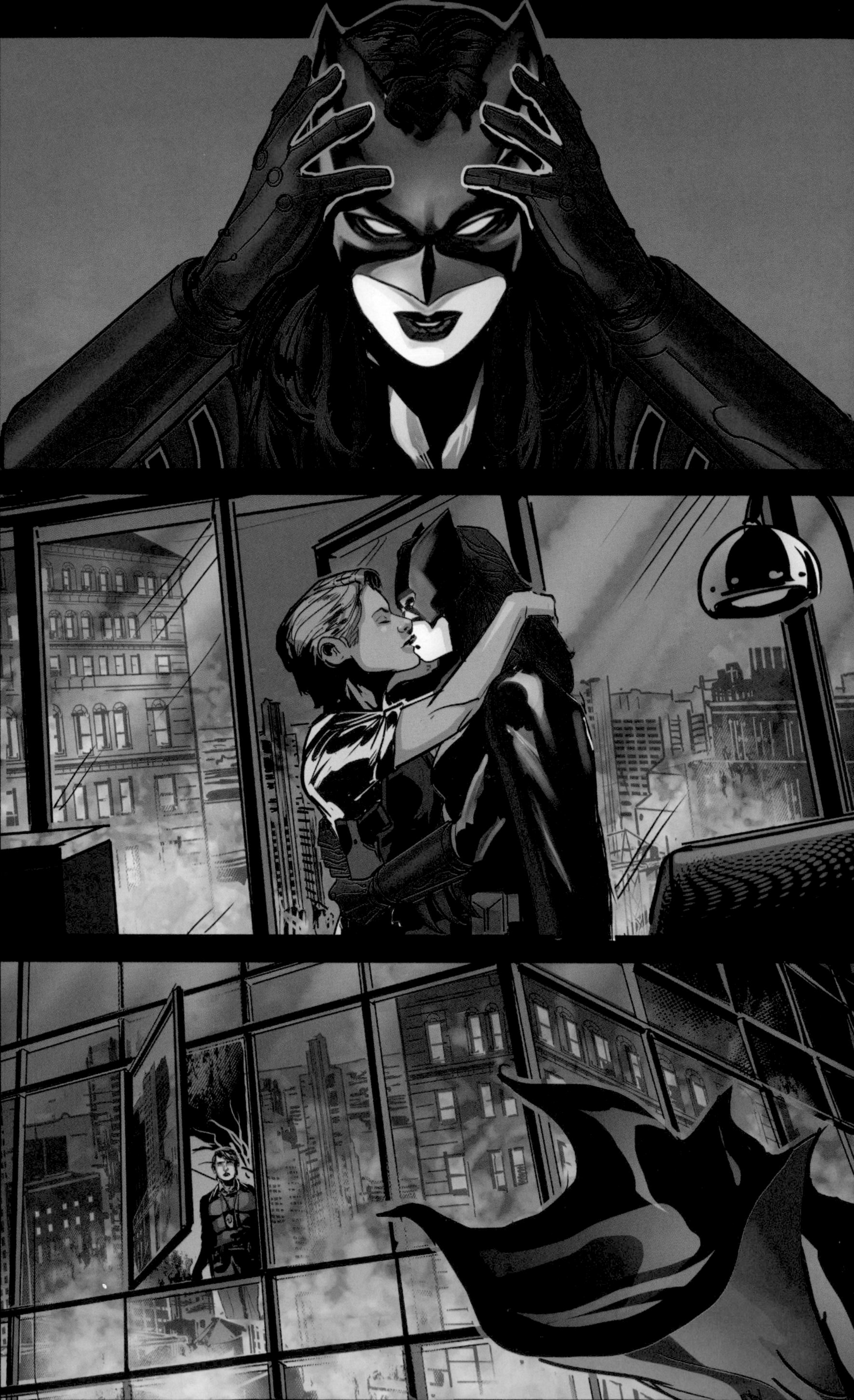

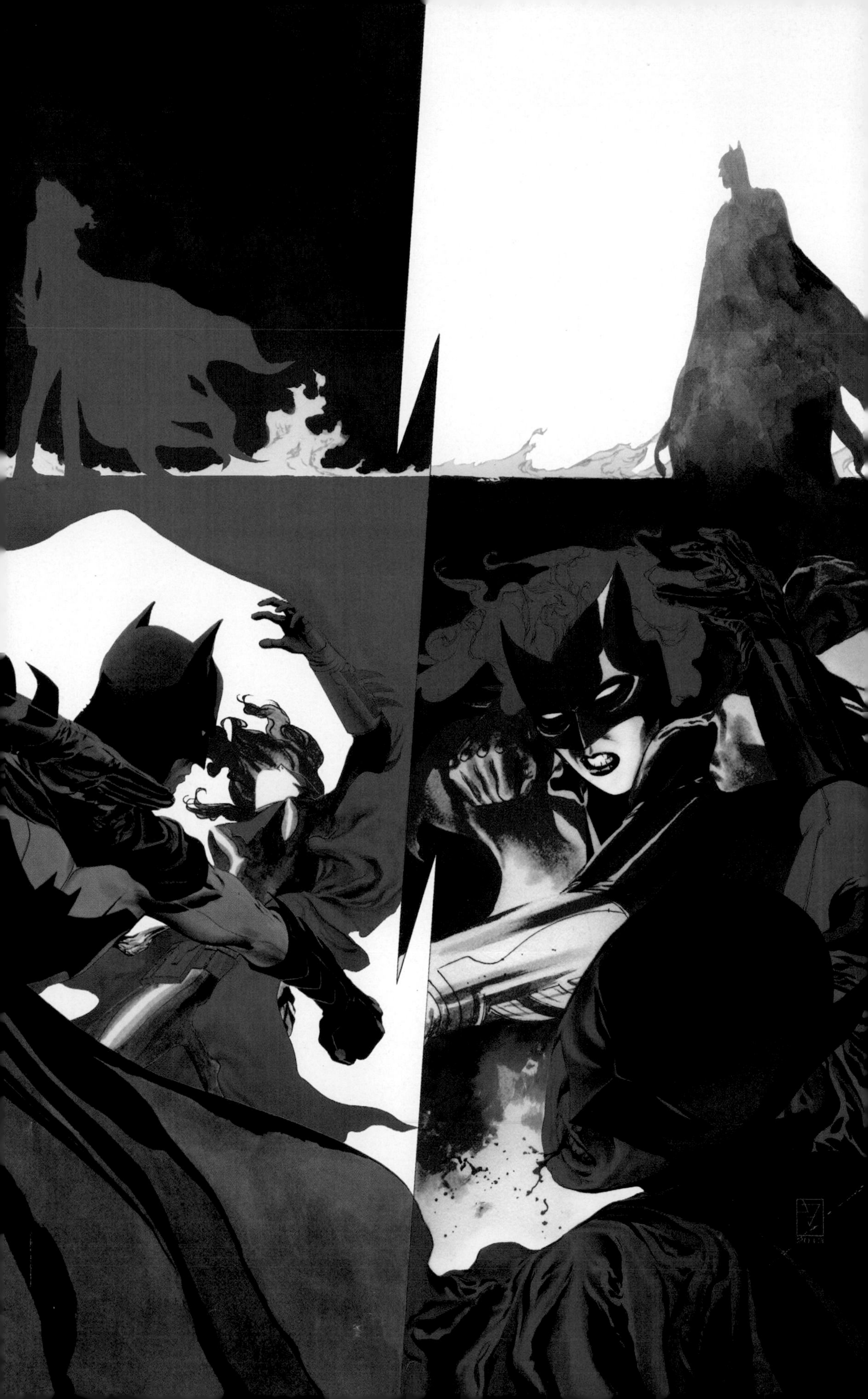

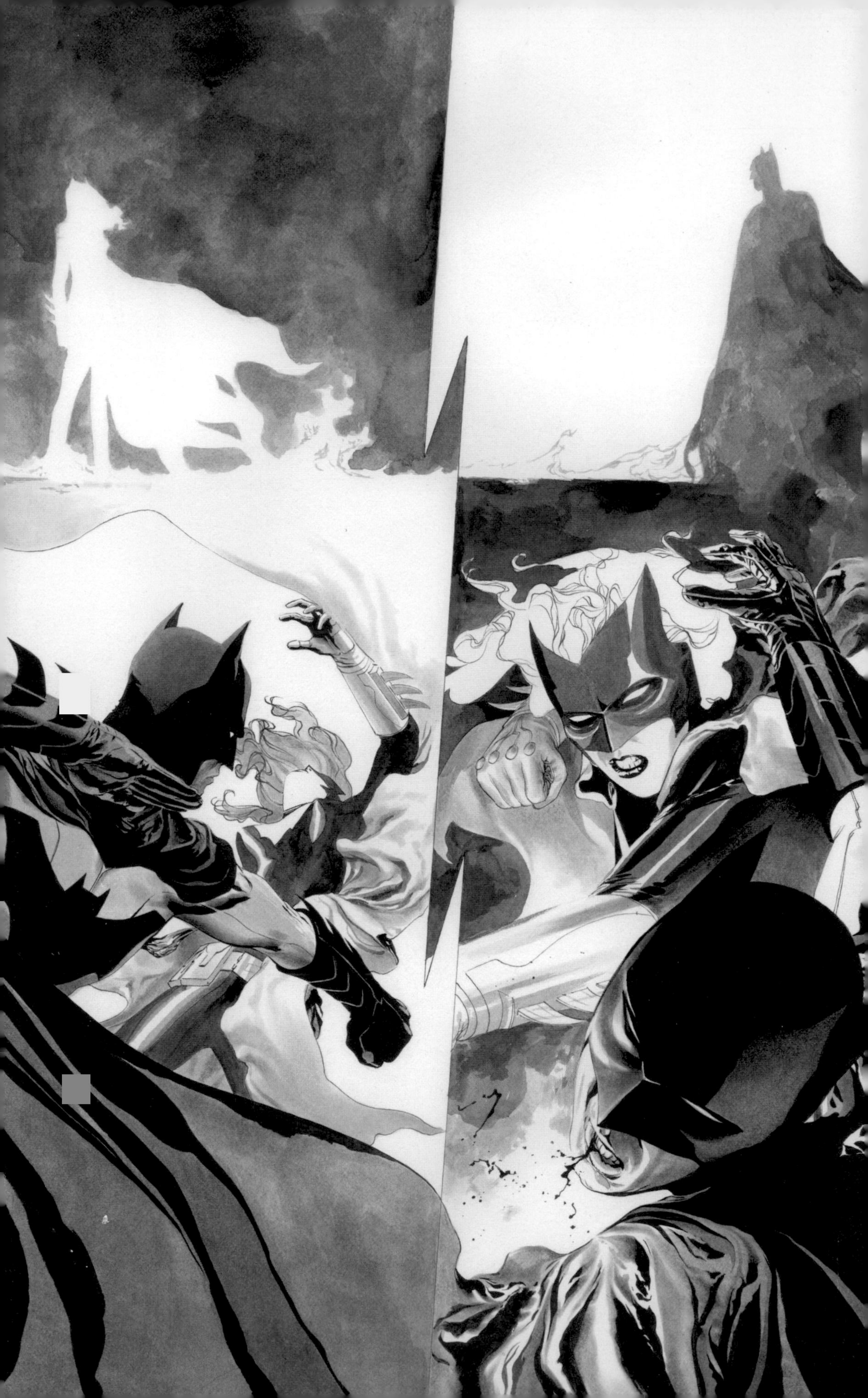

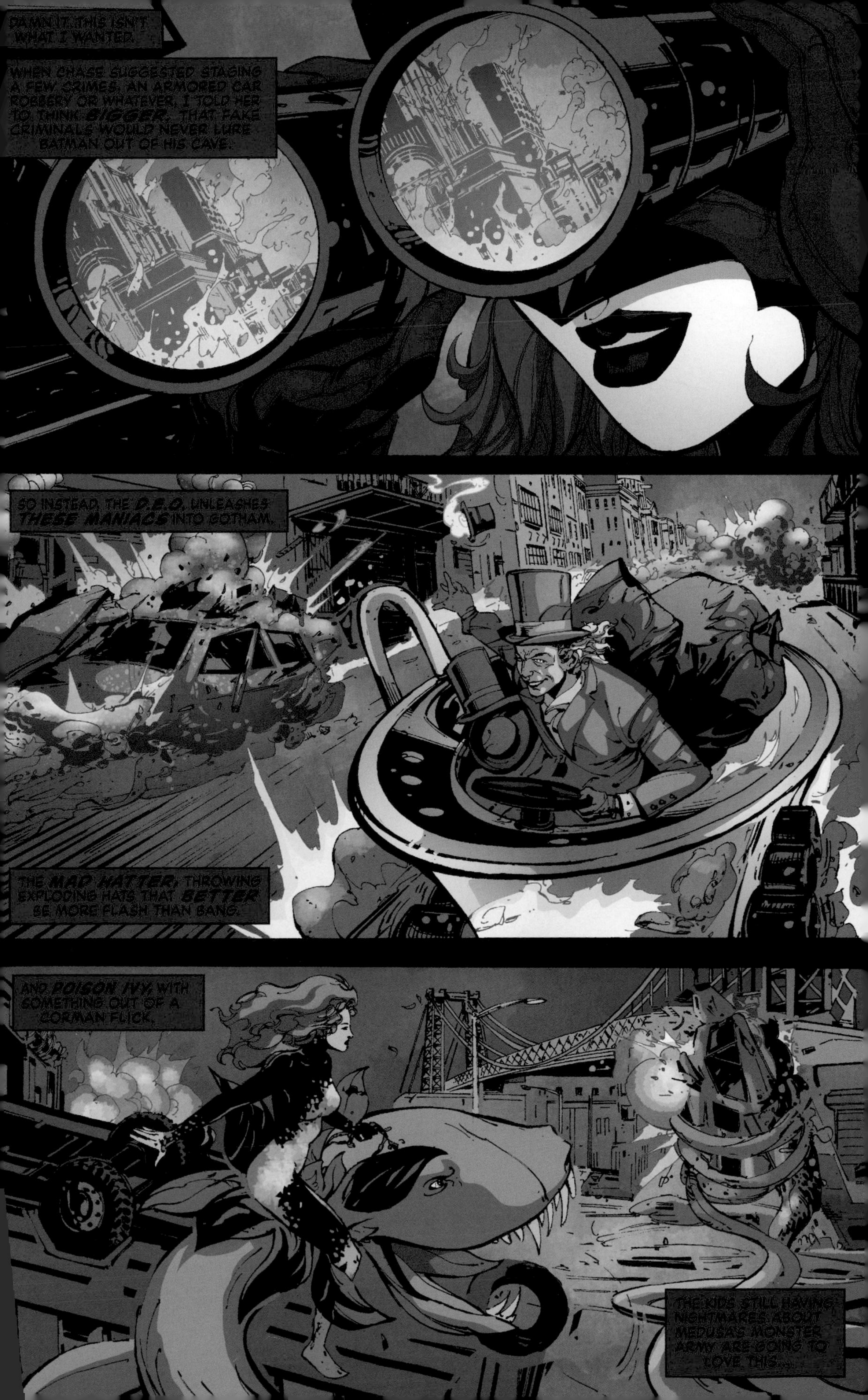
DAMN IT. THIS ISN'T WHAT I WANTED.
WHEN CHASE SUGGESTED STAGING A FEW CRIMES, AN ARMORED CAR ROBBERY OR WHATEVER, I TOLD HER TO THINK BIGGER. THAT FAKE CRIMINALS WOULD NEVER LURE BATMAN OUT OF HIS CAVE.
SO INSTEAD THE D.E.O. UNLEASHES THESE MANIACS INTO GOTHAM.
THE MAD HATTER, THROWING EXPLODING HATS THAT BETTER BE MORE FLASH THAN BANG.
AND POISON IVY, WITH SOMETHING OUT OF A CORMAN FLICK.
THE KIDS STILL HAVING NIGHTMARES ABOUT MEDUSA'S MONSTER ARMY ARE GOING TO LOVE THIS...

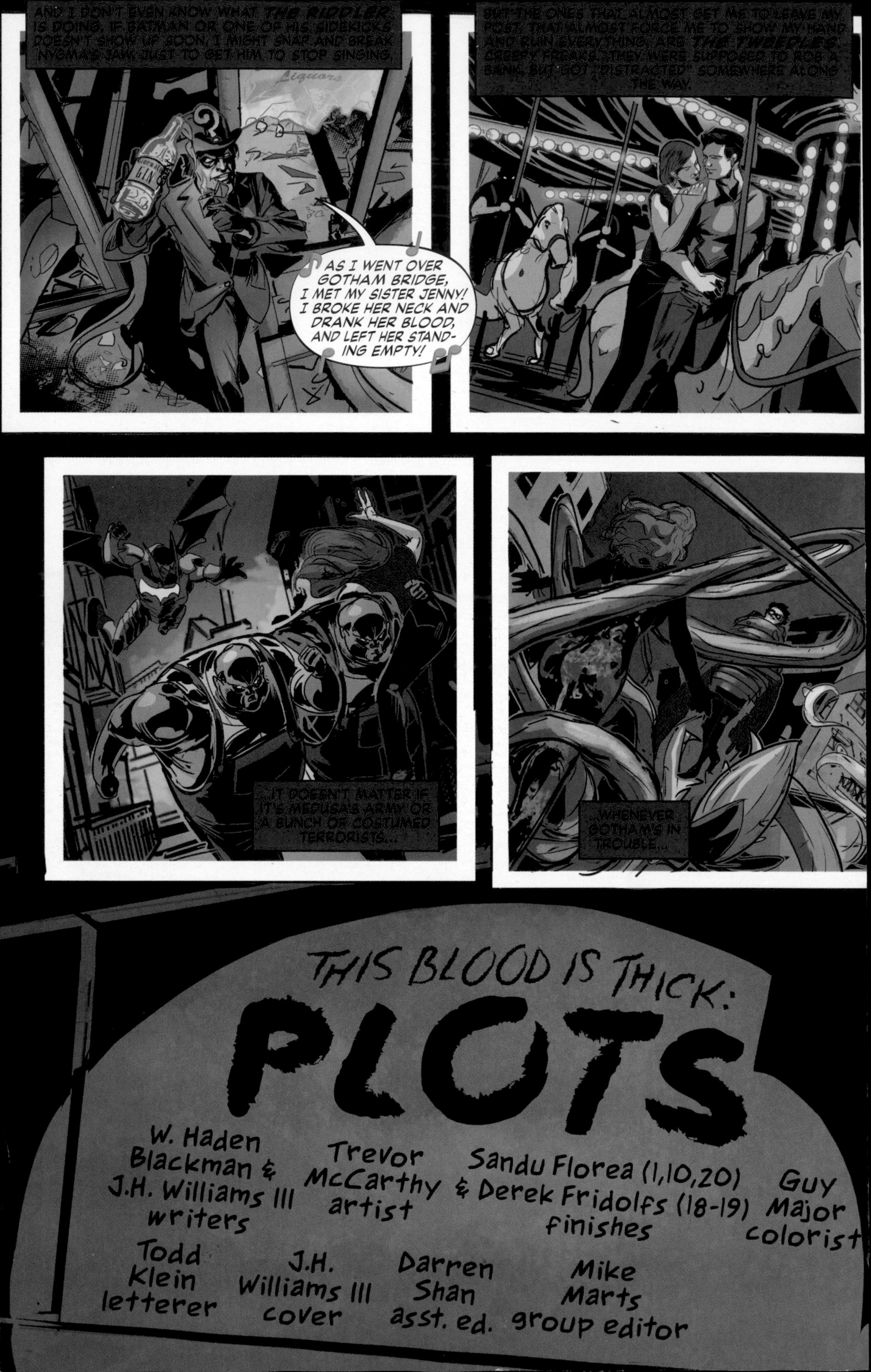

AND I DON'T EVEN KNOW WHAT THE RIDDLER IS DOING. IF BATMAN OR ONE OF HIS SIDEKICKS DOESN'T SHOW UP SOON, I MIGHT SNAP AND BREAK NYGMA'S JAW, JUST TO GET HIM TO STOP SINGING.
Liquors
GIN
AS I WENT OVER GOTHAM BRIDGE, I MET MY SISTER JENNY! I BROKE HER NECK AND DRANK HER BLOOD, AND LEFT HER STANDING EMPTY!
BUT THE ONES THAT ALMOST GET ME TO LEAVE MY POST, THAT ALMOST FORCE ME TO SHOW MY HAND AND RUIN EVERYTHING, ARE THE TWEEDLES. CREEPY FREAKS...THEY WERE SUPPOSED TO ROB A BANK, BUT GOT "DISTRACTED" SOMEWHERE ALONG THE WAY.
...IT DOESN'T MATTER IF IT'S MEDUSA'S ARMY OR A BUNCH OF COSTUMED TERRORISTS...
...WHENEVER GOTHAM'S IN TROUBLE...
THIS BLOOD IS THICK:
PLOTS
W. Haden Blackman & J.H. Williams III writers
Trevor McCarthy artist
Sandu Florea (1,10,20) & Derek Fridolfs (18-19) finishes
Guy Major colorist
Todd Klein letterer
J.H. Williams III cover
Darren Shan asst. ed.
Mike Marts group editor

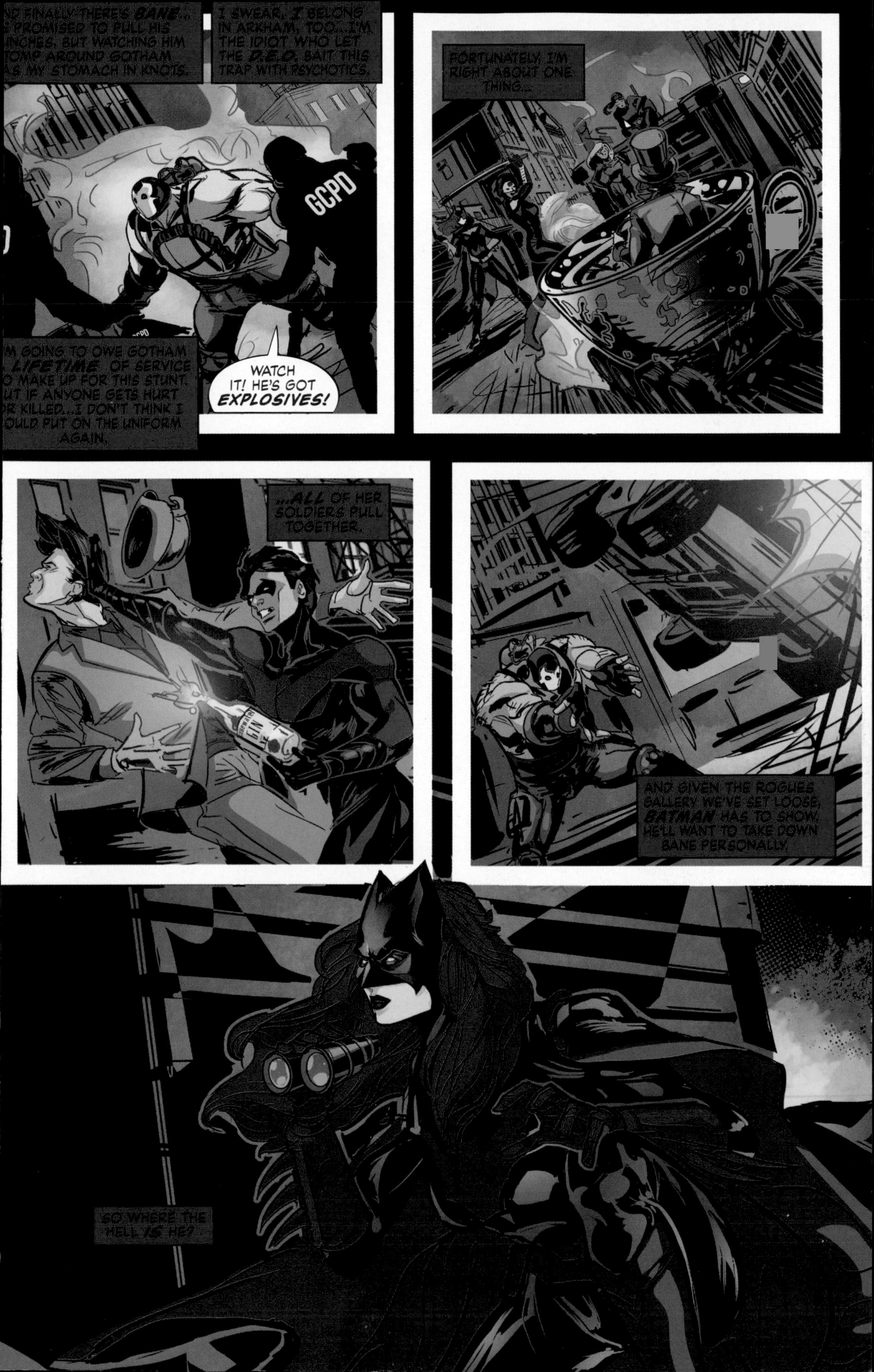
ND FINALLY THERE'S BANE...
E PROMISED TO PULL HIS
UNCHES, BUT WATCHING HIM
TOMP AROUND GOTHAM
AS MY STOMACH IN KNOTS.
I SWEAR, I BELONG IN ARKHAM, TOO...I'M THE IDIOT WHO LET THE D.E.O. BAIT THIS TRAP WITH PSYCHOTICS.
GCPD
M GOING TO OWE GOTHAM
LIFETIME OF SERVICE
O MAKE UP FOR THIS STUNT.
UT IF ANYONE GETS HURT
R KILLED...I DON'T THINK I
OULD PUT ON THE UNIFORM
AGAIN.
WATCH IT! HE'S GOT EXPLOSIVES!
FORTUNATELY, I'M RIGHT ABOUT ONE THING...
...ALL OF HER SOLDIERS PULL TOGETHER.
AND GIVEN THE ROGUES GALLERY WE'VE SET LOOSE, BATMAN HAS TO SHOW. HE'LL WANT TO TAKE DOWN BANE PERSONALLY.
SO WHERE THE HELL IS HE?

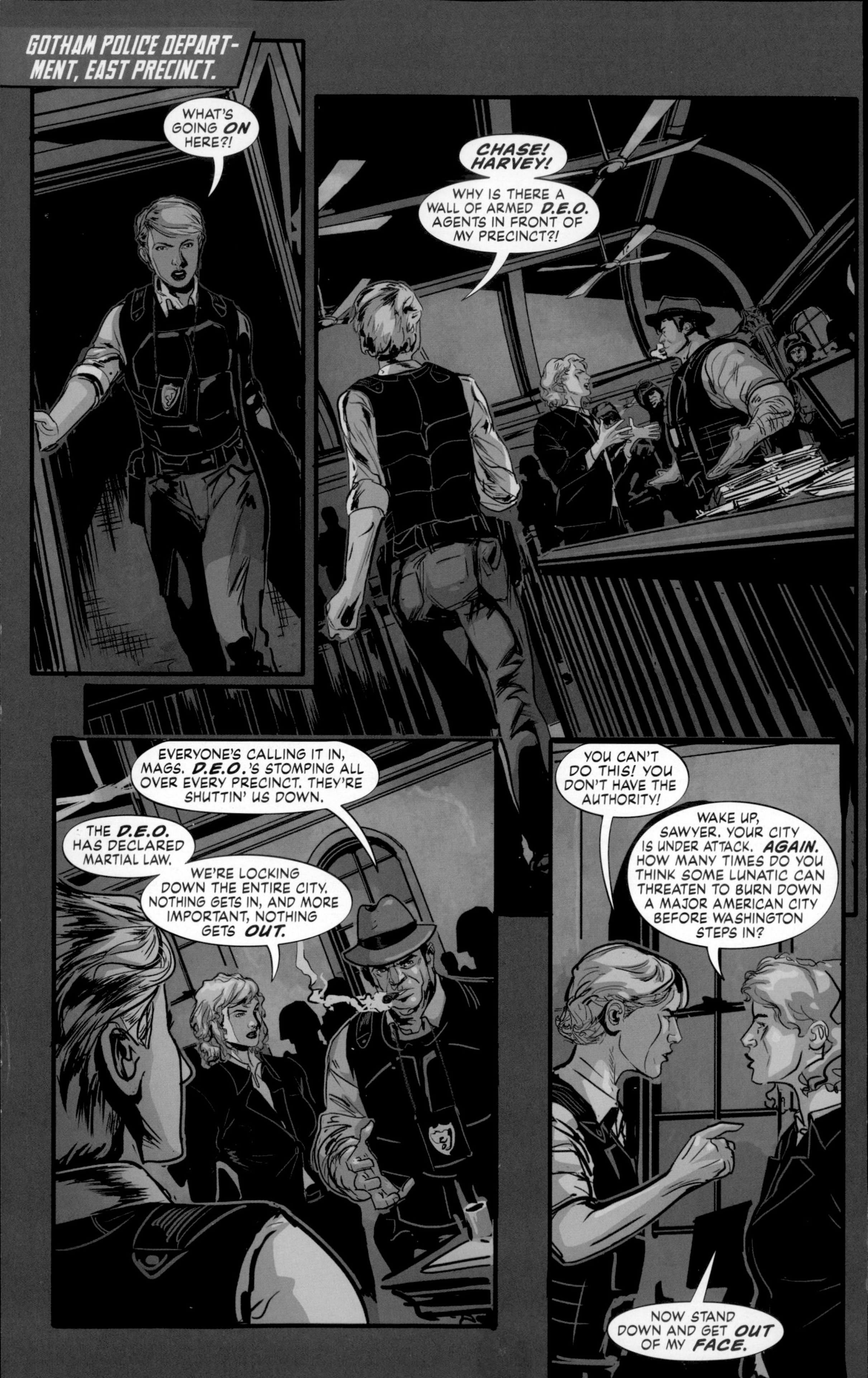

GOTHAM POLICE DEPARTMENT, EAST PRECINCT.
WHAT'S GOING ON HERE?!
CHASE! HARVEY!
WHY IS THERE A WALL OF ARMED D.E.O. AGENTS IN FRONT OF MY PRECINCT?!
EVERYONE'S CALLING IT IN, MAGS. D.E.O.'S STOMPING ALL OVER EVERY PRECINCT. THEY'RE SHUTTIN' US DOWN.
THE D.E.O. HAS DECLARED MARTIAL LAW.
WE'RE LOCKING DOWN THE ENTIRE CITY. NOTHING GETS IN, AND MORE IMPORTANT, NOTHING GETS OUT.
YOU CAN'T DO THIS! YOU DON'T HAVE THE AUTHORITY!
WAKE UP, SAWYER. YOUR CITY IS UNDER ATTACK. AGAIN. HOW MANY TIMES DO YOU THINK SOME LUNATIC CAN THREATEN TO BURN DOWN A MAJOR AMERICAN CITY BEFORE WASHINGTON STEPS IN?
NOW STAND DOWN AND GET OUT OF MY FACE.

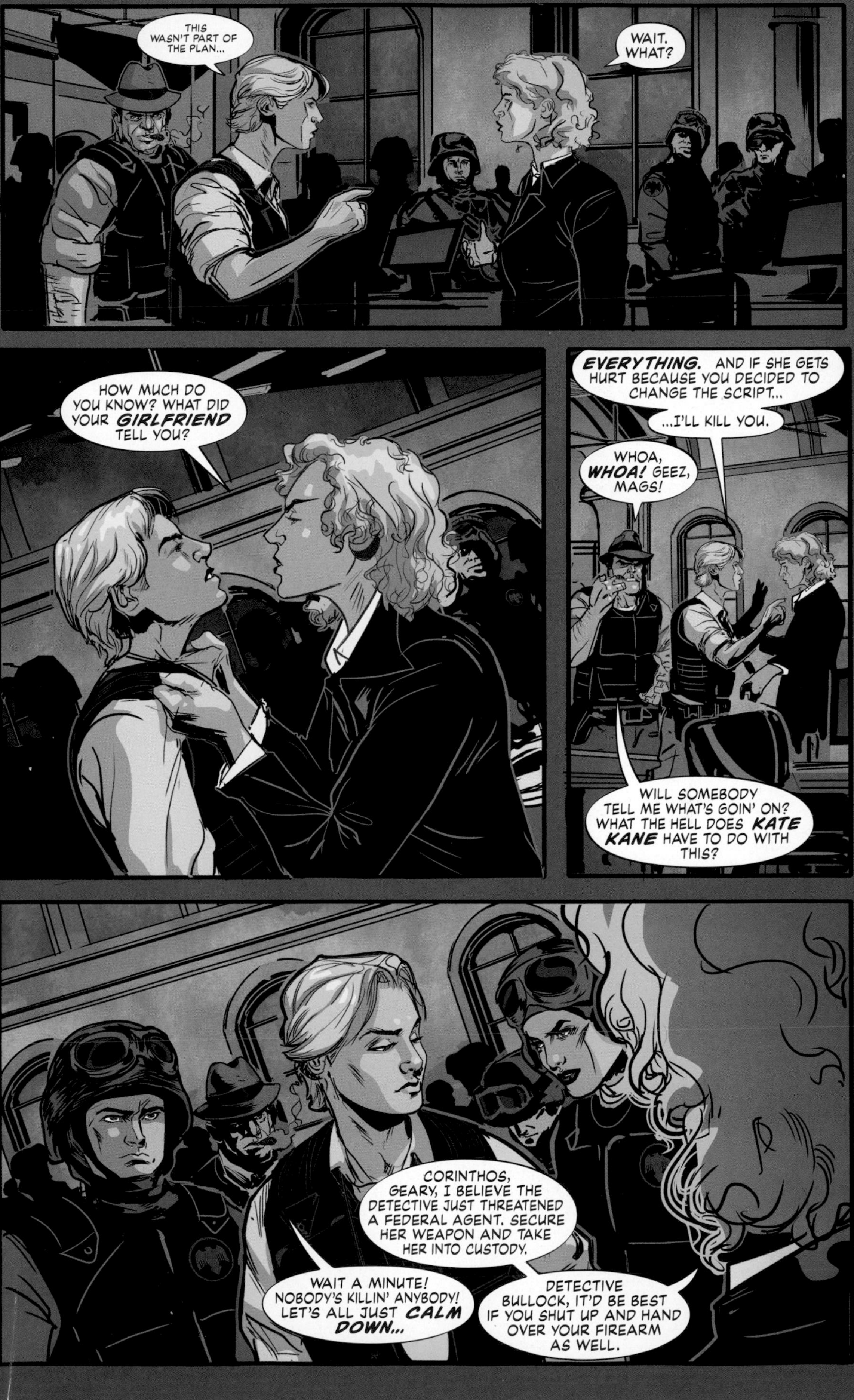
THIS WASN'T PART OF THE PLAN...
WAIT. WHAT?
HOW MUCH DO YOU KNOW? WHAT DID YOUR GIRLFRIEND TELL YOU?
EVERYTHING. AND IF SHE GETS HURT BECAUSE YOU DECIDED TO CHANGE THE SCRIPT...
...I'LL KILL YOU.
WHOA, WHOA! GEEZ, MAGS!
WILL SOMEBODY TELL ME WHAT'S GOIN' ON? WHAT THE HELL DOES KATE KANE HAVE TO DO WITH THIS?
CORINTHOS, GEARY, I BELIEVE THE DETECTIVE JUST THREATENED A FEDERAL AGENT. SECURE HER WEAPON AND TAKE HER INTO CUSTODY.
WAIT A MINUTE! NOBODY'S KILLIN' ANYBODY! LET'S ALL JUST CALM DOWN...
DETECTIVE BULLOCK, IT'D BE BEST IF YOU SHUT UP AND HAND OVER YOUR FIREARM AS WELL.

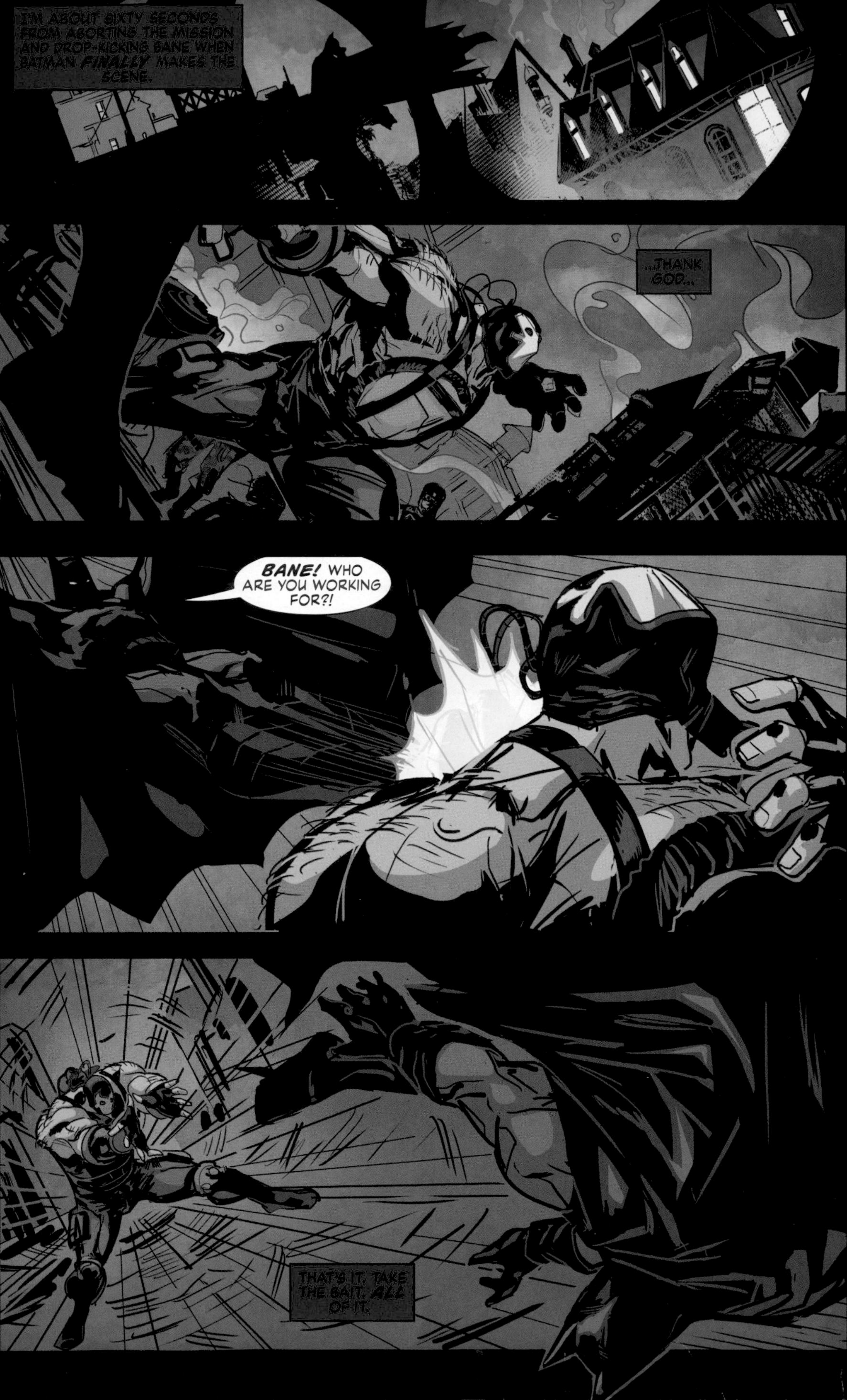
I'M ABOUT SIXTY SECONDS FROM ABORTING THE MISSION AND DROP-KICKING BANE WHEN BATMAN *FINALLY* MAKES THE SCENE.
...THANK GOD...
BANE! WHO ARE YOU WORKING FOR?!
THAT'S IT. TAKE THE BAIT. *ALL* OF IT.

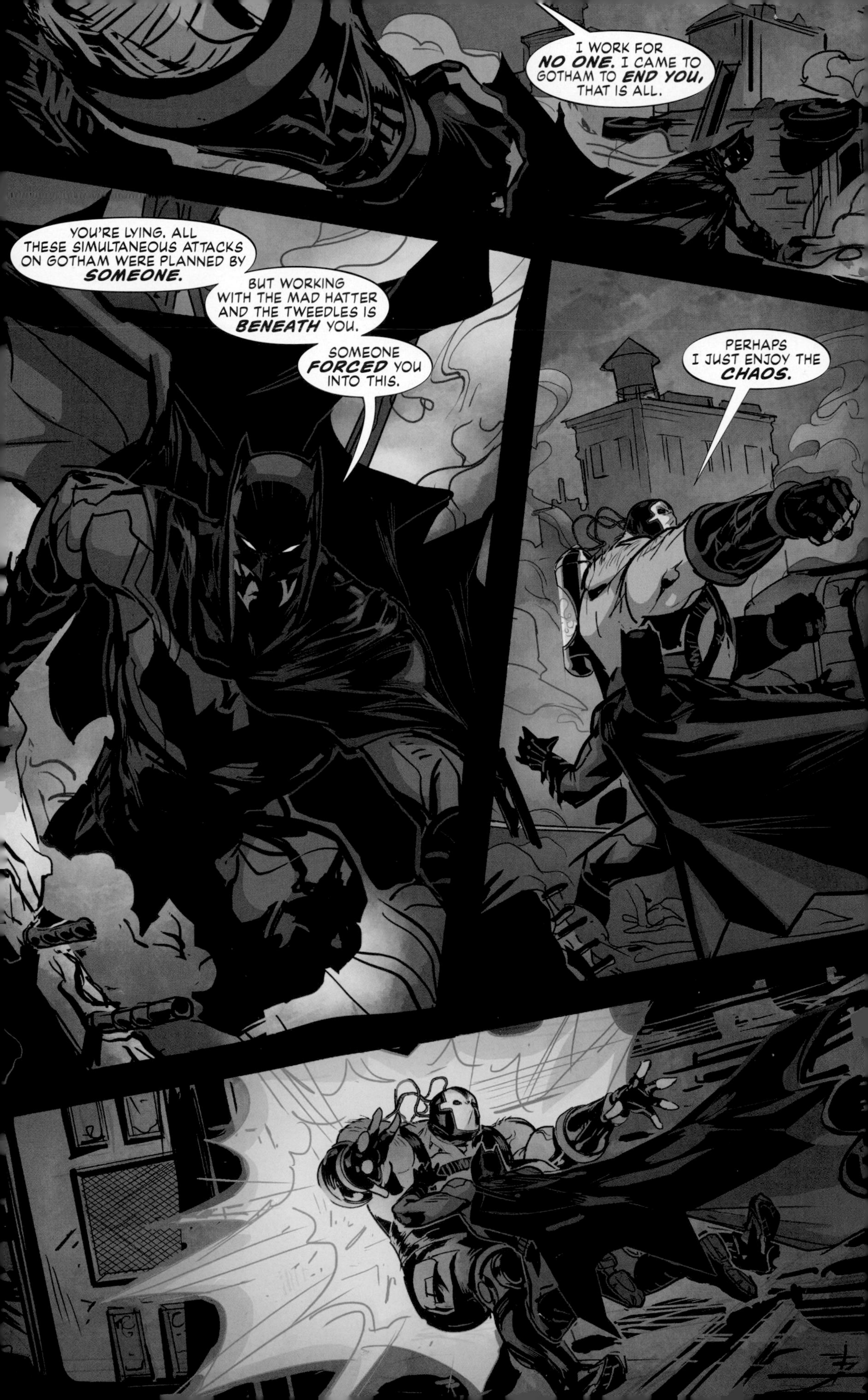
I WORK FOR NO ONE. I CAME TO GOTHAM TO END YOU, THAT IS ALL.
YOU'RE LYING. ALL THESE SIMULTANEOUS ATTACKS ON GOTHAM WERE PLANNED BY SOMEONE.
BUT WORKING WITH THE MAD HATTER AND THE TWEEDLES IS BENEATH YOU.
SOMEONE FORCED YOU INTO THIS.
PERHAPS I JUST ENJOY THE CHAOS.

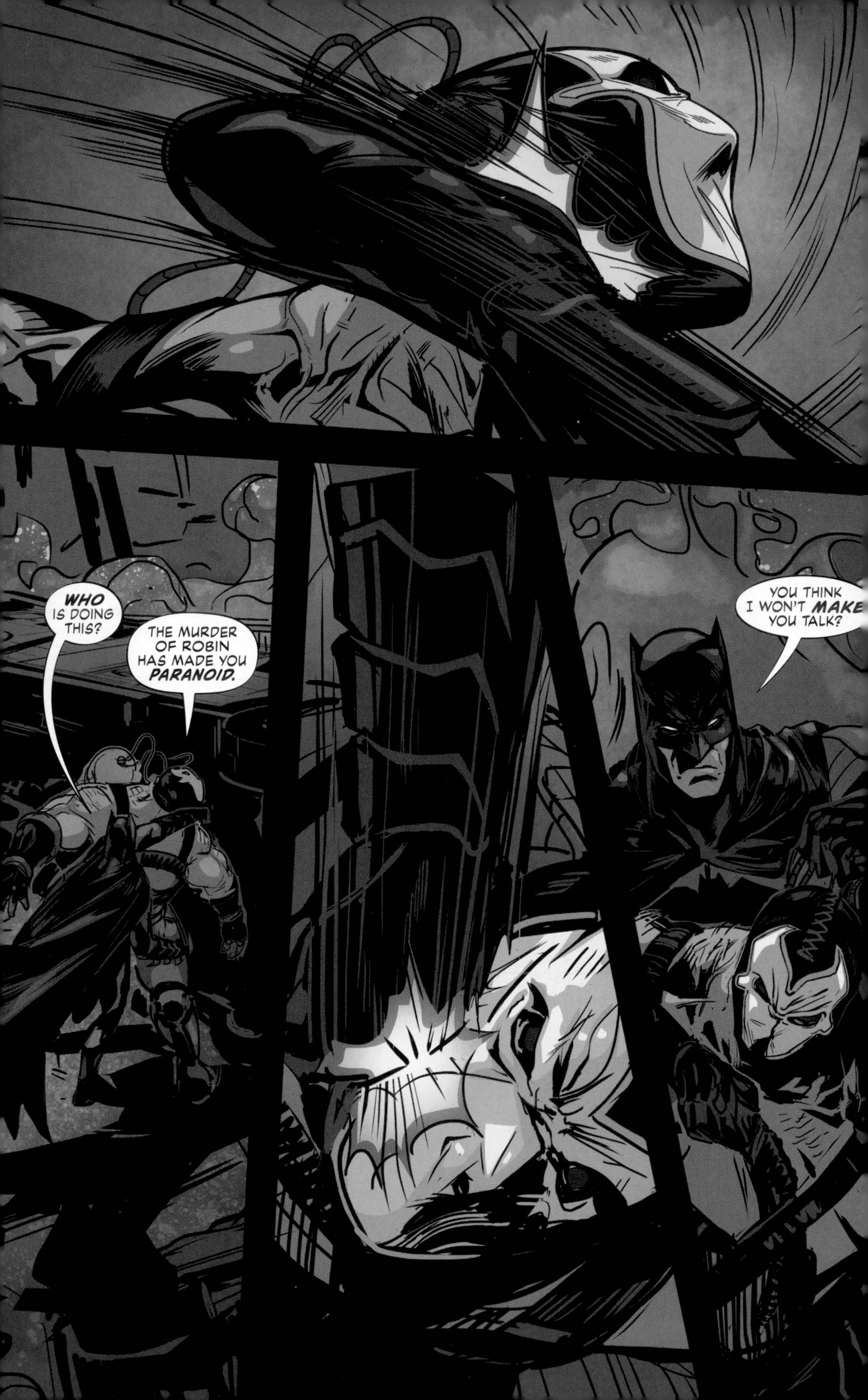
WHO IS DOING THIS?
THE MURDER OF ROBIN HAS MADE YOU PARANOID.
YOU THINK I WON'T MAKE YOU TALK?

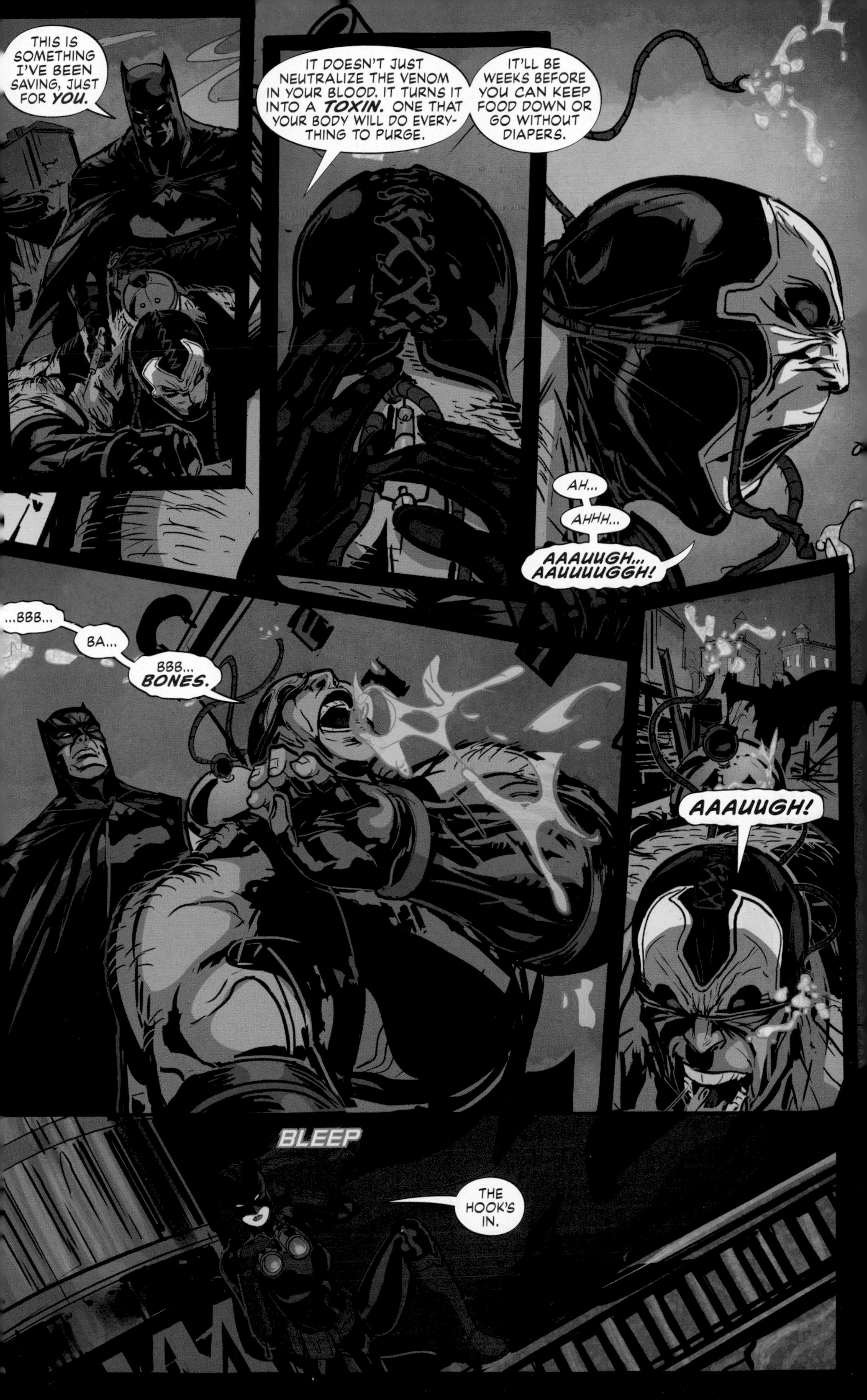
THIS IS SOMETHING I'VE BEEN SAVING, JUST FOR YOU.
IT DOESN'T JUST NEUTRALIZE THE VENOM IN YOUR BLOOD. IT TURNS IT INTO A TOXIN. ONE THAT YOUR BODY WILL DO EVERYTHING TO PURGE.
IT'LL BE WEEKS BEFORE YOU CAN KEEP FOOD DOWN OR GO WITHOUT DIAPERS.
AH...
AHHH...
AAAUUGH... AAUUUUGGH!
...BBB...
BA...
BBB... BONES.
AAAUUGH!
BLEEP
THE HOOK'S IN.

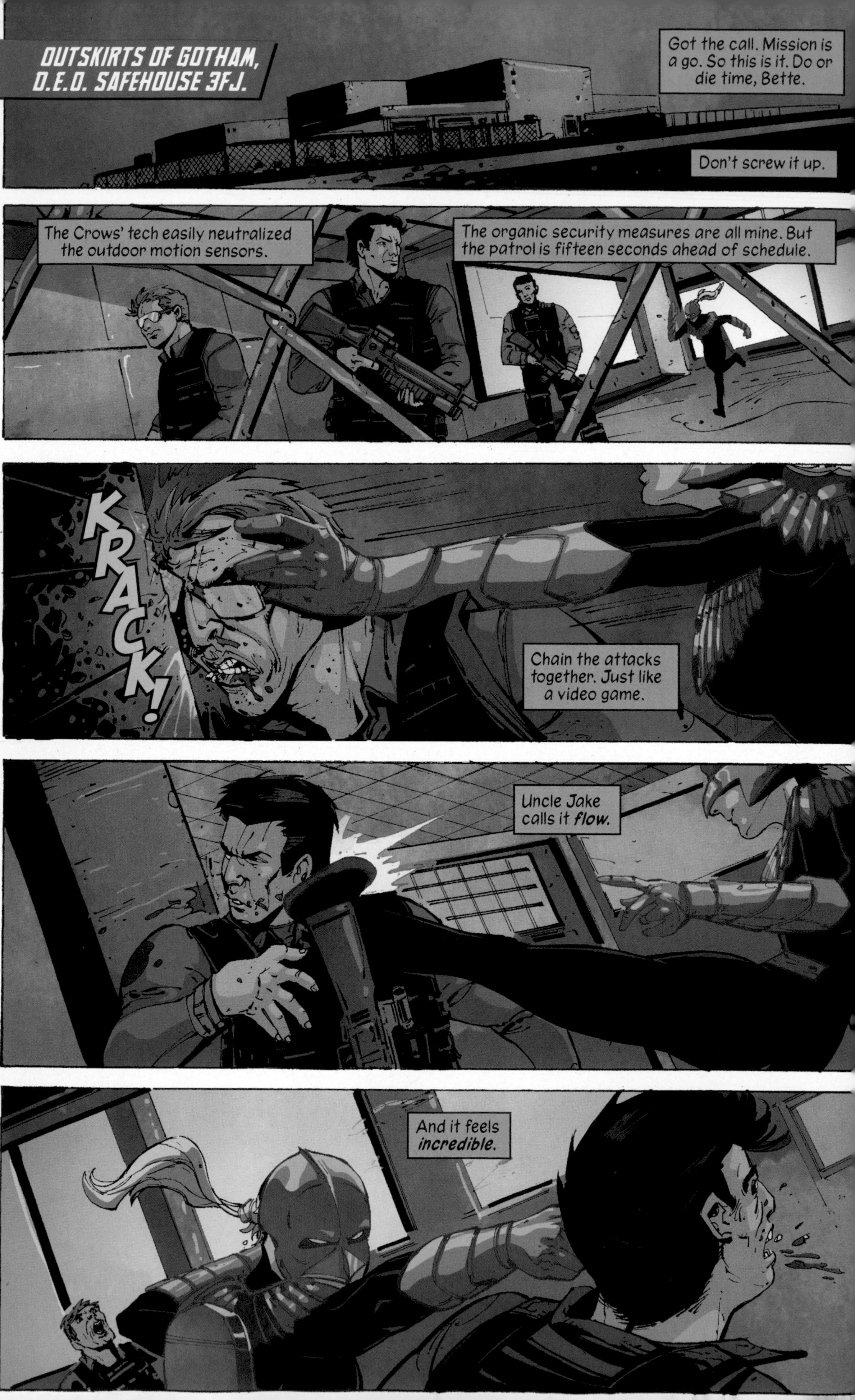
OUTSKIRTS OF GOTHAM, D.E.O. SAFEHOUSE 3FJ.
Got the call. Mission is a go. So this is it. Do or die time, Bette.
Don't screw it up.
The Crows' tech easily neutralized the outdoor motion sensors.
The organic security measures are all mine. But the patrol is fifteen seconds ahead of schedule.
KRACK!
Chain the attacks together. Just like a video game.
Uncle Jake calls it *flow.*
And it feels *incredible.*

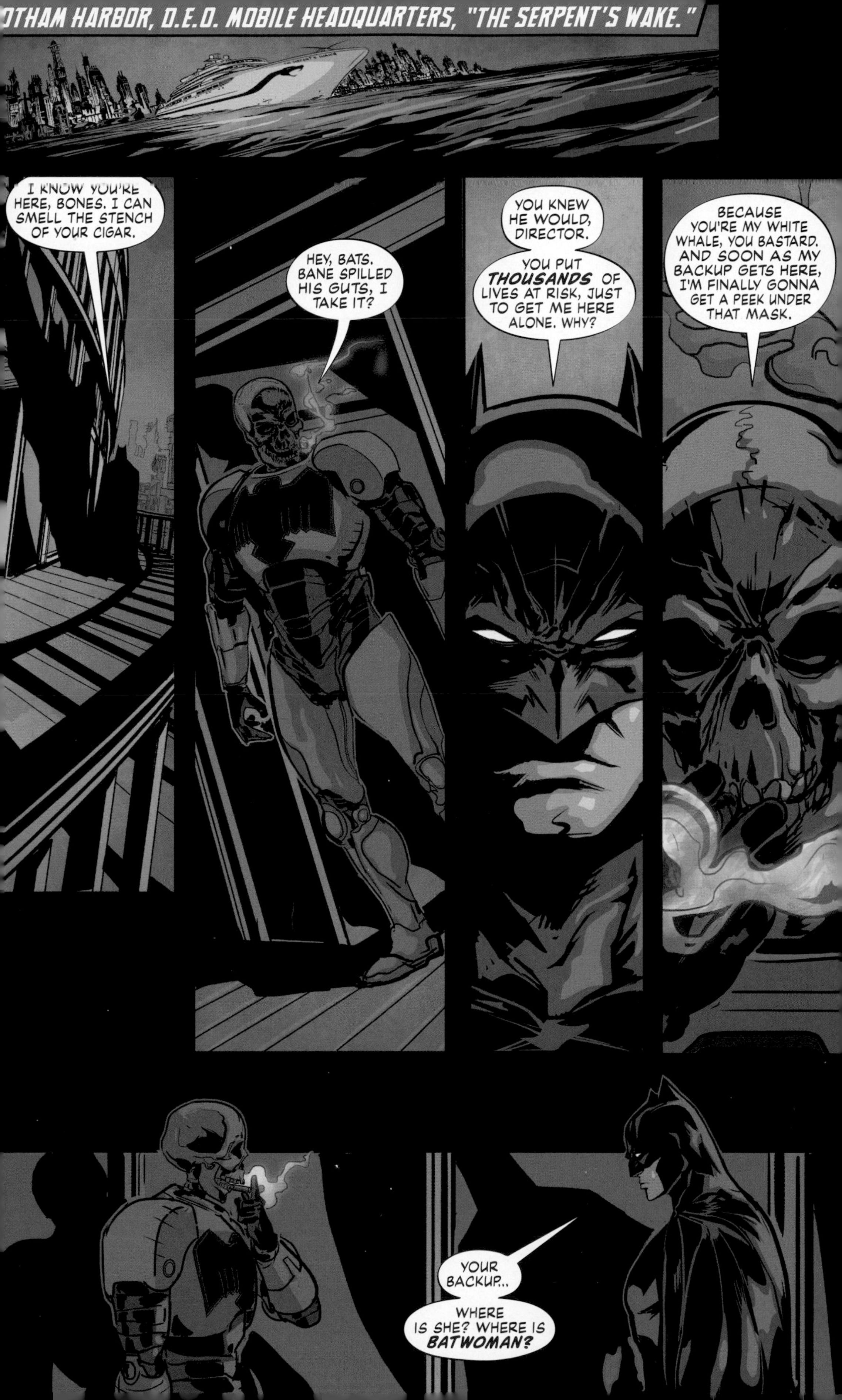
OTHAM HARBOR, D.E.O. MOBILE HEADQUARTERS, "THE SERPENT'S WAKE."
I KNOW YOU'RE HERE, BONES. I CAN SMELL THE STENCH OF YOUR CIGAR.
HEY, BATS. BANE SPILLED HIS GUTS, I TAKE IT?
YOU KNEW HE WOULD, DIRECTOR.
YOU PUT THOUSANDS OF LIVES AT RISK, JUST TO GET ME HERE ALONE. WHY?
BECAUSE YOU'RE MY WHITE WHALE, YOU BASTARD. AND SOON AS MY BACKUP GETS HERE, I'M FINALLY GONNA GET A PEEK UNDER THAT MASK.
YOUR BACKUP..
WHERE IS SHE? WHERE IS BATWOMAN?

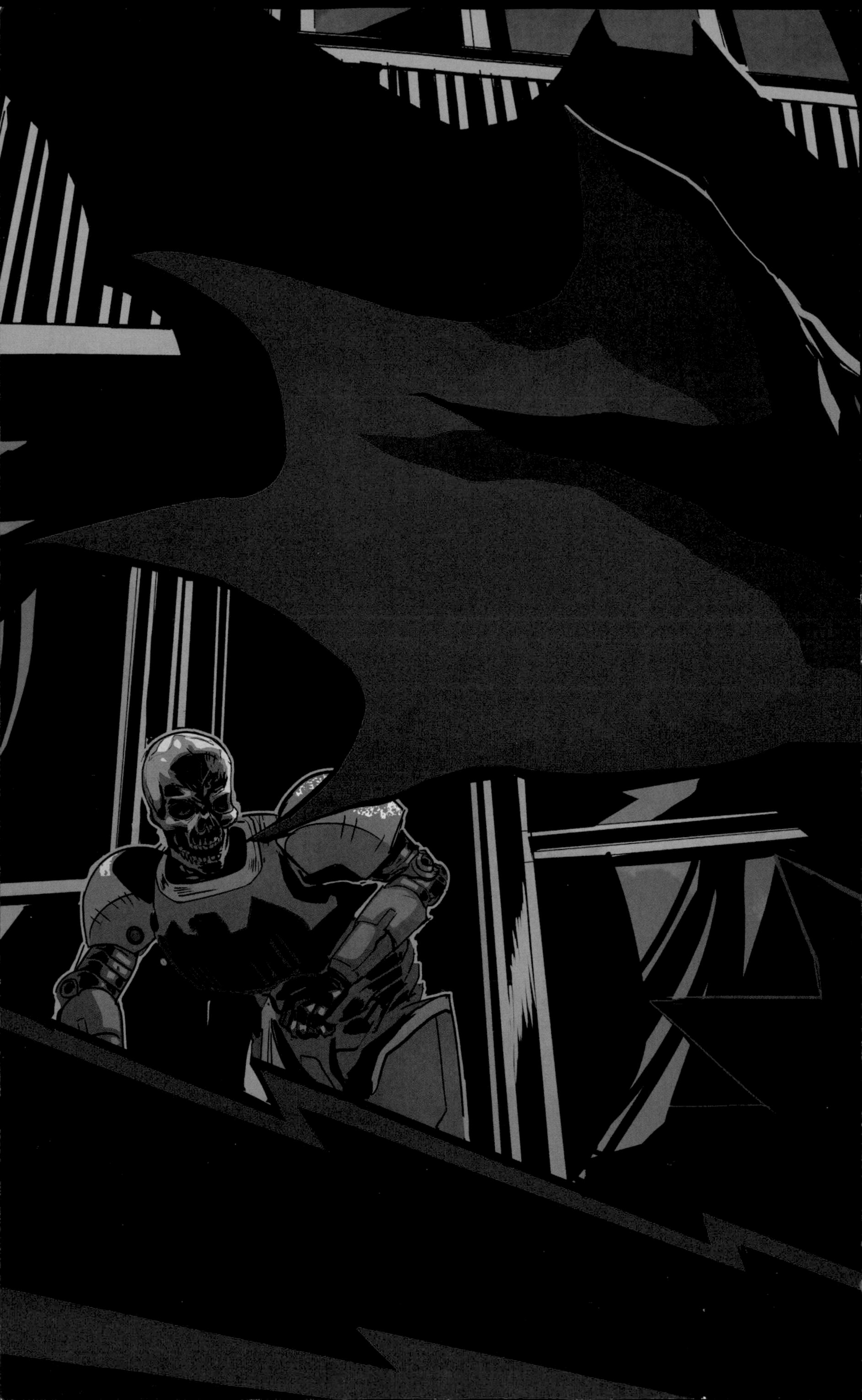

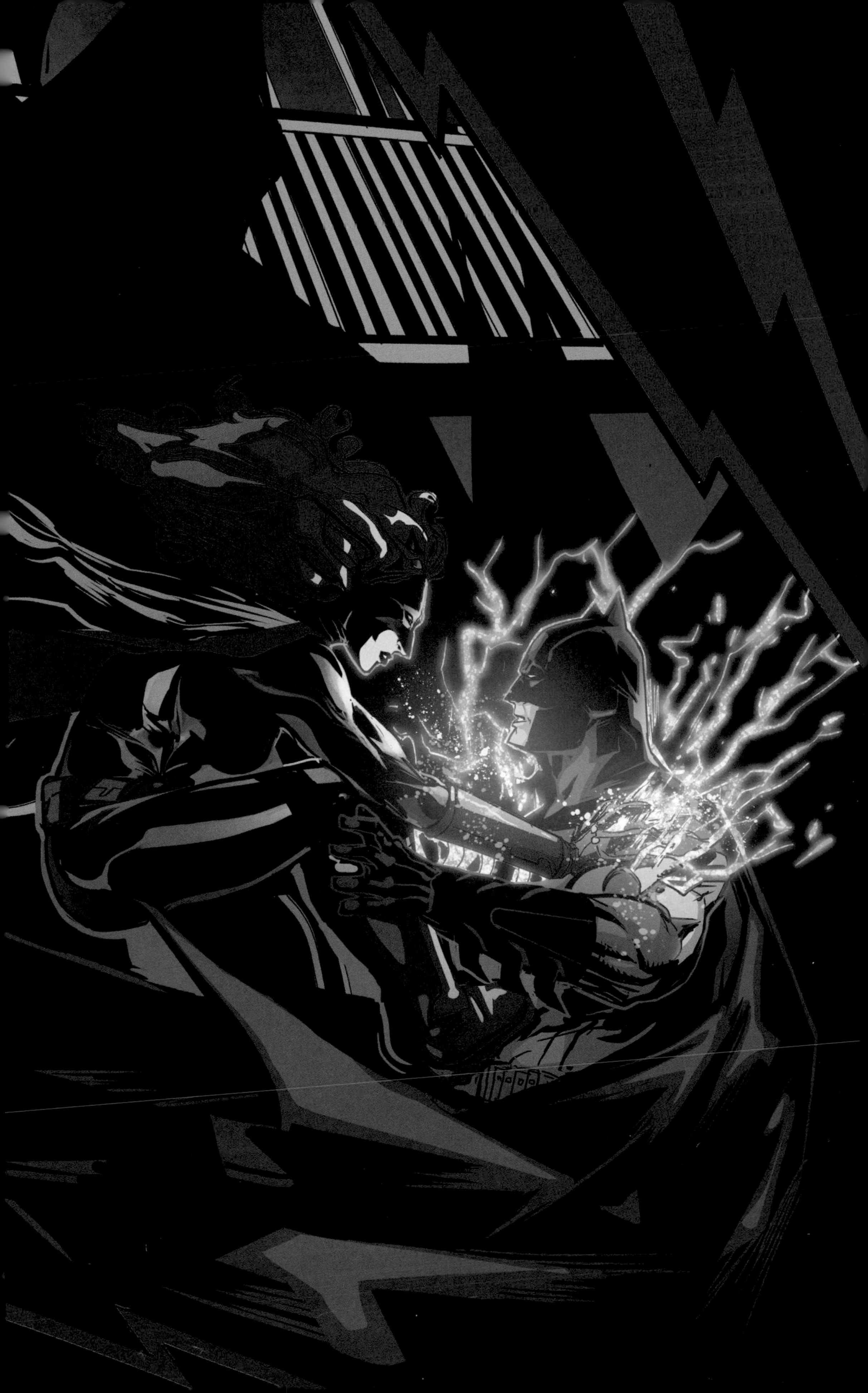

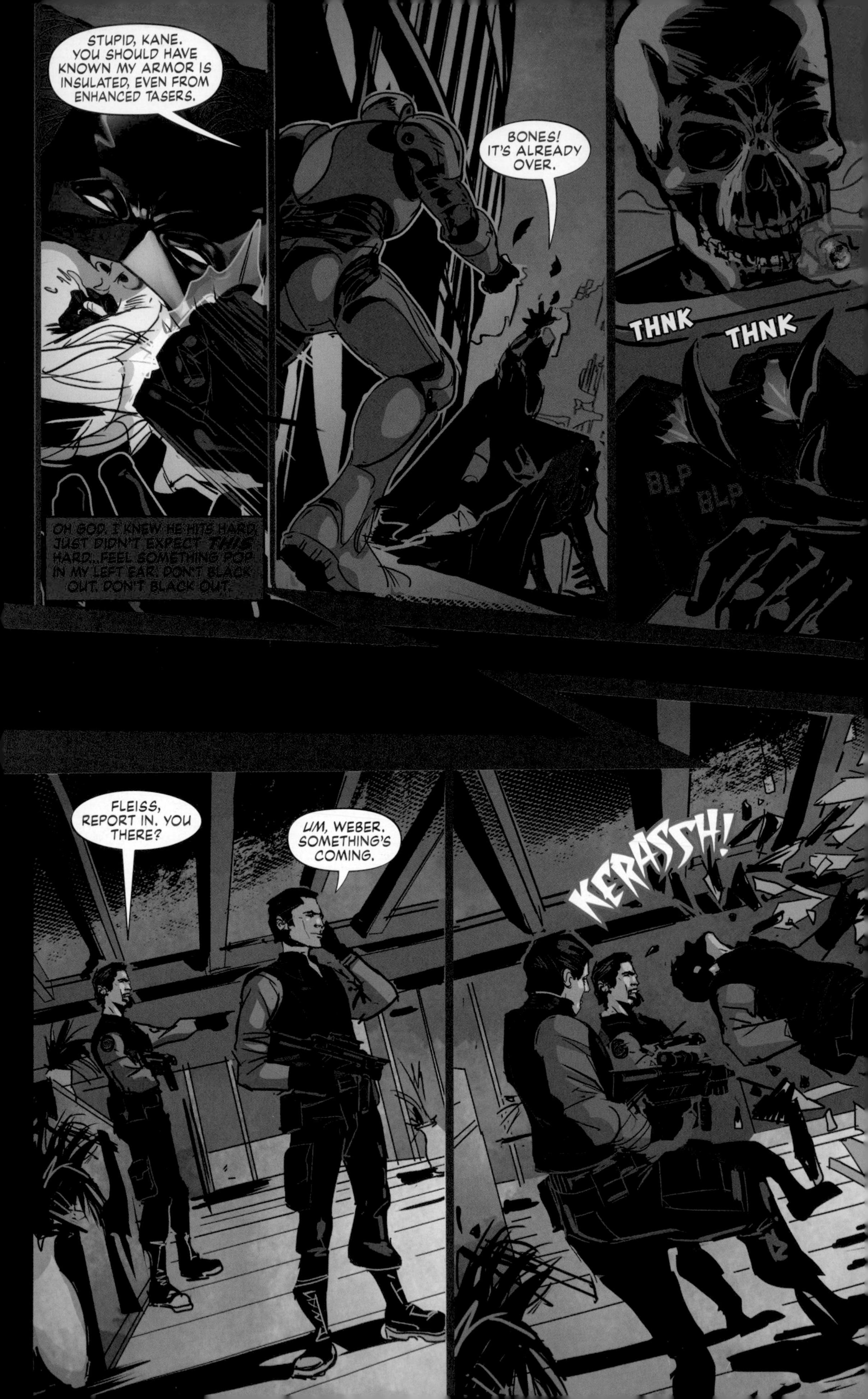
STUPID, KANE. YOU SHOULD HAVE KNOWN MY ARMOR IS INSULATED, EVEN FROM ENHANCED TASERS.
OH GOD. I KNEW HE HITS HARD. JUST DIDN'T EXPECT THIS HARD...FEEL SOMETHING POP IN MY LEFT EAR. DON'T BLACK OUT. DON'T BLACK OUT.
BONES! IT'S ALREADY OVER.
THNK
THNK
BLP
BLP
FLEISS, REPORT IN. YOU THERE?
UM, WEBER. SOMETHING'S COMING.
KERASSH!

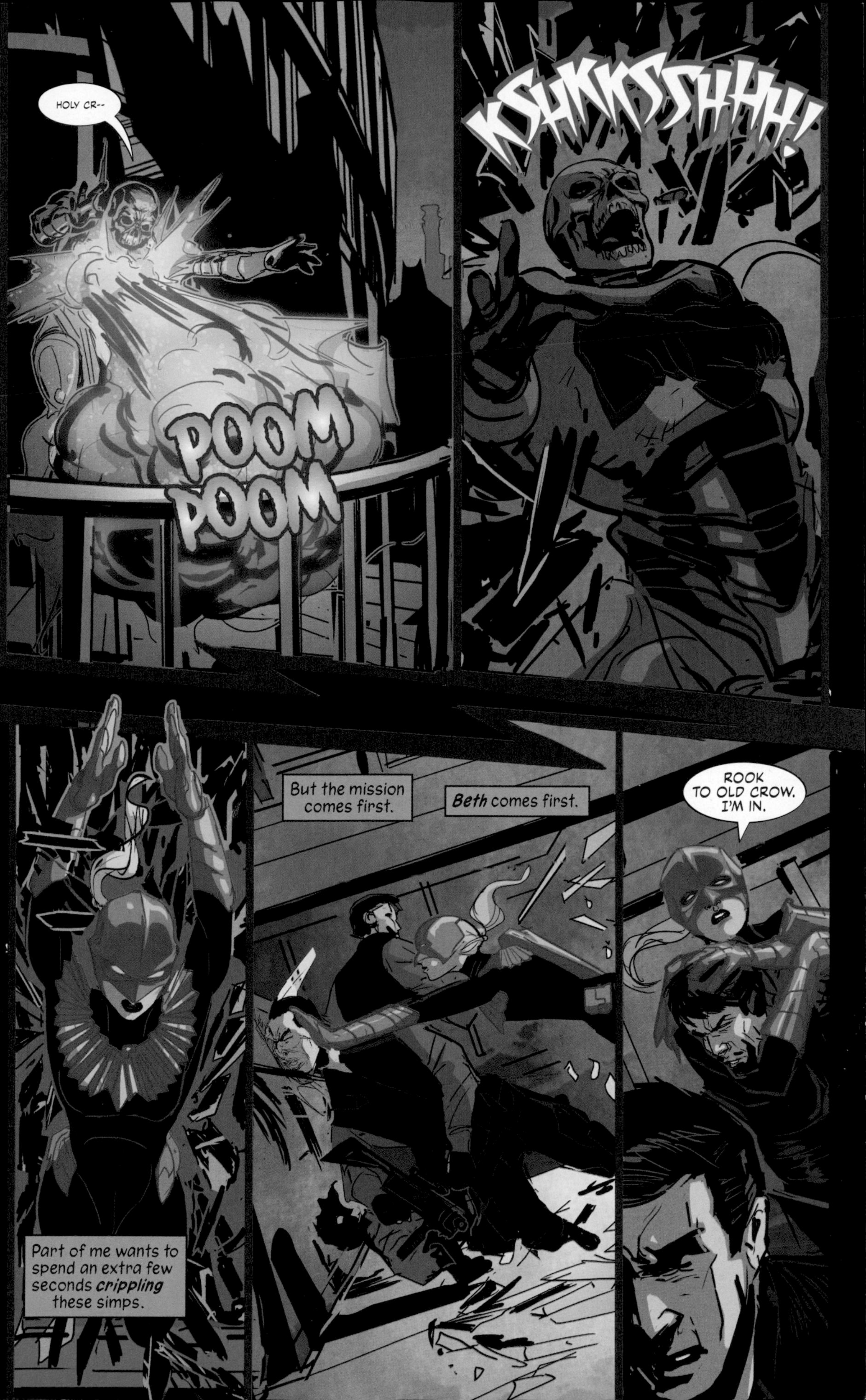
HOLY CR--
POOM POOM
KSHKKSSHHH!
Part of me wants to spend an extra few seconds *crippling* these simps.
But the mission comes first.
Beth comes first.
ROOK TO OLD CROW. I'M IN.

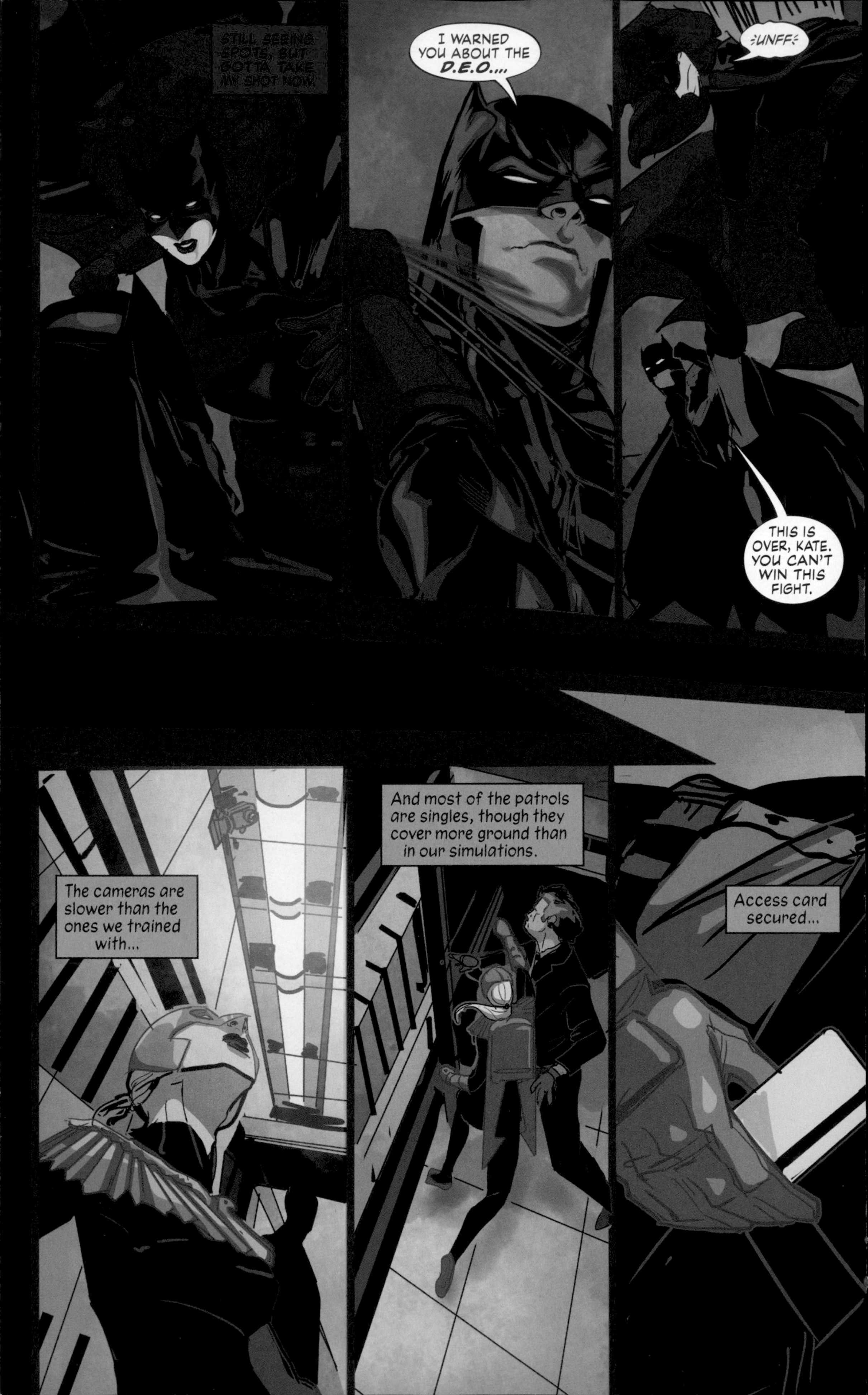
STILL SEEING SPOTS, BUT GOTTA TAKE MY SHOT NOW!
I WARNED YOU ABOUT THE D.E.O....
UNFF
THIS IS OVER, KATE. YOU CAN'T WIN THIS FIGHT.
The cameras are slower than the ones we trained with...
And most of the patrols are singles, though they cover more ground than in our simulations.
Access card secured...

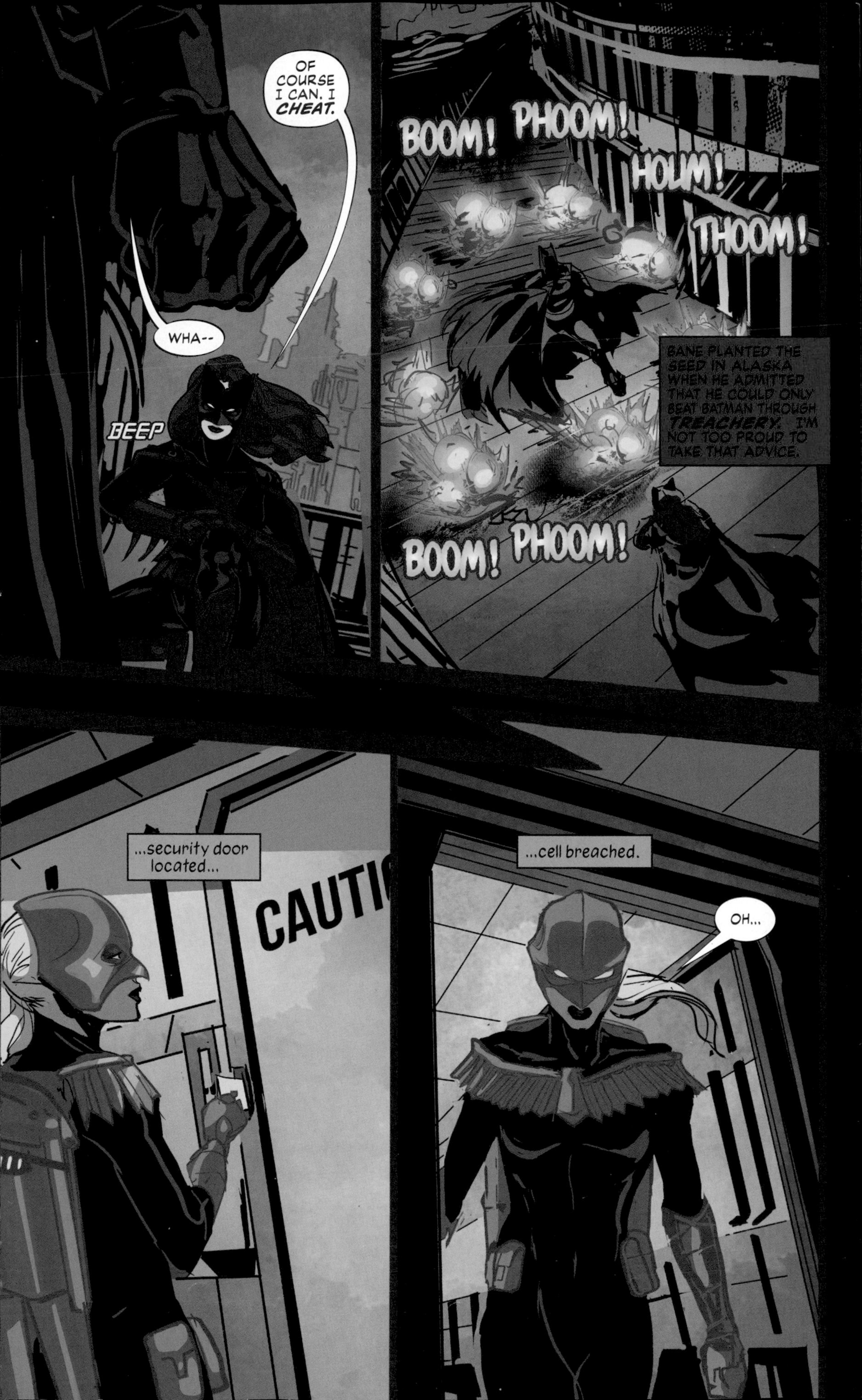
OF COURSE I CAN. I CHEAT.
WHA--
BEEP
BOOM! PHOOM!
HOUM!
THOOM!
BANE PLANTED THE SEED IN ALASKA WHEN HE ADMITTED THAT HE COULD ONLY BEAT BATMAN THROUGH TREACHERY. I'M NOT TOO PROUD TO TAKE THAT ADVICE.
BOOM! PHOOM!
...security door located...
CAUTI
...cell breached.
OH...

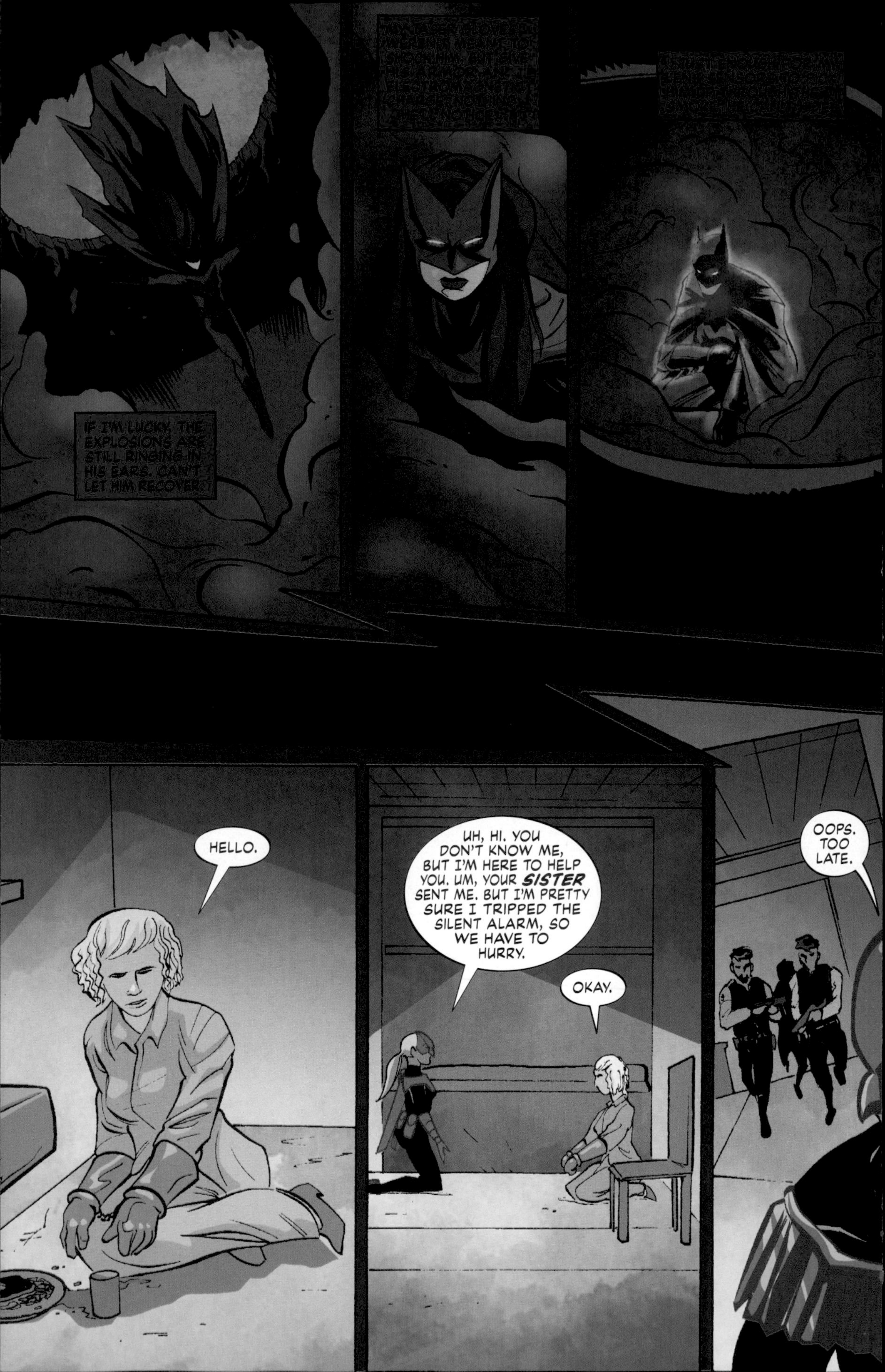

IF I'M LUCKY, THE EXPLOSIONS ARE STILL RINGING IN HIS EARS. CAN'T LET HIM RECOVER.
HELLO.
UH, HI. YOU DON'T KNOW ME, BUT I'M HERE TO HELP YOU. UM, YOUR *SISTER* SENT ME. BUT I'M PRETTY SURE I TRIPPED THE SILENT ALARM, SO WE HAVE TO HURRY.
OKAY.
OOPS. TOO LATE.

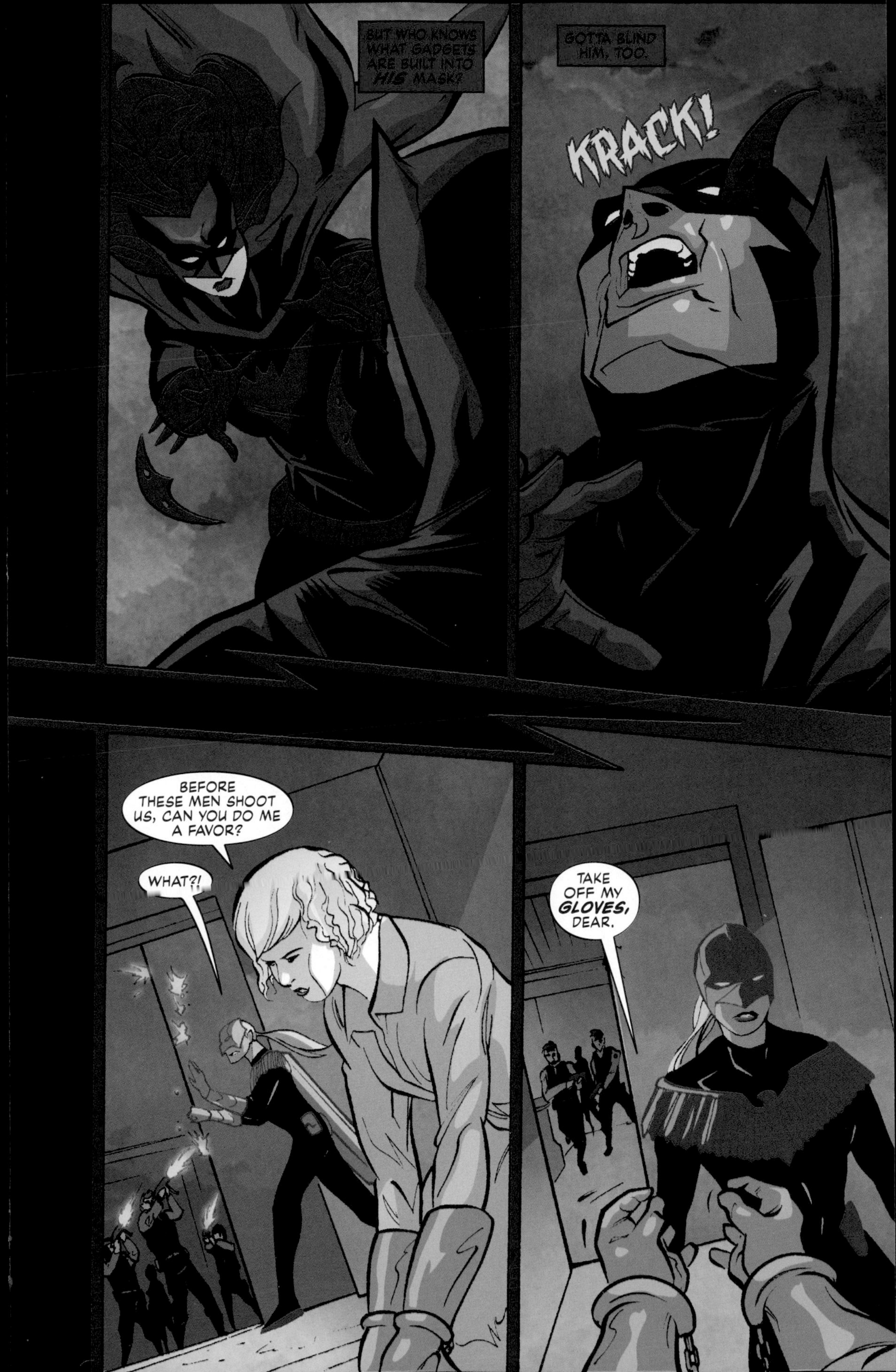
BUT WHO KNOWS WHAT GADGETS ARE BUILT INTO HIS MASK?
GOTTA BLIND HIM, TOO.
KRACK!
BEFORE THESE MEN SHOOT US, CAN YOU DO ME A FAVOR?
WHAT?!
TAKE OFF MY GLOVES, DEAR.

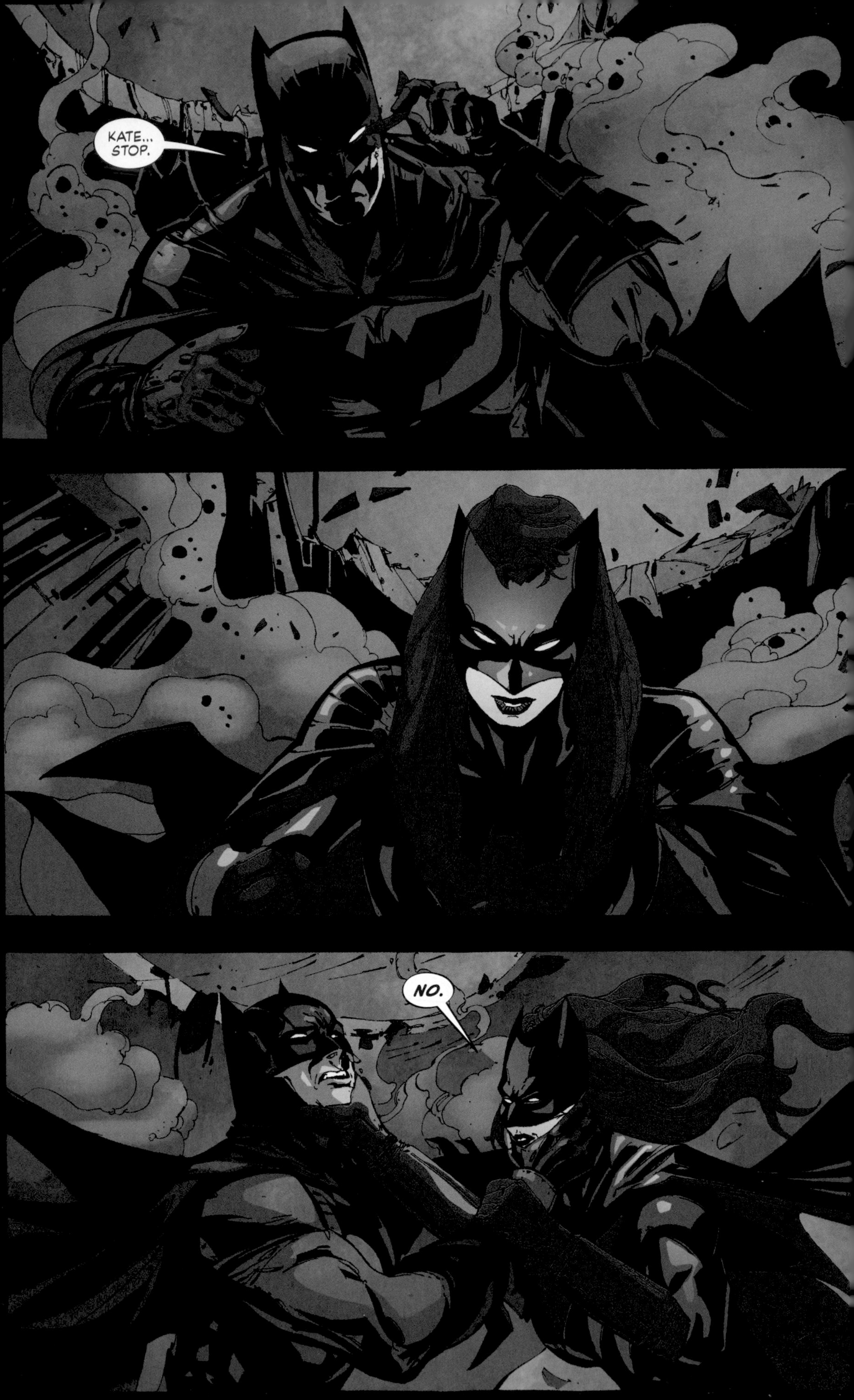
KATE... STOP.
NO.

Batwoman #19 Mad variant cover by Rick Tulka & Carl Peterson

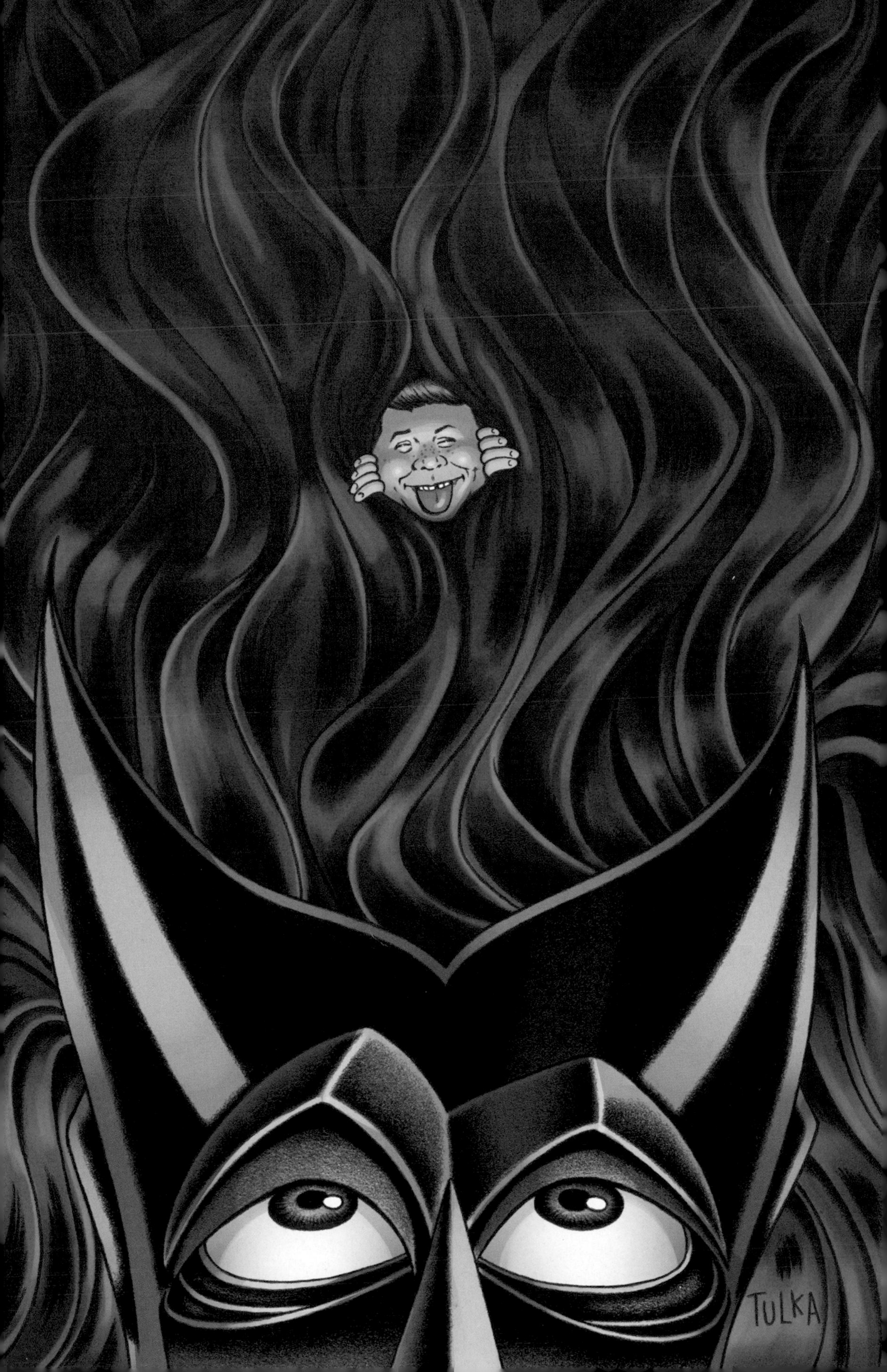
TULKA

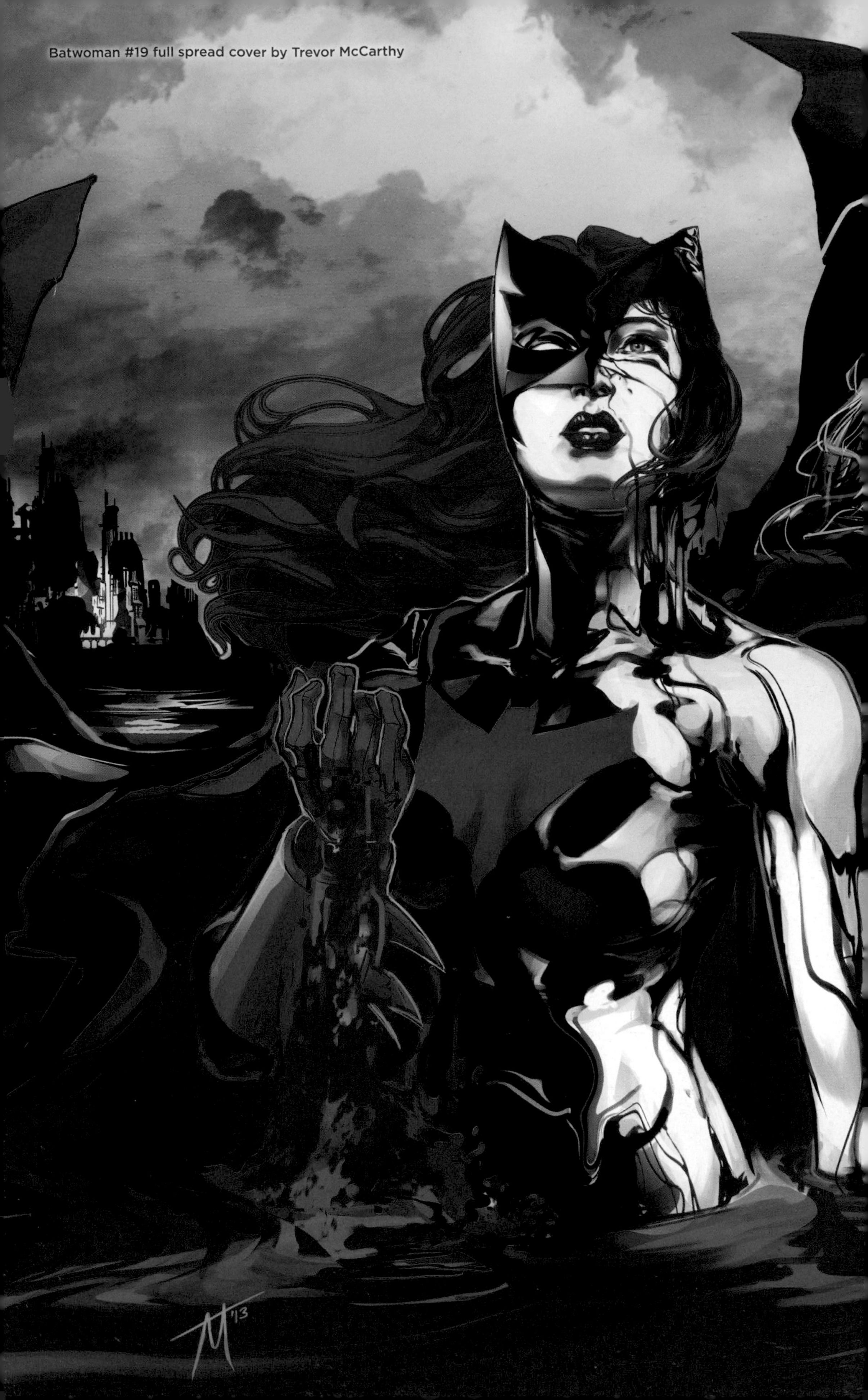

Batwoman #19 full spread cover by Trevor McCarthy

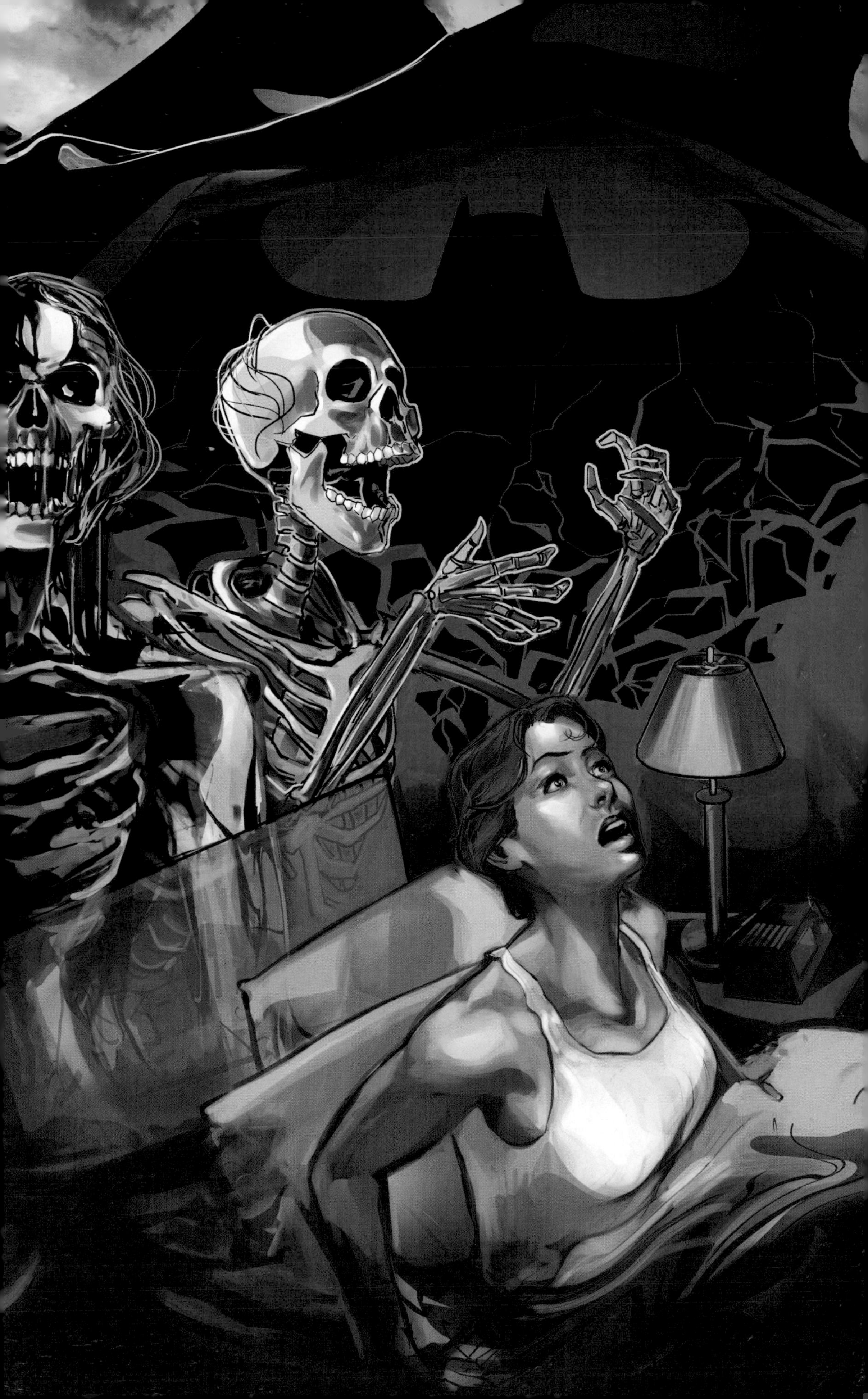

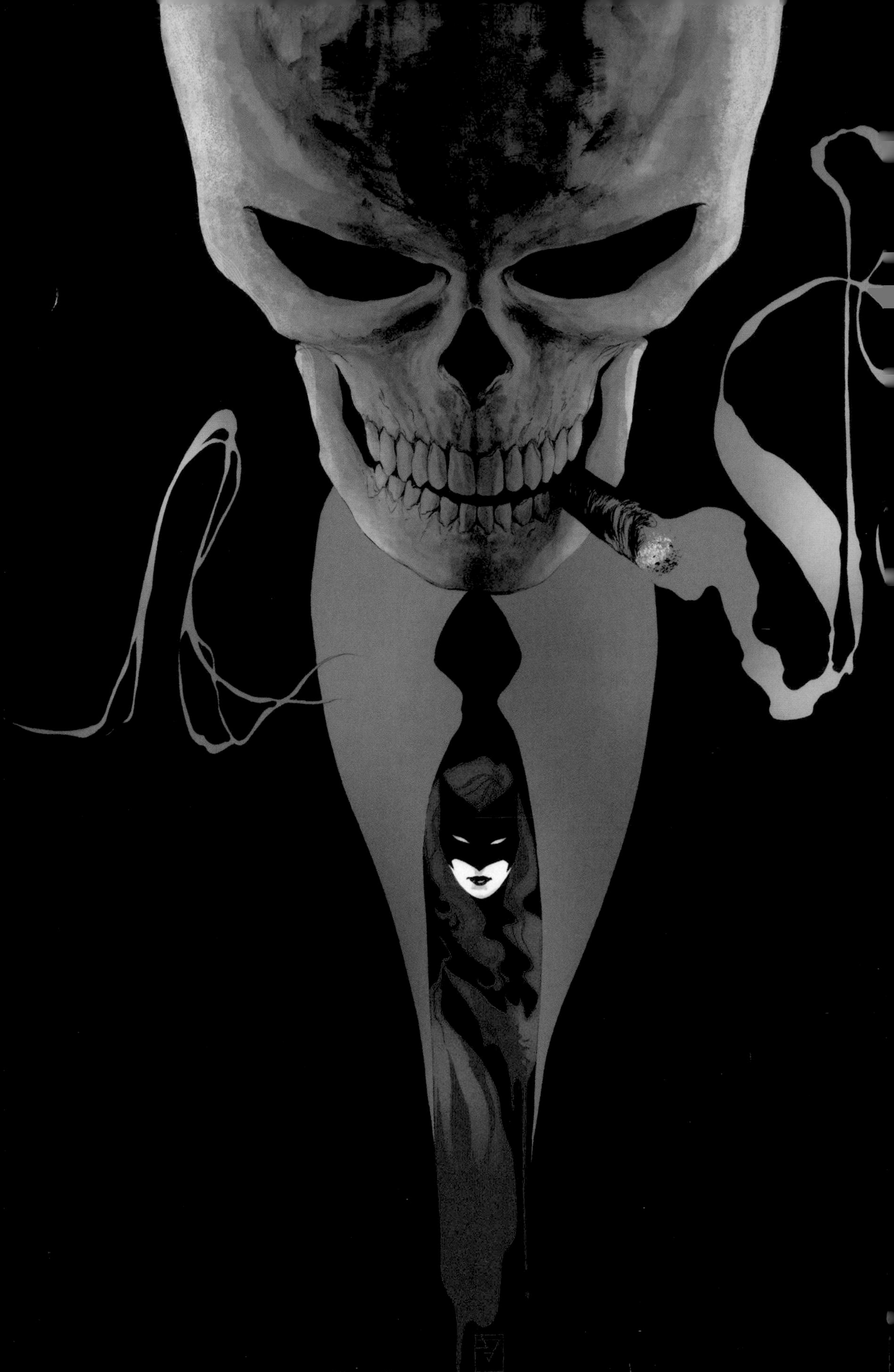

Batwoman #25 unused cover by J.H. Williams III